DYNASTY AND DIPLOMACY IN THE COURT OF SAVOY

This book is the first major study in English of the duchy of Savoy during the period of the Thirty Years' War.

Rather than examining Savoy purely in terms of its military or geo-strategic role, *Dynasty and Diplomacy in the Court of Savoy* comprises three interwoven strands: the dynastic ambitions of the ruling House of Savoy, the family interests of an elite clan in ducal service, and the unique role played by one member of that clan, Abate Alessandro Scaglia (1592–1641), who emerged as one of Europe's most widely known diplomats. Scaglia, the focus of the book, affords insights not only into Savoyard court politics and diplomacy, but more generally into a diplomatic culture of seventeenth-century Europe. With his image fixed by a remarkable series of Van Dyck portraits, Scaglia is emblematic of an international network of princes, diplomats, courtiers and artists, at the point of contact between dynasticism, high politics and the arts.

TOBY OSBORNE is Lecturer in History, University of Durham.

CAMBRIDGE STUDIES IN ITALIAN HISTORY AND CULTURE

Edited by GIGLIOLA FRAGNITO, Università degli Studi, Parma

CESARE MOZZARELLI, Università Cattolica del Sacro Cuore, Milan

ROBERT ORESKO, Institute of Historical Research,
University of London

and GEOFFREY SYMCOX, University of California, Los Angeles

This series comprises monographs and a variety of collaborative volumes, including translated works, which concentrate on the period of Italian history from late medieval times up to the Risorgimento. The editors aim to stimulate scholarly debate over a range of issues which have not hitherto received, in English, the attention they deserve. As it develops, the series will emphasize the interest and vigour of current international debates on this central period of Italian history and the persistent influence of Italian culture on the rest of Europe.

For a list of titles in the series, see end of book

DYNASTY AND DIPLOMACY IN THE COURT OF SAVOY

POLITICAL CULTURE

AND THE THIRTY YEARS' WAR

TOBY OSBORNE

CAMBRIDGE
UNIVERSITY PRESS

PUBLISHED BY THE PRESS SYNDICATE OF THE UNIVERSITY OF CAMBRIDGE
The Pitt Building, Trumpington Street, Cambridge, United Kingdom

CAMBRIDGE UNIVERSITY PRESS
The Edinburgh Building, Cambridge CB2 2RU, UK
40 West 20th Street, New York, NY 10011-4211, USA
477 Williamstown Road, Port Melbourne, VIC 3207, Australia
Ruiz de Alarcón 13, 28014 Madrid, Spain
Dock House, The Waterfront, Cape Town 8001, South Africa

http://www.cambridge.org

First published 2002

Printed in the United Kingdom at the University Press, Cambridge

Typefaces Bembo 11/12.5 pt and Bodoni   *System* LaTeX 2_ε [TB]

A catalogue record for this book is available from the British Library

Library of Congress Cataloguing in Publication data
Osborne, Toby.
Dynasty and diplomacy: the court of Savoy during the Thirty Years' War /
Toby Osborne.
p.   cm. – (Cambridge studies in Italian history and culture)
Includes bibliographical references and index.
ISBN 0 521 65268 5 (hc.)
1. Savoy (France and Italy) – History.   2. Savoy (France and Italy) – Foreign relations.
3. Scaglia, Alessandro, 1592–1641.   4. Savoy, House of.   5. Thirty Years' War, 1618–1648.
I. Title.   II. Series.
DG618.4 .O83   2002
327.44′585′009032–dc21   2002016576
ISBN 0 521 65268 5

CONTENTS

FIGURES

ACKNOWLEDGEMENTS

From the inception of my doctoral thesis to the completion of this book I have been very fortunate to have been helped and advised by a number of historians and friends, and I would like to express my gratitude to a number of them in particular. First and foremost I would like to thank my supervisor at Oxford, Sir John Elliott. It was his advice from the very beginning of my postgraduate work that directed me to focus on Savoy during the seventeenth century, and it goes without saying that his expertise on Spain and Europe in the age of Olivares remains unparalleled. Robert Oresko has always been a friend and a superb source of knowledge on Sabaudian history from my days as a postgraduate through to the editing of the book, which has also benefited inestimably from the expertise and insights of Geoffrey Symcox. David Parrott has similarly been a source of advice and information and I would like to thank both Robert Oresko and David for many fruitful discussions, and Roger Clark for his constant kindness. Arabella Cifani and Franco Monetti have been of such energy and warm support that without them I would simply not have been able to complete my research in Turin, or indeed to learn so much about Piedmontese culture. Similarly, Luc Duerloo's enthusiastic help and advice over issues relating to the Spanish Netherlands has always been welcome and indispensable. I would like to give particular thanks to William Davies at Cambridge University Press, who has been more than patient with me and has been a most civilised source of advice.

I would also like to thank the staff in various archives in which I have worked, in particular the archivists and staff at the two branches of the Archivio di Stato in Turin, Charles Burns of the Archivio Segreto Vaticano and the archivists at the Archives Générales du Royaulme, Brussels. In addition I have benefited from the support of various bodies that has enabled me to complete my work, most importantly the trustees of the Isaiah Berlin Scholarship in Oxford, the Scouloudi Foundation at the Institute of Historical Research, the Department of History at Durham University and the British Academy for providing me with grants of money and sabbatical leave. Finally a number of individuals have given me help, advice and ideas from the time of writing the doctoral thesis, and I would like to thank some of them by name: Miguel-Angel Echevarría Bacigalupe, Robin Briggs, José-Luis Colomer, Edward Corp, Bart de Groof, Lord Dacre of Glanton, Robert Evans, Alan Ford, Daniella Frigo, Margaret Harvey, David Hunt, James Inglis-Jones, H. G. Koenigsberger, Randall Lesaffer, Pierpaolo Merlin, Ricardo Merolla, Cesare Mozzarelli, Bruno Neveu, Mattias Oberli, Geoffrey Parker, Louise Rice, Claudio Rosso, R. Malcolm Smuts, Patrick Williams, Blair Worden.

ABBREVIATIONS

AAE	Archives du Ministre des Affaires Etrangères, Paris
CP	Correspondance Politique
ACM	Archivo de la Casa Miraflores, Madrid
AGR	Archives Générales du Royaulme, Brussels
SEG	Sécrétairerie d'Etat et de Guerre
AGS	Archivo General, Simancas
Est.	Sección de Estado y Guerra
ASB	Archivio di Stato, Biella
AST	Archivio di Stato, Turin
Art.	Articoli (Sezione Riunite)
LDS	Lettere Duchi e Sovrani
LFI	Lettere Forestieri: Inghilterra
LMF	Lettere Ministri: Francia
LMI	Lettere Ministri: Inghilterra
LMM	Lettere Ministri: Milano
LMR	Lettere Ministri: Roma
LMS	Lettere Ministri: Spagna
LMV	Lettere Ministri: Venezia
LP	Lettere Particolari
LPD	Lettere Principi Diversi
NF	Negoziazioni colla Francia
NI	Negoziazioni coll'Inghilterra
PCF	Patenti Controlli Finanzi (Sezione Riunite)
fasc.	fasciculo
m.	mazzo
ASV	Archivio Segreto, The Vatican
SS	Segretario di Stato
Arm.	Armarium
BA	Biblioteca Apostolica, The Vatican
Barb. Lat.	Barberini Latini

BL	British Library, London
Add. MS	Additional Manuscript
Eg. MS	Egerton Manuscript
BN	Bibliothèque Nationale, Paris
CSPD	Calendar of State Papers, Domestic
CPSV	Calendar of State Papers, Venetian
HMC	Historical Manuscripts Commission
PRO	Public Records Office, London
SP	State Papers

NAMES AND DATES

The terms used to describe the territories under the control of the duke of Savoy are deliberate, with implicit reference to the peculiar difficulties of discussing what was in essence a composite state. In general, the English terms 'Savoy' and the 'Savoyard state' are used as collective titles of these transalpine states, and it is furthermore defined primarily as a north Italian sovereignty, even though it was not limited to the Italian side of the Alps. Where the text refers to specific elements of this composite state, non-English terms are used, such as 'Savoie' to describe that duchy alone and 'Piemonte' for the principality in isolation. More generally I have employed English for places and proper nouns where there is a common and accepted usage; otherwise I have used the proper nouns according to the appropriate language – thus, 'Philip IV of Spain', while 'Carlo Emanuele I of Savoy'. For major individuals I have, at the first appropriate occasion, given birth and death dates (including ruling sovereigns, rather than their regnal dates). All dates, including those taken from English sources, are given according to the New Style with the year beginning 1 January.

INTRODUCTION

In September 1999 the National Gallery in London proudly announced the acquisition of the magnificent full-length portrait of Abate Alessandro Cesare Scaglia (1592–1641), 'without question one of Van Dyck's greatest achievements'.[1] Felicitously, the 'Camrose' portrait came into the National Gallery's permanent collection in the same year that marked the four-hundredth anniversary of Anthony van Dyck's (1599–1641) birth, adding to the gallery's other portrait of Abate Scaglia by Van Dyck in devotion to the Virgin and Child, and establishing the abate not only as a major patron of Van Dyck but also as a figure of exceptional importance in the history of collecting. Scaglia was indeed positioned at the heart of an international network of courtiers, collectors, artists and writers who gave seventeenth-century Europe a distinctive character, among them the artists Peter Paul Rubens (1577–1640) and Jacob Jordaens (1593–1678), the collector Cassiano dal Pozzo (1588–1657), the duke of Buckingham (1592–1628), Balthasar Gerbier (1592–1663) and Endymion Porter (1587–1649), and the writers Emanuele Tesauro (1592–1675), Virgilio Malvezzi (1595–1654), Fulvio Testi (1593–1646) and Alessandro Tassoni (1565–1635).

This was a remarkably wide-ranging cultural network. However, it would be wrong simply to view the abate in the reflected glory of such undeniably renowned names as Van Dyck or Rubens alone, divorcing artistic patronage from its early modern social and political context. Alessandro Scaglia was also of major importance in seventeenth-century international relations. For Scaglia, like many of his cultural contacts, the acquisition of pieces of art and patronage more generally were integral to early modern diplomacy rather than separate phenomena as academic categorisations

---

[1] National Gallery, press release, September 1999. It had been given to the gallery in lieu of death duties from the estate of the second Viscount Camrose, following his death in 1995, and his wife, who herself died in 1997 and who had formerly been married to Prince Aly Khan.

of 'history' and 'art history' possibly imply. Collecting and patronage created a cultivated and agreeable environment in which courtiers and diplomats shared in what approached a common language across both national and even confessional boundaries. While it would be too crude to suggest that this had direct or compelling political significance, shared interests created international networks of friends and contacts that could influence negotiations or facilitate policy-making, a factor of crucial importance to Alessandro Scaglia's role on the stage of European power politics. A synthesis of the history of collecting with diplomatic history would indeed move beyond traditional conceptions of narrative studies where the pursuit of foreign policies often meant little more than the signing of treaties or the writing of despatches, borrowing instead from studies in what might be described as 'new' diplomatic history, the very titles of which reflect a discernible change of historiographical emphasis.[2]

International relations in seventeenth-century Europe operated in various, often complex, ways. Early modern diplomacy should be seen as a multi-layered process rather than a linear series of events as purely narrative accounts might suggest. True enough, there were formal points of diplomacy that might for instance have included the public entrance of ambassadors to courts, with different levels of ceremony according to the status of the representative, public audiences, the signing of formal agreements and the exchange of gifts. It was during the sixteenth and seventeenth centuries that these ceremonial elements began to be formalised into coherent systems in a variety of European courts, including Turin, not least with the introduction of the office of Master of Ceremonies who was concerned with the regulation of court protocol.[3] However this did not constitute the sum total of diplomacy and diplomatic culture. The less tangible elements of early modern diplomacy, encompassing both the individual personality and personal interests of diplomatic representatives, also had their parts to play. In respect of personality, more attention should be given to studies of what might be described as 'creativity' in public affairs, that is to say what role an individual might have played in contrast to or perhaps in conjunction with

---

[2] In particular, Lucien Bély, *Espions et ambassadeurs au temps de Louis XIV* (Paris, 1990); Daniela Frigo, *Principe, ambasciatori e 'jus gentium': l'amministrazione della politica estera nel Piemonte del Settecento* (Rome, 1991); Miguel Angel Echevarría Bacigalupe, *La diplomacia secreta en Flandes, 1598–1643* (Leoia, 1984); Jocelyne G. Russell, *Peacemaking in the Renaissance* (London, 1986). Two 'classic' studies in a similar vein are Garrett Mattingly, *Renaissance Diplomacy* (London, 1955) and Charles Howard Carter, *The Secret Diplomacy of the Habsburgs, 1585–1625* (New York and London, 1964).

[3] Albert Loomie, 'The *Conducteur des Ambassadeurs* of seventeenth century France and Spain', *Revue Belge de Philologie et d'Histoire*, 43 (1975); Albert Loomie (ed.), *Ceremonies of Charles I: The Notebooks of John Finet, 1628–1641* (Fordham, 1987).

the influence of impersonal or structural forces in diplomacy such as economic imperatives or a state's 'quest for security'. By drawing on Linda Levy Peck's work on the Jacobean court and by taking account of the mental world of a diplomat like Alessandro Scaglia – through a synthesis of his cultural and political sensibilities recorded by the Van Dyck commissions – a more subtle picture of early seventeenth-century diplomatic culture emerges where the agency of the individual assumes a greater role in the formulation and execution of state policies.[4]

But what of 'state' policy-making? Alessandro Scaglia was a subject of the duke of Savoy, the ruler of a complex composite sovereignty that straddled the Alps. More correctly known in the period as *les états du Duc de Savoie*, Savoy had taken shape over a span of centuries and encompassed most importantly the francophone duchy of Savoie and, across the Alpine mountains, its social and political rival, the Italian principality of Piemonte, where the abate's family was based.[5] Through Alessandro Scaglia's career this book presents the first major account in English of Savoy's role in the diplomacy of the Thirty Years' War, redressing a balance that too often has weighed in favour of larger states. Of course Europe in the sixteenth and seventeenth centuries was undeniably dominated by France and Spain and the rivalries of their sovereign dynasties for territory and prestige across the continent, while the Austrian Habsburgs through the Holy Roman Empire maintained and possibly increased their power in central Europe. Other states also waxed and waned in greatness during this turbulent period. Sweden increasingly dominated the Baltic, Britain gradually emerged as a global trading power, while the Dutch Republic enjoyed its relatively brief but spectacular Golden Age of economic might and cultural brilliance in the seventeenth century. But narrowly focused

---

[4] Linda Levy Peck (ed.), *The Mental World of the Jacobean Court* (Cambridge and New York, 1991), especially the introduction.

[5] See Robert Oresko's introduction to Arabella Cifani and Franco Monetti, *I piaceri e le grazie: collezionisimo, pittura di genere e di paesaggio fra Sei e Settecento in Piemonte* (Turin, 1993). See also Lino Marini, *Libertà e tramonti di libertà nello stato sabaudo del Cinquecento* (Bologna, 1968), chapter 1, and Lino Marini, *Libertà e privilegio dalla Savoia al Monferrato da Amedeo VIII a Carlo Emanuele I* (Bologna, 1972), pp. 9–10; Stuart Woolf, *Studi sulla nobiltà Piemontese nell'epoca dell'assolutismo* (Turin, 1963), p. 7. For a clear introduction in English to Savoy's territorial portfolio that also included the county of Nice to the south of Savoie, the alpine duchy of Aosta, and the small principality of Oneglia which was surrounded on all sides by the republic of Genoa and which Emanuele Filiberto bought from Giovanni Girolamo Doria in 1576, see Geoffrey Symcox, *Victor Amadeus II: Absolutism in the Savoyard State 1675–1730* (London, 1983), chapter 2. On the rivalry between Savoie and Piemonte see Lino Marini, *Savoiardi e Piemontesi nello stato sabaudo, 1418–1601* (Rome, 1962), and more recently, Alessandro Barbero, 'Savoiardi e Piemontesi nel ducato sabaudo all'inizio del Cinquecento: un problema storiografico risolto?', *Bollettino Storico-Bibliografico Subalpino*, 87 (1989).

views of European history from this great-power perspective alone have distorted the ways in which historians have considered relations between them and other, seemingly 'smaller', states and dynasties. The effects have been almost entirely deleterious as some 'second-rank' states (for want of a better term), not least Savoy, have become the victims of neglect and misunderstanding.

Much of the difficulty in assessing Savoy's importance lies with its particular and burdensome historiography, a theme addressed in the first chapter of this book. While historians from Italy have often viewed Savoy in the light of its role in the *Risorgimento* (with contradictory results), many non-Italian historians have until recently neglected to lend any significant weight at all to the Italian peninsula in their accounts of seventeenth-century political history. Both groups have often failed to appreciate that the states of the peninsula, not least Savoy, were distinct and discrete identities with their own regional interests and internal politics in an age when there was no one unified Italian sovereignty. Indeed, archival research into Italian political history for the period after 1530 has hitherto remained woefully inadequate apart from the admirable tradition of north Italian local erudition, and the special case of the Venetian Republic which has long attracted the attention of economic and social historians. Only in recent years, with the research of a number of Anglo-American historians such as Robert Oresko, David Parrott, Christopher Storrs and Geoffrey Symcox, is the enormous but untapped potential of the north Italian archives for political history in the post-Renaissance period at last being exploited and placed in context for Anglophone scholarship.[6] It has, moreover, been accepted too often that Savoy only began to emerge from the long shadow of Franco-Spanish rivalry under the guidance of Vittorio Amedeo II (1666–1732), the sovereign who successfully exchanged his ducal title for that of a king following the War for the Spanish Succession (1701–13). A study of the duchy of Savoy during the early part of the seventeenth century presents a markedly different picture, showing that it was more than capable of holding its own in a Europe of leading and secondary powers; even 'small states', as Daniela Frigo has written, could 'play a political role of much greater weight than their military and territorial size might warrant'.[7]

---

[6] See for instance Robert Oresko, 'Bastards as clients: the House of Savoy and its illegitimate children', in Charles Giry-Deloison and Roger Mettam (eds.), *Patronages et clientélismes 1550–1750 (France, Angleterre, Espagne, Italie)* (London, 1995); D. A. Parrott, 'The Mantuan Succession, 1627–31: a sovereignty dispute in early modern Europe', *English Historical Review*, 112 (1997), 20–65; Christopher Storrs, *War, Diplomacy and the Rise of Savoy, 1690–1720* (Cambridge, 2000); Symcox, *Victor Amadeus II*.

[7] Daniela Frigo, 'Introduction', in Daniela Frigo (ed.), *Politics and Diplomacy in Early Modern Italy: The Structure of Diplomatic Practice, 1450–1800* (Cambridge, 2000), p. 4.

There were indeed a number of similar states in Europe, all of which can be described as being of the second rank through their geo-strategic, military, economic or political assets. The duchy of Lorraine was situated on the politically sensitive cross-roads between the Low Countries and southern and central Europe and had a complex dynastic relationship with France; the Saxon Electorate had valuable resources in silver mines, as well as its juridical position in the Empire; both the duchy of Bavaria and the Brandenburg Electorate had troops that could be of critical importance in central Europe; the duchy of Mantua controlled crucial fortresses that could influence movements through north Italy; the grand-duchy of Tuscany, on the other hand, had the wealth of the Medici family and a galley fleet that, although of decreasing importance, could be used in the Mediterranean.

What defined Savoy as a 'second rank' or 'small' state? The provinces under the duke of Savoy as a whole were not especially rich in terms of natural or economic resources. Of all the provinces, Piemonte had the greatest concentration of economic activity and wealth with its textile industries in towns such as Biella, a centre of wool production, and the silk-producing Racconigi. The principality was also the location from 1563 of the ducal capital, Turin, which was itself a significant silk producer, while beyond the city were the fertile plains around the River Po that gave way to wine-producing vineyards in the surrounding hills. But aside from Piemonte, much of the Savoyard patrimony was mountainous and undeveloped.[8] The Savoyard state also lacked a viable Mediterranean port that could rival Genoa or Leghorn, despite its control of Nice-Villafranca and, from the late sixteenth century, of Oneglia, which was never really developed. More promising was the fact that Savoy's population seems to have been one of the largest of the independent states of north Italy, though precise comparisons are difficult. In 1700 there were an estimated 1,396,000 inhabitants in the ducal states of Savoy. This can be compared with the Venetian Republic (with its Greek and Croatian populations beyond the peninsula) that had an estimated 2 million inhabitants by 1700, though it has also been suggested that Spain ruled over 5 million of the Italian peninsula's entire 13 million inhabitants in 1600.[9] Revenue systems, gradually developed from the mid-1550s and after Duke Emanuele Filiberto's restoration of 1559, combined direct and indirect taxes. These included a taille (from which the nobility and church were exempt) and various gabelles, though the collection and 'efficiency' of the most important gabelle, the salt gabelle, was not straightforward in what Mathew

---

[8] Symcox, *Victor Amadeus II*, chapter 2.
[9] *Ibid.*, p. 245; Gregory Hanlon, *Early Modern Italy, 1550–1800* (Basingstoke and London, 2000), chapter 4, and p. 74.

Vester has characterised as a 'polycentric' state where ducal power was mediated through local and non-state interest groups.[10] Whatever the limitations of the taille, it nevertheless enabled dukes of Savoy from the second half of the sixteenth century to raise troops with greater surety. During the Thirty Years' War Savoy was indeed a significant regional military power, even if, again, it lacked the kinds of European-wide resources available to the French and to the Spanish and Austrian Habsburgs – the armed forces, including mercenaries, available to the dukes during the early decades of the seventeenth century could total as many as 25,381 infantry and 1,213 cavalry (excluding militia), raised in 1625. To place this in context, Venice raised 11,000 troops in 1621 when it considered joining the German Protestant Union and Dutch Republic, and could raise up to 30,000 troops, though this mainly consisted of militia. With Spanish aid, Genoa managed to raise 15,000 to oppose Savoy and France in 1625; a year before, the papacy mobilised its own army of 12,000 in the vicinity of Ferrara, augmented by an additional 6,000 around Rome.[11] Perhaps more significantly, the Savoyard state also enjoyed a crucial geo-strategic position as the 'gatekeeper to the Alps', which made it such an important ally for the leading powers to court both politically and dynastically. Through a series of fortresses that included Pinerolo and the capital city of Turin itself, Piemonte controlled the main passes across the western Alps, over the Mont-Cénis and its subsidiary, the Mont-Genèvre, and through the Val di Susa, which lay to the west of the capital. To the south of Turin, between the county of Nice and the principality of Piemonte, lay the pass of Tenda, and the Great and Little Saint Bernards were to the north, through the duchy of Aosta.[12]

Savoy's geographical position in northern Italy meant that both France and Spain went to great lengths to gain the favour of the duchy, and this allowed successive dukes to play the rival ambitions of the leading powers for their own recurrent dynastic and political interests. Even the rhetoric of Franco-Spanish rivalry afforded opportunities for Savoy to improve its standing in the Italian peninsula and further afield. French foreign policy under Richelieu was faced with curious ideological tensions, at

---

[10] Mathew Vester, 'Territorial politics in the Savoyard domains, 1536–1580', (PhD thesis, UCLA, 1997), especially section 1.

[11] For some estimates of the numbers of troops Savoy could muster see Gregory Hanlon, *The Twilight of a Military Tradition: Italian Aristocrats and European Conflicts, 1560–1800* (London, 1998), pp. 106–9, 280–1; Hanlon, *Early Modern Italy*, p. 256. The impressive numbers mustered by Savoy in 1625 can be put into further perspective – the duchy only attained comparable numbers again at the end of the seventeenth century, during a period of sustained military expansion. Storrs, *War, Diplomacy and the Rise of Savoy*, p. 24.

[12] Symcox, *Victor Amadeus II*, p. 14.

once claiming to be founded on Catholic ideals yet also recognising the legitimate existence of Protestant states and allying with them and other states to oppose the Habsburgs. The Spanish argued in similarly defensive political language that the stability of 'Christendom', with its pre-Reformation resonances, essentially needed to be based on limiting French power while regaining the rebellious Dutch provinces. These different conceptions of how European power should be balanced played an important role in Savoyard diplomatic strategies, revealing how a seemingly regional power like Savoy was never isolated from wider issues of power politics. To France, the duchy was crucial because it potentially controlled access to the peninsula while the Spanish were equally aware of Savoy's significance to their logistics and the Spanish Road.[13] What is more, the very rhetoric of this Franco-Spanish rivalry, where both powers sought the moral highground for domestic and international audiences, clearly implied that it was necessary to work with independent states like Savoy to avoid charges of 'betraying' Catholicism or, particularly in Spain's case, of pursuing 'universal monarchy'. Neither France nor Spain therefore felt able or indeed willing to sideline Savoy. This in turn enabled the duchy to manipulate them by alternating alliances and dynastic affiliations, preferably keeping the two leading powers as rivals for Savoy's loyalty.

Military and geo-strategic resources undoubtedly proved important to Savoy's identity as a regional power in north Italy. Yet where this book discusses Savoy's role in Europe, most particularly in the first chapter, it is not primarily in terms of men or material, important though they were, but more from a dynastic viewpoint. Dynasticism might not have been the sole consideration in foreign policy-making but, in an age when ruling dynasties around Europe were acutely aware of responsibilities to family and posterity, Savoyard relations with other powers in the sixteenth and seventeenth centuries were formulated in the first instance around issues of family interest. They lay at the heart of its most important international disputes that often dated back centuries. The marriage alliances of different members of the ruling House moreover locked the duchy into a system of European courts and sovereign families. There were two practical implications of this dynastic system that directed the ruling family of Savoy to pursue particular foreign policies and a distinctive style of diplomacy. First, the Savoyard House could claim rights of inheritance to various territories within the Italian peninsula and also further afield at a time when there were often no codified laws of succession governing

---

[13] A subject elucidated by Geoffrey Parker's *The Army of Flanders and the Spanish Road, 1567–1659* (Cambridge, 1972).

them, while Europe more generally still did not have totally fixed state borders. These claims, among them to Monferrato, the shadow kingdom of Cyprus, the Spanish Netherlands, and even the Spanish composite monarchy itself, were in the early seventeenth century dangled before successive dukes by the leading powers as incentives for alliances. That is not to say that north Italy and the independent states of the region were under the sway of the leading powers. Unresolved territorial claims had the inherent energy to mobilise Savoyard rulers to action, something neither France nor Spain could necessarily prevent even with their superior material assets. But while Savoy's unfulfilled territorial ambitions meant that the duchy was neither a neutral nor a passive power in certain diplomatic disputes, dukes of Savoy could none the less mediate between other sovereigns precisely because of the criss-crossing family connections between the ruling House and dynasties that principally included the Habsburgs, Bourbons and Stuarts. These family webs were in this sense more extensive, and possibly of greater importance, than Savoy's formal diplomatic network in Europe; effectively, the dynasty's only permanent diplomatic missions in the seventeenth century were to the papal court, France, the Wittelsbach cousins in Bavaria and the Imperial court, with frequent (if not permanent) missions to Spain.[14] Playing the role of mediator became in itself a key element in Savoy's international strategies during the Thirty Years' War as the duchy pursued support for its territorial claims, and mediation was one of the characteristic signatures of Alessandro Scaglia's diplomacy as he moved around different European courts.

Relations with other powers in north Italy and further afield therefore were shaped by Savoy's geographical position and its military resources, though equally by family interest. There were other factors affecting the formulation of foreign policies in the early modern period. 'State' policies, closely connected as they were to the strategies of the ruling dynasty and at least formally by the seventeenth century seen as the expression of the sovereign's will, were to a significant degree also shaped by ministers and representatives in the service of the state or sovereign. In discussing the complexities of diplomacy in early modern Italy, Daniela Frigo has gone so far as to suggest not only that retrospective distinctions between 'interior' and 'exterior' spheres of politics are artificial, but also that diplomacy itself was much more than the expression of state power invested in the sovereign prince alone. Diplomacy, she argues, was subject to various complex influences that reflected the interests of court factions, families,

---

[14] This diplomatic system was not significantly expanded until after 1690. Storrs, *War, Diplomacy and the Rise of Savoy*, chapter 3.

individuals, local feudatories, cities and even peasantries.[15] While this might be stretching the case a little far, Frigo makes the important point that state and foreign policies often reflected the outcome of a process of interaction between the prince and at least some subjects within his patrimonial state. This study correspondingly argues that the conduct of Savoyard international relations needs to be understood in terms of personal and structural forces, and of the relationship between domestic and external forces, and as cultural and social history in addition to a narrowly defined conception of politics. By considering Alessandro Scaglia's career through his various interconnected identities, as a collector and diplomat and as a member of the Scaglia di Verrua, an elite noble family, and by examining the public and political roles of his family in conjunction with the dynastic interests of the sovereign House of Savoy, further insights can be gleaned into the processes that were involved in the pursuit of foreign policies. In this book 'dynasty and diplomacy' is examined as the interaction between two families, the sovereign dynasty and the Scaglia di Verrua.

The book argues that Alessandro Scaglia, as an experienced, wealthy and articulate member of an elite noble family on the social level immediately below that of his sovereign House, had a conception of what he should do as an ambassadorial representative of the duke of Savoy while advancing his own interests and those of his family. State service and personal interest constantly overlapped. Of course as with so many of the categories in this book, a distinction between public and private spheres of politics in early modern history needs to be considered with caution. For an individual like Scaglia, from a leading court clan, his entire public career was an expression of the intimately related ideas of service to the prince and service to his own family. Like sovereign dynasties, the elite noble families of early modern Europe directed their own strategies in the court context and also in the international arena to further their particular concerns. The pursuit and preservation of aristocratic power within the court was certainly influenced by the politics of the ruling family and by the changing patterns of alliances with other sovereign dynasties. One effect of Savoyard marriage alliances was the presence at different points in the Turinese court of members of the Spanish and French royal families which, coupled with the policy of playing Spain and France constantly against one another, encouraged the formation of different (and flexible) court loyalties that could be sympathetic to one state or the other. As families and individuals sought to establish their positions at court, they were also keenly aware of each other's fortunes. Not only did competition

---

[15] Frigo, 'Introduction', in Frigo (ed.), *Politics and Diplomacy*, pp. 7–8.

for power exist between different factional groups and groups associated with particular members of the ruling House; it also came from within them where individual and family affiliations proved powerful.

The importance of the individual as a political actor can be appreciated further by drawing on other lines of historical investigation. In the first place the structural characteristics of international relations enhanced the importance of a personalised style of diplomacy. This was a period in which the existence of semi-permanent embassies in European courts became a more normal element of international affairs, but where regimes still had problems in exerting immediate control over their diplomats resident in embassies. As Fernand Braudel has argued, time and space had a profound influence on early modern power politics, which in turn affected basic diplomatic practicalities such as the transmission of information from an embassy to the home state.[16] It took, for instance, roughly a week for a letter to pass between Turin and Paris during the early seventeenth century, though this was obviously subject to weather conditions across the Alps. More particularly, the relative slowness of communications meant that representatives had to know who and what they were serving while they were in the field, given the relative autonomy of action they might have while serving on missions. These practical problems coincided not by chance with a general interest in the conduct of state policies, especially diplomacy, which became a category for discussion in its own right because it was becoming a normal element of sovereign power, and because of the particular dilemmas faced by Catholic sovereigns in negotiating with other powers, including heretical Protestants. Political theorists in a discernible Catholic Europe, many of whom were themselves experienced diplomats or public figures, were in agreement in emphasising the moral content of state service, including diplomatic service. There was a general consensus that the role of the diplomat was in essence to serve the interests of his Christian prince for the pursuit of peace in a context where there was no definite division between what was useful and what was good.[17]

There is of course a perceived difficulty in connecting this commonplace rhetoric of seventeenth-century political conduct with what public

---

[16] Fernand Braudel, *The Mediterranean and the Mediterranean World in the Age of Philip II*, 2 vols. (London, 1986), I, part 2, chapter 1.

[17] There were a number of treatises written on the conduct of state affairs in this period. Three of direct interest to this book are Giovanni Botero, *Della ragion di stato*, ed. Luigi Firpo (Turin, 1947); Juan Antonio de Vera y Figueroa, count of la Roca, *El enbaxador* (Seville, 1620); Gasparo Bragaccio, *L'Ambasciatore in sei libri* (Padua, 1627). For a brief discussion of early modern diplomatic treatises more generally, consult François de Callières, *The Art of Diplomacy*, ed. H. M. A. Keens-Soper and Karl W. Schweizer (Leicester, 1983), pp. 19–41.

figures actually did. Language or the articulation of aims did not always correlate with actions. Two recent essays on the strategic aims and foreign policies of Cardinal Richelieu (1585–1642) indeed illuminate some of the problems faced by historians in dealing with this slippery subject. On the one hand Herman Weber has suggested that Richelieu fundamentally aspired to peace in Christendom, basing his arguments on the cardinal's memoirs and memoranda, while Robin Briggs has taken a more critical view of the cardinal's language from the same types of documentary evidence, arguing that he employed rhetoric to underpin a new approach to *raison d'état* in power politics.[18] It will clearly remain difficult to discuss the interplay between political rhetoric, personal belief and action without necessarily dividing them and perhaps introducing imbalances in their relationship. At one extreme, accepting public language, expressed through letters, tracts and memoirs, as completely true in its own terms would probably distort an understanding of motivation in favour of a simplistic face-value approach to politics.[19] The opposite however would be equally misleading. A strong distinction between language and action would portray political figures as having had complete freedom to separate at will what they said and did. These general problems are particularly relevant for this study because of the use of diplomatic correspondence where ambassadors had obvious reasons for 'spinning' information in writing to their princes. Yet one of the book's themes is that early modern international relations, as seen through the paradigmatic figure of Alessandro Scaglia, operated within a coherent conceptual and a moral framework. That did not mean that an ambassador like Scaglia was reluctant to pursue policies that to some appeared to be immoral, such as encouraging wars between sovereign states, as he did through his diplomatic involvement in England's concurrent conflicts with France and Spain during the crucial years of the 1620s. Rather, such tactics were pragmatic means to moral political ends. Alessandro Scaglia generally operated according to clear political premises that fundamentally shaped his actions and also fostered his ability to operate independently of others. What complicated his position was that these premises changed and moreover were affected by personal prejudices, especially his animosity towards Richelieu after the treaty of Monzón and particular Savoyard political ambitions in Italy and Europe, which he believed in themselves gave a justification to his

---

[18] Herman Weber, ' "Une bonne paix": Richelieu's foreign policy and the peace of Christendom', and Robin Briggs, 'Richelieu and reform: rhetoric and political reality', in Joseph Bergin and Lawrence Brockliss (eds.), *Richelieu and His Age* (Oxford, 1992).

[19] As Joseph Bergin and Lawrence Brockliss have quite reasonably observed, Weber reveals only 'how Richelieu wished to present his policy to his monarch and the outside world'. Joseph Bergin and Lawrence Brockliss, 'Introduction', *ibid.*, p. 7.

diplomatic tactics and language. Alessandro Scaglia, as with so many political figures of his age, always expressed his wish for European stability,
but with the heavy condition that it satisfied his concept of a peace with
reputation for his home state, with all that this entailed. The abate was
consequently involved in debate and confrontation with other public
figures such as Richelieu about the relative morality of given policies,
merging personal interests with state policy-making.

Turning to the presentation of this book, one important consideration
has been that of structure. I have restricted the central sections of this
study to the period of the Thirty Years' War, or more precisely to the
period from the beginning of Alessandro Scaglia's mission to Paris in
April 1624 until his death in May 1641 as an exile in Antwerp. While
the choice of dates might seem arbitrary in relation to his life and to
European events, it follows a coherent pattern for his career and more or
less coincides with the ministries of both Cardinal Richelieu and the
count-duke of Olivares (1587–1645). It also covers the transfer of power
in Savoy from Duke Carlo Emanuele I (1562–1630) to Vittorio Amedeo
I (1587–1637) in 1630 and the civil war that followed the untimely death
of Vittorio Amedeo I in 1637, until its eventual conclusion in 1642. The
work is based on a variety of European archives that document relations
between dynastically linked courts of Turin, Paris, Madrid, Brussels and
London. The two obvious absences from this list are the Imperial and
papal courts. Because Alessandro Scaglia did not serve in any diplomatic
missions to Vienna, I have chosen not to work on the Empire as such. The
role of the papal court in Rome is limited to the use of nuncio reports,
papal briefs and the anonymous *avvisi* in the Archivio Segreto Vaticano
and Biblioteca Apostolica. That is not to say, though, that neither was
important, for both persisted as rival and overlapping sources of power in
the seventeenth century. The role of Imperial jurisdiction in matters of
legal questions and dynastic disputes within the *Reichsitalien* – that grey
area of the Italian peninsula legally within the Holy Roman Empire – has
not been adequately understood by historians of the period.[20] Like the
Holy Roman Empire, Rome had a role as both a tangible and a symbolic
source of international influence to which Catholic powers turned in
times of dispute, and it indeed had a duty to mediate in disputes between
co-religionists. This study considers indirectly Savoy's relationship with
both the Austrian Habsburg and papal courts, most obviously during the
Gonzaga succession dispute.

---

[20] Robert Oresko and David Parrott, 'Reichsitalien and the Thirty Years' War', in Klaus
Bussmann and Heinz Schilling (eds.), *1648: War and Peace in Europe*, 3 vols. (Munich,
1998), I, pp. 141–2.

The documentation employed is mainly diplomatic and political. The use of ecclesiastical and family records is relatively limited since this is neither a study of Alessandro Scaglia in his role as an abate, nor purely a study of the Scaglia di Verrua as a family clan. Church and family papers, as well as financial and legal documents, have been employed where they contribute to an understanding of Alessandro Scaglia's career and the interaction between his family and the House of Savoy. On the whole the archival material has been very rich, aside from a few frustrating, though understandable, gaps, notably for some aspects of the abate's years in exile. In particular, Alessandro Scaglia's personal papers, such as private correspondence and financial records, which might yield significant insights not only into his political career but also into his habits as a patron and collector, still remain elusive. The majority of the papers of the Scaglia di Verrua can be found in the Archivio di Stato of Biella, the patrimonial family seat to the north of Turin, but there is very little material in the archive directly relating to Alessandro Scaglia.[21] Since in 1632 he went into exile to Brussels, one might alternatively have expected his papers to have entered the Spanish Netherlands. But neither the Archives Générales du Royaume in Brussels nor the Bibliothèque Royale reveal much, only that letters to the abate from Olivares, which would presumably have been among his personal papers, found their way into those archives; nor is there extensive material in the Staatsarchief of Antwerp, the city in which the abate retired from public life and died. As for the documentation that has been used, the diplomatic correspondence of the abate himself has been of central importance. This study initially developed from an interest in Scaglia, as viewed from the few secondary studies that refer to him as a patron of Van Dyck and diplomat, though I was subsequently directed towards an enormous amount of correspondence in the very underused Archivio di Stato in Turin, and also in the state archives in Brussels. Aside from other writings, it seems that the abate wrote at least one letter virtually every day, of varying length and detail from a single folio to very close discussions of political events that ran into tens of pages. The majority of these have survived and have formed the foundation of the research for the book.

While the use of one individual's correspondence is extremely useful, especially as it is so extensive and detailed, it nevertheless carries its own risks. It was, on the whole, diplomatic, 'public' correspondence; it was therefore written with a particular choice of language and for a specific audience, and furthermore it was obviously subject to Scaglia's own

---

[21] For a descriptive list of the papers see Maurizio Cassetti, 'L'Archivio S. Martino-Scaglia', *Studi Piemontesi*, 10 (1981).

awareness of events and his own political agenda. These limitations are important in one sense and moreover form a constant theme of the book where it addresses the abate's perceptions as a diplomat and the way in which he represented his actions, primarily to his sovereign prince. None the less, the book needs to move beyond the individual to place him in a wider political and cultural context, not least because the sheer detail of the correspondence might threaten to turn this study into a microscopic discussion of events. I have consequently taken care to place the Scaglia documentation in the context of what others were saying and doing. The use of a variety of archives in different countries has also allowed a more rounded understanding of how policy-makers in different courts inter- preted the same sets of events and thereafter formulated their diplomatic strategies.

The study of an individual such as Alessandro Scaglia might inevitably entail a biographical approach, while a broad study of international rela- tions or the policies of a state might be presented as a narrative history of the period. Both of these approaches have advantages, though also inherent limitations. A biographical study would be too restrictive in it- self, as this book combines the examination of an individual career with wider issues regarding Savoy and the conduct of international diplomacy. On the other hand, a purely narrative structure would be inadequate in explaining *how* Scaglia's style of diplomacy operated within its distinctive cultural and social system. Yet a possible alternative, a totally thematic or analytical study of Scaglia, Savoy and seventeenth-century interna- tional relations, would also be inappropriate. The course and structure of Savoyard politics in the early seventeenth century is too little known in the English-speaking world (and even to some extent in the Italian world) to assume sufficiently detailed knowledge on the part of the reader. This book consequently draws on all three of these approaches: it uses a narrative framework that is none the less founded on certain fundamen- tal premises about how international relations worked in dynastic and cultural frameworks, and about Scaglia's own recognisable approach to diplomacy.

It is fortunate for a work that seeks to move beyond a purely narrative structure that the chapters not only coincide with specific chronological periods but also mirror the central thematic aspects of Alessandro Scaglia's career. This book charts the rise of a diplomat to a position of international importance, and his actions and reactions in relation to the shape of state policy-making. The first part of the book is divided into two chapters and sets the fundamental parameters within which Savoy's role during the Thirty Years' War must be considered. The first of these considers the background of Savoy's international profile, emphasising the particular importance of dynasticism to the foreign policies of the duchy during the reign of Carlo Emanuele I. The second chapter shifts attention from the sovereign House to the Scaglia di Verrua, elaborating the role played by the family as a central clan at the ducal court operating its own cultural and political agendas while in constant and close interaction with the ruling dynasty.

The second and third parts focus on international relations between 1624 and 1632. The second part covers the mission to Paris from 1624 to 1627, the period when Scaglia began to establish both his international reputation and also the political ideas that he carried to the end of his life. It charts the relationship between Scaglia and the courts of Paris and London at a time when Savoy shifted from a clear anti-Habsburg stance to one of ambivalence in the wake of the treaty of Monzón. The settlements of Monzón in 1626 and Regensburg and Cherasco in 1630–1 were indeed pivotal not only to Savoy but also to the Thirty Years' War. They showed how the duchy conducted diplomacy in the context of dynastic and political ambitions within both the Italian peninsula and Europe, and also how it interacted with the leading powers. This period saw the death of Duke Carlo Emanuele I and the accession of his son Vittorio Amedeo I, an important juncture when Savoy moved towards an alignment with the Habsburgs, and then back towards France. In turn this raised questions about the relative strategic benefits of alliance with Spain or France, whether the dukes of Savoy in fact saw France as a more natural ally than Spain, given the duchy's geographical proximity to France and Savoy's dynastic claims to territories under Spanish protection in north Italy. In doing so, these chapters demonstrate the manner in which Alessandro Scaglia conducted a pragmatic form of diplomacy in response to the seeming anarchy of international relations in this period. This involves considering the most difficult and significant diplomatic problems of the period, among them England's wars with France and Spain and the war in north Italy, all of which involved Scaglia and his home state of Savoy. More broadly these sections consider the importance of Scaglia's reputation and image as a culturally sophisticated diplomat with a range of like-minded contacts and friends, who was capable of mediating in European disputes, while increasingly pursuing his own political agenda in the context of Savoy's changing relations with France and Spain.

The concluding part of the book addresses the period of Alessandro Scaglia's exile in the Spanish Netherlands, from 1632 until 1641, return-ing to the themes of state and family interest, diplomacy and cultural patronage, and the role of the individual in power politics. Through the lens of Alessandro Scaglia the international fortunes of the Savoyard state

again come into focus. Both chapters in the section deal with the relationship between Scaglia and Savoy in the 1630s, a difficult topic to
discuss since the surviving archival evidence dealing with these years is
by its nature equivocal about the extent and form of informal contact
between the exile and his home state. More generally, this section exam-
ines the concept of exile from an individual's home state, considering the
role of Scaglia's own political interests, whether he employed exile and
his connections with the Spanish to create a more favourable political
climate in Savoy. The book argues that exile should be viewed neither
purely as a negative gesture, nor as a representation of utter isolation, a
position the abate himself never seems to have accepted. These were years
in which two members of the ruling House of Savoy and two members
of the Scaglia di Verrua turned to Alessandro as a means of dealing with
crisis in Savoy, while he himself maintained a high profile through an
ostentatious manner of life and major artistic patronage, highlighted by
the remarkable string of commissions from Van Dyck. These chapters argue that for Scaglia the Spanish Netherlands offered different and indeed
positive opportunities for securing political objectives as his home state
descended into dynastic crisis and civil war.

Writing as an exile from Brussels in 1633, Alessandro Scaglia mem-
orably declared that, 'we are in the most public theatre, so to speak, of
Europe'.[22] Even beyond its immediate context, this well-turned phrase
remains appropriate for the abate's career as a whole. This book looks at
international relations one step away from the stance of the great powers,
aside from a purely French or Spanish point of departure, from the perspective of Savoy as a European state of the second rank, and from the
viewpoint of Scaglia as a subject of the duke of Savoy. It argues that a study
of the court of Savoy through Alessandro Scaglia and his family clan represents a way of reconsidering how foreign policies were formulated as the
outcome of the three intertwined strands of state dynasticism, aristocratic
family interest and individual creativity. In doing so the book addresses
with different priorities a number of the most important problems of
the Thirty Years' War, from the involvement of England in Europe to
the succession crisis in Mantua and Monferrato. In the minds and words
of contemporaries, Abate Alessandro Scaglia was a diplomat of the first
importance who remained at the centre of European diplomacy throughout most of his career. By studying his career one can gain insights into
how early modern international relations worked not only in a political
framework but also in a broad social and cultural context from which it
was never separated.

---

[22] AGR SEG 596, f. 219, Scaglia to Olivares, 24 June 1633.

PART I

DYNASTIC POWER: THE HOUSE OF SAVOY AND THE SCAGLIA DI VERRUA

1

DYNASTIC POWER: SAVOY AND EUROPE

After the treaty of Câteau-Cambrésis in 1559 and the conclusion of the Habsburg–Valois rivalries in the Italian peninsula, north Italy supposedly enjoyed some fifty years of relative peace. But by the early decades of the seventeenth century, north Italy was again one of the most unstable regions in Europe. Not only was it the scene of a renewed and intense rivalry between the ruling dynasties of France and Spain, but the independent states of the peninsula themselves engaged in frequent struggles for territorial, political and cultural superiority against each other, often in alliance with the two Catholic 'super powers'. Some states were perhaps more culpable than others in generating instability. Of the major conflicts that shook the region in the first decades of the seventeenth century, the wars in Mantua and Monferrato (1613–17 and 1628–31) and the wars in the Valtelline and Genoa (1625–6) were all instigated, at least in part, by the duchy of Savoy. Accounts of the Thirty Years' War indeed have rarely been kind to the duchy, and not only because of its frequent interventions in regional conflicts. From the seventeenth century through to the *Risorgimento* of the mid-nineteenth century and beyond, Savoy has been subjected to numerous, if typically misleading, historiographical traditions, its role in the international arena of diplomacy and power politics in turn raising fundamental questions about how the duchy and the entire Italian peninsula have been integrated into accounts of early modern Europe.

The most important historiographical traditions have followed the political unification of the Italian peninsula into a single nation-state during the nineteenth century. In the wake of national unification, Savoy was portrayed by some patriotic post-*Risorgimento* historians as a haven of political independence in a peninsula riven by conflicts and cowering under the long shadow of Habsburg military power. The duchy, so it was argued, enjoyed both political and cultural superiority over its lesser Italian neighbours because of the unflinching desire of the dukes of Savoy to assert themselves against foreign domination, even to the point of war.[1] Following the treaty of Câteau-Cambrésis Duke Emanuele Filiberto of Savoy (1528–80) was restored to his patrimonial land that had experienced occupation from the 1530s by French, Bernese and Imperial troops, prefiguring the national unification of the nineteenth century. Emanuele Filiberto's sole son and heir, Carlo Emanuele I, was in turn elevated to an exalted position as the lone defender of native Italian liberties against the interventions of outside powers. Accordingly, through the actions of these Savoyard dukes, the House of Savoy itself was viewed as the nationalistic prototype of the dynasty that eventually unified Italy.[2]

This traditional view of valiant Savoyard independence was inextricably coupled with the notion of liberty and had at least part of its origins well before the nineteenth century. Liberty, a multi-faceted concept, was hardly new in the Italian peninsula. As Quentin Skinner has elaborated, one conceptual tradition of political liberty enjoyed a history in the republican civic-states of the Italian peninsula that dated back to the middle ages, while the Italian historian Lino Marini has directed attention to the struggles in the later middle ages between the constituent territories of the duchy of Savoy over constitutional and economic rights or liberties.[3] The specific notion of liberty employed by dukes of Savoy, not least by Carlo Emanuele I, differed from those traditions of civic or economic rights. It was more concerned on a state level with addressing the extent of Spanish power that claimed control over the kingdoms of Naples and Sicily and the duchy of Milan, as well as an effective protectorate over the republic of Genoa. In essence this meant political freedom from Spanish dominion even if the Spanish Habsburgs were not in fact concerned with imposing their supposedly tyrannical will over all the states of Italy, let

---

[1] Giuseppe Olmi, 'La corte nella storiografia Italiana dell'Ottocento', in Cesare Mozarelli and Giuseppe Olmi (eds.), *La corte nella cultura e nella storiografia: immagini tra Otto e Novecento* (Rome, 1983), p. 81. For some classic statements of this view see Luigi Cibrario, *Origine e progressi delle istituzioni della monarchia di Savoia sino alla costituzione del regno d'Italia* (second edition, Florence, 1869), pp. 148–9; Domenico Carutti, *Storia della diplomazia della corte di Savoia (dal 1494 al 1773)*, 4 vols. (Rome, 1875–80), II, book VI, p. 310. A more moderate expression of this sentiment can be found in R. Quazza, 'La politica di Carlo Emanuele I durante la guerra dei trent'anni', *Carlo Emanuele I Miscellanea*, 1 (1930), 4–5.

[2] Olmi, 'La corte nella storiografia', in Mozarelli and Olmi (eds.), *La corte*, pp. 72–6, 84; Ruth Kleinman, 'Carlo Emanuele I and the Bohemian election of 1619', *European Studies Review*, 5 (1975); Daniela Frigo, 'L'affermazione della Sovranità', in Cesare Mozarelli (ed.), *'Familia' del principe e famiglia aristocratica*, 2 vols. (Rome, 1988), p. 295. Even the foundation of a national collection of the arts was affected by *Risorgimento* views of Italian history. Jaynie Anderson, 'National museums, the art market and Old Master paintings', *Wolfenbütteler Forschungen, Kunst und Kunsttheorie 1400–1900*, 48 (1991).

[3] Quentin Skinner, *The Foundations of Modern Political Thought*, 2 vols. (Cambridge 1978); Marini, *Libertà e privilegio*.

alone with creating a feared 'universal monarchy' across the entirety of Christian Europe.[4]

Certainly, the violent confrontations between Savoy and Spain in north Italy during the early seventeenth century provided ample opportunities for the Savoyard duke to tap into this version of political liberty, as he himself became 'the symbol and point of reference to all those who aspired to a return of the peninsula to Italians', according to Franco Barcia.[5] In December 1614 Duke Carlo Emanuele I commissioned the Modenese poet Alessandro Tassoni, who was then resident in Rome, to write a defence of Savoy's military incursion into the duchy of Monferrato following the death in 1612 of Carlo Emanuele I's son-in-law, Duke Francesco IV of Mantua and Monferrato.[6] The conflict began with Savoy's invasion of Monferrato in the spring of 1613 and had little to do with notions of liberty as such, and more to do with the duke's own territorial claims to that separable duchy. But the extreme sensitivity of north Italy to Madrid's own strategic considerations, added to the fact that Carlo Emanuele also attacked Genoa, dragged the Spanish Habsburgs into confrontation with Savoy. The conflict lasted beyond the two efforts to conclude the war at the treaties of Asti in 1615, until 1617, by which time Savoy, facing direct attack from Spanish forces, no longer had the support of France or Venice that had been offered earlier.[7] Inevitably the war activated the familiar anti-Habsburg rhetoric of the defence of Italian freedom against foreign, primarily Spanish, interference.[8] Divided into two sections, the *Filippiche* were initially circulated in manuscript because of their more than controversial message in criticising other Italian states; they were eventually published in four different editions in May 1615.[9] Tassoni's aim was straightforwardly to eulogise the role of the Savoyard

---

[4] See also the rather dated account of liberty defined against Spanish dominance in Vittorio di Tocco, *Ideali d'indipendenza in Italia durante la preponderanza spagnuola* (Messina, 1926).

[5] Franco Barcia, 'La Spagna negli scrittori politici italiani del XVI e XVII secolo', in Chiara Continsio and Cesare Mozzarelli (eds.), *Repubblica e virtù: pensiero politico e Monarchia Cattolica fra XVI e XVII secolo* (Rome, 1995), p. 191. Even though the war was not ultimately successful, Carlo Emanuele seemed to be a valient loser, for, as Romolo Quazza has written, 'when the war of Monferrato was finished [Carlo Emanuele I] was materially vanquished, morally victorious'. *Storia politica d'Italia: preponderenza spagnuola, 1559–1700* (Milan, 1950), p. 432.

[6] *Storia politica d'Italia*, book III, part II, chapter 2.

[7] For the treaties of Asti to terminate Savoy's incursions into Monferrato see Jean Dumont (ed.), *Corps universel diplomatique du droit des gens, contenant un receuil des traitez d'alliance, de paix, etc. faits en Europe depuis le régne de Charlemagne jusques à présent*, 8 vols. (Amsterdam, 1726–31), V, part II, pp. 263, 271–2.

[8] Di Tocco, *Ideali d'indipendenza*, p. 89; Pietro Pulliati, *Bibliografia di Alessandro Tassoni*, 2 vols. (Florence, 1969-70), I, p. 94.

[9] *Ibid.*, p. 95.

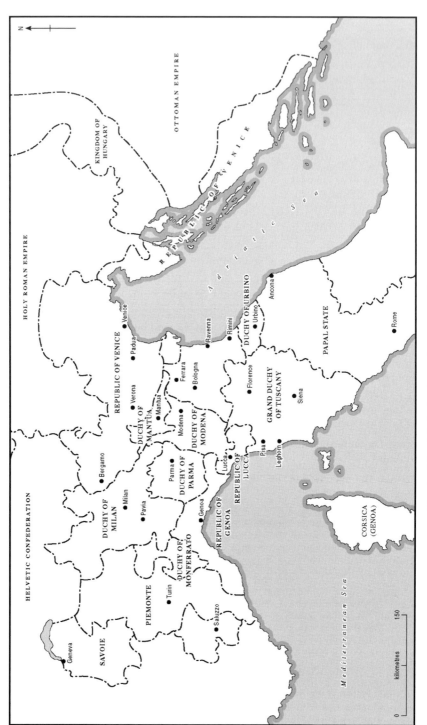

Fig. 1   North Italy in the early seventeenth century.

Fig. 2   The duchy of Savoy *c.* 1627.

duke as the tireless and typically lone defender of Italian liberties in opposition to the Spanish Habsburgs, his work evoking the orations of Demos-
thenes against Philip of Macedon, oppressor of the Greeks. Accordingly,
in the first half of the *Filippiche* Tassoni praised Carlo Emanuele I for
'fighting for the reputation of the princes of Italy and for our common
liberty', repeating stock anti-Habsburg phrases.[10] He did not end there.
Tassoni concluded the second part of the tract by castigating other Italian
sovereign states not under Spanish control – principally the republic of

[10] *Ibid.*, p. 345.

Venice, the grand-duchy of Tuscany and even the Papal state – for their reluctance to support the duke of Savoy in his, and possibly by implication their, time of acute political need.[11]

While this positive interpretation of Savoy's role as the defender of the Italian peninsula has had a persistent influence on numerous Italian writers, it was not the only account of early modern Savoy's role in international relations. Writing at the beginning of the twentieth century, the historian Luigi Randi for one mixed the view of Savoy as the lone voice against Spanish power with a second powerful tradition that has been equally influential in shaping conceptions of Savoyard and Italian political and cultural history. In his biography of Cardinal Maurizio (1593–1657), Duke Carlo Emanuele I's fourth son Randi wrote that 'only the House of Savoy stood out as a contrast to the domination of foreigners', especially Spain, 'the natural enemy of every independent Italian prince'. Savoy's struggle to maintain independence, according to Randi, came in a period not only when the domination of Spain had effectively undermined political liberty but also when the Italian peninsula was itself languishing in the trough of decline.[12]

The crucial theme of decline, a fundamental opposite to the dynamic force of political liberty, has been equally resonant in histories of the Italian peninsula. Like the theme of liberty, it nevertheless derived in part from the early modern period, with the perpetual rivalries between the Habsburgs and French ruling dynasties over north Italy. While this rivalry had initially focused on gaining control of the duchy of Milan, culminating in the Holy Roman Emperor Charles V's campaigns of the 1530s, the entire peninsula remained one of the key strategic theatres of the leading powers, certainly until the War for the Spanish Succession at the beginning of the eighteenth century when the Spanish composite monarchy was effectively partitioned. The fortunes of the Burgundian inheritance of the Spanish Netherlands and the Franche-Comté in northern Europe were linked with those of the Italian and Iberian peninsulas, creating a complex political relationship between the Spanish and Austrian

---

[11] Alessandro Tassoni, *Filippiche contra gli spagnuoli*, in *Prose politiche e morali*, 2 vols. (Rome and Bari, 1978), II, p. 361. The tract seems to have been enlarged to seven parts, though not by Tassoni, and was reprinted with an anonymous response, *Risposta alle scritture intitolate Filippiche*, which inverted his argument by blaming Carlo Emanuele I for bringing war to the Italian peninsula. Pulliati, *Bibliografia*, p. 97 for bibliographical information.

[12] Luigi Randi, *Il Principe Cardinale Maurizio* (Florence, 1901), pp. 8, 10, 12. The idea of decline was perhaps most importantly expressed by Benedetto Croce, who was preoccupied in the first place with the seemingly woeful state of Italian literature in the first half of the seventeenth century, a trough from which he argued Italian writers only emerged towards the end of the century. Benedetto Croce, *Storia dell'età barocca in Italia* (Milan, 1993), especially chapter 1.

branches of the Habsburgs. With the revolt in the Netherlands from 1566 and continuing rivalries between Spain and France over the Italian peninsula, which were only temporarily halted by the French Wars of Religion, the Spanish monarchy was set the monumental task of defending its territorial possessions and prestige across continental Europe.

Neither of the two Catholic 'super powers' was willing, or indeed able, to exclude Italy from its strategic calculations, not least because the logistics of the Spanish composite monarchy depended to a large degree on open lines of communication between the peninsula and the Low Countries in northern Europe. One of the routes of the Spanish Road passed directly through Savoyard territory and the key Alpine pass through the Val di Susa to the west of the ducal capital and its fortress, giving the duchy a crucial role in regional geo-politics, especially when the other major Alpine route, through the Valtelline, was itself frequently insecure.[13] Although this meant that the leading powers were in fact highly sensitive to preserving good relations with states such as Savoy, some more nationalistic Italian historians like Randi were nevertheless confronted with the problem of how to discuss the open involvement of these leading powers in a peninsula that from the mid-nineteenth century had effectively rejected foreign intervention. The seventeenth century, coming after the apparent glories of the Renaissance but before the satisfaction of territorial unification and full political independence, was nothing less than embarrassing.

In this light the Italian states of the seventeenth century were stereotypically listless, with little energy or capability for affecting their individual and collective political destinies.[14] Indeed, while Randi argued that Savoy was effectively alone in rising above this political turpitude, to other historians the duchy was as much, if not more, a victim of decline than the other states of the peninsula. The evidence for political decline, like that of liberty, again seemed to exist in abundance, not least during the first half of the seventeenth century when Carlo Emanuele I was on the ducal throne. As Emanuele Filiberto had in 1553 inherited a duchy suffering from war and foreign interventions so his son Carlo Emanuele I bequeathed Savoy in a piteous state to his successor. At the time of Carlo Emanuele I's death in July 1630 north Italy was being ravaged by virulent plague (to which he himself succumbed) and the patrimonial Savoyard lands were once more occupied by French, Spanish and Imperial troops following the seemingly disastrous involvement in the war for the

---

[13] Parker, *The Army of Flanders*, p. 71, for an indication of the logistical route.

[14] See Giuseppe Olmi's comments, 'La corte nella storiografia dell'Ottocento', in Mozarelli and Olmi (eds.), *La corte*, pp. 65–75. See also Pierpaolo Merlin *et al.* (eds.), *Il Piemonte sabaudo: stato e territori in età moderna* (Turin, 1994), p. 174, and Guido Quazza, *La decadenza italiana nella storia europea* (Turin, 1971), part I.

succession of Mantua and Monferrato. Even by early modern standards such a direct contravention of territorial integrity seemed to break what were arguably the golden rules of good government. When in 1580 Carlo Emanuele I assumed the ducal throne from his dying father, Emanuele Filiberto reportedly advised his son that 'your age had already made you capable of governing the states that I leave you; take care to conserve them for your heirs'.[15] The Piedmontese Jesuit Giovanni Botero (1544–1617), employed by Carlo Emanuele I as a tutor to the ducal sons at the beginning of the seventeenth century, also had a relatively clear conception of the duties of the prince which he elaborated in his highly influential treatise on political statecraft, *Della ragion di Stato* (1589). The good prince acting according to the precepts of 'reason of state' was expected to defend both his subjects and his territorial state; 'the state', according to Botero in the opening sentence of the treatise, was 'firm rule over people, and reason of state the means of creating, protecting and increasing such a territory'.[16] This high moral and political responsibility effectively entrusted to the sovereign as a guardian of his dynasty, subjects and patrimonial lands was something that Carlo Emanuele I had arguably failed to fulfil on his death.

Given these factors, Carlo Emanuele I's dubious legacy to his successor Vittorio Amedeo I seemingly implied that he was not in control of his own political destiny, and by extension the destiny of the duchy of Savoy. Political impotence has indeed been a crucial component of the historiography of Italian decadence. Yet according to a third tradition of historical interpretation this view of decline has itself been turned on its head to suggest that Carlo Emanuele I was in fact fundamentally reckless and overambitious, hot-headedly pursuing policies that cost the duchy heavily in the early seventeenth century and moreover destabilised the entire region of north Italy.[17] His siege of the city of Geneva in December 1602 which culminated in the infamous *Escalade*, the botched attempt to take the Reformed city by force of arms when Savoyard troops were thwarted in scaling the city's defensive walls, has been taken as but one spectacular example of ill-considered Savoyard territorial ambitions. The duke's still more ambitious plan to obtain both the vacant Bohemian and Imperial crowns at the head of a makeshift anti-Habsburg coalition following the death of Emperor Matthias in 1619, on the other hand, has

---

[15] Samuel Guichenon, *Histoire généalogique de la Royale Maison de Savoie*, 2 vols. (Lyons, 1660), I, p. 697.

[16] Botero, *Della ragion di stato*, p. 55.

[17] For instance, see Quazza, 'La politica di Carlo Emanuele I', 3; Quazza *Preponderanza spagnuola*, p. 431; Litta, *Celebri famiglie Italiane*, 'Duchi di Savoia', table XV (Milan, 1844).

been viewed as fanciful, if not faintly ridiculous.[18] It seems hardly surprising that a recent study of early modern Italy has characterised Carlo Emanuele I as 'one of the most incautious rulers of the age'.[19] Even Samuel Guichenon, a Savoyard subject whose monumental genealogical history of the House of Savoy written in the 1650s heaped praise on the exploits of successive dukes to rank the dynasty with the royal families of Europe, addressed Carlo Emanuele I's apparently insatiable appetite for war with the awkward gloss that

> his enormous courage evident in so many episodes gave him such great aspirations that he could not contain his ambitions within the borders set for his lands, and he let loose his designs of which only the Caesars and Alexanders had been capable, having such a high opinion of his conduct, his spirit and his bearing that he believed nothing could block them.[20]

Looking over Carlo Emanuele I's fifty-year reign from 1580 until 1630 it would be hard to deny that he was a political opportunist. By nature the 'chameleon', as he has been described, was willingly involved in territorial and international disputes at virtually any opportunity, and when circumstances demanded he tapped into an established stock of political and cultural images about liberty and foreign tyranny (principally Spanish tyranny) to rationalise his ambitions.[21] Yet taking the three broad historiographical strands together, Carlo Emanuele I was not the selfless defender of Italian liberties, nor was he languishing in a decline, and finally he was neither reckless nor entirely cynical. The Savoyard duke had no evident conception of a single Italian nation-state, even of a unitary territorial state under the direction of the Savoyard dynasty as eventually emerged during the *Risorgimento*. Moreover, while the language of 'liberty' implied that his international aspirations were in line with those

---

[18] Much of the historiography on the siege of Geneva has been written by Genevans, which has obviously led to some bias. See the comments in Kleinman's article, 'Carlo Emanuele I and the Bohemian election of 1619'. For Carlo Emanuele I's attempts on Geneva, Saluzzo and Provence in the sixteenth century see Merlin *et al.* (eds.), *Il Piemonte*, pp. 182–7.

[19] Hanlon, *Twilight of a military tradition*, p. 278.

[20] Guichenon, *Histoire généalogique*, I, p. 866. See also *ibid.*, I, p. 708. For a similarly ambivalent judgement of Carlo Emanuele I see Vittorio Siri, *Memorie recondite dall'anno 1601 sino al 1640*, 8 vols. (Lyons, 1677–9), VII, pp. 197–8, and Quazza, 'La politica di Carlo Emanuele', 4. The nineteenth-century historian Domenico Carutti, author of one of the classic histories of Savoy, was himself candid about the ambitions of Carlo Emanuele I and the problems facing Savoy at the point of his death, but gave him the benefit of the doubt by arguing that if the French had not entered Casale in 1630 the duke's reputation would have been 'raised to the stars'. Carutti blamed the invasion of French troops into north Italy on an inept local commander. Carutti, *Storia della diplomazia*, II, p. 310.

[21] Domenico Sella, *Seventeenth Century Italy* (London, 1997), p. 5.

of other Italian states in a common cause they in fact placed the duke
in direct competition with them for territory and prestige. The picture
that emerges from Carlo Emanuele I's foreign policies suggests an underlying consistency towards foreign polcies where he, like other dukes of
Savoy, viewed his state as a potential leader of a group of different and
independent sovereign territories within the peninsula, each one vying
for power and prestige, often in alliance with either France or Spain.
That these independent states remained rivals was evident in certain key
flashpoints during the early seventeenth century, most strikingly over the
contentious issue of the succession to Mantua and Monferrato, where
Savoy's unresolved territorial claims brought the duchy into diplomatic
and military confrontation with rival Italian sovereign powers.

   Far from operating without regard to wider principles, Duke Carlo
Emanuele I was invariably motivated and guided by his dynastic priorities,
and it is on them that the rest of the chapter will focus. While not the only
factor in the formulation of foreign policies, dynasticism was arguably of
greater importance than 'material' considerations such as his military
resources, or the duchy's pivotal geographical position, as outlined in the
Introduction. It was certainly the case that so long as Savoy maintained
its position as the 'gatekeeper of the Alps', with independent control of
the west Alpine passes, the duchy enjoyed some tangible leverage over
France and Spain. Savoy's importance to France and Spain was, at least
on a basic level, governed by the duchy's geographical position. But the
power afforded to Savoy by its control of passes through the Alps, and
its capacity as a regional military force, were primarily used by Carlo
Emanuele I as tools in his foreign policies, the means to dynastic ends.
If during the early seventeenth century Carlo Emanuele I had calculated
in terms of his material power alone, he would perhaps have been less
willing to push his state (and north Italy by extension) repeatedly to war
and crisis. Dynasticism established, energised and justified the territorial
ambitions of Savoyard dukes within the Italian peninsula and further
afield in Europe, in a context where many disputed territories were not
subject to codified laws of succession and were thus open to negotiation.
Indeed, even if unresolved dynastic interests remained dormant for years
or even generations, they could be activated at any appropriate time with
a strong semblance of legitimacy, although it was rarely in the interests of
sovereigns to let any of them lapse for too long.[22]

   If the duke's dynastic and territorial strategies are taken into account,
the assumptions and aspirations of Savoy's foreign policies certainly become more comprehensible. Duke Carlo Emanuele I was not a political

---

[22] For a near-contemporary assessment of Savoy's various territorial claims consult
Guichenon, *Histoire généalogique*, I, pp. 96–111.

chancer but a sovereign who was always alert to his unfulfilled dynastic rights, and who was willing, and perhaps even compelled, to fight for them as his particular responsibility to his House. Within the Italian peninsula the duke of Savoy's most important and politically sensitive territorial claim was to the duchy of Monferrato, one part of the Gonzagan collection of territories that also included Mantua. The issue of the Gonzaga succession flared up twice in the early seventeenth century with massive international consequences, first in 1613, following Duke Francesco IV's death, and then after the death of Duke Vincenzo II in December 1627. As will be seen in chapter 5, Mantua and Monferrato were essentially two separate states that had been linked following the dynastic union in 1531 between Federico II Gonzaga, duke of Mantua, and Margherita, daughter of Guglielmo IX Paleologo of Monferrato. Though linked (not formally unified) under a single ruler, each sovereignty had different customs of succession, of partible inheritance in Mantua and of inheritance through both the male and female lines in Monferrato.[23] The particular status of Monferrato as a *feudo feminino* provided the basis for the claim of the House of Savoy to that duchy alone. Duke Carlo Emanuele I repeatedly argued that female succession was permissible in Monferrato and that consequently he had a claim through a Savoyard connection that predated the marriage in 1531 of Federico and Margherita. The origins of Savoy's claims to Monferrato dated back to the marriage between Aimone, count of Savoy, and Iolanda, daughter of Teodoro Paleologo, marquis of Monferrato, in 1330. According to their marriage contract, all of the Paleologo inheritance would pass to Savoy in the event of the male line of Teodoro becoming extinct. The claim to portions of Monferrato was revived following the marriage in 1485 of Carlo I of Savoy (died 1490) to Bianca, daughter of Guglielmo VI Paleologo, and again in 1533 following the death of Giovanni Giorgio Paleologo, and lastly by the marriage in 1608 of Margherita, a legitimate daughter of Carlo Emanuele I, to Francesco IV, who ruled as duke of Mantua and Monferrato for an unexpectedly brief period in 1612.[24]

---

[23] The issue of Mantua and Monferrato has recently been examined by David Parrott, 'The Mantuan Succession'.

[24] Litta, *Celebri famiglie Italiane*, 'Duchi di Savoia', table VII (Milan, 1841), and 'Paleologo, Marchesi di Monferrato', table I (Milan, 1847). Guichenon, *Histoire généalogique*, I, p. 645; Pietro Giovanni Capriata, *The history of the wars of Italy from the year MDCXIII to MDCLIV in XVIII books, rend'red into English by Henry, earl of Monmouth* (London. 1663), pp. 7–9. See also Parrott, 'The Mantuan Succession', 32–3, and footnote 14 in David Parrott and Robert Oresko, 'The sovereignty of Monferrato and the citadel of Casale as European problems in the early modern period', in D. Ferari and A. Quondam (eds.), *Stefano Guazzo e Casale tra Cinque e Seicento* (Mantua, 1997), which strongly reinforces the closeness of dynastic ties between the House of Savoy and the Paleologo family, before even those of the Gonzaga House.

THE SAVOYARD SUCCESSION DURING THE SEVENTEENTH CENTURY

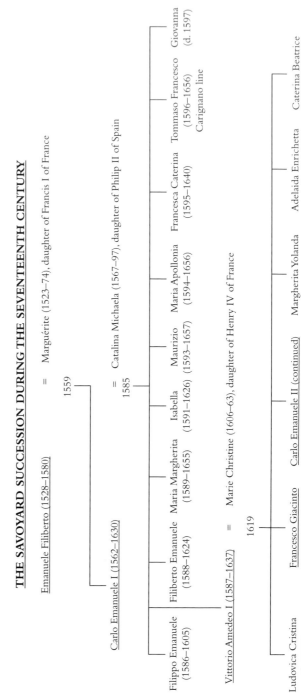

Emanuele Filiberto (1528–1580) = Marguérite (1523–74), daughter of Francis I of France

1559

Carlo Emanuele I (1562–1630) = Catalina Michaela (1567–97), daughter of Philip II of Spain

1585

Filippo Emanuele (1586–1605)

Filiberto Emanuele (1588–1624)

Maria Margherita (1589–1655)

Isabella (1591–1626)

Maurizio (1593–1657)

Maria Apollonia (1594–1656)

Francesca Caterina (1595–1640)

Tommaso Francesco (1596–1656) Carignano line

Giovanna (d. 1597)

Vittorio Amedeo I (1587–1637) = Marie Christine (1606–63), daughter of Henry IV of France

1619

Ludovica Cristina (b. 1629)

Francesco Giacinto (1632–8)

Carlo Emanuele II (continued) (1634–75)

Margherita Yolanda (1635–63)

Adelaida Enrichetta (1636–76)

Caterina Beatrice (?)

Carlo Emanuele II (1634–75) = 1). Françoise-Madeleine, daughter of Gaston d'Orléans

1664 2). Maria Giovanna Battista, daughter of Duke Charles Amadée of Neamours

Vittorio Amedeo II (1666–1732) = Anne-Marie, daughter of Philippe d'Orléans
king of Sicily, 1713; 1684
king of Sardinia, 1720

Maria Ludovica Gabriella (1688–1714)
m. Philip V of Spain

Vittorio Amedeo (1699–1715)

Carlo Emanuele III (1701–73)
king of Sardinia, 1730

Maria Adelaïde (1685–1712)
m. Louis, duke of Burgundy

Fig. 3 The House of Savoy during the seventeenth century.

Fig. 4   Anthony van Dyck, *Prince Filiberto Emanuele of Savoy* (1624). This portrait was completed following Van Dyck's invitation in 1624 to travel to Palermo by Filiberto Emanuele, who had recently been appointed as viceroy of Sicily. The portrait served several purposes. Most obviously, it recorded Filiberto Emanuele's elevation as viceroy by Philip III, important to both Savoy and Spain for improving dynastic and political relations between the Savoyards and Habsburgs. The timing of the portrait may also have been linked to the project for a marriage between the prince and his niece, Maria Gonzaga, whose marital status potentially governed the fate of Mantua and Monferrato, where Savoy had a dynastic claim. Filiberto Emanuele died in August 1624, within months of the completion of the portrait.

The complexity of relations between the duchies of Savoy and Monferrato was increased by their ill-defined borders. As Peter Sahlins' suggestive study of the seemingly 'fossilised' Pyrenean boundary between France and Spain has indeed argued, borders were more complex in early modern Europe than their modern counterparts too often suggest. They could signify more than simply territorial delimitations, but also different borders of jurisdiction, where loyalties were defined primarily by the relationships between rulers and subjects above and beyond territorial divisions.[25] Some ecclesiastical benefices under Savoyard jurisdiction, for instance, enjoyed rights outside the territorial limits of the duchy, while dioceses in Monferrato held property in the Savoyard state, a problem that remained unresolved until the reforms conducted by Pope Benedict XIII Orsini (1649–1730) in 1727 following pressure by Vittorio Amedeo II.[26] Similarly, in the realm of secular territorial interest some leading noble families who were subjects of the duke of Savoy also held land in Monferrato, which had the potential of raising searching questions about their political loyalties. The Valperga di Rivara were one of the most distinguished family clans from Piemonte and enjoyed considerable favour at the Savoyard court, particularly after the restoration of Duke Emanuele Filiberto. The marriage of one member into a family from Monferrato nevertheless had serious consequences for the Valperga during the Gonzaga succession disputes of 1612 and 1627, since as part of the marriage dowry he acquired land outside Savoy's jurisdiction. With properties in both Savoy and Monferrato the family divided, though as Alessandro Scaglia's exile will suggest, families faced with political crisis could place their members in different political camps to safeguard their collective interests.[27]

Savoy's second major disputed territorial interest in north Italy was the region of Zuccarello, which was at least formally in the possession of the Spanish-protected republic of Genoa. Carlo Emanuele I had bought Zuccarello from its previous owner, Scipione del Carretto, in 1588. However, the sale of Zuccarello, which stood within the *Reichsitalien*, that part of the Italian peninsula under the feudal guidance of the Holy Roman Emperor, had not been recognised formally by the Emperor.

[25] Peter Sahlins, *Boundaries: The Making of France and Spain in the Pyrenees* (Berkeley, Los Angeles and Oxford, 1989), especially the introduction.

[26] Achille Erba, *La Chiesa sabauda tra Cinque e Seicento: ortodossia tridentina, gallicanesimo savoiardo e assolutismo ducale (1580–1630)* (Rome, 1979), pp. 28–9. Though see Carlo Marco Belfadi and Marzio Achille Romani, 'Il Monferrato: una frontiera scomoda fra Mantova e Torino (1536–1707)', in Carlo Ossola, Claude Raffestein and Mario Ricciardi (eds.), *La frontiera da stato a nazione: il caso Piemonte* (Rome, 1987), which argues that the period in fact saw a rationalisation of Savoy's territorial borders.

[27] Woolf, *Studi sulla nobiltà Piemontese*, pp. 83–93.

This allowed Scipione's brother Ottavio to contest the sale with the support of the republic of Genoa, while arguing that since Scipione had been accused of a murder he had consequently forfeited any legal rights over the property.[28] Subsequent attempts by Carlo Emanuele I to obtain an unequivocal Imperial decision over the matter of the sale came to nothing. Like the issue of Monferrato, control of Zuccarello remained unresolved into the seventeenth century, the source of potentially serious military conflict in north Italy and a sticking point in relations between Turin and Madrid.[29]

The zeal with which Carlo Emanuele I pursued the claims to Monferrato and Zuccarello during the early seventeenth century has led some historians to conclude that in the first decades of the century Savoy's borders on the French side of the Alps were consolidated once and for all, with the possibilities of territorial expansion thereafter limited solely to the Italian peninsula. Stuart Woolf for one concluded that Emanuele Filiberto and Carlo Emanuele I were in fact concerned with rationalising their states by effectively dropping the claims to Geneva, which Emanuele Filiberto had lost as a result of the 1536 invasion of his duchy by French and Bernese troops, and diverting their attention solely to interests on the Italian side of the Alps.[30] This view of territorial, and by extension political, rationalisation indeed seems to be supported by the example of Carlo Emanuele I's agreement with Henry IV (1553–1610) of France through their treaty signed at Lyons in 1601. The treaty saw the exchange of Savoy's properties of Bugey, Bresse, Valromey and Gex, which were west of the river Rhône, for the French enclave of Saluzzo in the Piedmontese Alps, a territory which had dominated Savoyard ambitions at the close of the sixteenth century when France was riven by civil conflict. The treaty also marked a phase of Savoyard diplomacy that raised the possibility of aligning with France against Spain and Spanish-controlled territory in the Italian peninsula, a project that was only temporarily put

---

[28] Carutti, *Storia della diplomazia*, II, book V, p. 4; Guichenon, *Histoire généalogique*, I, pp. 715, 833. Vittorio Siri also recorded that Savoy claimed rights to Zuccarello because the territory had paid homage to Luigi of Savoy until 1448. Siri, *Memorie recondite*, V, p. 797.

[29] Pietro Rivoire, 'Un diplomatico Piemontese del secolo XVII', *Bollettino Storico-Bibliografico Subalpino*, 2 (1897), 318–19.

[30] Stuart Woolf, 'Sviluppo economico e struttura sociale in Piemonte da Emanuele Filiberto a Carlo Emanuele III', *Nuova Rivista Storica*, 46 (1962), 2–3; Belfadi and Romani, 'Il Monferrato', in Ossola, Raffestein and Ricciardi (eds.), *La frontiera*. For the enormous complexities of Savoyard-Genevan relations during the reign of Emanuele Filiberto see Robert Oresko, 'The question of the sovereignty of Geneva after the Treaty of Câteau – Cambrésis', in Helmut G. Koenigsberger (ed.), *Republiken und Republikanismus im Europa der Frühen Neuzeit. Schriften der Historischen Kollegs Kolloquien 2* (Berlin, 1988).

on hold by the assassination of Henry IV in 1610.[31] Such a view might however fall into a trap of historical inevitability, for contrary to the assumption that early modern Europe saw the final consolidation of territorial borders into a recognisably rational shape, borders in north Italy remained far from stable, let alone formalised, during the seventeenth century.[32] The sheer variety of Savoy's unresolved dynastic claims meant that the duchy could potentially expand in any geographical direction. To the south lay the republic of Genoa and Zuccarello, while Monferrato was to the east; Languedoc lay west and had been the target of Carlo Emanuele during the 1590s, before Henry IV had been able to reassert control over France, while the city of Geneva, lost in 1536, was to the north.

The House of Savoy's potential rights to lands beyond the Italian peninsula were equally wide-ranging and they too were retained by successive dukes in the hope that they might be realised. The Portuguese succession crisis of 1578–80 brought to the fore the House of Savoy's right to the royal throne through Duke Carlo II's (1504–53) marriage in 1521 to Maria Beatriz (1504–38), daughter of King Manuel I (1469–1521) of Portugal, a claim that was as strong if not stronger than that of Philip II of Spain, who of course obtained the crown in 1580 through force of arms as much as by dynastic argument.[33] Carlo Emanuele I's marriage in 1585 to Catalina Michaela (1567–97), the younger of Philip II's two daughters, opened other avenues for dynastic advancement into the Spanish composite monarchy, and the Spanish king himself suggested that the first male child of the union might inherit the Milanese territories under his rule, with the title of king of Lombardy.[34] The marriage in 1598 of Philip II's elder daughter, Isabella Clara Eugenia (1566–1633), to her cousin Archduke Albert VI (1559–1621) of Austria and the recognition that the Spanish Netherlands as a distinct territorial unit was potentially alienable from the Spanish composite monarchy, on the other hand, left open the possibility that Carlo Emanuele I, as the widowed husband of

---

[31] Dumont (ed.), *Corps universel diplomatique*, V, part II, pp. 10–13. On the issue of Saluzzo see G. Vita, 'Carlo Emanuele I e la questione del marchesato di Saluzzo (1598–1601)', *Bollettino Storico-Bibliografico Subalpino*, 24 (1922) and 25 (1923). On Franco-Savoyard relations after the treaty of Lyons see Romolo Quazza, *Preponderanza spagnuola*, book III, part II, chapter 1.

[32] On the borders of Savoy see Claude Raffestein, 'L'evoluzione del sistema delle frontiere del Piemonte dal XVI secolo al XIX secolo', in Ossola, Raffestein and Ricciardi (eds.), *La frontiera*.

[33] Guichenon, *Histoire généalogique*, I, pp. 102–6.

[34] Though this was seemingly restricted to the first male child only and was not extended to any following sons. Litta, *Celebri famiglie Italiane*, 'Duchi di Savoia', table XV (Milan, 1844).

Isabella's younger sister, might in turn inherit the Spanish Netherlands in the event of Albert and Isabella dying without legitimate male issue.[35]

The potential claims to the Portuguese throne and to Spanish territories, formed one element of Savoy's burning ambition to obtain royal status, a tantalising prize for the ducal House throughout the sixteenth and seventeenth centuries; it was not formally achieved until 1713 with the treaty of Utrecht, when Savoy was accorded the royal crown of Sicily, followed more permanently in 1720 by the less significant kingdom of Sardinia.[36] Prior to this, most attention of the dukes of Savoy focused on obtaining the right to the so-called kingdom of Cyprus with the associated royal territories of Jerusalem and Armenia, a claim that was based on its donation to Savoy by the last legitimate member of the Lusignan dynasty, Carlotta (d. 1487), who in 1458 had married Luigi of Savoy (1431–82). However, international recognition of Savoy's ambition proved to be an insurmountable problem. The kingdom of Cyprus was also claimed by the republic of Venice and the issue almost continuously divided the duchy and the republic throughout the early modern period, raising difficult and immensely controversial questions of their relative precedence among the states of the Italian peninsula, and not just those two powers.[37] Savoy's claims to pre-eminence seemed strong. As Robert Oresko has suggested, reiterating a point made as early as 1633 by the Piedmontese polemicist Pietro Monod when justifying the *trattamento reale* of the previous year, it had already become customary for the head of the ducal House to marry daughters of kings, implying closeness between the Savoyard dynasty and the royal dynasties of Europe; Vittorio Amedeo I wedded a daughter of Henry IV, Carlo Emanuele I's father had of course married a daughter of Francis I, while his grandfather Duke Carlo II had taken the daughter of the king of Portugal as a bride.[38] In addition, successive rulers of Savoy from Amedeo VIII (1383–1451), the first duke, secured the privilege of the Imperial vicariate in those parts

---

[35] On Savoy's potential claim to the Spanish Netherlands consult Guichenon, *Histoire généalogique*, I, p. 106; V. Ansaldi, 'Giovanni Botero coi principi sabaudi in Ispagna (da lettere inedite)', *Bollettino Storico-Bibliografico Subalpino*, 35 (1935), 322, 328.

[36] For further information on Savoy's royal ambitions see Robert Oresko, 'The House of Savoy in search for a royal crown in the seventeenth century', in Robert Oresko, G. C. Gibbs and H. M. Scott (eds.), *Royal and Republican Sovereignty in Early Modern Europe: Essays in Memory of Ragnhild Hatton* (Cambridge, 1997), and Luigi La Rocca, 'L'aspirazione del duca Carlo Emanuele I al titolo di re di Piemonte', *Archivio Storico Italiano*, series 5, 46 (1910).

[37] On Venice's claim see, for instance, Siri, *Memorie recondite*, VI, p. 193.

[38] Oresko, 'The House of Savoy', in Oresko, Gibbs and Scott (eds.), *Royal and Republican Sovereignty*, p. 285; Pietro Monod, *Trattato del titolo regio dovuto alla serenissima Casa di Savoia. Insieme con un ristretto delle rivolutioni del Reame di Cipro appartenente alla corona dell'Altezza Reale di Vittorio Amedeo, Duca di Savoia* (Turin, 1633), p. 26.

of the Italian peninsula that were within the Empire following his abdication in 1449 as antipope Felix V (he had abdicated his ducal throne in 1440), while the court of Turin was the only one in the peninsula to have a regular nuncio from Rome. However, on the other side of the balance, the Holy Roman Emperor Maximilian II (1527–76) had in 1569 elevated Tuscany to a grand-duchy, despite the relative newness of the Medici family among the princely houses in Italy.[39] Even earlier than this, in 1560, Pope Paul IV Carafa (1476–1559) had granted the *sala regia* to Venice, primarily a ceremonial gesture though a bitter pill for Emanuele Filiberto and his son Carlo Emanuele I to swallow given the high importance they ascribed to issues of precedence.[40] Even though the Savoyard dynasty, at least, always saw itself above other sovereign powers in the Italian peninsula and as an equal to the royalty of Europe, few European sovereigns were willing to choose definitively between Savoy, Venice and Tuscany. The rivalries and disputes over prestige and status among these independent states could threaten the stability of north Italy.[41]

While Carlo Emanuele I bore the responsibility of promoting existing Savoyard claims across Europe, he was equally alert to the enormous dynastic possibilities afforded by his own children. He himself was the only legitimate son of Duke Emanuele Filiberto through his marriage to Marguérite de Valois.[42] In 1585, nearly five years after succeeding his father to the Savoyard throne, Carlo Emanuele I married Catalina Michaela, travelling to the Iberian peninsula to complete the dynastic transaction.[43] By his marriage Carlo Emanuele I was fortunate, and almost unique in early modern Savoyard history, in having a large number of legitimate

---

[39] For a discussion of the role of the Empire in the peninsula, in particular over issues of ceremonial and political precedence, consult Giovanni Tabacco, *Lo stato sabaudo nel sacro romano impero* (Turin, 1939). For the elevation of Tuscany see Alessandra Contini, 'Aspects of Medicean diplomacy in the sixteenth century', in Frigo (ed.), *Politics and Diplomacy*, pp. 78–9.

[40] Oresko, 'The House of Savoy', in Oresko, Gibbs and Scott (eds.), *Royal and Republican Sovereignty*, pp. 290-1. On the issue of the *sala regia* see for example AST, Cerimoniale, Roma, m. 1, fasc. 9.

[41] Guichenon, *Histoire généalogique*, I, p. 537; Litta, *Celebri famiglie Italiane*, 'Duchi di Savoia', table X (Milan, 1842). On the difficulties faced by Vittorio Amedeo I for obtaining recognition of his declaration of royalty see for instance A. Zanelli, 'Le relazioni fra il Ducato Sabaudo e la Santa Sede dal 1631 al 1637 nel carteggio della Nunziatura Pontificia', *Bollettino Storico-Bibliografico Subalpino*, 41 (1939) and 42 (1940); CSPV 1632–6, pp. 116, 126.

[42] Emanuele Filiberto also had three illegitimate sons, Don Amedeo (d. 1610), Don Filippo (d. 1599) and Othone (d. 1580), and three illegitimate daughters, Maria (1556–80), Matilda (d. 1639) and Beatrice (d. 1580). Guichenon, *Histoire généalogique*, I, pp. 703–6; Litta, *Celebri famiglie Italiane*, 'Duchi di Savoia', table XV (Milan, 1844).

[43] Dumont (ed.), *Corps universel diplomatique*, V, part I, pp. 437–41 for a text of the marriage contract.

sons and daughters who survived into adulthood. These legitimate off-spring were critically important political resources to the duke as the head of the main branch of the family, responsible as he was for planning domestic and foreign strategies; they were probably the most powerful tools available to the duke for maximising existing dynastic claims and creating new territorial and international interests, though given the number of legitimate children Carlo Emanuele I also had to take care in offsetting the considerable financial costs involved in providing for them with any wider benefits.[44]

The eldest of the five sons was Filippo Emanuele who was born in 1586. While the Infanta Catalina Michaela had formally renounced her own claim to the Spanish throne in her marriage contract to Carlo Emanuele I, the Savoyard duke nevertheless viewed his first-born legitimate son as a potential heir to parts of the Habsburg patrimony, or indeed to its entirety.[45] Filippo Emanuele's first name appropriately evoked that of the king of Spain, and his godparents included his cousin, the future Philip III, and maternal aunt, Isabella Clara Eugenia, underlining still further the dynastic connections between the Savoyard and Habsburg Houses.[46] In 1603 the young Filippo Emanuele travelled with his younger brothers, Vittorio Amedeo and Filiberto Emanuele, to Madrid under the charge of Filiberto Gherardo Scaglia and the didactic supervision of the Jesuit Giovanni Botero. The ostensible purpose of the trip was one of goodwill, though the Savoyard duke clearly had his eyes fixed on greater things. At the time of the mission Philip III was, as his father had been, subject to considerable dynastic insecurity, lacking a male heir. Although the Spanish were extremely reluctant formally to recognise Filippo Emanuele as a claimant to the Habsburg territorial inheritance because of the obvious implication that the composite monarchy might pass out of the direct control of the Habsburg dynasty, the House of Savoy nevertheless saw itself as a fall-back option for Spain in the event of a break in the direct line of succession. Filippo Emanuele's journey to Madrid thus reminded the Habsburgs of his potential significance as a dynastic safeguard. Unfortunately for Carlo Emanuele I, however, his young son caught the plague and died on the mission at the same time that Philip III succeeded in fathering a legitimate son and heir, the future Philip IV.

---

[44] Enrico Stumpo, *Finanza e stato moderno nel Piemonte del Seicento* (Rome, 1979), p. 133.

[45] Dumont (ed.), *Corps universel diplomatique*, V, part I, pp. 438–9. See also Carutti, *Storia della diplomazia*, I, pp. 413–14.

[46] Guichenon, *Histoire généalogique*, I, p. 870. As Guichenon recorded here, Filippo Emanuele also had two other godparents, Pope Gregory XIII Boncompagni (1502–85) and the French dowager consort Catherine de' Medici (1519–89).

Filippo Emanuele's death stalled Savoyard ambitions on the glittering prize of the Spanish Habsburg inheritance, though it remained a distant possibility during the seventeenth century. Carlo Emanuele I's third son, Filiberto Emanuele (1588–1624), was himself groomed to continue the special relationship with Spain, serving as a point of contact between the respective courts at Turin and Madrid. In 1597 he was naturalised by Philip II as a prince of the blood and in the following year he was nominated as prior of Castile and León, an honour that was followed by that of the grand-mastership of the order of St John of Jerusalem. On the face of it the promotion was surprising, given the variable relations during the first decades of the seventeenth century between Savoy and Spain over Spanish-protected territory in north Italy. It is quite possible however that both Houses viewed Filiberto Emanuele as an acceptable figure who could potentially straddle the differences that separated Savoy and Spain, particularly in the early 1620s. It was in the interests of both dynasties to maintain a controlled level of contact, for Spain because of the intrinsic strategic importance of Savoy, and for Savoy because of its general policy of playing the leading powers against each other and because of the distant claim to the Spanish composite monarchy. In 1620 Filiberto Emanuele was elevated to the principality of Oneglia, a title associated with Savoy's territorial enclave in the Spanish-protected republic of Genoa. More importantly Philip III appointed the Savoyard prince as viceroy of Sicily in December 1621, a position Filiberto Emanuele marked for posterity with the spectacular portrait commissioned from Anthony van Dyck in 1624 depicting him bearing armour decorated with Savoyard emblems and insignia (Fig. 4).[47] His untimely death due to a plague that swept Sicily in the same year, like that of Filippo Emanuele's death in Madrid in 1603, was undeniably a blow to Savoy's dynastic relations with Spain at what was an important and delicate juncture in the military conflict engulfing Europe after 1618.

The remaining three sons all outlived their father. The eldest of these, the second son, was Vittorio Amedeo (1587–1637), who was established as the prince of Piemonte, heir to Carlo Emanuele I, following Filippo Emanuele's death in 1605. In February 1619 Vittorio Amedeo took as his bride Marie Christine (1606–63), one of the two legitimate sisters of Louis XIII of France. That two sons of the duke of Savoy were groomed

---

[47] Van Dyck, who was in Genoa at the time, was requested by Filiberto to execute the portrait in the Sicilian capital of Palermo. The portrait is now in the Dulwich Picture Gallery. Christopher Brown and Hans Vlieghe (eds.), *Van Dyck, 1599–1641* (London, 1999), p. 172. For further details on Filiberto consult G. Claretta, *Il Principe Emanuele Filiberto di Savoia alla corte di Spagna* (Turin, 1872); Litta, *Celebri famiglie Italiane*, 'Duchi di Savoia', table XVI (Milan, 1844).

to further relations with the court of Spain while another married in the ruling House of France is in itself a testament to the importance of the Savoyards in early modern dynastic politics, as an established Catholic dynasty that controlled a geographically sensitive region. Not only did the union repeat the custom of Savoyards marrying royal daughters, but it also served to mirror the Habsburg dynastic affiliations of two of his brothers, Filippo Emanuele and Filiberto, and thus balance Savoy's interests between France and Spain, albeit at a time when Carlo Emanuele I was inclining to a position of hostility towards the Habsburgs.

Placing legitimate sons into advantageous marriages was evidently crucial to the success of the House of Savoy, as it was for any dynasty responsible for heritable patrimonies in early modern Europe, whether sovereign or noble. Nevertheless, where primogeniture was practised for transmitting land, rather than the main alternative of partible inheritance, a careful balancing of family resources was necessary. Cadet branches of the sovereign House that might follow from the marriages of younger sons could certainly serve as fall-back options during moments of dynastic uncertainty if the eldest son failed to produce his own heirs. Yet the head of the House had to ensure that if any cadet branches of the dynasty were established they would not threaten the greater part of the family's patrimony destined for the eldest legitimate son. The potential problem of creating autonomous cadet branches by dividing the Savoyard patrimony had already become evident in the example of the Nemours family, which was established with its own appanages and titles by Savoy and France from the end of the fifteenth century, and which had settled at the French court during the reign of Francis I.[48] Through the family's connections with the Guise dynasty in France it became clear that the Nemours clan was powerful enough to pursue its own strategies independent of France or Savoy, with the potential of creating a separate sovereignty encompassing both Languedoc and Geneva. The lingering problem was only resolved following the death of Henri, the last Nemours duke, in 1657 and the marriage of the elder of the nieces to Carlo Emanuele II of Savoy, bringing the clan's patrimony back into the hands of the main branch of the Savoyard House.[49]

---

[48] Guichenon, *Histoire généalogique*, II, p. 1051.

[49] *Ibid.*, II, pp. 1049–76; Litta, *Celebri famiglie Italiane*, 'Duchi di Savoia: Duchi del Genevese e di Nemours', tables XII–XIII (Milan, 1842); Robert Oresko, 'The Sabaudian Court 1563–c. 1750', in John Adamson (ed.), *The Princely Courts of Europe, 1500-1750* (London, 1999), pp. 239–40; Romolo Quazza, 'Nevers contra Nemours nel 1624', *Atti e Memorie dell'Accademia Virgiliana*, 30 (1920). See also Vester, 'Territorial politics', section 2, on Jacques de Savoie-Nemours and his role as a cadet of the Savoyard House and a potential claimant to the ducal throne.

In spite of these potential dangers, suitable provision still had to be made for other legitimate sons to ensure that they could enjoy an appropriate position within the dynasty, and moreover that they could contribute to the wider political, social, cultural and financial fortunes of their House. Maurizio, as the fourth son in line, did not marry and instead was granted in 1607 at the age of fourteen a cardinal deaconate by Pope Paul V Borghese.[50] Significantly he did not take full priestly orders, so that as a dynastic 'spare' he remained available for marriage in the event of an unforeseen crisis within the Savoyard House or a diplomatic opportunity, a strategy not uncommon among the elites of early modern Catholic Europe. In 1624 Maurizio was touted as a potential spouse for his niece, Maria Gonzaga, daughter of Margherita of Savoy and Duke Francesco IV of Mantua and Monferrato (to bolster Savoy's claim to Monferrato), and he eventually married another niece, Ludovica Cristina, a daughter of Marie Christine, as part of a process of reconciliation within the Savoyard dynasty after the civil war of 1637–42.[51] Maurizio's position as a prince of the church also conferred other benefits on Savoy by providing the sovereign House with an ecclesiastical source of power at a time when it did not have an automatic cardinalate. It was not until the eighteenth century that the House of Savoy gained this power as a right, and up to that point successive dukes had to rely on the support of other Catholic dynasties and the papacy for nominations to the Sacred College.

Savoy's dependence on other powers for entry to the College of Cardinals did little to dampen Maurizio's tireless energy in promoting what he considered to be his rightful ceremonial status. His career as a prince of the church and a patron of the arts indeed encapsulates the ways in which the House of Savoy sought to place itself at the centre of a cosmopolitan court that ranked not only as a leading dynasty in the Italian peninsula, but also as a significant presence in Europe. His visit to the French court in 1618 to mark the conclusion of the negotiations for the marriage of his elder brother Vittorio Amedeo to Marie Christine was reportedly a 'very solemn affair', with 150 carriages and 800 followers.[52] The occasions of his visits to the papal court were if anything even more

---

[50] He was also granted in succession three titular churches, S. Maria Nuova, S. Eustachio and S. Maria in Via Lata. G. B. Adriani, *Memorie della vita e dei tempi di Monsignor Gio. Secondo Ferrero-Ponziglione Referendario Apostolico, primo Consigliere e Auditore Generale del Principe Cardinale Maurizio di Savoia* (Turin, 1856), p. 221.

[51] The idea emerged after the death of Carlo Emanuele I's eldest son, Filiberto Prince of Oneglia. Romolo Quazza, *Mantova e Monferrato nella politica europea alla vigilia della guerra per la successione, 1624–1627* (Mantua, 1922), p. 63.

[52] ASV Avvisi, 8, f. 335, 7 November 1618. For another contemporary description of Louis XIII's welcoming party see G. Romano (ed.), *Le collezioni di Carlo Emanuele I di Savoia* (Turin, 1995), p. 352.

spectacular and critically important to Savoy in its efforts to assert relative political and cultural superiority among the states of the Italian peninsula.[53] In 1623 he rented an elaborately decorated palace on the Monte Giordano, where he established 'a very stylish court of more than two hundred people'. Three years later, in 1626, Maurizio formed the artistic and literary Accademia dei Desiosi under his direction. It was one of the most significant of the Roman academies that served to rank with other social circles and patronage networks, and his second academy after his Accademia dei Solinghi, which had been formed in Turin and which met at the *Vigna*, later the suburban residence of Duchess Marie Christine.[54] The so-called *Magnificentia Principis* was integral not only for asserting Cardinal Maurizio's own position as a sophisticated and significant patron of the arts, but also for emphasising the fundamental importance of his family as members of a cosmopolitan European court system.[55]

Maintaining this level of display was financially very costly.[56] On more than one occasion Maurizio delayed visits to Rome because, so he claimed, he lacked funds sufficient to reflect his dignity.[57] When he eventually made his entrance in 1631 following a delay ostensibly for financial reasons, he went to great pains to seek the elevation of his ceremonial title from *Eminenza* to *Altezza*, to reflect the reform introduced by Pope Urban VIII Barberini on 10 June 1630 over terms of address at the Sacred College. The reform was intended to place a control on the inflation of titles among the clergy and to mark out those cardinals from royal families, and Maurizio accordingly argued that he should also enjoy this status since he was not only a prince of the church but also the son of a sovereign, with explicit reference to Savoy's royal pretensions over the shadow kingdom of Cyprus.[58] The birth in October 1632 of Francesco

---

[53] For example Adriani, *Memorie*, pp. 149–51 on Maurizio's visit of 1621. See also p. 225.

[54] ASV Avvisi, 9, f. 164, 17 June 1623; f. 172v, 24 June 1623; ff. 178–82, 1 July 1623. I am grateful to Professor Riccardo Merolla of La Sapienza University for directing me to his article, 'L'Accademia dei Desiosi', *Roma moderna e contemporanea*, year III (1995); Adriani, *Memorie*, pp. 222–5. While the career of Cardinal Maurizio encompassing both his ecclesiastical and family strategies in Savoy and at the papal court needs a more focused study based on both Turinese and Roman archives, consult Randi, *Il Principe Cardinale Maurizio di Savoia*; Matthias Oberli, *Magnificentia Principis: Das Mäzenatentum des Prinzen und Kardinals: Maurizio von Savoyen (1593–1657)* (Weimar, 1999).

[55] *Ibid., passim.*

[56] *Ibid.*, pp. 288–93 for tabulated information on Maurizio's expenditure on artistic patronage.

[57] Adriani, *Memorie*, pp. 227–33. Though Oberli's work suggests that the period immediately before Maurizio's journey to Rome was one of the leanest in terms of expenditure on art. Oberli, *Maurizio von Savoyen*, p. 291.

[58] For example, AST Cerimoniale, Roma, m. 1, 'Raisons par lesquelles le Ser^me Prince Cardinal de Savoye ne peut accepter autre Titre, que celuy d'Altesse', 1631; P. Brayda

Giacinto (1632–8), a male heir to Duke Vittorio Amedeo I, provided further opportunities for the uncle, Maurizio, to make visible statements about both his status and that of the House of Savoy at the papal capital. In recognition of this important dynastic event, Maurizio organised a series of elaborate and extravagant celebrations outside his palace on the Monte Giordano lasting a month, which, according to the anonymous *avvisi* of Rome, included bonfires, artificial machines, fireworks and a fountain of red wine.[59]

While Maurizio's position within the church highlighted one critically important strategy employed by Catholic dynasties in early modern Europe, the career of the youngest ducal son, Tommaso Francesco (1596–1656), bore witness to another. In January 1625 Tommaso Francesco married Marie de Bourbon-Soissons, the sister of Louis, count of Soissons (1604–41), who, as a French prince of the blood, again reinforced the connections between the Houses of Savoy and the ruling Bourbons of France. Tommaso Francesco was subsequently established as the prince of Carignano, a title associated with appanages in Piemonte and which presented him with the opportunity of establishing a legitimate cadet branch of the sovereign House. Because Tommaso Francesco was the youngest son with two surviving elder brothers, Carlo Emanuele I may well have felt safe in doing so, given that his immediate prospects of emerging as a rival to the main branch of the Savoyard House at that point seemed remote, though also because his appanages were not consolidated into a coherent and potentially threatening geographical unit.[60] He was also placed in a socially acceptable career, for while Maurizio had entered the church, Tommaso Francesco was effectively marked for military service. At the age of sixteen he accompanied his father Carlo Emanuele I at the siege of Trino and went on to see combat at Asti. His military career was to reach a peak when in 1634 he entered Habsburg service in the Spanish Netherlands as a general of the army of Flanders, albeit in a complex set of political circumstances.[61]

In addition to his five sons Carlo Emanuele I also had five legitimate daughters, and like the sons they too were integrated into his dynastic

di Soleto, 'Il titolo di Eminenza ai Cardinali ed i Duchi di Savoia (tre documenti inediti del 1630)', *Bollettino Storico-Bibliografico Subalpino*, 24, (1922); Oresko, 'The House of Savoy', in Oresko, Gibbs and Scott (eds.), *Royal and Republican Sovereignty*, pp. 287–8.

[59] ASV Avvisi, 80, ff. 256v–6, 9 October 1632, f. 280, 23 October 1632.

[60] Guichenon, *Histoire généalogique*, II, pp. 1035–44; Litta, *Celebri famiglie Italiane*, 'Duchi di Savoia', table XXIII (Milan, 1844); Oresko, 'The Sabaudian Court', in Adamson (ed.), *Princely Courts*, p. 240.

[61] Litta, *Celebri famiglie Italiane*, 'Duchi di Savoia', table XVI (Milan, 1844). For a generous thumbnail character sketch of Tommaso Francesco see Hanlon, *Twilight of a military tradition*, pp. 103–4.

strategies, similarly presenting both dynastic benefits and potential costs to the head of the House. Given the fact that any marriages involving daughters entailed the outlay of potentially expensive dowries, Carlo Emanuele I had to take care so that in organising the marriage of any of his daughters there would be significant political or dynastic returns. In 1608 two of his daughters married, Maria Margherita (1589–1655) to Francesco IV of Mantua and Monferrato, and Isabella (1591–1626) to Alfonso III d'Este of Modena (d. 1644). The marriage of Margherita was of obvious significance to Savoy's dynastic pretensions in the Italian peninsula, reinforcing Savoy's long-standing claim to Monferrato as a separable duchy. After the death of her husband she, like her deceased brothers Filippo Emanuele and Filiberto, attached herself to the Habsburg cause and in 1634 she was appointed by Philip IV as regent of Portugal, the last Spanish regent before the Portuguese revolt of 1640.[62] Two other daughters, Maria Apollonia (1594–1656) and Francesca Caterina (1595–1640), again fulfilled quite typical dynastic roles for younger daughters as they were placed in convents under the order of St Francis, though as with Cardinal Maurizio they also remained available for marriage as circumstances dictated.[63] The last daughter, Giovanna, died at birth in 1597 with her mother.[64]

Apart from his legitimate offspring Duke Carlo Emanuele I had eleven illegitimate sons and daughters and again, like the legitimate children, they also had particular dynastic and political roles to play for the House of Savoy. Significantly, the bastard sons all remained unmarried apart from Carlo Umberto (1601–63), who married in 1645 a daughter of the prince of Masserano. By keeping these *signori del sangue* unmarried, the duke avoided the need for the duke to create appanages that would have eroded his patrimony.[65] In contrast to the legitimate sons, they were totally excluded from the *Annunziata*, reflecting the conscious decision of the ducal regime to preserve the purity of the order's membership. The supreme *Annunziata* was the chivalric order of the House of Savoy, with the head of the dynasty as the order's master. It could date its origins back to 1374, if not earlier, and as such was one of the oldest in Europe, comparable to sovereign orders from other courts including the English Garter (1348) and the Burgundian *Toison d'Or* (1430).[66] Like

[62] The best biography is Romolo Quazza, *Margherita di Savoia, Duchessa di Mantova e Vice-Regina del Portogallo* (Turin, 1930).

[63] Litta, *Celebri famiglie Italiane*, 'Duchi di Savoia', table XVI (Milan, 1844).

[64] *Ibid.*; Guichenon, *Histoire généalogique*, I, p. 873.   [65] *Ibid.*, I, p. 874.

[66] Vittorio Amedeo Cigna-Santi suggested 1361 as a date of foundation, adding that others had suggested 1362, 1355 and 1344, in his *Serie cronologica de' cavalieri dell'ordine supremo di Savoia detti prima del collare indi della Santissima Nunziata* (Turin, 1786), p. 4. A copy of this rare book can be found in the Biblioteca Reale in Turin.

the Garter, the *Annunziata* was revived in the early modern period to invigorate court ceremony and to function as an important source of patronage, with creations taking place at moments of political or dynastic importance such as for marriages of members of the sovereign House, significant diplomatic missions from Turin to other courts, and the accession of dukes to the throne. One of Emanuele Filiberto's first acts on returning to his patrimonial states after Câteau-Cambrésis, for example, was to convene a chapter of the order, while subsequent chapters were called when Carlo Emanuele I acceded to the throne in 1580, when his children were married and, in 1648, when Duke Carlo Emanuele II (1634–75) reached his formal majority.[67] The *Annunziata* was furthermore defined by its exclusivity. Apart from the head of the order and other sovereign members, its knights could hold only the *Annunziata*, and the total membership was fixed, though the upper limit was periodically changed, and it was this sense of exclusivity that precluded the illegitimate sons of Carlo Emanuele from elevation.

Having said that, two of the recognised natural sons, Don Emanuele (1600–52) and Don Silvio (d. 1644), were admitted to the order of SS. Maurizio e Lazzaro and two others were promoted to the order of Malta, the precise reasons for which remain unclear.[68] The order of SS. Maurizio e Lazzaro was an amalgamation of two lesser orders which obtained a papal bull of approval from Gregory XIII Boncompagni (1502–85) on 15 October 1572, and which was modelled in part on the secular Tuscan order of S. Stefano, founded as recently as 1562.[69] In contrast to the senior order of the *Annunziata*, it was not exclusive and the total membership was not limited, reflecting the differences in its functions. Rather than serving solely as a point of contact between the sovereign duke and the Savoyard elites, the order of SS. Maurizio e Lazzaro acted as a hinge between the sovereign, as the order's grand-master, his subjects and the church in the duchy. Like that of S. Stefano, it brought together military and religious functions; with its naval associations it was promoted to defend the western reaches of the Mediterranean from the threat of Islam, while to emphasise the order's religious identity Carlo Emanuele I had the body of St Maurizio, the Roman soldier of the Theban Legion martyred around 287 during the reign of Emperor Maximian Herculius and Piemonte's patron saint, transferred in 1591 from Chablais to Piemonte and placed in his capital and ducal seat of Turin.[70] The order was also

---

[67] See for instance *ibid.*, pp. 65, 107, 154.
[68] Guichenon, *Histoire généalogique* I, p. 874.
[69] Erba, *La Chiesa sabauda*, section II, chapter 2; G. Claretta, *Dell'Ordine Mauriziano nel primo secolo della sua ricostruzione e del suo grand'ammiraglio Andrea Provana di Leyni* (Turin, 1890).
[70] *Ibid.*, pp. 155–8.

integrated into the system of ducal patronage and power. Donations made in the name of the order for establishing priories or chapels *in commendam* conferred enormous secular influence over religious foundations in the duchy, thereby serving as an additional source of patronage to the duke for rewarding his subjects. Ecclesiastical benefices, which were not of course juridically heritable as property, were more easily controlled by the dukes of Savoy once placed under its guidance, though in turn this had the potential to generate friction between the ducal regime seeking to extend influence over the church and the implementation of Tridentine reforms within Savoy.

While certain limits were placed on the illegitmate sons as associate members of the sovereign dynasty, with their inclusion only in the House's lesser order, they were none the less formally recognised as bastards of the duke, with the accompanying epithet of *di Savoia*, and were placed in military and ecclesiastical positions as suitable forms of employment. Don Felice (*c.* 1602–43), for example, was nominated in 1625 as lieutenant-general of the county of Nice and in 1634 he became lieutenant-general and governor of Savoie. Don Antonio (d. 1688), on the other hand, was granted three abbeys, also serving as governor and lieutenant-general of Nice.[71] At the same time the illegitimate daughters were used as a means of extending ducal patronage within Savoy. Once they had been recognised and preferably 'legitimised' they were able to marry into Savoyard noble families, binding those family clans closer to the ducal House. Margherita, for example, married in 1645 Francesco Filippo d'Este, marquis of Lanzo and S. Martino.[72] Unlike the bastard sons these daughters could marry without causing unacceptable *mésalliances* and, given the application of primogeniture principally through the legitimate male line, they were unlikely to present a dynastic challenge to the main branch of the House.

The provisions made for each of the children formed a wider dynastic strategy of calculating the social, political and financial costs and benefits involved in providing for the large number of legitimate and illegitimate offspring, including appanages for the legitimate married sons and dowries for the married daughters.[73] The marriages of the legitimate sons and daughters effectively increased the diplomatic fortunes of the dynasty

---

[71] Litta, *Celebri famiglie Italiane*, 'Duchi di Savoia', table XVI (Milan, 1844).

[72] *Ibid.*, table XV.

[73] Stumpo, *Finanza e stato*, p. 133. For further information about the households of the legitimate princes and princesses see Pierpaolo Merlin, *Tra guerre e tornei: la corte sabauda nell'età di Carlo Emanuele I* (Turin, 1991), pp. 16–23. On the ducal bastards see Oresko, 'Bastards as clients', in Giry-Deloison and Mettam (eds.), *Patronages et clientèlismes*; Litta, *Celebri famiglie Italiane*, 'Duchi di Savoia', table XV (Milan, 1844).

by ensuring that the House of Savoy enjoyed dynastic connections with other sovereign dynasties in Europe. The sons in particular reinforced the familial connections with the royal Houses of the Bourbons, the Spanish Habsburgs and (through the Bourbons) the Stuarts. It was precisely these connections that shaped the nature of Savoyard diplomacy in the early modern period and to some degree the reciprocal diplomacy of those other powers, locking them all into a distinctive structure of international relations based not merely on the demands of narrowly defined 'power politics' but also on the more intangible force of dynastic affinity.

Ties of marriage could certainly encourage warmer diplomatic relations between sovereign dynasties and their states, as was hoped of Vittorio Amedeo's marriage in 1619 to the Bourbon Marie Christine. The point is perhaps made more vividly still through the growing intimacy between the Stuart and Savoyard Houses during the first decades of the seventeenth century. As states with similar geo-strategic roles and with comparable levels of military resources, both England and Savoy faced the same types of problems in dealing with the leading powers, and they both pursued their own international objectives by exploiting the rivalries between those powers. In the first decades of the seventeenth century James I and Carlo Emanuele I worked to establish a dynastic network that included the Habsburg and Bourbon Houses. For James I, a union with the Savoyard dynasty would have linked his dynasty with the Habsburgs as part of his broader aspiration of establishing himself as a European paternal figurehead, given Carlo Emanuele I's own marriage to Catalina Michaela (even though she had died in 1597).[74] For his part, Duke Carlo Emanuele I hoped that the marriage of one of his children with a member of the Stuart House would satisfy one of his constant ambitions of ranking with the royal dynasties of Europe. Two dynastic projects were discussed to unite the Stuart and Savoyard Houses. The first in 1611 involved Elizabeth Stuart (1596–1662) and Vittorio Amedeo I, the eventual successor to the Savoyard state, and the second, Henry (1594–1612), prince of Wales and one of Carlo Emanuele I's daughters.[75] Of course neither of these ambitious projects was fulfilled – in 1613 Elizabeth married the Protestant Elector Frederick of the Palatinate while Henry unexpectedly died in the previous year – and the two Houses never forged direct links. Nevertheless, the marriage in January 1619 between Marie Christine (1606–63) (Louis XIII's younger sister) and Vittorio Amedeo I, together with the marriage of

---

[74] Consult Oresko, 'The House of Savoy', in Oresko, Gibbs and Scott (eds.), *Royal and Republican Sovereignty*.

[75] E. Passamonti, 'Relazioni Anglo-Sabaudi dal 1603 al 1625', *Bollettino Storico-Bibliografico Subalpino*, 36 (1934), and 37 (1935).

Henrietta Maria (1609–69) and Charles Stuart (1600–49) in 1625, joined the Stuart and Savoyard dynasties indirectly through the Bourbons and placed them in a structure of international relations that made use of kinship ties as a means of pursuing political objectives, one of the abiding themes of Savoy's diplomacy during the Thirty Years' War.

In the summer of 1625, a secretary of Alessandro Scaglia, Savoyard ordinary ambassador in Paris, raised the possibility of Marie Christine writing to Henrietta Maria as *ma sœur*, 'as a title of special affection between two sisters for reason of their blood as well as for the fact that they come from royal houses [*sic*]'.[76] Later in the same year the English king reportedly said that he 'wished to have the duke as his father and the prince of Piemonte [Vittorio Amedeo] as his true and loved brother, recognising him as the son of the greatest prince of the age'.[77] Such language was deliberately calculated to transmit what would have been comprehensible dynastic and political signals to the House of Savoy and to a potentially wider audience. Certainly, it referred to the fact that Henrietta Maria and Marie Christine were full sisters, which might equally explain Charles I's familiarity in addressing other members of the Savoyard House. Charles I himself occasionally wrote to the Savoyard duke as *mon père* rather than *mon cousin*, the customary form of address in correspondence between legitimate sovereign princes.[78] Yet it was equally understood that *ma sœur* was a typically royal address to which Marie Christine as an individual might have been entitled as a sister of Louis XIII but which also played on the wider aspirations of the ducal Savoyard House to royal status. The title of address used by Marie Christine indeed provoked a lively debate precisely because of its royal connotations. Eventually as a compromise it was agreed that the two sisters should correspond with each other as *mon cœur, ma sœur*, emphasising their affection while perhaps retaining the ambiguity about royal status.[79] The willingness of Charles I to express affection for the House of Savoy, and by implication to flatter

---

[76] AST LMI m. 4, fasc. 1, Barozzio to Scaglia, 29 October 1625; AST LMF m. 26, fasc. 1, 271, Scaglia to Carlo Emanuele I, 15 November 1625.

[77] AST LMF m. 26, fasc. 1, 269, Scaglia to Carlo Emanuele I, 15 November 1625. See also 168, Scaglia to Carlo Emanuele I, 9 July 1625.

[78] For example, AST LFI m. 48, Charles I to Carlo Emanuele I, 1629; Charles I to Carlo Emanuele I, undated.

[79] AST LMI m. 4, fasc. 1, Barozzio to Scaglia, 29 October 1625; AST LMF m. 26, fasc. 1, 271, Scaglia to Carlo Emanuele I, 15 November 1625. In practice, Henrietta Maria appears to have used the abbreviated *mon cœur* in correspondence. Ermano Ferrero (ed.), *Lettres de Henriette Marie de France, Reine d'Angleterre, à sa sœur Christine, Duchesse de Savoie* (Turin, 1881) for some examples. The issue of terms of address as a signifier of royalty was repeated at great length by Pietro Monod in justifying Savoy's historical case for the *trattamento reale*. Monod, *Trattato del titolo regio*, chapter 1.

Savoyard royal claims, enabled the English sovereign to forge a special diplomatic relationship with a willing duke of Savoy without formally conceding anything over protocol that would have set unwelcome precedents. As will be seen, this was of particular importance in a diplomatic context where England and Savoy were negotiating a military alliance to combat the Habsburgs in continental Europe.[80]

Dynastic kinship, even expressed on a seemingly minor level like this epistolary etiquette, could strengthen political relationships, affinities that in turn were central to Savoyard international calculations throughout the early modern period. Foreign policies dominated the political agenda of Carlo Emanuele I's reign, and since the formulation of Savoy's foreign affairs remained at least formally his prerogative as the sovereign ruler of the Savoyard state, they intrinsically reflected the dynastic priorities of his family, as much as military or geo-strategic calculations. As the Savoyard House had sought to reclaim authority following the years of occupation in the sixteenth century, its growing confidence was reflected in the emphasis given to its international interests. During the remarkably long reign of Duke Carlo Emanuele I, the House of Savoy placed itself as a member of a 'club' that included the royal Stuarts, Bourbons and Habsburgs. This fundamentally dynastic identity proved centrally important in the seventeenth century. Unresolved territorial claims, marriages and new points of dynastic contact set some of the key parameters within which Savoyard diplomacy operated during the turbulent years of the Thirty Years' War.

---

[80] CSPV 1626–8, p. 314. On his part, Carlo Emanuele I also made reference to the dynastic ties by assuring Charles I of the 'service' due to him by the duke's children. For example, PRO SP 92/12/37, Wake to Conway, 19 February 1626.

2

POWER AND PATRONAGE: THE SCAGLIA DI VERRUA IN THE SERVICE OF SAVOY

In March 1619 Augusto Manfredo Scaglia (1587–1637), the elder of the two sons of Filiberto Gherardo Scaglia, the count of Verrua (1564–1619), wrote with 'tears from his heart' to Duke Carlo Emanuele I of the death of his father while serving as Savoy's ordinary ambassador in Paris. In his reflective letter Augusto Manfredo described in detail the years of faithful service to the House of Savoy given by his father, 'a stable column of faith, devotion, prudence and integrity'.[1] Augusto Manfredo's tone was clearly eulogistic, but he was also quite justified. The count of Verrua's entire life had encapsulated the close and constant interaction between family interest and public service, and the reciprocal relationship between the Scaglia di Verrua as an ambitious aristocratic family clan and the ruling family of Savoy. Without doubt, the fortunes of his increasingly cosmopolitan family closely mirrored those of the sovereign dynasty as in the mid-sixteenth century the ruling House regained power following the years of war and occupation with the support of the duchy's elites. Located at the very centre of Savoyard politics, Scaglia di Verrua family history was woven into the fabric of state history.

Yet so far the history of Savoy has been viewed solely from the perspective of its ruling sovereign dynasty, with the dynastic aspirations of the ducal House establishing some of the basic parameters within which foreign policies at least operated. To present this as a complete picture of how those policies were formulated and conducted during the early modern period would however suggest the Savoyard state was monolithic, with little regard to the subjects ruled by the duke, particularly the

---

[1] AST LMF m. 18, fasc. 2, 73, Augusto Manfredo Scaglia to Carlo Emanuele I, 14 March 1619. Alessandro Scaglia, the younger brother wrote a similar letter to the Savoyard duke. Alessandro Tassoni, *Lettere (a cura di Pietro Pulliati)*, 2 vols. (Rome, 1978), I, p. 403, while the Piedmontese Jesuit, poet and historian Emanuele Tesauro composed an *Elogium Sepulchrale* in Verrua's honour, presumably at the time of his death. Emanuele Tesauro, *Inscriptiones, quotquot reperiri potuerunt* (third edition, Brandenburg, 1671), pp. 232–3.

aristocratic elites like the Scaglia di Verrua who played a major role in the political culture of the duchy during and beyond the seventeenth century. But quite how they should be incorporated into Savoyard history has itself become subject to particular historiographical assumptions. After the Second World War, as historians of early modern Savoy became increasingly interested in socio-economic history, some studies of the duchy shifted away from the nationalistic agenda set by the *Risorgimento* to one that concerned the processes of what amounted to internal social and political modernisation.[2] At a time when the borders of the duchy had been stabilised, so this line of argument has suggested, the regime also monopolised power within the duchy, fundamentally redefining the relationship between the duke and his subjects to the benefit of the ruler over the ruled. As a recent book on early modern Italy has claimed, Carlo Emanuele I, in affirming his authority, 'reduced once-mighty feudal lords to mere ornaments or loyal lieutenants'.[3] Accounting for Savoyard history in terms of the growth of state power alone nevertheless has its own limitations, tacitly assuming that the relationship between the ruling House and social groups under its sovereignty was a rerun of the questionable 'centre versus periphery' conception of early modern state formation. Moreover, and more broadly, it does little to account for the 'polycentric' nature of the composite Savoyard duchy, where local loyalties could be defined in a variety of complex and overlapping ways, though perhaps this was less so for elite clans who committed themselves to the court and who were thus in close and regular contact with the ruling family.[4]

While it cannot be doubted that the Savoyard ruling House gradually succeeded in extending its authority within its patrimony as the most significant source of power after Emanuele Filiberto's restoration to the duchy in 1559, some further qualifications must be made. The extension of Savoyard power was not necessarily a process of confrontation or containment from the later sixteenth century; the history of early modern Savoy was more than just a destructive struggle between ducal institutions seeking to extend the range of their influence over interest groups like noble families who had to be coerced into loyalty to an ever-expanding state. Rather, it was one of interaction between the ruling House, with its access to patronage, and members of the nobility, who, far from existing as a homogeneous social group, typically operated with sets of individual

---

[2] A point recently made by Claudio Rosso in Merlin *et al.* (eds.), *Il Piemonte sabaudo*, p. 175.

[3] Hanlon, *Early Modern Italy*, p. 271. See the historiographical comments in Merlin *et al.* (eds.), *Il Piemonte sabaudo*, pp. 175–8.

[4] The conceptual difficulties of state history and early modern Savoy have been carefully considered in Vester's introduction to 'Territorial politics'.

and family interests, often in direct competition with one another. In offering their service to the sovereign family, they monopolised many of the high offices of government. In turn they influenced ducal policy-making while also extending their cosmopolitan outlooks beyond the borders of the duchy through cultural patronage and brokering.[5]

These terms of reference have already been employed in a variety of studies beyond Savoy which have focused on the histories of courtiers and ministers as much as the systems of state power or even of sovereigns in isolation from those in their service. The very personalities of ministers have become the subject of close scrutiny as some historians have come to view them as more than just 'empty shells' with little or no individual identity or interest, for as Alessandra Contini has quite reasonably suggested through her work on early modern Italian diplomacy, 'restoring a human and political physiognomy to these representatives [diplomats] – to these men – dispels the monolithic image of power exercised exclusively by the prince, and it restores substance and weight to the system's protagonists'.[6] The family histories of office holders and courtiers in particular seem to offer an additional approach to the study of power politics in early modern Europe, shedding important light also on how regimes formulated, and thereafter conducted, domestic and foreign policies. Research into family papers, financial and legal records, diplomatic correspondence, literary works and the visual arts has shown how political figures operated with various assumptions about duty and interest, public service (in this case, serving the sovereign and the sovereign's administrative systems) and private gain. Serving sovereigns intrinsically meant self-service at a time when the precise relationship between public and private spheres remained uncertain, especially given the absence of impersonal state bureaucracies supposedly guided by the principle of meritocracy.[7]

That is not to say that there was no conception of what was 'moral' and what was not in the realm of early modern politics. There were certainly occasions when individuals or ministers were thought to have abused their institutional or ministerial power, crossing an invisible, though typically ill-defined, boundary that was felt to separate the acceptable from the corrupt. Work on the Jacobean court has for some time directed

---

[5] For examples of noble cosmopolitanism see Oresko, 'The Sabaudian court', in Adamson (ed.), *Princely Courts*, pp. 241–2. See also the comments in C. Storrs, 'Savoyard diplomacy in the eighteenth century (1684–1798)', in Frigo (ed.), *Politics and Diplomacy*, p. 244.

[6] Contini, 'Medicean diplomacy', in Frigo (ed.), *Politics and Diplomacy*, p. 64.

[7] Though Mathew Vester has claimed that 'there is good evidence that a public–private distinction already existed in the mid-sixteenth century, and was even used to differentiate between the various kinds of activities engaged in by a single individual, whether a state official or not'. Vester, 'Territorial politics', p. 468.

attention to the grave concerns felt by some contemporaries that negative self-interest was eating away at the heart of a political system.[8]
Elsewhere, Jean-Claude Waquet's important case study of early modern
Florence has in the first place illuminated the conceptual problems that
existed in disentangling personal and public interest, and more broadly
how early modern historians have addressed the slippery subject of corruption.[9] Waquet has argued that corruption, while condemned at the
time as an invidious product of human sin, still had an important latent
function to play within the political system of Florence. According to
his model, corruption redistributed money and power among individuals and interest groups who might otherwise have grown hostile to the
existing political order by their economic and social difficulties. Perhaps
Waquet presents too tidy an explanation for how ministers, and indeed
the rulers of Florence, squared by a process of mental casuistry the benefits of corruption with the inescapable view that it was sinful. Yet he
nevertheless makes the important point that public ministers could simultaneously be considered guilty as individuals of corruption (however
defined) while personally justifying their crimes, exposing what was still
the fundamental 'fragility' of the early modern state, as he puts it.[10]

   This ambiguity, or closeness, between different types of service and
interest has also been examined through a number of important examples drawn from seventeenth-century France. Without doubt the most
spectacular example of supposed corruption was that of Nicolas Fouquet
(1615–80) who emerged as the *Surintendant des finances* during Mazarin's
ministry in the 1650s. Fouquet's dramatic fall from power and arrest in
1661, soon after Louis XIV assumed his personal rule, came as the minister was accused of using his office to fill his own pockets at the expense of
the crown. While his disgrace is now understood as much in terms of his
ministerial rivalry with Jean-Baptiste Colbert (1619–83) and his network
of clients, Fouquet had seemingly crossed the boundary dividing private
interest from public service.[11] For their part, the two cardinal-ministers
Richelieu and Mazarin (1602–61) saw holding office as about establishing and extending the influence of their family clans as much as about

---

[8] For example Linda Levy Peck, *Court Patronage and Corruption in Early Stuart England*
(Boston and London, 1990); David Wootton, 'Francis Bacon: Your Flexible Friend',
in J. H. Elliott and L. W. B. Brockliss (eds.), *The World of the Favourite* (New Haven
and London, 1999).

[9] Jean-Claude Waquet, *Corruption: Ethics and Power in Florence, 1600–1770* (Worcester,
PA, 1991).

[10] *Ibid.*, pp. 190–6.

[11] For a discussion of the Fouquet-Colbert rivalry see Daniel Dessert, *Fouquet* (Paris,
1987); M. Fumaroli, 'Nicolas Fouquet, the Favourite *Manqué*', in Elliott and Brockliss
(eds.), *World of the Favourite*.

operating according to a narrowly defined, and possibly anachronistic, conception of state service. Joseph Bergin's studies of Richelieu's rise to power and subsequent ministry have presented a credible picture of how the cardinal operated according to various assumptions about service and interest that intrinsically included furthering the fortunes of his own family network.[12] In striking contrast to Richelieu, Jules Mazarin lacked crucial advantages of being a native Frenchman from a noble background and accordingly turned to dynastic strategies to compensate for his weak social position. As Robert Oresko has elaborated, the marriages of his nieces to members of the high French aristocracy, not least Armand de Bourbon (1629–66), the prince of Conti and a prince of the blood (albeit the most junior), served both to establish the cardinal's own position within French society and to strengthen his power as a minister during Anne of Austria's (1601–66) insecure regency from 1643 until Louis XIV assumed personal power in 1661. He even sought to use his nieces to strengthen France's international relationships with Savoy and Modena, integral to his aspiration of creating a strong anti-Habsburg powerbase in north Italy.[13] Mazarin's strategy of mixing family aspirations with ministerial power certainly paid off. While the cardinal was confronted with the violent opposition culminating in the Frondes, and he indeed went into self-imposed exile on two occasions, he still managed to amass one of the greatest fortunes of any individual other than the crown in the entire history of pre-revolutionary France. In turn his wealth enabled him to cultivate the longed-for attributes of nobility through a programme of cultural patronage and collecting art, in particular by buying up works from Charles I's extensive collection as it was dispersed after his execution.[14]

In contrast, the integration of family and state history arguably has had until recently a comparatively limited impact on studies of early modern Savoy, influenced as many of them have been by particular historiographical legacies of Italian unification where there was little role for interests other than a compelling nationalistic sentiment and, more recently, of the inexorable expansion of the state. There are nevertheless

[12] Joseph Bergin, *Cardinal Richelieu: Power and the Pursuit of Wealth* (New Haven and London, 1985); Joseph Bergin, *The Rise of Richelieu* (New Haven and London, 1991).

[13] Robert Oresko, 'The marriages of the nieces of Cardinal Mazarin: public policy and private strategy in seventeenth century Europe', in Reiner Babel (ed.), *Frankreich im europäischen Staatensystem der frühen Neuzeit* (Sigmaringen, 1995). For other examples relating family and state power see Jean-Louis Bourgeon, *Les Colbert avant Colbert: destin d'une famille marchande* (Paris, 1973); Mozzarelli (ed.), *'Familia' del principe*.

[14] For a view of Mazarin as a patron and collector see Jonathan Brown, *Kings and Connoisseurs: Collecting Art in Seventeenth-Century Europe* (New Haven and London, 1995), chapter 5.

some valuable exceptions. Antonio Manno's indispensable, if occasionally unreliable, genealogical research into the leading families of the states of Savoy still provides an excellent reference point for the study of those elites, while Stuart Woolf's classic case study of family clans from early modern Piemonte elaborated the complexities of family economic strategies for maintaining and extending properties, albeit in the context of the supposedly absolutist Savoyard state.[15] More recently the works of Pierpaolo Merlin, Claudio Rosso and Daniela Frigo have in different ways, and to varying degrees, acknowledged the significance of contextualising the careers of political figures and ministers with the histories of their particular families. All of these studies have directed attention to the mutually beneficial relationships formed between the House of Savoy, looking to maintain and extend its power within the patrimonial lands of Savoy and more broadly on the international stage with the aid of its elites and ministers associated with its court, and those individuals who saw service to the sovereign House as the best (if not, perhaps, sole) means for extending their own interests.[16] As Frigo has argued, the resurgent interest in the political history of early modern Italy has come as 'the boundaries marking out the "political" in the *ancien régime* have been extended, while the distinctions between the public and private have faded'.[17]

There is no better example of this close interaction between state and family history than the Scaglia di Verrua, one of the great social, cultural and political success stories of early modern Savoy. The Scaglia di Verrua could trace their line at least back into the thirteenth century when their patrimonial seat was established in 1274 in the Piedmontese town of Biella, 60 miles to the north of Turin. But while the family clan was long established in Piemonte it was in fact a fairly recent arrival at the still-young ducal capital of Turin, a city that had only been established as the seat of the Savoyard court in 1563, replacing the previous capital of Chambéry in Savoie that was perhaps a little too close to the potentially unstable French borders.[18]

---

[15] Antonio Manno, *Il Patriziato Subalpino*, 32 vols. (manuscript copies in the Archivio di Stato and Biblioteca Reale, Turin); Woolf, *Studi sulla nobiltà Piemontese.*

[16] In particular Merlin, *Guerre e tornei*; Claudio Rosso, *Una burocrazia di Antico Regime: i segretari di stato dei duchi di Savoia, I (1559–1637)* (Turin, 1992); Frigo, *'Jus gentium'.*

[17] Daniela Frigo, 'Introduction' in Frigo (ed.), *Politics and Diplomacy*, p. 6. However Christopher Storrs has recently argued that Savoy, at least in the late seventeenth century, underwent a process of modernisation where its state institutions came to dominate over private power as its military efficiency improved. Storrs, *Rise of Savoy*, pp. 8–9.

[18] Merlin *et al.* (eds.), *Il Piemonte sabaudo*, p. 93. For further details consult Geoffrey Symcox, 'From commune to capital: the transformation of Turin, sixteenth to eighteenth centuries', in Oresko, Gibbs and Scott (eds.), *Royal and Republican Sovereignty.*

THE SCAGLIA DI VERRUA DURING THE SEVENTEENTH CENTURY

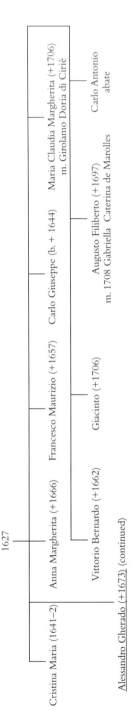

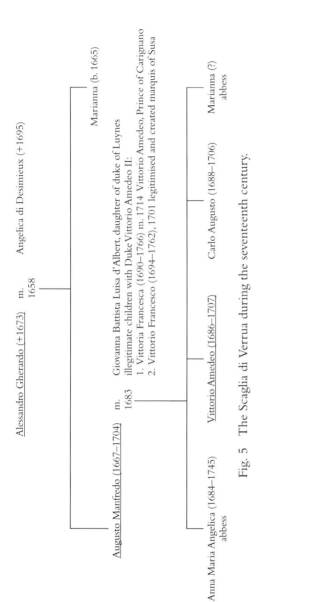

Fig. 5 The Scaglia di Verrua during the seventeenth century.

Alessandro Gherardo (+1673)   m.   Angelica di Desimieux (+1695)
                               1658

Augusto Manfredo (1667–1704)   m.   Giovanna Battista Luisa d'Albert, daughter of duke of Luynes
                               1683   illegitimate children with Duke Vittorio Amedeo II:
                                       1. Vittoria Francesca (1690–1766) m. 1714 Vittorio Amedeo, Prince of Carignano
                                       2. Vittorio Francesco (1694–1762), 1701 legitimised and created marquis of Susa

Marianna (b. 1665)

Anna Maria Angelica (1684–1745)   Vittorio Amedeo (1686–1707)   Carlo Augusto (1688–1706)   Marianna (?)
abbess   abbess

The move of the Scaglia di Verrua to Turin reflected some of the major changes in the social and political history of the Savoyard state. Writing in the middle of the seventeenth century the Piedmontese Jesuit, historian and tutor to Duke Vittorio Amedeo II, Emanuele Tesauro (1592–1675), described the ancient origins of Turin. Central to his foundation myth were eulogistic, if somewhat fanciful, references to Faetante or Erídano, a wandering prince of Egypt who had travelled along the Italian peninsula from its southern tip to establish the city in 1523 BC. As Tesauro was keen to point out in his efforts to establish the newly created capital's historical pedigree within the Italian peninsula, this was well before the dates given for both the foundation of Rome and the Trojan wars.[19] A more recent and considerably more sober account of Turin's architectural history has dated its foundation to 30 BC, adding that well into the middle ages the city was of relatively little importance even in Piemonte where other urban centres such as Asti and Chieri enjoyed considerably greater influence.[20] The transformation of Turin into the dominant city both in Piemonte and in the wider Savoyard state was due entirely to its foundation as the ducal capital by Emanuele Filiberto, a *tabula rasa*, as Geoffrey Symcox has put it, on which the restored sovereign dynasty effectively stamped its own distinctive mark.[21] Soon after Emanuele Filiberto moved to Turin, the city was developed as a crucial military strongpoint that could exercise control not only over the city but also over the surrounding region and the strategically important Val di Susa with its key points of access to the Alps.[22] With astute sense he also sited his court in the capital, adjacent to the city's cathedral. The ducal palace, which was initially located in the palace of the archbishop of Turin, began to take shape at the end of the century, with more significant architectural expansion continuing under Emanuele Filiberto's son, Duke Carlo Emanuele I, in the face of difficult relations with the city's communal council and the archbishop. To emphasise still further the importance of the city as the seat of the restored dynasty, the Shroud of Christ was transferred from Chambéry to Turin, albeit in 1578, a calculated time gap that

[19] Emanuele Tesauro, *Historia dell'Augusta Città di Torino*, 2 vols. (Turin, 1679–1712), I, pp. 1–2.

[20] Martha D. Pollak, *Turin 1564–1680. Urban Design, Military Culture, and the Creation of the Absolutist Capital* (Chicago and London, 1991), p. 14.

[21] Symcox, 'From commune to capital', in Oresko, Gibbs and Scott (eds.), *Royal and Republican Sovereignty*, p. 245. The significance of the restoration of the court in a new capital has been further emphasised by Oresko, 'The Sabaudian court', in Adamson (ed.), *Princely Courts*, pp. 232–3.

[22] The fortress that provided one of the city's pivotal centres was elaborated by Carlo Emanuele I when he undertook a programme of urban building in 1619. Pollak, *Turin*, chapter 3.

avoided alienating those elites who had previously been based in the pre-restoration capital. Emanuele Filiberto was seeking to merge the roles of the House of Savoy as both a sovereign dynasty and the custodian of one of Christendom's most sacred objects, which eventually established Turin firmly on the map of Catholic pilgrimage.[23]

The creation of a new capital with a restructured court underlined the desire of the House of Savoy to assert its pre-eminence within its dynastic territories following the disastrous years of war and occupation in the middle of the sixteenth century. By the beginning of the seventeenth century the expanding court and capital under Carlo Emanuele I also served to strengthen the ties between the dynasty and the social and political elites of the Savoyard state, particularly those from the surrounding province of Piemonte who were 'bullied, threatened, lured and bribed' to buy land and establish their family *palazzi* in Turin, while seeking the patronage and power associated with the ducal House.[24] A close relationship between the sovereign dynasty and the elite noble families who dominated Savoyard society during the sixteenth and seventeenth centuries was crucial to the success of the restored sovereign dynasty, given the divisions of loyalty within those elites during the years of occupation from the 1530s until 1559. The Scaglia di Verrua were indeed one of these clans drawn to the city in the early decades of the seventeenth century. The family only acquired a permanent base in proximity to the court in 1617 when the count of Verrua bought a *palazzo* that had previously belonged to the count of Solaro and that had been expanded and decorated with frescoes at the end of the sixteenth century.[25] The family's ascent to the highest echelons of wealth, social status and power in the duchy of Savoy was of equally recent origins. The first signs of a significant rise in the family fortunes can be dated to the middle of the sixteenth century when in 1534 the territory of Verrua was bought by Gherardo Scaglia from the count of Savoia di Tenda, who came from an illegitimate branch of the House of Savoy. It was granted the status of

---

[23] Ostensions of the shroud took place on 4 May, its feast day, on important dynastic occasions and to important visitors, though a permanent chapel was not begun until after Carlo Emanuele I's order of 1607. John Beldon Scott, 'Seeing the Shroud: Guarini's Reliquary Chapel in Turin and the ostentation of a dynastic relic', *The Art Bulletin*, 77 (1995); Oresko, 'The Sabaudian court', in Adamson (ed.), *Princely Courts*, pp. 236–7; Symcox, 'From commune to capital', in Oresko, Gibbs and Scott (eds.), *Royal and Republican Sovereignty*, p. 243.

[24] Oresko, 'The Sabaudian court', in Adamson (ed.), *Princely Courts*, p. 244; Daniella Frigo, 'L'affermazione della sovranità: famiglia e corte dei Savoia tra Cinque e Settecento', p. 298, in Mozzarelli (ed.) *Familia del principe*.

[25] The Palazzo Verrua was damaged during an allied bombing raid in 1942 and a number of family papers were consequently destroyed, though the building has recently been restored. See the newspaper article in *La Stampa* (24 May 1992).

contado by Duke Emanuele Filiberto in 1561, from which the head of the Scaglia family effectively drew his title as it was inherited by the eldest legitimate son of the main branch of the House.[26]

During the late sixteenth and early seventeenth centuries, when Duke Carlo Emanuele I was on the Savoyard throne, the political fortunes of the Scaglia di Verrua rose at a spectacular pace. This was due almost entirely to Filiberto Gherardo Scaglia, the count of Verrua, described by Pierpaolo Merlin as 'undoubtedly one of the most important figures in Savoyard politics during the first two decades of the seventeenth century'.[27] As his son Augusto Manfredo Scaglia had elaborated in his letter written on his father's death, Verrua's life was defined by service to Duke Carlo Emanuele I and members of the ruling family, and highlighted by a succession of significant diplomatic missions. In 1593 he was ambassador of the duke to the Venetian Republic; in 1598 he was the Savoyard ordinary ambassador in Rome; in 1604–5 he represented the duke of Savoy in Madrid; finally, he was Carlo Emanuele I's ordinary ambassador in Paris until his death there in 1619.[28] Augusto Manfredo went on to record that his father also held several key offices at the Turinese court. In 1604 he was appointed *Maggiordomo* of the separate household of the ducal princes, allowing some considerable influence over the princes at a time when they were in childhood, while in 1614 he was appointed to the office of *Maggiordomo maggiore* of the ducal household, a position concerned with the regulation of ceremonies at the court at a time when there was no official Master of Ceremonies as such.[29] Service to Duke Carlo Emanuele I afforded still further rewards to Verrua and his family. On 18 March 1608 Filiberto Gherardo Scaglia was created a knight of the Savoyard order of the *Annunziata*, the timing of which clearly pointed to his diplomatic success in negotiating the marriage in the same year between one of Carlo Emanuele I's daughters, Isabella, and Alfonso d'Este of Modena.[30]

---

[26]   AST Sezione Riunite PCF 1561, ff. 135–9, 'Lettere de rattificationi di contado per monsignor di Verrua', 6 July 1561.

[27]   Merlin, *Guerre e tornei*, p. 67. Manno describes Verrua as the 'primo e solo ministro di Carlo Emanuele I', though this is ambiguous given that no such position existed at the Savoyard court. *Patriziato Subalpino*, XXIV, p. 245. There is a small, albeit error-prone, political biography of the count: M. Lusso, 'Filiberto Gherardo Scaglia, conte di Verrua, 1561/2–1619' (tesi di laurea, University of Turin, 1957–8; copy in the Biblioteca Provincia, Turin).

[28]   AST LMF m. 18, fasc. 2, 73, Augusto Manfredo Scaglia to Carlo Emanuele I, 14 March 1619.

[29]   AST Sezione Riunite PCF 1614–15, f. 190, 13 January 1615; Merlin, *Guerre e tornei*, pp. 67–8.

[30]   There were two other creations in the same year, including a member from the S. Martino d'Agliè family who was named before Verrua and thus took ceremonial precedence. No doubt Duke Carlo Emanuele I was seeking to maintain a balance

Verrua's promotion to the *Annunziata*, the highest honour he could hold as a subject of the duke, marked his position at the pinnacle of Savoy's political elite, placing him in close proximity to his sovereign prince as the head of the order. While Verrua was the most obvious beneficiary of the promotion, it also served his sovereign prince. The *Annunziata* was a powerful instrument for bestowing ducal favour and forging links between the sovereign and elite subjects, 'a noble means of establishing the authority of the sovereign', according to the seventeenth-century genealogical historian Samuel Guichenon, who also saw it as a key component for the glorification of the House of Savoy as a leading European dynasty.[31] By placing Verrua in the *Annunziata* Carlo Emanuele I could link his family more closely to the ducal court in the capital city of Turin. It should be added, however, that promotions to the order were also something of a political balancing act. Because of the *Annunziata's* potency as a sign of favour, dukes of Savoy had to exercise caution in making promotions to avoid alienating leading aristocratic families or creating dangerous factional imbalances at the court. This careful control of political power was accordingly reflected in the individuals who were promoted and the sequence in which their promotions took place. *Principi del sangue* always assumed precedence to promotions as legitimate members of the Savoyard House, followed by those with lesser claims to the ducal succession, then by the elite noble clans that surrounded the ruling dynasty, like the Scaglia di Verrua. From these noble creations the same names reappear throughout the sixteenth and seventeenth centuries, illustrating the intimate relationships cultivated by the sovereign House with particular families connected to their court, and the balances Savoyard dukes had to strike between them. Among these promotions were the Valperga di Rivara and the S. Martino d'Agliè, two elite Piedmontese noble families who had significantly benefited from the shift of power to Piemonte after 1559 and who, with the Castellamonte family, could claim a possible descent from Arduino, the last king of Italy.[32] Another prominent name among the promotions was the Chabod, a clan from Savoie that in recognition of this shift of influence had re-established its base close to the restored ducal court in the capital of Turin.[33]

between competing noble clans at the Turinese court. Cigna-Santi, *Serie cronologica*, pp. 107–11.

[31] Guichenon, *Histoire généalogique*, I, p. 989. Cigna-Santi also noted several occasions when dukes of Savoy used the *Annunziata* to reward the loyalty of important subjects, thereby binding them more closely to the sovereign dynasty. *Serie cronologica*, pp. 79, 97, 117, for example.

[32] C. Gallina, 'Le vicende di un grande favorite (Filippo di S. Martino d'Agliè)', *Bollettino Storico-Bibliografico Subalpino*, 21 (1919), 185.

[33] Merlin *et al.* (eds.), *Il Piemonte sabaudo*, pp. 118–19. The Valperga were unusual as a Piedmontese clan that broke into the patronage system of the Savoyard House at an

As a responsible head of his clan, the count of Verrua also secured land for his family through his own marriage, purchases and ducal gifts, and through the marriage of his elder son. Land remained a fundamental building-block of heritable power for the family, as it did for nobilities elsewhere in early modern Europe, though the process of acquisition by Filiberto Gherardo did not lead in the first instance to the creation of consolidated estates in a single geographical area. Significantly some properties gained through his son's marriage were located beyond Savoy and within Monferrato, pointing again to the complexity of relations between the two states and more widely to the differences between territorial and jurisdictional borders illuminated by the work of Peter Sahlins.[34] That the Scaglia di Verrua held land outside the limits of the Savoyard state certainly had the potential to complicate Filiberto Gherardo's position as a minister of Duke Carlo Emanuele I. Claudio Rosso has written with some justice of 'the long pre-eminence of his [the count of Verrua's] family clan, that until the middle of the 1620s guided the foreign policy of the duchy', emphasising the role individuals from the family could play in state politics.[35] Yet the count was suspected of abusing this influence for personal gain, crossing that invisible boundary between what could be perceived as acceptable service on the one hand and unacceptable private interest on the other, even though the Scaglia di Verrua had come to define themselves as a court clan in proximity to the ruling prince. Foreign policies could be more than just the expression of the sovereign's will but also the outcome of a potentially complex process of interaction between the prince and other interest groups, albeit under the great arch of Sabaudian dynasticism. In 1613, following the death of Duke Francesco IV of Mantua and Monferrato, Carlo Emanuele I's son-in-law through the marriage to Margherita, and the refusal of the new Mantuan duke, Ferdinando, to allow Carlo Emanuele custody of Francesco IV's daughter, Maria, the duke invaded Monferrato to push his claim to the duchy.[36] Filiberto Gherardo was given command of one

early stage, with their first elevation in 1519. Prior to the shift of power to Turin, the *Annunziata* was dominated by nobles from outside the principality of Piemonte. Cigna-Santi, *Serie cronologica*, p. 54.

[34] 'Redditi lasciati dal fu signor Conte di Verrua', enclosure in AST LMF m. 18, fasc. 2, 73, Augusto Manfredo Scaglia to Carlo Emanuele I, 14 March 1619, for an assessment of their value. Further information on the acquisitions of land can be found in Manno, *Patriziato Subalpino*, XXIV, pp. 243–51.

[35] Rosso, *Una burocrazia*, p. 138. Pierpaolo Merlin concurs with this assessment: 'lo Scaglia si adoperò per favorire la pace con la Francia, continuando poi ad essere uno dei principali artefici della politica estera del ducato'. Merlin, *Guerre e tornei*, p. 67.

[36] Maria Gonzaga's dynastic importance was all the greater as she was a potential key not only to the future of Monferrato but also to Mantua. Parrott, 'The Mantuan Succession', 34–5.

of three invading columns, and he fully supported the duke's war strategy. Some of his (unnamed) opponents condemned Filiberto Gherardo's
hawkish policy for being motivated less for a desire to pursue the territorial claims of his prince than to consolidate the family's particular
properties under Savoyard jurisdiction. The charge prompted Filiberto
Gherardo to defend himself in writing, though whether the quite plausible suspicions ever fully dissipated is unclear.[37] It is certainly tempting
to view Augusto Manfredo Scaglia's eulogistic letter written to the duke
of Savoy after his father's death as a final attempt to preserve Verrua's
reputation for posterity.

While the count of Verrua accumulated offices and land to establish his family's social power he was equally concerned as head of his
House to ensure the succession of his biological line by primogeniture
through a senior legitimate male heir, and furthermore to organise financial provision for any younger children without substantially eroding his
patrimony, just like his sovereign prince, Carlo Emanuele I.[38] Through
his marriage to Bianca, daughter of Cesare Ponte di Scarnafigi, Verrua
had two sons, Augusto Manfredo and Alessandro Cesare. As the elder
son, Augusto Manfredo was marked out to assume the role of head of
the main branch of the House which transmitted the bulk of the family's
patrimony through primogeniture. He was also the first member of the
Scaglia di Verrua to enjoy the title of marquis of Caluso which he acquired
through his marriage in 1605 to the widowed Margherita, daughter of
Count Teodoro Biandrate di S. Giorgio, and which was thereafter effectively established as the title of the family's heir apparent.[39] His marriage,
for which Verrua had sought Carlo Emanuele I's approval and that of the
duke of Mantua and Monferrato because of the division of Margherita's
properties and dowry between the two states (threatening to raise questions of divided loyalty), itself contributed to the strategy of family power
at the ducal court.[40] Not only did the union bring the dowry of land
in Monferrato to the Scaglia di Verrua from his wife's first marriage, but
Margherita extended the family's power in her own right, demonstrating
the role female members of the clan could play themselves. At least in

---

[37] Biblioteca Reale di Torino, Archivio Scarrampi, 3755, 'un volume di scritture risguadᵗⁱ
   il Conte di Verrua', ff. 53–64, spring 1614; Quazza, *Preponderanza spagnuola*, p. 409;
   Rosso, *Una burocrazia*, pp. 150–1. See also AST LMR m. 21, fasc. 4, 266, Filiberto
   Gherardo Scaglia to Carlo Emanuele I, 30 October 1605.
[38] Providing for 'il mantenimento della casa' was a theme of Verrua's will. ASB Archivio
   Scaglia, Testamenti 2530, will of Filiberto Gherardo Scaglia, 7 March 1619.
[39] Margherita was the widow of Carlo Guglielmo Valperga di Caluso who had died in
   1596. Manno, *Patriziato Subalpino*, XXIV, p. 246.
[40] AST LMR m. 21, fasc. 4, 266, Filiberto Gherardo Scaglia to Carlo Emanuele I,
   30 October 1605; fasc. 2, Aldobrandini to Carlo Emanuele I, 30 October 1605.

1623 and 1624 she served as a *fille d'honneur* in Marie Christine's separate household in Turin, a court obviously marked by its predominantly female identity.[41] Like his father, Augusto Manfredo Scaglia also served in a sequence of diplomatic missions and offices that included the *Gran Scudiere*, one of the three main positions in the ducal household. Augusto Manfredo furthermore held army offices as general of the ducal infantry and governor of the fortress of Vercelli, reflecting the particular importance of military service as an acceptable form of employment for the elites of the Savoyard duchy throughout the early modern period.[42] Carlo Emanuele's energetic foreign policies in the first decades of the seventeenth century provided ample opportunities for military experience. It was as an infantry commander that Augusto Manfredo demonstrated his military credentials in the famed, though ultimately unsuccessful, defence of Vercelli of 1617 against overwhelming Spanish forces, and later at the sieges of the fortresses of Verrua and Alessandria in 1625, once more against Spanish forces.[43] He also managed to repeat one of his father's greatest successes in service to the House of Savoy when in 1619 he was himself nominated as a knight of the *Annunziata*, the reward for successfully concluding the marriage negotiations between Vittorio Amedeo and Marie Christine which had been initiated in Paris by his father.[44] It is indeed worth adding that Augusto Manfredo was the only knight elevated by Carlo Emanuele I in 1619, underscoring the importance of his involvement in the French marriage negotiations and also the rising fortunes of the Scaglia di Verrua more generally.

While Augusto Manfredo's career was a story of social and political success in its own right, his younger brother, Alessandro Cesare Scaglia, remains the best-known and most important member of the Scaglia di Verrua, even though he was never the head of his House (raising

[41] AST Sezione Riunite, Art. 219 (1623), f. 2; (1624), f. 5. Unfortunately these household accounts give no indication as to what happened to Margherita after 1624. For details of the territories obtained through the marriage see Manno, *Patriziato Subalpino*, XXIV, p. 246.

[42] AST Sezione Riunite, Art. 219 (1620), f. 13, for the first mention regarding the *Gran Scudiere*, and subsequent volumes thereafter. On the importance of military employment to the Savoyard elites in the early modern period consult Walter Barberis, *Le armi del principe: la tradizione militare sabauda* (Turin, 1988), and Hanlon, *Twilight of a military tradition*, chapter 7.

[43] For two contemporary accounts see 'Difesa del Marchese di Caluso Governatore di Vercelli per la dedizione di questa Città nel 1617 scritta da esso stesso ed esposta al Duca Carlo Emanuele I', *Archivio Storico Italiano*, 13 (Florence, 1847), pp. 519–28, and the 'Relazione dell'assedio della Città di Vercelli fatto nell'anno 1617 dell'esercito di Spagna', by Antonio Berado and dedicated to Augusto Manfredo Scaglia, *ibid.*, pp. 453–519.

[44] Manno, *Patriziato Subalpino*, XXIV, p. 245; Cigna-Santi, *Serie cronologica*, p. 129.

interesting parallels with the familial roles of Cardinals Richelieu and Mazarin). In the words of both contemporaries and historians, Alessandro was a remarkable figure, one of the most widely known diplomats in Europe during the early seventeenth century, and, as will be seen, a figure of exceptional importance in the history of collecting, in particular because of his Van Dyck commissions dating from the 1630s. One of most influential early modern accounts of diplomatic practice, Abraham de Wicquefort's (1606–82) *L'ambassadeur et ses fonctions* (1681), included a section towards the end on 'some noteworthy contemporary ambassadors', Alessandro among them (the only Savoyard diplomat to be included). De Wicquefort in fact was fairly critical of the abate, primarily because of the inconstancy of Carlo Emanuele I, reiterating one of the most persistent historiographical images of the duke: 'but as for him [Scaglia] one can well apply the proverb: like master, like servant. The duke, who was the most ambitious and unsettled of all princes, had him as his confidant and he served him [the duke] in his most delicate negotiations.' The author added that Alessandro Scaglia 'had spirit, but it was muddle-headed, very like his master, and more suited to doing things than to resolving them, so that while one can not consider him the wisest of ambassadors, one ought to place him amongst the most crafty'.[45] De Wicquefort has not been alone in this negative opinion. In his study of James Hay earl of Carlisle, Roy Schreiber was similarly disparaging in equal measure to Alessandro as an ambassador and to Savoy as a second-rank state, saying of the abate that there 'was something of the jackal about Scaglia always sniffing the air for a kill, hoping to claim a small piece of it. In justice he was surrounded by lions, and did not have much choice.'[46] However, few other historians have shared this opinion. The Piedmontese historian Romolo Quazza generously said of Alessandro Scaglia that he was a minister of 'unequalled astuteness and versatility', while Arabella Cifani and Franco Monetti have described him as a 'subtle and talented diplomat', though also as 'sceptical, cynical, ironic and intelligent'.[47] H. G. R. Reade, one of the few English historians to have

[45] Abraham de Wicquefort, *L'ambassadeur et ses fonctions*, 2 vols. (The Hague, 1681), II, pp. 418–19.

[46] Roy Schreiber, 'James Hay. The First Earl of Carlisle', *Transactions of the American Philosophical Society*, 74 (1984), p. 44. With equal negativity L. Cust described Alessandro as 'one of the most slippery among the political agents in the tortuous intrigues of the Spanish court', though given his assertion that Alessandro came from a Genoese family his views should perhaps be taken with caution. L. Cust, *Anthony van Dyck: An Historical Study of His Life and Works* (London, 1900), p. 93.

[47] R. Quazza, *La guerra per la successione di Mantova e del Monferrato, 1628–1631*, 2 vols. (Mantua, 1926), I, p. 68; A. Cifani and F. Monetti, 'New light on the Abbé Scaglia and Van Dyck', *The Burlington Magazine*, 134 (August, 1992).

used (however badly) archival material from Turin, described him in even more glowing terms:

> According to his Mantuan rivals, Scaglia was a born intriguer, who had nothing of the priest about him, and who by his conduct had rendered himself impossible in the eyes of the French Government. Yet, to judge from his despatches the 'Abate', as Englishmen called him, was one of the farthest sighted diplomats of his age, and history has confirmed the justice of his predictions.[48]

As for his elder brother, Alessandro's career was plotted out by his father, Filiberto Gherardo Scaglia, and integrated into his strategy of organising and deploying the resources of the family clan – his future was simply too important to be left to chance. As the cadet, Alessandro Cesare did not marry, serving instead a different function within the structure of the family's power. Where primogeniture was practised a younger son like Alessandro was understandably less likely to receive and transmit the bulk of the family's patrimony – that remained the prime dynastic responsibility entrusted to the eldest son and principal heir. Alessandro nevertheless had to be compensated appropriately (not least so that he would not drain the family's resources) and given a socially acceptable role, just like the younger sons from other elite families around Catholic Europe. One established tradition was to place them in the church, a strategy that could indeed extend the range of family power, more so if families could establish a hold upon ecclesiastical benefices that could be closely associated with their Houses and eventually passed on to their younger nephews. Alessandro was the first member of the Scaglia di Verrua to be placed into this system of income distribution marking his role as the family's link with the church, like Cardinal Maurizio of Savoy in whose household the abate, at the age of seventeen, was placed as a gentleman of the chamber.[49]

In 1603 Alessandro Scaglia, then aged eleven, was accorded the abbey of S. Maria di Staffarda, one of the wealthiest benefices in the principality of Piemonte. The abbey, as with the other ecclesiastical benefices obtained by the Scaglia di Verrua, was a gift from Duke Carlo Emanuele I as a reward for the services of the count of Verrua. This nomination was followed by that to a second abbey in 1613, S. Giusto di Susa, and

---

[48] H. G. R. Reade, *Sidelights on the Thirty Years' War*, 3 vols. (London, 1924), III, p. 44. For a similarly generous contemporary opinion see Francesco Agostino della Chiesa, *S.R.E. cardinalium, archiespiscoporum, episcoporum, et abbatum Pedemontanae regionis chronologica historia* (Turin, 1645), p. 284, where Scaglia was described as a 'vir consilii, morumque suavitate, doctrina, prudentia, & in rebus arduis gerendis summa dexteritate admirabilis prudentissime, & laudabiliter apud praecipuos Christianae Reipublicae'.

[49] AST Sezione Riunite PCF 1608–10, f. 271, 4 December 1609.

finally in 1616 Alessandro received a third abbey, S. Pietro di Muleggio, both again located in Piemonte.[50] Of course ecclesiastical benefices were not in themselves juridically heritable, making them potentially insecure as a source of lasting family power that could be transferred across generations. If however they could be brought more firmly into the gift of the duke of Savoy then the chances that the Scaglia di Verrua might secure them for future second sons would improve, so long as the family retained ducal favour. The Savoyard order of SS. Maurizio e Lazzaro provided the opportunity to increase control over the family's benefices by placing them in the gift of the duke, and Alessandro's father Count Filiberto Gherardo, as a knight of the order, succeeded in bringing his son's benefices under its guidance (benefiting both the Scaglia di Verrua and the ducal House). Eventually two of the three abbeys, S. Giusto and S. Pietro, were successfully transferred to Alessandro's second nephew, Filiberto Scaglia.[51] The third and most significant abbey, Staffarda, was not retained within the family after Alessandro's death and returned to the gift of the duke; it was presented in 1643 to a son of the rival S. Martino d'Agliè, very possibly reflecting the special favour they enjoyed with Duchess Marie Christine, in particular after 1630 when she became the ducal consort.

The ecclesiastical career of the abate, with his pattern of benefice holding, was integral to a family strategy that was both social and political, but this was not the limit of the Scaglia di Verrua's clerical ambitions. Under Filiberto Gherardo's guidance the family clan was establishing itself amongst the highest noble families in Savoy, ranking just beneath the members of the sovereign dynasty itself and those clans which had lesser claims to sovereign status. As a reward for the success of Filiberto Gherardo and Augusto Manfredo in brokering the marriage between Vittorio Amedeo and Marie Christine in 1619, the family's hopes were raised that Alessandro might obtain a cardinal's hat with the sponsorship of the French court. The promotion would quite obviously have represented a significant advance in the family's social and political status, immediately placing the Scaglia di Verrua above most of its rivals at the Savoyard court. Alessandro's promotion would also have benefited the House of Savoy at a time when it had only one representative, Cardinal Maurizio, at the Sacred College; the dynastic union between Savoy and France could have served as an appropriate pretext for the pope bestowing a gift of a second red hat on the Savoyard court, thereby increasing Carlo Emanuele I's prestige and influence in Rome.

[50] Erba, *La chiesa sabauda*, p. 226; della Chiesa, *S.R.E. Cardenalium*, pp. 246, 248.
[51] Erba, *La chiesa sabauda*, pp. 225–6; Claretta, *Dell'Ordine Mauriziano*, pp. 247–8.

Alessandro however never received his cardinal's biretta. Filiberto Gherardo Scaglia's death in March 1619 was in itself a serious setback to the family's ecclesiastical ambitions because so much of its success had up to that point been channelled through him, though at least initially Duke Carlo Emanuele I, Vittorio Amedeo and Cardinal Maurizio continued to petition Pope Paul V Borghese (1552–1621) in support of Alessandro's advancement.[52] In replying to these requests the pope made repeated excuses, that Alessandro would be elevated when the opportunity arose but that there were no suitable vacancies at that time.[53] There were further problems facing his promotion. The simmering but quite evident tensions between the courts of Rome and Turin over questions of etiquette and the relative status of the duchy amongst the Italian states complicated any possibility of a Savoyard nomination directly from the papal court. The most immediate way for Alessandro to have entered the Sacred College would therefore have been through the nomination of another European power, such as France; it was not until the eighteenth century that the House of Savoy acquired the right to name its own crown cardinals, despite a regular stream of petitions during Carlo Emanuele I's reign requesting the elevation of the archbishopric of Turin to a cardinalate.[54] But while members of the French royal family were willing to support Alessandro's candidacy when Filiberto Gherardo was alive, they were not it seems willing to push the request with the necessary vigour after his death in 1619. Added to this, the Scaglia di Verrua had seemingly irritated the ruling papal clan since Filiberto Gherardo and Alessandro enjoyed the support of Cardinal Pietro Aldobrandini (d. 1621) whose own relations with the Borghese during the pontificate of Paul V Borghese seemed fragile.[55] Aldobrandini after all was a cardinal-nephew of the last-but-one pope, Clement VIII Aldobrandini (1536–1605), and thus a member of a rival family group at the Roman court.

Given these problems it seems hardly surprising that Alessandro Scaglia was not nominated in 1619. That did not however signal the end of his

---

[52] The Savoyard half of these petitions can be followed in AST Materie Ecclesiastiche categoria 28, nomina del Cardinale, which includes some papal responses.

[53] For example, ASV Arm. XLV, 13, f. 582, Paul V Borghese to Carlo Emanuele I, 7 December 1619; f. 583, Paul V Borghese to Marie Christine, 7 December 1619.

[54] For an example see ASV SS Francia 52, f. 79, Carlo Emanuele I to Paul V Borghese, 20 November 1620. Gregory XV Ludovisi expressed his sympathy for the idea but was equally quick to stress the same difficulties. ASV Arm. XLV, 19, f. 379, Gregory XV Ludovisi to Carlo Emanuele I, 25 December 1621.

[55] BA Barb. Lat. 5883, ff. 118, Bentivoglio to Borghese, 16 June 1619. It is evident that Bentivoglio, the papal nuncio in France, was also ill disposed to the Scaglia di Verrua and to Augusto Manfredo 'il quale doveva esser giudato in tutto, e per tutto dal frescia.' BA Barb. Lat. 5884, f. 29v, Bentivoglio to Borghese, 7 January 1620. The precise reasons for this antipathy remain unclear.

aspirations for a red hat, or indeed for an alternative clerical promotion. And even though again nothing ultimately came of any of these
prospects, for much of his life the abate was seen as someone who remained on the verge of obtaining a major position within the Catholic
church, most often in recognition of his own political skills (rather than,
as before, as a reward for the activities of other members of his family).[56]
Following the death of Pope Gregory XV Ludovisi (b. 1554) in 1623,
Alessandro Scaglia was proposed as a papal nuncio to the French court.[57]
The mission would not only have strengthened the newly forged connections between the Scaglia di Verrua and Paris but would also ultimately
have guaranteed the abate a longed-for cardinalate since a nunziatura
to Imperial or royal courts customarily concluded with the bestowal of
the biretta for the departing papal envoy. Three years later, in 1626,
Cardinal Richelieu again raised the possibility of Scaglia's promotion to
the Cardinals' College following the apparent success of his diplomatic
negotiations with England over the Huguenot problem, though once
more without any definite outcome, and thereafter the possibilities of
advancing with the support of France quickly waned as Alessandro's own
relationship with Richelieu deteriorated. There was to be one last significant opportunity for clerical promotion when Alessandro's political
affinities shifted towards the Habsburgs in the course of the late 1620s.
The prospect of a Spanish candidacy was raised, again with the intention
of rewarding Abate Scaglia for his diplomatic services, though as before
without any definitive outcome.[58]

    As Filiberto Gherardo groomed his elder son as his heir and placed the
second son in the church as an alternative career and source of income
for the family, he also raised them both to serve as central members of
the duke of Savoy's clientele to ensure that as adults they would perpetuate
the relationship of service to the ducal House and gain for the Scaglia
di Verrua. When in 1603 the count travelled on a mission to Madrid
with the three eldest sons of Carlo Emanuele I as Maggiordomo to the
princes, it seems that he also brought Augusto Manfredo and Alessandro
with him. Unfortunately it remains unclear in the frustrating absence of
documentary evidence as to whether Verrua also had his sons educated

[56] For example, ASV SS Savoia, 46, ff. 224v–5, Albertini to Barberini, 31 May 1627;
    f. 232v, Albertini to Barberini, 7 June 1627. On one occasion Richelieu asked Bagno
    about a report that Philip IV had given his support to Scaglia's promotion; the cardinal
    wished to know whether Urban VIII Barberini would support it. ASV SS Francia, 68,
    f. 267v, Bagno to Barberini, 29 December 1628.
[57] Adriani, *Memorie*, pp. 193–4, 446–7.
[58] PRO SP 94/35/77, Cottington to Carlisle, 1 November 1630; CSPV 1626–8, pp. 617,
    624; J. H. Elliott and José F. de la Peña (eds.), *Memoriales y cartas del Conde Duque de
    Olivares*, 2 vols. (Madrid, 1978–80), II, pp. 28–9.

with the ducal children when they were under the didactic supervision of the Jesuit political theorist Giovanni Botero. That would certainly add a fascinating and important dimension to understanding the mental world of Alessandro Scaglia as a political figure in Counter-Reformation Europe, perhaps as Robert Bireley has suggestively done at a higher level for Emperor Ferdinand II through his relationship with his Jesuit confessor William Lamormaini.[59] It is nevertheless striking that the ages of the Scaglia di Verrua and the ducal sons were almost identical. It should be emphasised that Augusto Manfredo Scaglia was born in 1587 and Alessandro Scaglia in 1591; the ducal sons who travelled to Madrid were Filippo Emanuele (b. 1586), Vittorio Amedeo (b. 1587) and Filiberto Emanuele (b. 1588). What can be said with more certainty is that the Scaglia di Verrua attached particular significance to diplomatic service, as a way of serving both the sovereign and, equally importantly, themselves. In the first place it offered opportunities for raising sons at a time when there were no institutional means for educating the nobility in Savoy – it was not until 1677 that the Turin Academy for nobles was founded, while the University of Turin was only re-established in the following century. Moreover, diplomacy in early modern Savoy was seen as a socially acceptable avenue for noble state service, a *cursus honorum* well into the eighteenth century that could bring significant benefits to the family unit in terms of international prestige and honours closer to home, if not necessarily in terms of financial rewards then as offices and grants of land.[60] At a time when there was no 'professional' Savoyard diplomatic corps as such, ambassadors not only in Savoy but across early modern Europe were typically seen as the embodiments of their sovereigns, and accordingly had to be of a suitable social status to represent their princes, quite apart from needing sufficient resources to offset the inevitable costs of diplomatic missions. Writing in 1627, the Modenese writer Gasparo Bragaccio for one stated that 'truly, the purpose of the ambassador is so intrinsic and connected to the person of his master, that he cannot be seen as separate from the prince'.[61] Both of Verrua's sons had their first individual experience of state service as ambassadorial agents of Carlo Emanuele I, allowing the family also to widen its sphere of influence

---

[59] Robert Bireley, *Religion and Politics in the Age of the Counterreformation: Emperor Ferdinand II, William Lamormaini, S.J., and the Formation of Imperial Policy* (Chapel Hill and London, 1981).

[60] Storrs, 'Savoyard diplomacy', in Frigo (ed.), *Politics and Diplomacy*, pp. 244–5. For the comparative cases of Mantua and Ferrara see the comments by Frigo, ' "Small states" and diplomacy. Mantua and Modena', in *ibid.*, p. 157. On the persistence of the elites in early modern diplomatic service see Bély, *Espions et ambassadeurs*, pp. 291–301.

[61] Bragaccio, *L'Ambasciatore*, p. 36.

into the international arena by establishing links with other sovereign courts. Augusto Manfredo joined his father in the Savoyard embassy in Paris where he assumed control following Verrua's death in 1619, while in 1614 Alessandro undertook his first mission as ordinary ambassador to the papal court where he remained almost permanently until 1623, apart from a brief break in 1622–3.[62] The Savoyard embassy in Rome was effectively the duchy's only permanent diplomatic presence in an Italian court during the early seventeenth century, and a symbolically crucial one as the focal point for Savoy's rivalry for status with other Italian sovereign powers – indeed, Turin was also the only Italian court to receive a regular papal nuncio during the period. Alessandro's selection for the mission at such an early stage of his career reflected perhaps a degree of confidence in his abilities, though also a recognition of the Scaglia di Verrua's importance to the ducal regime as a reliable and capable elite family.

While members of the family served in diplomatic missions across a variety of European courts, the Scaglia di Verrua became closely associated most particularly with the French court as a result of repeated missions to Paris. Importantly, this quickly created the impression of the family as a francophile clan with a cosmopolitan profile, an image that was to feature throughout the seventeenth century and which culminated in the marriage in 1683 between Augusto Manfredo Scaglia (1667–1704) and Giovanna Battista, daughter of the duke of Luynes, one of the members of the high French nobility.[63] Indeed, the perception that members of the Scaglia di Verrua had a particular expertise in dealing with the Bourbon court in itself became a reason for the House of Savoy to send them to serve in France, inscribing itself in a broader pattern of early modern diplomatic culture. There were certainly comparable figures from the court of Charles I for instance who were identified according to certain political affiliations and whose very selection for particular missions was seen as a means of potentially influencing the fortunes of international relations because of the favour as individuals they might enjoy in their resident courts. Francis Cottington (1578–1652) made three journeys as a diplomatic representative to Madrid despite complaining about the personal expense his missions incurred, and he enjoyed some considerable favour with the Habsburg

---

[62] The purpose of his missions to Rome can be understood from his instructions, transcriptions of which can be found in Eugenio Passamonti, 'Le "instruttioni" di Carlo Emanuele I agli inviati sabaudi in Roma con lettere e brevi al duca dei pontefeci suoi contemporane', *Bollettino Storico-Bibliografico Subalpino*, 32 (1930).

[63] G. de Léris, *La comtesse de Verrue et la cour de Victoire-Amadée II de Savoie* (Paris, 1881); Symcox, *Victor Amadeus II*, pp. 74–5; Manno, *Patriziato Subalpino*, XXIV, p. 249.

regime; the enigmatic artist and sculptor Balthasar Gerbier, a native Zeelander, spent most of his diplomatic career as an agent at the court of the Spanish Netherlands in Brussels, initially as a client of the duke of Buckingham, while Thomas Roe's (1581–1644) background as a merchant in the towns of the Hanse and the Levant was seen as a clear qualification for missions as Charles I's representative to Denmark, the Low Countries, Sweden and the Imperial court, as well as good experience for missions to Persia and to the Ottoman court.[64] Perhaps more interesting still was Endymion Porter who, like Gerbier, emerged with a reputation for dealing with the Spanish Habsburgs during the 1620s in part through his membership of the duke of Buckingham's network of clients. With his Spanish grandmother, Porter was, unusually for an English ambassador, fluent in Spanish, and in 1623 he was involved in the aborted negotiations for Charles' marriage to a Spanish Infanta, thereafter serving in a string of missions to Madrid and Brussels during the 1620s and 1630s. Again like Gerbier, Porter also cultivated an image as a knowledgeable collector of the arts which in turn was integral to his career as a cosmopolitan courtier-diplomat and which had significant parallels with Alessandro Scaglia's own career. Porter was closely involved in the acquisition of the Mantuan collection for Charles I in 1628, probably the greatest cultural achievement of his reign, and he was a friend to Daniel Mytens I (1590–1647) and Orazio Gentileschi (1563–1639), two painters employed at the Stuart court, while his friendship with Anthony van Dyck, who superseded Mytens as the leading portrait painter in London, was recorded for posterity in the remarkable double portrait of Porter with the artist painted in 1635.[65]

However, for a family like the Scaglia di Verrua the benefits of diplomatic service away from Savoy still had to be balanced with the need to retain a continuous presence at the sovereign court. That after all was where the greatest opportunities for acquiring power and patronage were to be found, primarily through closeness to the ruling duke. In August 1624 Augusto Manfredo Scaglia returned to Turin from his diplomatic mission in Paris, five years after the death of his father. Filiberto Gherardo had been central to establishing the fortunes of the Scaglia di Verrua as a court clan during the first two decades of the seventeenth century and Augusto Manfredo bore the responsibility as the new head of the House of ensuring the important transition of power and favour from father to

[64] Martin J. Havran, *Caroline Courtier: The Life of Lord Cottington* (London, 1973); Michael Strachan, *Sir Thomas Roe, 1581–1644: A Life* (Salisbury, 1989).
[65] Gervas Huxley, *Endymion Porter: The Life of a Courtier, 1587–1649* (London, 1959); Brown and Vlieghe (eds.), *Van Dyck*, pp. 298–9. The portrait is now in the Prado, Madrid.

son.[66] At least he and Alessandro were fortunate to enjoy the continuing support of two of the ducal sons whom they had known since childhood; Vittorio Amedeo and Tommaso Francesco both wrote to Alessandro expressing their sense of loss on Verrua's death, while Vittorio Amedeo also contacted his ducal father, asking him to maintain the favour he had already bestowed on the Scaglia di Verrua.[67] Augusto Manfredo was nevertheless all too aware that both he and his younger brother, who was still serving in his mission to the papal court, were the targets of attacks from unnamed opponents in Turin, while Augusto Manfredo's wife herself wrote to Duke Carlo Emanuele I that she and her husband were facing criticism from 'a certain leading minister' over the family's property in Caluso.[68] While no names were given, this alone implied that the Scaglia di Verrua had rivals for power at the Savoyard court, just as the attacks on Filiberto Gherardo's ministerial integrity in 1614 over the invasion of Monferrato had done. To preserve ducal favour and the possible integrity of his own estates, Augusto Manfredo had to ensure his personal presence as the new head of his family clan at the court in Turin, reiterating the significance of physical proximity to the sovereign.

Given this need for Augusto Manfredo Scaglia to be present in Turin, the important duty of preparing younger relatives for public service was assumed by Alessandro, who remained almost permanently abroad during his years of service as Duke Carlo Emanuele I's most experienced ambassador, displaying a sense of collective responsibility among family members. As early as 1618 all of Augusto Manfredo's own four sons were with their uncle in Rome, and it is certain that two of them gained further diplomatic experience under the direction of Abate Alessandro.[69] In 1625 Carlo Vittorio (d. 1653), the eldest of Augusto Manfredo's three surviving sons (the fourth died sometime after 1621), was sent to the abate in Paris by Duke Carlo Emanuele I with military insignia, captured presumably from Spanish troops in north Italy. The ceremonial mission

---

[66] Augusto Manfredo Scaglia's departure from the Savoyard mission to Paris was also prompted by financial problems, which he claimed were affecting his capacity to represent the duke of Savoy with sufficient dignity. For example, AST LMF m. 23, fasc. 1, 35, Augusto Manfredo Scaglia to Carlo Emanuele I, 8 March 1623. It seems that he was not properly paid until 1627. AST Sezione Riunite PCF 1627, f. 35, 11 July 1627; f. 77, 1 November 1627.

[67] AST LMR m. 31 fasc. 2, 14, Tommaso Francesco to [Alessandro] Scaglia, 8 May 1619; 24, Vittorio Amedeo to Scaglia, 16 October 1619; AST LDS 48, 614, Vittorio Amedeo to Carlo Emanuele I, 8 March 1619; 618, Vittorio Amedeo to Carlo Emanuele I, 17 March 1619.

[68] For example AST LMF m. 19 fasc. 2, Augusto Manfredo Scaglia to Carlo Emanuele I, 28 September 1620; 21, Augusto Manfredo Scaglia to Carlo Emanuele I, 4 February 1620; 28, countess of Verrua to Carlo Emanuele I, 25 February 1620.

[69] ASV Avvisi, 8, f. 355v, Rome, 14 November 1618; f. 372v, Rome, 21 November 1618.

may also have emphasised the fact that Carlo Vittorio was himself destined for a career in military service to Savoy. In 1630 the second son, Abate Filiberto (d. 1658), served in the Savoyard embassy in Madrid under his uncle Alessandro, where the nephew eventually concluded a settlement of the duke of Savoy's long-running dispute with the republic of Genoa over possession of Zuccarello.[70] The abate was effectively perpetuating the cycle of diplomatic service in his family clan so that its power would in turn be carried across the generations.

While members of the Scaglia di Verrua worked both collectively and individually to obtain court offices, diplomatic posts and gifts from the duke of Savoy, together with heritable land, they also operated as political patrons and brokers within the duchy and further afield on the European stage. Three secretaries of state in service to the duke owed their positions directly to the patronage of the Scaglia di Verrua while two others also served for long periods under members of the family. The most important was Pietro Barozzio (d. 1660), described by Claudio Rosso in his prosopographical study of the Savoyard state secretaries as one of the leading secretaries at the court of Savoy, at least until the death of Duke Vittorio Amedeo I in 1637. Through his attachment to the Scaglia clan and his service to the House of Savoy, Barozzio obtained grants of land that could be inherited through his own family line, in addition to a newly created barony established in 1629 and associated with the estate he acquired at Lessona.[71] The two other secretaries of state in the clientele of the Scaglia di Verrua, Bernardino Almerigi (d. 1628) and Bernardino Baretti (d. 1626), also obtained heritable territorial possessions. For all three clients, office holding under the guidance of the Scaglia di Verrua represented a stepping stone to the advancement of their own families, with the broad ambition of securing heritable landed wealth and increased social status.[72]

Through state service members of the Scaglia di Verrua constantly operated as mediators between individuals seeking some kind of gain or patronage and the court of Turin. This was especially true while they served on diplomatic missions since as ambassadors they could operate as both formal and informal points of contact between the courts in which they served and their home state. Alessandro Scaglia repeatedly wrote letters of recommendation and pleading letters for various individuals and for the sponsors of third parties both from within Savoy and further

---

[70] AST LMF m. 26, fasc. 1, 152, Scaglia to Carlo Emanuele I, 7 June 1625; LMS m. 24, fasc. 1, 40, Scaglia to Vittorio Amedeo I, 3 June 1631.
[71] Rosso, *Una burocrazia*, pp. 174–9, 368–9.   [72] *Ibid.*, pp. 145–6, 368.

afield. To take one example, Pietro Barozzio, client of the Scaglia di Verrua, had a brother, Michele Barozzio, who as captain of a regiment of soldiers was imprisoned in 1624 with his son because his troops burnt a house belonging to someone described as a personal enemy. On Pietro Barozzio's request, Alessandro wrote to Carlo Emanuele I seeking his brother's release, arguing that Pietro had served as an able secretary of state to the duke and that his brother had himself served the duke for twenty-four years and commanded a regiment that would still be of use to Carlo Emanuele I in time of war. While it is not actually clear from surviving evidence as to whether Michele Barozzio was duly released, the incident alone shows how the abate could use his ambassadorial position as a channel for petitions of third parties to reach the duke and other members of the ruling dynasty.[73]

Political patronage and brokering were one potentially important means for the Scaglia di Verrua to further their network of influence and for channels of patronage to remain open to the Savoyard court. As leading members of the Savoyard elite with significant diplomatic experience, individuals from the clan also functioned as cultural patrons and brokers, particularly in the realms of the visual arts and literature. This in turn contributed to the family's increasingly cosmopolitan presence on a stage beyond the duchy, and in retrospect it marks its significance in the history of collecting and patronage. As the duke of Savoy's ordinary ambassador to the Venetian Republic, Carlo Emanuele Scaglia, the younger brother of Filiberto Gherardo Scaglia, was in contact with Vincenzo Scamozzi (1548–1616), architect and pupil of Andrea Palladio (1508–80), and he sent the frontispiece of Scamozzi's important theoretical treatise, *L'idea dell'architettura universale* (1615), to the duke of Savoy. Carlo Emanuele Scaglia recorded that Scamozzi had wished to dedicate one of the twelve books from his treatise to Carlo Emanuele I, like Palladio before him, who had dedicated two volumes of his immensely influential *I quattro libri dell'architettura* (1570) to Duke Emanuele Filiberto. The Savoyard ambassador had considered the section on military architecture to be the most suitable, adding in another letter that Scamozzi should be duly rewarded for his offer. The timing of the book's publication coincided with Savoy's military confrontation against Spain in north Italy and four years before Carlo Emanuele I embarked on expanding Turin and its fortress, and, in dedicating the book to the duke, Scamozzi himself drew attention to the age of his House, its marriages to the leading dynasties of Europe

---

[73] AST LMF m. 26, fasc. 1, 99, Scaglia to Carlo Emanuele I, 19 April 1625; 105, Scaglia to Carlo Emanuele I, 30 April 1625. For a few other examples of diplomatic brokering involving the abate see Tassoni, *Lettere*, I, pp. 391, 394.

and, most relevantly, the virtues of Carlo Emanuele I in war and peace.[74] Further work is required to assess the full extent of Filiberto Gherardo Scaglia's and his elder son Augusto Manfredo's roles as collectors and patrons, though during Augusto Manfredo's mission to Paris he negotiated the acquisition of a series of cloths showing the story of Artemesia from the leading tapestry workers at the Gobelins workshop, and he also noted a rich tapestry of the story of Diana, together with another showing the flight of Arion, the immortal horse of Greek mythology. This was to be the beginning of a process where Augusto Manfredo sought to woo tapestry makers from Paris to Turin, while continuing to acquire tapestries for the Savoyard House.[75] He also brokered the commission for the French painter Fernand Elle (1580–1649) to paint members of the Savoyard House, along with Marie Christine whose portrait was sent to Turin to further the marriage negotiations with the prince of Piemonte, Vittorio Amedeo. The prince of Piemonte in turn looked to the Paris market to acquire jewelry, precious objects and landscapes, the latter through Augusto Manfredo, who was also instructed by Turin to acquire any sort of oriental curiosity there.[76]

The most important member of the family as a cultural patron and broker was without doubt Alessandro Scaglia, whose exceptional credentials were established at the very outset of his career. As early as 1614, the year of his first diplomatic mission as Carlo Emanuele I's ordinary ambassador to the papal court, Alessandro was the recipient of a dedication by one of the major Piedmontese historians of the seventeenth century, Francesco Agostino della Chiesa. Della Chiesa claimed that in dedicating his book *Catalogo di tutti li scrittori Piemontesi et altri dei stati dell'altezza sereniss. di Savoia* (1614) to Alessandro, he felt compelled to produce a work on Piedmontese authors to give them their deserved praise in the face of undeserved literary criticism. He went on to write that because of his desire to seek a virtuous protector and his family's existing devotion to the Scaglia di Verrua, Alessandro was the natural choice for the

---

[74] Cifani and Monetti, 'New light', footnote 38; AST LMV m. 6, 13, Carlo Emanuele Scaglia to Carlo Emanuele I, 14 July 1615; 92, Carlo Emanuele Scaglia to Carlo Emanuele I, 19 December 1615. For the dedication to Duke Carlo Emanuele I see Vincenzo Scamozzi, *L'idea dell'architettura universale* (Venice, 1615), part I, book II. The dedication was dated 15 August 1615.

[75] Romano (ed.), *Le collezioni*, pp. 268–72.

[76] Alessandro Baudi di Vesme, 'L'arte negli stati sabaudi', *Atti della Società Piemontese di Archeologia e Belli Arti*, 14 (1932), 304–8; Romano (ed.), *Le collezioni*, pp. 251–2, 353. On his departure from Paris, Augusto Manfredo Scaglia tried unsuccessfully to persuade Elle to return with him to Turin. AST LMF m. 24, fasc. 2, 42, Augusto Manfredo Scaglia to Carlo Emanuele I, 4 April 1624; m. 25, 119, Scaglia to Carlo Emanuele I, 8 November 1624.

dedication.[77] Quite why this should have been so remains open to speculation. Perhaps because Della Chiesa was himself a Jesuit he saw Alessandro, a commendatory abate in the church, as the obvious member of the family with whom he should be associated. It is also quite possible that Della Chiesa saw the young Alessandro Scaglia as a potentially lucrative patron for the future and, given the timing of the dedication, as a link to a wider pool of patrons in Rome where the abate was dispatched by Carlo Emanuele I.

During Alessandro's mission to Rome between 1614 and 1623 his expertise as a cultural patron and broker was significantly enhanced, helped no doubt by the sheer concentration of artistic activity in what was the most important European centre for patronage and commissions, and one of Carlo Emanuele's principal sources of art for his growing gallery in Turin.[78] The abate's diplomatic correspondence reveals a figure who rapidly established friendships and contacts among a number of significant artists, writers and patrons; according to the great nineteenth-century Piedmontese art historian Alessandro Baudi di Vesme, the abate was looked on by Carlo Emanuele I as an 'expert connoisseur' in paintings who could help the duke expand his own collection, so important to his identity as the leading Italian sovereign, that was housed in the newly built gallery in his Turinese palace.[79] Scaglia is known to have spent the summers of 1618 and 1619 in the circle of Cardinal d'Este at the Villa d'Este in Tivoli outside the papal capital, and during his stay there the abate counted among his friends the patron and collector Cassiano dal Pozzo and the writer Fulvio Testi.[80] Dal Pozzo was of course one of the most significant private patrons of seventeenth-century Europe, by birth from an illustrious Piedmontese family – the Dal Pozzo family originated in Biella, the same town as the Scaglia di Verrua – although from 1612 he had resided in Rome.[81] For his part, Testi had already established contact with the Turinese court in 1617 when he emulated his friend Alessandro

---

[77] Francesco Agostino della Chiesa, *Catalogo di tutti li scrittori Piemontesi et altri dei stati dell'altezza sereniss. di Savoia* (Turin, 1614), preface.

[78] Romano (ed.), *Le collezioni*, p. 245.

[79] Alessandro Baudi di Vesme, 'La regia pinacoteca di Torino', *Le Gallerie Nazionale Italiane*, III (Rome, 1897), 6.

[80] Scaglia wrote afterwards to the cardinal thanking him for his hospitality. Tassoni, *Lettere*, I, p. 401. While in Rome the abate was known to have had three residences of his own, the Palazzo Cenci alla Dogana, the Palazzo Caprianica and the Palazzo Ricario alla Lungara. J. A. F. Orbanni, *Documenti sul barocco in Roma*, (Rome, 1920), pp. 227, 238–9, 253.

[81] Like the Scaglia di Verrua family archive, that of the Dal Pozzo can still be found in Biella. Other members of the family remained in Savoy and indeed made their own contributions to the patronage of the arts.

Tassoni by dedicating a collection of verse to Carlo Emanuele I, including a poem in which an oppressed Italy called on the Savoyard duke to avenge her against foreign troops. In a letter written in 1641 in which Testi reflected at length on his career, he implied that the abate had in fact operated as the mediator with the duke for the work.[82] While in Rome Scaglia also established contact with Antonio Tempesta (1555–1630), a painter and engraver from Florence who specialised in pastoral scenes, and the Sienese painter Antiveduto della Grammatica (1571–1626).[83] Through these points of contact the abate purchased works both for the duke of Savoy and for his daughter Margherita, and Giovanni Romano has suggested that the failed attempt to woo Della Grammatica to Turin in 1621, and Carlo Emanuele I's and Vittorio Amedeo's wider interest in Carravagist painters had coincided with their plans from 1619 of building new apartments in the growing ducal palace.[84] The abate also bought works from Della Grammatica for himself. According to a letter to the abate of 1625, it seems that Alessandro Tassoni was in possession of a number of paintings which, presumably, he had made available to Scaglia, among which were 'four *chiariscuri* by Tempesta and two in colour, a hunt scene and a battle'.[85]

Alessandro Scaglia also collected other works of art and goods for the duke of Savoy in the course of the mission, and his diplomatic correspondence deposited in Turin serves as an important guide to his cultural sensibilities. While in Rome he looked to complete the purchase of a number of classical sculptures, some of which were later transported back to the Savoyard duke in Turin.[86] He bought books and illuminated manuscripts, that included a book illustrated with fish that the prince wanted by a writer called Ippolito Salviano, and which has been located in the Biblioteca Nazionale in Turin. In a later letter, Scaglia noted another work on natural history, illustrated by Salviano and his son.[87]

---

[82] Fulvio Testi, *L'Italia all'invittissimo e gloriosissimo prencipe Carlo Emanuel Duca di Savoia* (Rome, 1617); Fulvio Testi, *Lettere (a cura di Maria Luigi-Doria)*, 3 vols. (Bari, 1967), I, p. 57; III, p. 241.

[83] On Tempesta see Alessandro Baudi di Vesme, *Schede Vesme: l'arte in Piemonte dal XVI al XVIII secolo*, 3 vols. (Turin 1963–8), III, p. 1040. On Grammatica consult *ibid.*, II, p. 537.

[84] Romano (ed.), *Le collezioni*, p. 247.

[85] AST LMR m. 30, fasc. 2, 94, Scaglia to G. Crotti, 3 August 1619; Tassoni, *Lettere*, II, p. 136, which also made reference to a 'nativity in amethyst and a baptism in lapislazuli' by Turpino. For further information on Alessandro's artistic activities in Rome see Cifani and Monetti, 'New light', 509.

[86] *Ibid.*, 509. They included some nude figures which he considered to be the best. AST LMR m. 26, fasc. 4, 143, Scaglia to Carlo Emanuele I, 30 January 1615.

[87] AST LMR m. 29, fasc. 2, 79, Scaglia to 'His Highness', 13 October 1618, 117, 14 December 1618; Romano (ed.), *Le collezioni*, p. 325.

Alessandro also kept his eye open for other potential commissions. In 1619 he informed Carlo Emanuele I of some goldsmiths at the Altemps residence who had a collection of works valued which included twenty-four silver fruit dishes – twelve with figures of emperors with bass reliefs showing their deeds and victories, four with figures of the seasons, four of the elements and four of the world's 'monarchies' – and also tankards, and vases decorated with flowers and festoons and 'naturalistic' enamels of fruits.[88] In 1623 the abate was in touch with an unnamed engineer and a fountain designer, who sent a variety of plans for fountains back to Carlo Emanuele I, though Scaglia did not later say whether anything came of this potential commission.[89] Carlo Emanuele I too wrote to the abate of his collecting habits. In a letter to Scaglia written in 1620, the duke recommended two artists to the abate, the Flemish painter Ludovico Susio and Guglielmo Nef, who had worked in Turin and had then moved to Rome.[90]

Duke Carlo Emanuele I was not alone in drawing on Alessandro's growing expertise, as other members of the House of Savoy contacted the abate with requests for works of art and finished goods. The most significant collector from the ruling House other than the duke was Cardinal Maurizio, who earnestly wished to establish his own cultural credentials as part of his campaign for both self-promotion and the advancement of the dynasty. He employed Alessandro to purchase classical sculptures and manuscripts – it was Scaglia who looked to acquire in 1617 the collection of sculptures at the villa of Cardinal Altemps, although the villa eventually went to the Borghese family. It was in this context that Maurizio wrote to the abate of his particular interest in the classical sculptures and 'other antiquities' in the collection.[91] Elsewhere, Scaglia looked to procure a book of verse and three classical marble busts for another, though unspecified, member of the Savoyard dynasty (possibly Maurizio). The abate recorded that the verse, while in a beautiful hand, was of a mediocre quality, while the busts, said to have included Achilles, Anacreon and Archimedes, were in bad condition.[92]

One of the most significant, well-documented and abiding of Alessandro's friendships established at Rome was with the writer Alessandro Tassoni who distinguished the abate as his 'particular lord [mio

---

[88] AST LMR m. 30, fasc. 1, 27, Scaglia to Carlo Emanuele I, 9 March 1619.
[89] AST LMR m. 33, fasc. 8, 18, Scaglia to Carlo Emanuele I, 21 June 1623.
[90] Romano (ed.), *Le collezioni*, p. 224.
[91] AST LMR m. 29, fasc. 1, 51, Maurizio to Scaglia, 14 December 1617; fasc. 2, 79, Scaglia to Maurizio, 13 October 1618; Cifani and Monetti, 'New light', 509; Romano (ed.), *Le collezioni*, p. 171.
[92] AST LMR m. 29, fasc. 2, 79, Scaglia to 'His Highness', 13 October 1618.

signore particulare]', and who had already known the abate's father since at least 1599.[93] Duke Carlo Emanuele I's commission from Tassoni to defend Savoy's claim over Monferrato was brokered by the abate in 1614.[94] Subsequent to the initial commission of the *Filippiche*, the Scaglia di Verrua family, and Alessandro in particular, maintained a special interest in Tassoni, securing for him the position in 1618 of secretary to the abate and gentleman in Cardinal Maurizio's household.[95] Three members of the family were also involved in the publication of what today has become Tassoni's best-known literary work, the mock poem *La sechia rapita* (1622), the first of its kind in Italian. Because of the stringency of the Inquisition in the papal capital, Tassoni wished to have his poem published outside Rome. Alessandro Scaglia negotiated to have it printed in the city of Lyons probably because of its less-restricted publishing culture and proximity to the Italian peninsula, while Pietro Barozzio, who was then at the French court as secretary to Augusto Manfredo Scaglia, did the same in Paris. In the meantime Alessandro's uncle, Carlo Emanuele Scaglia, who was still resident as the duke of Savoy's ordinary ambassador in Venice, circulated manuscript copies of the work there prior to its full publication.[96]

Although the Scaglia di Verrua, primarily under Alessandro's direction, actively promoted Tassoni's career, the writer's experience of service to the House of Savoy was marked by constant and ultimately terminal problems. The *Manifesto di Alessandro Tassoni intorno le relazioni passate tra esso e i principi di Savoia*, a scathing attack against the ruling family, written between 1626 and 1627 (though not published until the nineteenth century), after Tassoni's departure from Savoyard service, catalogued his frustration at dealing with Duke Carlo Emanuele I and his sons, especially Maurizio.[97] While Tassoni complained about Carlo Emanuele I's apparent indifference to him, not least on an occasion when he had attempted to seek an audience with the duke for his unpaid stipend as a gentleman to Cardinal Maurizio, the author's position within Maurizio's household proved certainly no more satisfactory. Tassoni was subjected to sharp attacks from the cardinal's existing clients, no doubt suspicious of

[93] Tassoni, *Lettere*, I, pp. 8–9, 87, 130–1. He also described Alessandro and Augusto Manfredo Scaglia as 'two leading individuals – perhaps the leading ones – of the duke of Savoy'. *Ibid.*, I, p. 132.

[94] That Alessandro was supportive of Tassoni can be inferred from his letter to the duke of Savoy praising the writer and asking for Carlo Emanuele I to give him due reward. AST LMR m. 26, fasc. 4, 140, Scaglia to Carlo Emanuele I, 20 December 1614.

[95] AST Sezione Riunite PCF 1618–19, f. 25, 2 June 1619.

[96] Tassoni, *Lettere,* II, pp. 99, 109, 111–12, 114, 137; Pulliati, *Bibliografia*, I, pp. 94–7; 163–85.

[97] *Ibid.*, I, pp. 426–30.

him as a potential rival for favour, and the cardinal's own unsympathetic attitude did nothing to alleviate the tensions. In 1621 the bitterly disillusioned Tassoni left the cardinal's household, also severing his formal ties with the House of Savoy for good. Back in the papal capital he went on to serve first Cardinal Ludovico Ludovisi, nephew to Pope Gregory XV Ludovisi, and then from 1632 Duke Francesco I of Modena (d. 1658), a grandson of Carlo Emanuele I. Tassoni's poor experiences in Savoy's service, however, did little to sour his relations with the abate and the Scaglia di Verrua, as his *Manifesto* made equally clear. When the writer travelled to Turin in 1620 he remained as a guest of Alessandro Scaglia in the abbey of Staffarda to avoid what he claimed were his enemies in Turin, and the abate's hospitality was later reciprocated for Scaglia and his nephews. When the 'four quick witted putti [quattro putti molto spiritosi]', as he described the nephews, journeyed between their uncle in Rome and Turin via the shrine of Loreto, Alessandro Tassoni ensured that they were introduced to the court in Modena.[98] For the abate and his brother in 1623, Tassoni ensured that they were accommodated in Modena when they undertook a journey from the papal capital to Turin.[99]

After the abate departed from the Savoyard mission in Rome he left a number of his personal belongings in Tassoni's care, to which the writer drew attention when in May 1632 he composed his sixth will. The writer noted that these included 'paintings, seats and small tables' which had become mixed up with the author's own possessions, so that, apart from a few specific pictures, he intended to leave all the remaining pictures, 'all the stone frames, all the chairs, all the small tables, sideboards, desks, all the *lettiere di noce* and all the *casse da campagna*' to his long-standing friend. The abate had also deposited with Tassoni two tapestries of a 'new French allegory and the other of a Flemish woodland scene [una nuova figurata di Francia, l'altra a boscaglie di Fiandra]', a 'large carpet and a baldacchino with moth-eaten and threadbare green cloth and a letter chest'.[100] As Tassoni recorded in a series of letters written in the following year, Alessandro Scaglia intended to sell his tapestries, which were valued at 4,000 ducats. Significantly the correspondence was directed to Cassiano dal Pozzo, adding to the impression once more that Dal Pozzo also knew the abate directly as another link in Scaglia's network of friends, artists and writers from Rome.[101]

---

[98] Tassoni, *Lettere*, II, p. 86.   [99] *Ibid.*, II, pp. 87–8, 92, 139–40, for example.
[100] *Ibid.*, II, pp. 327–8.
[101] Tassoni, *Manifesto*, in *Prose politiche*, p. 407; Tassoni, *Lettere*, II, pp. 327–8; Pulliati, *Bibliografia*; Joseph Cooper Walker, *Memoirs of Alessandro Tassoni* (London, 1815), pp. 120–67.

Alessandro Scaglia was equally energetic as a cultural patron and broker during his second major diplomatic mission, to the French court between 1624 and 1627. There is evidence, again from his formal diplomatic correspondence, that he was active in commissioning works of art and buying finished goods for the Savoyard court. Fernand Elle, who had been approached by Alessandro's father and brother to purchase a collection of portraits by him for the Turinese court, was employed through the abate to paint a portrait of Marie de Bourbon-Soissons, Tommaso Francesco's bride-to-be.[102] Aside from acquiring paintings, the abate also purchased diamonds for Carlo Emanuele I, while a revealing list of diplomatic expenses drawn up in Paris during 1626 and included in his correspondence shows that he also bought tapestries from an individual named Valcheria at the Gobelins workshops, thirty pairs of shoes, and buttons from two goldsmiths named Giardin and Pigiard.[103] In addition he bought a variety of animals for export to Savoy. From the duke of Angoulême (1573–1650) he purchased a number of dogs and horses, reflecting the importance of hunting in sovereign courts, including the Savoyard court; from the menagerie of the duke of Chevreuse, Alessandro also sought the transport to Turin of more exotic animals, among which were parrots and an elephant.[104]

It would be hard to deny that Alessandro's rapidly acquired experience in buying and commissioning pictures, literary works, sculptures, furniture, jewels and animals enabled him to develop with great speed a personal expertise and a reputation as a sophisticated and knowledgeable collector at an early stage in his career. This is certainly one of the abiding images of the abate, confirmed most importantly by the Van Dyck commissions dating from his period of exile in the 1630s. But nor should the potential diplomatic significance of collecting and the interchange of political and artistic patronage be overlooked, however difficult mapping specific connections between politics and patronage might seem.

---

[102] Baudi di Vesme, 'L'arte negli stati sabaudi', pp. 308–9. The portrait of Marie de Bourbon-Soissons would probably have formed part of the ducal collection in the Galleria Sabauda in Turin. However, the collection was partially broken up and divided between Turin and the palace at Stupinigi. There is currently no authoritative catalogue of the Stupinigi collection and the portrait that has tentatively been identified as being of Soissons at the Galleria Sabauda was evidently painted at a later date; the whereabouts of the Elle portrait thus remains elusive.

[103] AST LMF m. 25, 119, Scaglia to Carlo Emanuele I, 8 November 1624; 114, Scaglia to Carlo Emanuele I, 1 November 1624.

[104] AST LMF m. 27, fasc. 3, 195, Scaglia to Carlo Emanuele I, October 1626, with list of expenses attached; 248, Scaglia to Carlo Emanuele I, 8 December 1626; 259, Scaglia to Carlo Emanuele I, 21 December 1626. On Carlo Emanuele I's evident interest in exotic animals see Romano (ed.), Le collezioni, p. 325.

By establishing informal connections with courtiers and creating networks of artists and writers across Europe, ambassadors like Alessandro
Scaglia could effectively increase their potential political influence in their
diplomatic missions. Cultural links between courtiers could operate like
dynastic affinities between courts, albeit on a potentially weaker level.
While Alessandro Scaglia's friendships with courtiers did not necessarily
create compelling political bonds in themselves, they could none the less
establish favourable conditions for influencing policy-makers who shared
his interests or aspired to them. Friendship is indeed central to understanding Alessandro Scaglia's world as a cultural patron and broker, and
more broadly his entire career as a diplomat and political figure from his
first mission to Rome in 1614 until his death in 1641 in Antwerp. In his
study of Francis Bacon (1561–1626), David Wootton has emphasised the
importance of friendship in early modern political culture. He argues that
friendship in the context of court politics was distinct from its idealised
Ciceronian version, what Sharon Kettering has described as 'personal
friendship' in her work on sixteenth-century France.[105] Political friendship, or 'social friendship' to use Kettering's terminology again, had very
different connotations in the sixteenth and seventeenth centuries when
set against its less convention-bound modern counterpart: 'Friendship
is thus inseparable', Wootton writes, 'in the early modern period, from
alliance, clientage and favouritism – concepts which are to us antithetical
to friendship, because in our view friendship is a matter for private life,
while public life is ostensibly governed by the revolutionary principles of
impartiality and the career open to talents.'[106]

Clearly, both Wootton and Kettering have a structural approach to
friendship; as Wootton acknowledges, his methodology draws on ideas
already applied to gift-giving in early modern Europe, themselves informed by anthropological conceptions of carefully controlled, if often
implicit, social conventions.[107] In an age when there was a specific and
widespread literature on the subject, Wootton suggests, acts of friendship
had a functional role within politics, though a role that was also inherently
dangerous and which could play on the early modern anxieties of service
and self-interest. Alessandro's own father, Filiberto Gherardo Scaglia, has
been credited with an unpublished political treatise, *Avvertimenti politici*

---

[105] Sharon Kettering, 'Friendship and clientage in early modern France', *French History*,
6 (1992), 152. For another interpretation of Stoicism and friendship in early modern Europe see Mark Morford, *Stoics and Neostoics: Rubens and the Circle of Lipsius*
(Princeton and Oxford, 1991).

[106] Wootton, 'Flexible friend', p. 188; Kettering, 'Friendship and clientage', 158.

[107] For a recent account of gift giving in its different social, religious and political contexts
see Natalie Zemon Davis, *The Gift in Sixteenth-Century France* (Oxford, 2000).

per quelli che vogliono entrare nella corte, a work on court life that encompassed similar ideas about the importance of choosing patrons with care, and which likewise assumed that there was political give and take in friendship. The treatise included chapters on how a courtier should seek an appropriate patron and how he should guard his words and actions, trusting in few yet remaining patient and prudent in dealing with his patron and rivals, all fairly familiar themes – his own son Alessandro took a personal motto of *Quiescendo Sapimus*, with its early modern resonances of political reticence and self-control.[108] Most relevantly in chapter three, Verrua wrote of the care with which friends should be chosen, echoing the concerns expressed by Bacon that friendships with other aspiring political figures could lead to dangerous rivalries for patronage:

> In the courts where you serve, you should have no-one for a confidant or a friend. Yet because it is not possible to exist without a friend, you should elect one from beyond [the court] with mature consideration, who, among his other qualities, should above all never pretend to have interests with your patron.[109]

While Alessandro himself was silent on the subject of friendship as an explicit topic for discussion, his own acts of gift-giving and, more broadly, the sharing of cultural interests with political figures, at the least established intangible affinities with other influential courtiers, if not the kind of functional political reciprocity assumed by Bacon and perhaps also his father. Through the friends he cultivated around Europe – both 'personal' and 'political' friends – the abate could move more freely among courts and make contact with courtiers not least because he often shared their cultural interests, though also because he was in a position of giving, buying or receiving finished goods like paintings, tapestries and furniture from them. One of Alessandro's key friendships during the 1620s was with George Villiers, the duke of Buckingham. A record of their closeness was provided by the duke himself who, in an extraordinary piece of hyperbole, wrote on one occasion to the abate of a bundle of over fifty letters that arrived in London from which Alessandro's favourite dog had miraculously recognised his particular letter.[110] As will be seen, their relationship had much to do with common political goals and the Stuart and Savoyard dynastic affinities during the complex period of active English engagement in Europe, though Buckingham's efforts to establish

---

[108] Filiberto Gherardo Scaglia, 'Avvertimenti politici per quelli che vogliono entrare nel corte', *Miscellanea di Storia d'Italia* (1889).
[109] Verrua, 'Avvertimenti politici', 354.
[110] PRO SP 78/80/3, Buckingham to Scaglia, 17 January 1627.

himself as a cultivated courtier also drew him to the abate, revealing how politics and patronage could merge in early modern diplomacy. Late in 1625 Scaglia's secretary was negotiating with the duke in London while Buckingham was planning to return to France for a second time, to advance the international anti-Habsburg coalition – the abate and duke had met when Buckingham was in Paris in May 1625, with the intention of representing Charles I at his marriage in proxy to Henrietta Maria. Knowing Buckingham's interest in collecting, Alessandro wrote to Duke Carlo Emanuele I that:

> You will see from the enclosed letter of Barozzio the news from England; I believe that he will not be back without achieving something, for the duke of Buckingham has always expressed himself well-disposed to serving you, to whom one thought appropriate to give a gift of a good painting, which may be all he desires. When [Vittorio Amedeo] was here I gave him a *Carità Romana,* which might be very valuable, for one I had by the same artist was greatly appreciated [by Buckingham] when he was here, and the style of that painter is infinitely pleasing to him [Buckingham]. It might be appropriate to give him another by an old master.[111]

While the painter was not named, it seems that he was possibly Bartolomeo Manfredi (1582–1622), one of Caravaggio's (1571–1610) closest followers. Caution has to be exercised in linking the abate's letter with specific works that were in Turin or London, but an inventory of the Sabaudian collection from 1635, drawn up by Antonio della Cornia, included a *Carità* by Manfredi, depicting a woman giving her breast to an imprisoned old man, while an inventory of Buckingham's collection, also from the 1630s, mentioned a *Carità romana* by Manfredi.[112]

This was not to be the last occasion on which Alessandro used a gift of paintings to please the duke. Early in 1628 the abate inadvertently became involved in the bungled attempt to have Frances Coke, Lady Purbeck, arrested. Purbeck, whose residence at York House on The Strand was next to that of the abate, was Buckingham's sister-in-law and was reputedly an adulteress. Given the obvious doubts over the legitimacy of her children, the duke was extremely reluctant to see his own possessions pass to his brother's line at a time when he had no heirs of his own. When constables hid in the grounds of Scaglia's residence to arrest Purbeck following a sentence of adultery against her in the Court of High Commission, Scaglia's

[111] AST LMF m. 26, fasc. 1, 258, Scaglia to Carlo Emanuele I, 1 November 1625.
[112] Baudi di Vesme, 'La regia pinacoteca di Torino', 43; Randall Davies, 'An inventory of the duke of Buckingham's pictures, etc., at York House in 1635', *The Burlington Magazine*, 10 (1906), 380; Romano (ed.), *Le collezioni*, p. 362. I am grateful to Arabella Cifani and Franco Monetti for alerting me to these points.

followers used a page boy dressed in women's clothing as a decoy to have the unwelcome constables removed. Buckingham – at least in public – was furious with the abate for this 'carnival trick' and refused even to see him at court. It was only following the intercessions of the earls of Carlisle and Holland and, most significantly of all, a gift of two paintings from Scaglia, that the abate and Buckingham were publicly reconciled.[113]

Common interests expressed through collecting and the practice of patronage could therefore help to create or reinforce friendships among courtiers from different states and, in the case of the Stuart court, across confessional boundaries. In turn these friendships could serve as diplomatic or political points of contact. They gave a distinctive shape to the Scaglia di Verrua's cosmopolitan profile in the seventeenth century, reflecting both the growing power of the family clan and the ways in which that power could be put to use in the service of Savoy. During the first two decades of the seventeenth century the Scaglia di Verrua had indeed reached a high point of political and cultural influence both within the duchy and further afield, most particularly in France. That influence had been obtained through a productive relationship with the ruling House of Savoy which in return drew on the expertise and loyalty of members of the Scaglia family in diplomatic and military service. Even the names given to members of the Scaglia di Verrua explicitly copied those of the ruling House, no doubt to underline a sense of affinity between the two families – Carlo Emanuele Scaglia (brother of Filiberto Gherardo), Carlo Vittorio Scaglia, Maurizio Scaglia and Filiberto Scaglia (three sons of Augusto Manfredo) were all names that resonated with those of the sovereign dynasty, while Filiberto Gherardo's sole daughter, Bianca, had remained unmarried, taking, appropriately enough, the name in 1629 of Maria Cristina (the name of Prince Vittorio Amedeo's consort) as a nun.[114]

Of all the members of the family clan, Alessandro Scaglia stands out as the prime example of the way in which a particular type of diplomacy both evolved and operated, employing informal lines of contact with other courtiers across Europe and furthering the particular interests of his family in the context of Savoy's international power profile. The abate's entire career brought together rapidly accumulated influence and cultural expertise to create a distinctive diplomatic profile. At this point it is perhaps useful to return to the themes of state history and state formation. Alessandro Scaglia's profile and the identity of his family presents an

[113] Toby Osborne, 'Abbot Scaglia, the Duke of Buckingham and Anglo-Savoyard relations during the 1620s', European History Quarterly, 30 (2000), 5–6.
[114] Manno, Patriziato Subalpino, XXIV, p. 245.

approach to the formulation of ducal policies, foreign policies in particular where the Scaglia di Verrua undoubtedly enjoyed most of their influence, that moves beyond institutional or impersonal power alone. True enough, the dynastic aspirations of the Savoyard duke set some of the essential parameters within which foreign policies operated, but he also needed the expertise of elite families like the Scaglia di Verrua to implement them, and individuals like Alessandro Scaglia were skilful and powerful enough to bring their own influence to bear on those policies. The Scaglia di Verrua's history as a family with collective aspirations and individual personalities was inseparable from that of the ruling dynasty of Savoy, and it was this complex relationship that was borne out by the career of Alessandro Scaglia during the Thirty Years' War. In March 1624 the abate received his formal credentials to travel to Paris as ordinary ambassador of Duke Carlo Emanuele I, replacing his father and brother, both of whom had held the position before him. The move to the French court marked the beginning of a new phase in his career that set him on the centre stage of international diplomacy until his death in May 1641.

PART II

THE TREATY OF MONZÓN, 1624–1627

3

SAVOYARD DIPLOMACY: ALESSANDRO SCAGLIA AND THE MISSION TO PARIS, 1624–1626

The interaction between two families, the sovereign House of Savoy and the aristocratic Scaglia di Verrua, affords a different approach to the state history of Savoy, and in particular to the duchy's role on the stage of international power politics. The ruling dynasty under the guidance of the ducal head had in the sixteenth century sought to reclaim control over its patrimonial territories and thereafter set about trying to gain yet more territories to which it felt legitimately entitled, primarily in north Italy. As the House of Savoy extended its power against domestic and foreign rivals so the Scaglia di Verrua had risen to the pinnacle of the Savoyard political world while furthering their own horizons beyond the duchy through diplomatic service and cultural patronage and brokering. Of all the members of the Scaglia di Verrua, Alessandro encapsulates how the tracks of state and family history interacted and the way in which a distinctive style of diplomacy operated. His very career as a commendatory abate and an ambassador depended on his father's service to Duke Carlo Emanuele I. His subsequent success in his own right owed much more to his own social and cultural qualities, and his emergence during the 1620s as one of Europe's most significant diplomatic figures in turn shaped Savoy's involvement in the Thirty Years' War.

Alessandro Scaglia arrived at the French capital in May 1624. While he had already accumulated nine years of diplomatic experience as the Savoyard ordinary ambassador to the papal court, and indeed had established himself there as an experienced and significant patron and broker of the arts, he still lacked an international network of political friends and contacts of his own outside the Italian peninsula. That gap in his expertise was soon filled. Shortly after arriving in France, political circumstance combined with the favour already acquired by other members of the Scaglia di Verrua to the abate's advantage. Even before 1624 the Scaglia di Verrua had created a distinctive identity as a francophile family clan with a recognised skill in dealing with the French court. Alessandro's father had served his last mission to Paris, followed by his elder son, Augusto Manfredo Scaglia, and the very selection of the abate by Duke Carlo Emanuele I to replace his father and brother in the Savoyard embassy in Paris pointed to the particular diplomatic expertise of the family. Certainly, that credit had been retained by Augusto Manfredo after his father's death in 1619. Since his own arrival at the French court, he had enjoyed good relations with the Bourbon regime, and significantly with visiting English representatives in Paris at a time when Savoy, France and England were negotiating an anti-Habsburg alignment, in part cemented by the dynastic alliance already made by the marriage in 1619 of Marie Christine to Vittorio Amedeo and the projected union between Henrietta Maria and Charles Stuart. The esteem in which the new count of Verrua (inheriting the title following his father's death) was held at the French court was seen most clearly on his return to the Savoyard court in Turin, necessary for his part to preserve the Scaglia di Verrua's personal presence at the ducal court there. After a meeting with Marie de' Medici, Alessandro Scaglia recorded her 'particular feelings on the departure of my brother, for his service with which they declared themselves greatly satisfied, and assured that the favour he enjoyed will be no less for me'.[1]

James Hay (c. 1580–1636), the earl of Carlisle and the English extraordinary ambassador in Paris between February 1624 and June 1625, was no less friendly to the Scaglia di Verrua.[2] Hay, renowned for his sense of magnificence and personal charm, had evidently got on well with Verrua, and while the English ambassador expressed his regrets on the count's departure from France, Alessandro Scaglia himself soon assumed the favoured position enjoyed by his elder brother.[3] In the context of increasing Anglo-Savoyard diplomatic co-operation that marked the mid-1620s, Verrua's friendship with James Hay, who at this point shared their commitment to the anti-Spanish alliance, furnished Alessandro Scaglia with a ready-made contact, a point the abate clearly appreciated.

> The count of Carlisle, the extraordinary ambassador of the king of England at this court, already known to you, professes particular confidence and friendship to my brother, as your minister, to whom he has continually demonstrated in the name of Charles I every sincere and warm

---

[1] AST LMF m. 25, 18, Scaglia to Carlo Emanuele I, 3 August 1624. See also, 20, Scaglia to Carlo Emanuele I, 5 August 1624.

[2] For a biography of the earl see Schreiber, 'James Hay'. Background information about his mission can also be found in Gary Bell, *A Handlist of British Diplomatic Representatives, 1509–1688* (London, 1990), pp. 106–7.

[3] Schreiber, 'James Hay', pp. 5, 21.

correspondence in your and everybody's interests, and as a close friend of my brother, he has visited me on numerous occasions.[4]

The Scaglia di Verrua were functioning as a family unit in service to Savoy. Their success as a collective interest group that could pool the resources, reputations and expertise of their individual members both for their own interests and for those of Savoy ensured that Abate Scaglia was able to gain access for the first time to a network of courtiers and diplomats beyond the Italian peninsula.

What he actually did, or was ordered to do, can be gauged from the instructions he took to Paris. Most importantly of all, Alessandro was to continue pressing for recognition of Carlo Emanuele I's territorial ambitions in the Italian peninsula.[5] Savoy's as yet unfulfilled campaign to obtain Zuccarello was to be incorporated into an international coalition against Spain involving England, the Venetian Republic and, of course, France. Scaglia was to build on the initiatives agreed in principle when Carlo Emanuele I and Louis XIII had met at Avignon in 1622, and put to paper in the following year by the treaty of Paris agreed between France, Savoy and Venice. In short, the three powers were committed to containing and reversing Habsburg power that in the aftermath of the battle of the White Mountain (8 November 1620) had made spectacular advances across Europe.[6] While a variety of possible military plans was considered from 1622, the coalition eventually focused on a two-pronged offensive in central Europe and the Italian peninsula, both to prevent the Habsburgs from concentrating their resources on either offensive and to obtain certain territorial objectives of the coalition members. The so-called 'German diversion' would involve England, now that the duke of Buckingham and Prince Charles were converted to a course of action against the Habsburgs following the breakdown of the Anglo-Spanish marriage negotiations, as James I's aspirations for a general European peace were left in tatters.[7] The mercenary-general Peter Ernst von Mansfeld (c. 1580–1626), it was hoped, would simultaneously command a land force to take control of the Franche-Comté and ultimately recapture the

[4] AST LMF m. 25, 30, Scaglia to Carlo Emanuele I, 12 August 1624. See also, AST LMF m. 25, 26, Scaglia to Carlo Emanuele I, 10 August 1624. Carlisle later described Verrua as 'my old friend in France, a great servant of our nation'. PRO SP 92/13/273, Carlisle to Carlton, 28 July 1628.
[5] The abate's written instructions can be found in AST NF m. 8, 12–13, 16 April 1624.
[6] Carutti, *Storia della diplomazia*, II, chapter 7; Dumont (ed.), *Corps universel diplomatique*, V, part II, p. 417.
[7] The transformation of England into a power at war with Spain can be followed in Thomas Cogswell, *The Blessed Revolution: English Politics and the Coming of War, 1621–24* (Cambridge, 1989).

Electoral Palatinate from Habsburg and Bavarian control. Meanwhile, the second element of the offensive, the Italian diversion involving Savoy, Venice and France, would secure the Grison passes in the Valtelline as a means of cutting the logistically critical Spanish Road. This would furthermore involve a push southwards to the republic of Genoa to satisfy Savoy's particular territorial claim to Zuccarello, a plan that dated back at least to the anti-Habsburg phase of Savoyard dynasticism when Henry IV had been on the French throne. As a link between the two offensives, the Savoyard regime pressed the English to provide ships for a joint naval attack on the port of Genoa – crucial to the Spanish as a link to Milan – from the Mediterranean with the aid of the fleet under the command of Charles, duke of Guise (1571–1640).[8]

It would be an understatement to say that this multi-national anti-Habsburg coalition was ambitious. The insurmountable problems of organisation, added to the widely different political circumstances and strategic interests of the coalition members, became all too apparent during the course of 1624 and 1625. Despite the initial enthusiasm in England for a war with Spain, Mansfeld's expedition into continental Europe at the beginning of 1625 proved to be a military and diplomatic disaster. It succeeded in generating heated political debate in England between the crown and Parliament, not least because the money granted by Parliament was given on the explicit understanding that it would not be used to fund a costly land campaign. In March 1625 French troops were mustered in north Italy, and combined with Savoyard troops to form an impressive army of an estimated 30,000 infantry and 3,000 cavalry, with a battery train of thirty-eight guns.[9] After the joint army captured Novi, on the edge of the Apennines, Carlo Emanuele I moved his forces south into Genoa, capturing Voltaggio and besieging Gavi. But as the marquis of Leganés, governor of Milan, reacted by rapidly mobilising defences in Genoa and then attacking the Savoyard state itself in April 1625, the ever-cautious Venetian Republic became increasingly reluctant to be drawn into a well-defined alliance that bound it to military action against Spain. Not only was the republic fearful of Spanish reprisals if it were to make any move on the duchy of Milan, but it was all too wary of Carlo Emanuele I's own territorial ambitions, given the intense and long-standing rivalry

[8] Discussions of these plans feature in virtually all of Scaglia's correspondence between 1624 and 1625. For some examples see AST LMF m. 25, fasc. 1, 10, Scaglia to Carlo Emanuele I, 25 July 1624; 48, Scaglia to Carlo Emanuele I, 26 August 1624, with enclosure, 'Articoli sopra la diversione'. On the plan to use English ships see, for instance, PRO SP 92/11/201-v, late December 1625; CSPV 1625–6, pp. 82, 139. David Parrott has seen the projected attack on Genoa as one of France's military priorities because of its geo-strategic significance. Parrott, 'The Mantuan Succession', 40.

[9] The estimates are taken from Hanlon, *Twilight of a Military Tradition*, p. 107.

with Savoy for power and prestige in the region.[10] But perhaps more serious still was the domestic tension within France over the acceptability of Richelieu's foreign policies, closely related as it was to factional rivalries within the Bourbon court over control of policy-making. Alessandro Scaglia for one realised that the French regime would be extremely hesitant to initiate open war against Spain, a factor that constantly hampered various anti-Habsburg coalitions, dependent to varying degrees on the support of Paris, until the outbreak of formal hostilities between France and Spain in 1635. 'Everything in France is easy', he wrote, 'except going directly and openly against the Spanish.'[11] Opposition to the Spanish Habsburgs constantly divided French political opinion, at this point exposing Richelieu to criticism when he was still establishing himself as Louis XIII's leading minister.[12]

The internal debate in France about Richelieu's foreign policies was in turn closely linked to the twin issues of England and the Huguenots, probably the two most serious problems facing the broad anti-Habsburg coalition. The marriage in May 1625 between Charles Stuart and Henrietta Maria, which had been intended in part to bolster the alliance against Spain, was laden with serious confessional and political difficulties even before the union had actually taken place. In his efforts to secure France's participation in the longed-for anti-Habsburg coalition, the duke of Buckingham had made matters worse by offering the French excessive concessions over the marriage contract, that included allowing the queen freedom of worship as a Catholic. The deterioration in relations between the Stuarts and Bourbons was moreover linked with the worsening crisis over the Huguenot community at La Rochelle, a problem that deeply concerned many Protestant Englishmen, not least because ships lent to the French crown as part of the marriage alliance were used during 1625 in military action against the Huguenot fleet.

Alessandro Scaglia clearly appreciated the deleterious effect the Huguenot question was having on the anti-Habsburg coalition, and

---

[10] AST LMF m. 25, fasc. 1, 42, Scaglia to Carlo Emanuele I, 22 August 1624; 101, Scaglia to Carlo Emanuele I, 16 October 1624; m. 26, fasc. 1, 8, Scaglia to Pasero, 13 January 1625; Quazza, *Prependerenza spagnuola*, p. 444.

[11] AST LMF m. 26, fasc. 1, 38, Scaglia to Carlo Emanuele I, 22 February 1625.

[12] AST LMF m. 25, fasc. 1, 69, Scaglia to Carlo Emanuele I, 15 September 1624; m. 26, fasc. 1, 287, Scaglia to Carlo Emanuele I, 29 November 1625. On the divisions over policy within France see Rémy Pithon, 'Les débuts difficiles du ministère de Richelieu et la crise de Valteline, 1621–1627', *Revue d'Histoire Diplomatique*, 74 (1960); A. D. Lublinskaya, *French Absolutism: The Crucial Phase, 1620–1629* (Cambridge, 1968). It is worth noting how closely the ministry of Richelieu and Scaglia's own career coincided – Richelieu's main rival, La Vieuville, was imprisoned shortly after Scaglia arrived in Paris, marking the beginning of Richelieu's ministry, while the cardinal died within eighteen months of the abate's death.

argued that it should be put to one side or settled by negotiation so that attention could be focused on the more important wider issues affecting so-called European liberty. When the papal nephew and legate Francesco Barberini, at the French court in May 1625 on a mission to resolve the conflict among Catholics in north Italy, criticised the abate for his seemingly lax attitudes to the heretics, Scaglia responded by drawing on the powerful rhetorical trope of anti-Spanish public liberty in Europe:

> Some have spread insidious rumours to the legate that in respect of the Huguenot negotiation, France is seeking to protect heretics. However, I spoke to that legate some time ago, and also to various ministers of his, saying that I would not hesitate to work with all my energy for the peace of this kingdom [France] while Christendom had such need of it, for the conservation of people and the salvation of his allies and friends at a time when others prowl around with nooses. It was true that your [Carlo Emanuele I] interests did not coincide with the Huguenots here, because of the issue of Geneva, but the Spanish compel us to take action since their ministers are working to your destruction.[13]

Just as Carlo Emanuele I had tapped into the language of liberty to justify his territorial ambitions in north Italy, not least through sponsoring Tassoni's *Filippiche*, so Alessandro Scaglia applied a brand of political pragmatism by presenting the Spanish threat as greater to Europe than that of the heretical Huguenots (although he was nevertheless careful to reiterate that Carlo Emanuele I was certainly no friend to the Protestant cause either in France or closer to home where he still longed for the return of the reformed city of Geneva to his patrimony). The abate's statement presents a neat summary of his thinking at that uncertain juncture, of a brand of moralised pragmatism applied directly to international power politics. It was this pragmatic approach to the dilemma of opposing

---

[13] AST LMF m. 26, fasc. 1, 183, Scaglia to Carlo Emanuele I, 27 July 1625. The best guides to the Anglo-French problems are (still) S. R. Gardiner, *History of England from the Accession of James I to the Outbreak of the Civil War, 1603–42*, 10 vols. (London, 1883–4), vols. V–VI; Roger Lockyer, *Buckingham: The Life and Political Career of George Villiers, First Duke of Buckingham, 1592–1628* (London, 1981), chapters 7–8; S. L. Adams, 'The Protestant cause: religious alliance with West European Calvinist communities as a political issue in England, 1559–1630' (DPhil thesis, University of Oxford, 1973), chapter 10; S. L. Adams, 'Spain or the Netherlands? The dilemmas of early Stuart foreign policy', in H. Tomlinson (ed.), *Before the English Civil War: Essays in Early Stuart Politics and Government* (London, 1983). For a French viewpoint see Gabriel Hanotaux and Duc de la Force, *Histoire du Cardinal Richelieu*, 6 vols. (Paris, 1893–1947), III. Carlo Emanuele I and Scaglia fully recognised the threat to Savoyard interests of a breakdown of Anglo-French relations. CSPV 1625–6, p. 272. Further information on Barberini's mission can be found in A. Malvezzi, 'Papa Urbano VIII e la questione della Valtellina', *Archivio Storico Lombardo*, 7 (1957), 18–37.

Catholic Spain that underpinned his efforts to interpose between the English and French courts.

To prepare the ground for a mission of mediation to London, Pietro Barozzio, his secretary in Paris and a family client, was sent ahead in October 1625, while the abate himself contacted Carlisle, who by mid-1625 had emerged as one of the abate's closest political friends at the Caroline court. The earl set himself the task of preparing for Scaglia's visit by organising coaches and also by seeking an English vessel for the Channel crossing, writing to the abate of his wish for his speedy arrival there.[14] Early in January 1626, after much delay, Scaglia eventually departed for a three-day extraordinary mission to England, and from start to finish the mission was marked by ostentatious displays of goodwill and favour.[15] When the abate, together with a Dutch naval commander, crossed the Channel in a Dutch boat, he was accompanied by fourteen English ships, if the Venetian ambassador in London is to be believed. On arriving at the English capital he was then entertained by the two courtiers then established as his closest friends, Buckingham and Carlisle, receiving favours far greater than he might ordinarily have expected. 'The expressions of honour this king has shown to you through me', Scaglia wrote to Carlo Emanuele I, 'have been exceptional. I can truly say that there has never been another representative who has been treated with such honours and showered with so many courtesies at the English court.' Obviously room has to be given for rhetorical exaggeration. After all, the abate knew in writing to the Savoyard duke that any favour he received as his ambassadorial embodiment at the Caroline court was by extension favour shown to Carlo Emanuele I. Yet there was more to this than the hyperbole of diplomatic rhetoric, and Scaglia was certainly not alone in believing that he enjoyed a seemingly unparalleled level of treatment. The Florentine agent Salvetti, based in London, recorded concern felt in some unspecified quarters that the abate's high-profile mission might have established an unwelcome ceremonial precedent for future diplomatic missions, not only for Scaglia as an individual but for all visiting ambassadors.[16]

Following public and private audiences with Charles I and Buckingham, Alessandro Scaglia took formal leave of the king to return to

---

[14] Carlisle had in fact invited the abate to England as early as July 1625. AST LMF m. 26, fasc. 1, 167, Scaglia to Carlo Emanuele I, 2 July 1625; CSPV 1625–6, p. 248; PRO SP 92/11/185, Scaglia to Sir John Apsely, governor of Dover, 29 December 1625.

[15] The course of Barozzio's negotiations, which primarily concerned obtaining English ships for use against Genoa, can be followed in his correspondence with Scaglia in AST LMI m. 4, fasc. 1.

[16] HMC Eleventh Report Appendix, Part I (Salvetti Correspondence) (London, 1887), p. 76; CSPV 1625–6, pp. 277, 284–5, 291.

France. Like the entry to a court, the formal departure of an ambassador in early modern Europe presented opportunities for the manipulation of diplomatic etiquette, and again the abate was marked out for special treatment. As was customary for a parting diplomat, Alessandro received what amounted to a standard diplomatic gift from Charles I of gilt silver plate.[17] More exceptionally Charles I ordered that Scaglia should be entertained with a 'very fine party [bellissimo festino]' at Buckingham's house in the company of the duke and Carlisle, the two courtiers who were closest to the abate. The king wished to attend the dinner but excused himself on the grounds of toothache, and in expressing his regret gave Scaglia a diamond ring from his hand, 'saying that I [Scaglia] should wear it with his Majesty in mind, as a testimony of the esteem in which he holds me'. By direct command of King Charles I, the abate was later escorted to the coast in specially prepared royal coaches with a guard of troops and sixty royal officials, including twelve 'highly qualified and accustomed to serving the king', and provided with transport back across the Channel in an escorted ship of the admiralty.[18]

The exceptional ceremonial treatment enjoyed by Scaglia did not pass unnoticed by the prickly Jean de Varignies de Blainville, Louis XIII's extraordinary ambassador sent to London shortly before the abate, and it was not intended to do so. While procedures of diplomatic protocol were gradually being codified in various courts during the sixteenth and seventeenth centuries as ambassadors were recognised as the embodiments of sovereign powers, those sovereigns and their regimes could still manipulate the ceremonial of diplomacy to transmit comprehensible, if typically implicit, political signals. The under-studied subject of diplomatic ceremony, of the rights to public and private audiences, of access to the court, and of gift-giving, indeed presents early modern historians with an additional perspective on international relations and power politics. If, for instance, an ambassador enjoyed exceptional favours then contemporaries understandably concluded that the ambassador's mission was

---

[17] On the formalisation of silver plate as a parting diplomatic gift from Charles I see Loomie (ed.), *Ceremonies of Charles I*, pp. 37–9.

[18] AST LMF m. 27, fasc. 1, 10, Scaglia to Carlo Emanuele I, 4 February 1626. The exceptional use of a royal coach as departing transport to Dover, rather than for its more customary use to travel to the first and last formal audiences with the king, can be inferred from Finet's comments in Loomie (ed.), *Ceremonies of Charles I*, pp. 52–3. Soon after returning to France, Scaglia wrote a letter of effusive thanks to Carlisle for the warmth of his welcome. BL Eg. MSS 2597, ff. 8–v, Scaglia to Carlisle, 5 February 1626, while Duke Carlo Emanuele I similarly thanked the English ordinary ambassador in Turin for 'the honours done unto his ambassador by his Majesty, the favours and caresses he received of my lord duke of Buckingham, my lord of Carlisle, and your lordship'. PRO SP 92/12/37, Wake to Conway, 19 February 1626.

met with calculated approval, and correspondingly if an ambassador were coolly received then it could imply that his objectives or presence were not well considered by his hosts.[19] The English regime had deliberately emphasised the importance of Scaglia's mission to make a clear diplomatic point to the French. Buckingham for one was bitterly offended by the refusal of Louis XIII to allow him to travel to France on a second personal mission in the autumn of 1625, and the sense of frustration was only exacerbated by the hostile and difficult behaviour of Blainville at the Caroline court.[20] By visibly favouring Scaglia beyond what was 'normal', the English regime was showing itself open to negotiation, even if through the mediation of an acceptable third party such as the abate. In public at least Cardinal Richelieu expressed his complete satisfaction with Scaglia's mediation, as he was perhaps compelled following the warmth of his reception in London, and in a truly remarkable display of confidence embraced the abate, declaring that he was nothing less than 'a messiah sent by God', presumably for preventing a war with England.[21]

The extent of Scaglia's welcome at the English court may also have had something to do with his personality and qualities as a wealthy and culturally sophisticated diplomat with the knowledge of a skilled and astute collector. Certainly, his sharp mind, refined qualities and smooth manners were ideally suited to cultivating contacts at the Caroline court, which had its dynastic affinity with the court of Savoy and which was positioned within a diplomatic structure that was receptive to informal negotiations. At least when domestic tensions with Parliament did not shackle him, Charles I approached foreign policies with a clear dynastic slant, underscored as they were by criss-crossing family connections that linked London with Paris and Turin, and ultimately with Madrid and Brussels. Charles and his favourite, Buckingham, at least, were moreover fascinated

---

[19] For a late seventeenth-century study of diplomatic protocol consult de Wicquefort, *L'ambassadeur*. There is little secondary work on this topic, though consult Loomie, 'The *Conducteur des Ambassadeurs*'. Loomie (ed.), *Ceremonies* also offers valuable information on issues of protocol. Diplomatic protocol evolved as embassies became permanent, particularly in the later seventeenth century, as examined by Bély in his study, *Espions et ambassadeurs*.

[20] Jean Armand du Plessis, duc de Richelieu, *Mémoires du Cardinal Richelieu*, 10 vols. (Paris, 1907–31), VI, p. 184. Blainville's poor behaviour in England was noted by the abate. AST LMF m. 26, fasc. 1, 273, Scaglia to Carlo Emanuele I, 18 November 1625, while Roy Schreiber has described Blainville as a 'spy and a plotter'. Schreiber, 'James Hay', p. 91.

[21] This remarkable incident is recorded by the abate. AST LMF m. 27, fasc. 1, 238, Scaglia to Carlo Emanuele I, 7 December 1626. However, it stands in complete contrast to the image of Scaglia as later reinvented in Richelieu's *Mémoires*, where it was claimed that 'Scaglia lived in England not as a churchman but as a courtier, nor as a Catholic'. *Mémoires*, V, p. 185.

by the courts of Catholic Europe. They wished to fashion themselves as significant collectors of art and to establish the English court as a centre of modern connoisseurship to assert both dynastic and cultural affinity with continental Europe, a point recently made by R. Malcolm Smuts who has suggested that 'some early seventeenth century [Caroline] collectors began to associate art collecting with a cosmopolitan aristocratic culture they wished to emulate'.[22] To the English king and his favourite, Alessandro Scaglia may therefore have represented the qualities of cultivation they themselves were so eager to display.

Whatever the immediate political value of the abate's brief mission for preserving Anglo–French relations and the anti-Habsburg coalition, it had much wider implications for the character and future of his diplomatic career. Through the rivalry between England and France he had succeeded in establishing direct contact with Charles I, the duke of Buckingham and (with the help of his elder brother) the earl of Carlisle. Since the English regime had favoured the abate so openly during his mission to England, the diplomatic intimacy between powerful English courtiers such as Buckingham and Carlisle and Scaglia was given substance. This too had implications. A distinctive pattern was taking shape where a special relationship was seen to exist between the abate, as an individual, and English policy-makers in the critical years of the 1620s, in a wider context where the English crown was making professions of its affection for the duke of Savoy as a reliable dynastic and political ally.[23] Within a very short period of time the abate had successfully made a transition from a diplomat based in Rome to a political figure with a distinctive international profile that mixed state dynasticism with elite court culture.

For Alessandro Scaglia and his sovereign duke, the growing political intimacy with the English court came at a crucial juncture in international relations. The abate's brief mission to England had taken place when the French regime under Cardinal Richelieu's direction was having serious misgivings about the confrontation with Spain in north Italy, given pressure from critics within France and from the papacy to give priority to the Huguenot problem over that of north Italy, and also the failure of the alliance with Savoy and Venice to capture Genoa. In late 1625 secret negotiations with Madrid to end the dispute over the Valtelline were begun

---

[22] R. Malcolm Smuts, 'Art and the material culture of majesty in early Stuart England', in R. Malcolm Smuts (ed.), *The Stuart Court and Europe. Essays in Politics and Political Culture* (Cambridge, 1996), pp. 96–7. See also Brown, *Kings and Connoisseurs*, especially chapter one.

[23] AST LMF m. 26, fasc. 1, 163, Scaglia to Carlo Emanuele I, 30 June 1625; 258, Scaglia to Carlo Emanuele I, 1 November 1625.

in Spain, to the complete exclusion of the other coalition allies. With no definite knowledge of the negotiations, the abate continued as if the anti-Habsburg coalition remained in place, while in February 1626 Vittorio Amedeo, the prince of Piemonte and brother-in-law to Louis XIII, arrived in Paris to obtain the command of French troops in north Italy. Though Vittorio Amedeo also suspected that the French wanted at least an end to the war in north Italy, both Richelieu and Louis XIII denied that there were any peace talks.[24] A written agreement between Monsieur de Fargis, representing France, and the count-duke of Olivares was nevertheless concluded at Monzón in Spain on 5 March 1626. According to the treaty, the Valtelline, source of so much tension between the leading powers, would return to its state as it had been in 1617 and would remain solely Roman Catholic, while all fortresses in the valley would be handed over to the surety of the pope as a neutral Catholic third party. In an attempt to defuse another explosive regional problem, France and Spain furthermore agreed that Savoy and Genoa should consent to a suspension of arms so that negotiations could settle their outstanding differences over Zuccarello.[25] These terms were nothing less than a terrible defeat for the members of the anti-Habsburg coalition, including Savoy – David Parrott has seen Savoy's interests as the 'first casualty' of the treaty that represented 'the outright abandonment by France of the Duke of Savoy and his claims', while the seventeenth-century commentator Vittorio Siri astutely observed that Carlo Emanuele's interests were best served by dividing France and Spain, a position effectively undercut by the treaty.[26] Nor did the almost total secrecy in which the treaty had been negotiated, and the particular insult of appointing Vittorio Amedeo to a military command in the full knowledge that it would amount to nothing, soften the blow. In fact Richelieu later argued that he was not responsible for the treaty. Fargis, so the cardinal argued, had acted beyond his formal powers in signing an earlier version of the written agreement. But while the cardinal had given the impression that he was actually angry with the terms, he also made it clear that he could do little but consent to them, not least because of the growing pressure at home generated both by the Huguenots and the *dévots*.[27]

---

[24] AST LPD m. 51, Vittorio Amedeo to Carlo Emanuele I, February 1626; March 1626. See this *mazzo* for further letters between the prince of Piemonte and his father.

[25] For a text of the treaty of Monzón see Dumont (ed.), *Corps universel diplomatiques*, V, part II, pp. 487–9.

[26] Parrott, 'The Mantuan Succession', 41; Siri, *Memorie recondite*, V, p. 115.

[27] The issue of the legality of the treaty has been touched upon by D. P. O'Connell. 'A cause célèbre in the history of treaty making. The case of the treaty of Regensburg, 1630', *British Yearbook in International Law*, 42 (1967), 72–3.

While the bold project of organising an international coalition to counter the threat of the long-feared Habsburg 'universal monarchy' – whatever the reality of that assumption – was in many respects too ambitious to succeed, the resulting failure of the anti-Habsburg coalition and the stunning blow of the treaty of Monzón still did not spell complete or lasting defeat for Savoy in a context where the weight of power and influence throughout Europe remained very much in the balance. The diplomatic techniques employed by Scaglia after Monzón illuminate one way in which a second-rank state of the early seventeenth century sought to affect the direction of international affairs, and how an individual used his particular profile to achieve this. Above and beyond its military power in north Italy and the influence Savoy's control of the west Alpine passes afforded, the duchy's diplomatic profile in Europe was strengthened by dynastic connections with other sovereign states, principally England. This was a period in which Alessandro Scaglia, reaching the height of his international career, sought to increase Savoy's influence by offering to mediate in England's wars with France and Spain. His diplomacy after Monzón was moreover set within a conceptual framework of prudent diplomacy that recognised the necessity for diplomats to exercise pragmatism to achieve favourable outcomes to their broader aims. The use of moderated forms of political deceit, of dissimulation and reticence, was reluctantly accepted as necessary where they contributed to the achievement of a good and reputable policy. Without the capability of responding to the mutability of politics in a fallen world of the untrustworthy, infidels and heretics, Catholic princes and their representatives would only fail in the pursuit of their policies.[28] This pragmatic, yet fundamentally moral, conception of how diplomatic means could be subjugated to longer-term strategic ends, by feigning interests and pursuing what appeared to be contradictory policies, was precisely what Alessandro Scaglia followed from the summer of 1626. It is this notion of defensible diplomatic pragmatism and flexibility, with an implied political agenda, that should be understood when considering the way in which Savoy operated in the critically important period between 1626 and 1628. While his aim remained the pursuit of Savoy's dynastic interests, primarily in north Italy, his method shifted with the currents of power politics.

---

[28] The issue of political deceit, particularly in the atmosphere of post-Reformation political mistrust, has received considerable attention from Robert Bireley, *The Counter-Reformation Prince: Anti-Machiavellianism or Catholic Statecraft in Early Modern Europe* (Chapel Hilll and London, 1990), and also J. A. Fernández-Santamaría, *Reason of State and Statecraft in Spanish Politiclal Thought, 1595–1640* (Lanham, 1983).

After the treaty of Monzón Cardinal Richelieu remained unavailable for comment because, so other French ministers claimed, of a sudden and serious illness. It seems that the burden of guiding French policy at such a difficult time had weighed heavily on the cardinal, though rather conveniently his loss of health also allowed him to avoid the understandably aggrieved Scaglia. Despite wishing to see the cardinal in person, for several days both Abate Scaglia and the equally indignant Venetian ambassador were forced to seek information elsewhere.[29] In their meetings with the abate, French ministers defended the treaty by pointing out how the internal pressures on the kingdom – unease among sections of the nobility, Richelieu's ministerial rivalries and the Huguenot question – had necessitated a settlement over the Valtelline. He replied by arguing that the treaty was to the detriment both of France's allies and of France's own reputation. When he eventually saw Richelieu, ill and lying restless in bed, Scaglia repeated his case against that 'greatest monstrosity', and when the cardinal asked the abate if he could accept Monzón, he bluntly criticised the French as the 'authors of all Spain's advantages'.[30]

Richelieu's efforts to appease Scaglia seem to have had little success. While in 1624 he had arrived in Paris with high hopes of cementing an anti-Habsburg coalition, Alessandro Scaglia's diplomacy from the summer of 1626 became much more pragmatic as he aimed either to temper Richelieu's policies or perhaps even to force his removal from power. There were certainly abundant opportunities to lean on the cardinal. The treaty had much to do with Richelieu's foreign and domestic problems, and Scaglia believed, however correctly, that the cardinal's ministerial position was precarious enough to be in doubt. French court politics, Scaglia wrote, was like a 'heaven full of comets'. If Richelieu were to be weakened, or even to fall from power, then the direction of French policy-making could change to Savoy's benefit. France, according to Alessandro Scaglia, was effectively governed by one minister, which by inference meant that his removal would change the direction of French politics, possibly with the reactivation of the military alliance with Savoy in pursuit of Carlo Emanuele's dynastic interests in Spanish-protected Genoa. Such a risky strategy of destabilising Richelieu, however, carried an equal portion of danger. Indeed, his removal might not automatically

---

[29] AST LMF m. 27, fasc. 3, 55, Scaglia to Carlo Emanuele I, 19 May 1626; 56, Scaglia to Carlo Emanuele I, 19 May 1626; 59, Scaglia to Carlo Emanuele I, 22 May 1626. Richelieu was notorious as a hypochondriac, a characteristic shared with Olivares (and Scaglia too). J. H. Elliott, *Richelieu and Olivares* (Cambridge, 1989), p. 18.

[30] AST LMF m. 27 fasc. 3, 68, Scaglia to Carlo Emanuele I, 31 May 1626; 80, Scaglia to Carlo Emanuele I, 9 June 1626.

entail improved relations with France or a more consistent set of French foreign policies. More immediately (and equally seriously), as Alessandro soon discovered, he also ran the risk of alienating the cardinal and turning him into an abiding political opponent.[31]

Scaglia kept a close watch on the tensions within France and the Bourbon court, a task that kept him extremely busy, and potentially raised opportunities for threatening Richelieu. The cardinal may not have had a deliberate intention of alienating the high nobility, but his policies, not least the priority he gave to international affairs and to a policy of Habsburg containment, still created considerable unease among sections of the French elites. Gaston d'Orléans (1608–60) was a perpetual source of concern for the cardinal as the king's sole legitimate brother and the first in line to the throne. His relationship with Louis XIII was far from secure, primarily because of his marital status, upon which the future of the kingdom potentially depended at a time when the king had no heirs of his own. Nor was Gaston an unequivocal supporter of Richelieu. With a less than certain temperament, Gaston remained at best cool to the cardinal-minister, establishing a fundamentally important dynamic of French political culture that lasted until the death of Richelieu in 1642. In the spring of 1626, soon after the completion of the treaty of Monzón, Jean-Baptiste d'Ornano (1581–1626) and César, duke of Vendôme (1594–1665), an illegitimate brother of the king, were arrested for their implication in a plot against Richelieu. Gaston's involvement was quickly suspected, and Scaglia reported a rumour that the prince was thinking of fleeing to the Huguenot stronghold of La Rochelle, apparently because he was disgusted with Richelieu's handling of France.[32] The cardinal-minister's style of government and the contentious issue of Gaston's marital status also managed to alienate other members of the *Grands*, the high French aristocracy. Scaglia wrote repeatedly of the tense relations between the cardinal, Vendôme and the count of Soissons, because of their opposition to the marriage which Richelieu had effectively brokered in 1626 between Gaston and the

---

[31] AST LMF m. 28, fasc. 6, 6, Scaglia to Carlo Emanuele I, 8 January 1627; 14, Scaglia to Carlo Emanuele I, 13 January 1627; 44, Scaglia to Carlo Emanuele I, 29 February 1627; 30, Scaglia to Carlo Emanuele I, 11 February 1627. It is worth adding that, despite their failure to participate with France and Savoy in the north Italian diversion, even the Venetians were reluctant to accept the treaty, leading Isaac Wake to comment that, '[A]s France did first delude their confederates with a clandestine treaty, so now these do requite them with dilatory answers, which are more equivocal and ambiguous than the ancient oracles.' BL Add. MS 34,311, f. 8, Wake to Conway, 11 September 1626.

[32] For further information about Gaston see Georges Dethan, *La vie de Gaston d'Orléans* (Paris, 1992), a reworking of an earlier publication, *Gaston d'Orléans: conspirateur et prince charmant* (Paris, 1959).

wealthy madame de Montpensier. Soissons, the brother-in-law of Prince Tommaso Carignano, had particular reason to feel aggrieved, since he had in effect been promised the hand of Montpensier as compensation for supporting the crown during the minority of his cousin Louis XIII. If such aristocratic opposition was not serious enough, Richelieu also had to contend with a powerful ministerial rival following the second major plot of his ministry, the Chalais conspiracy, in Michel de Marillac (1560–1632), who served as the *garde des sceaux*. Not only were they personal rivals but they also represented different approaches to French policy-making, as Marillac was known, much more than the cardinal, to favour domestic reforms over confrontation with Spain.[33]

It was however England that presented the best opportunities to Scaglia for coercing Richelieu immediately after Monzón. The deterioration in relations between the English and French seemed increasingly to exclude peaceful reconciliation in favour of open conflict, even though there were repeated attempts at negotiation. Despite his growing ambivalence about the value of allying with Richelieu, Scaglia still wrote that 'this is an evil that if left unchecked will make a settlement ever more difficult'.[34] The reasons for the rapid breakdown of relations between the two crowns were understood by contemporaries and are generally well known from the secondary literature. Buckingham's personalised dispute with Richelieu that dated back to the refusal to accept a second visit of the duke to Paris had a powerful impact on wider state relations, while disagreements over the Huguenot question deepened at a time when the Protestant community at La Rochelle was turning to rebellion. The retention of English ships by the French which, it seemed, were to be used against the Huguenots also generated sharp tensions, as did the composition of Queen Henrietta Maria's Catholic household in London.[35] The combination of Richelieu's domestic problems and this deterioration in Anglo-French relations was something Scaglia could not disregard, given their implications for Savoy's aspirations for gaining Zuccarello in the Spanish

---

[33] For example AST LMF m. 27, fasc. 3, 81, Scaglia to Carlo Emanuele I, 9 June 1626; 96, Scaglia to Carlo Emanuele I, 29 June 1626. On Richelieu's relationship with the *Grands* see Arlette Jouanna, *Le devoir de révolte: la noblesse française et la gestation de l'état moderne, 1559–1661* (Paris, 1989), and Jean-Marie Constant, *Les conjurateurs: le premier libéralisme politique sous Richelieu* (Paris, 1987). The articles by David Parrott, 'Richelieu, the *Grands*, and the French army', in Bergin and Brockliss (eds.), *Richelieu and His Age*, and Robin Briggs, 'Noble conspiracy and revolt in France, 1610–50', *ibid.*, present a somewhat different picture from that of Orest Ranum, 'Richelieu and the great nobility: some aspects of early modern political motives', *French Historical Studies*, 3 (1963).

[34] AST LMF m. 28, fasc. 6, 43, Scaglia to Carlo Emanuele I, 24 February 1627.

[35] Among the various accounts of Anglo-French relations at this point see Gardiner, *History*, VI, chapter 59; Lockyer, *Buckingham*, chapters 7 and 8.

protectorate of Genoa. True, he was concerned that as France's position worsened so the international standing of the Habsburgs appeared to improve, particularly it seemed in the Holy Roman Empire. But at this moment he did not look on in total horror at the prospect of a breakdown of the anti-Habsburg coalition which prior to the treaty of Monzón he had been instrumental in organising. Instead he opted for an alternative policy of exploiting Richelieu's difficulties, hoping most importantly to draw on the newly acquired strength of his informal connections at the English court. While Scaglia might not have been able to compel the English regime to follow his particular strategies, he could at least seek to influence particular ministers and courtiers through the more intangible force of friendship. The friendships Scaglia cultivated with English courtiers during their diplomatic missions to Paris in 1625, and his own successful and highly publicised mission to London in January 1626, had indeed won him powerful support.[36]

The shift from clear-cut support of the anti-Habsburg coalition to a more equivocal form of diplomacy seems to have marked the beginning of a much broader change in the direction of Carlo Emanuele I's foreign policies. In the instant after the treaty became public, Bernardino Spada, the papal nuncio at the French court, warned that 'the Savoyard ambassador, who is openly unhappy with the French, says that if nothing changes the duke of Savoy will have no option but to foment trouble with the English king, the disaffected nobles and the Huguenots'. The nuncio's concerns were not unfounded, as Scaglia began to articulate an even more important diplomatic strategy. Towards the end of May 1626 Scaglia advised the duke of Savoy to remain vigilant in case the English wished to settle with Spain given the fluidity of England's international interests, adding that the English ambassador in Turin should be consulted so that Savoy could mediate between the two crowns.[37] In June Scaglia wrote a detailed and important letter to the duke of Buckingham, fully aware that England and France were moving closer to war at a time when the English were simultaneously involved in open hostilities with Spain. In this double conflict the abate saw the means for putting pressure on Cardinal Richelieu. Scaglia suggested that Buckingham should seek to end the war with Spain to free the Spanish from one commitment so that in turn they could divert their resources elsewhere in Europe. But the abate was not endorsing a full political shift to the Habsburgs. To avoid

---

[36] AST LMF m. 27, fasc. 3, 100, Scaglia to Carlo Emanuele I, 12 July 1626; m. 28, fasc. 6, 43, Scaglia to Carlo Emanuele I, 24 February 1627; 51, Scaglia to Carlo Emanuele I, 4 March 1627.

[37] ASV SS Francia, 65, f. 156v, Spada to Barberini, 25 March 1626; AST LMF m. 27, fasc. 3, 63, Scaglia to Carlo Emanuele I, 31 May 1626.

giving the Spanish too much of an advantage and to force them to reason, he added that this should be done while still supporting Christian IV of Denmark (1577–1648), who had in the spring of 1626, with English and Dutch money, landed an army in the Empire. To complete the strategy, Scaglia advised that the English should persuade the Grisons to reject the treaty of Monzón, in effect to force France and Spain back into confrontation. Such a change in the international balance of power would prove all too sobering to Richelieu, and accordingly the cardinal would be forced to be more considerate to his true allies, England and, of course, Savoy. This pragmatic strategy of playing one war against the other through the possibility of negotiating a separate peace with Spain was without doubt insightful, and it was to become the central theme of Anglo-Savoyard diplomacy in 1627 and 1628. At this point, however, the abate's imaginative plan proved unacceptable to Buckingham, as he made clear in responding to Scaglia. The duke courteously praised him for his particular affection for Charles I and agreed with the general thrust of his letter. Buckingham added however that the idea of a peace with the Spanish could not be pursued, given their preparations for war against England, to which the abate himself had drawn attention. 'It is not the time to amuse ourselves with treaties', as the duke wrote. In any case, Charles I would not be guilty of the same treachery to his allies that the French had shown in their betrayal of England and Savoy.[38]

While Buckingham remained cautious about engaging in negotiations with Spain, Scaglia was more willing to take an initiative. So far as he believed, the extent of Richelieu's domestic and foreign difficulties had only advanced Spain's power in Europe, a perception that may well have been underlined by the various military successes in the early 1620s of both branches of the Habsburgs throughout Europe from north Italy to the Low Countries. Emperor Ferdinand II had successfully overcome Mansfeld, and Bethlen Gabor in Hungary, while keeping Christian IV of Denmark in check, defeating him at the battle of Lutter in August 1626. The year 1625 was Spain's *annus mirabilis*, in which the Dutch fortress of Breda was captured, while access to the Valtelline was effectively regained. Spain's successes alone presented dangers to the duke of Savoy at a time when his relations with the French were far from settled. If Scaglia were to reactivate diplomatic relations with Spain, it would in the first place act as a guarantee of Savoyard security even though Scaglia neither trusted

---

[38] PRO SP 92/12/113–5, Scaglia to Buckingham, June 1626; ff. 117–18, Buckingham to Scaglia, June 1626; Lockyer, *Buckingham*, pp. 335–6. The plan of opposing Monzón and of balancing Spain and France with the help of England was repeated in July when Scaglia sent his secretary to London. AST NI m. 1, fasc. 11, 'Memoria delle Proposizioni', July 1626.

the Spanish nor fully endorsed negotiating with them.[39] During the autumn of 1626 Scaglia had already been dropping hints to the Spanish ordinary ambassador in Paris, the marquis of Mirabel, that he wished to restore Savoy's severely damaged relations with Madrid and that the abate hoped to serve Philip IV in some way, very generalised remarks that may well have referred to mediating with England. Scaglia added his wish to resolve Savoy's differences with Genoa without the mediation of France, giving at least the impression not only of trust in Spain but also of a converse distrust in France. In the last place, the abate suggested that Spain should become involved in domestic difficulties within France by offering support to the count of Soissons, exiled from France after the Chalais conspiracy.[40]

The meeting with Mirabel marked the beginning of further contact between the two ambassadors. During another conversation Alessandro Scaglia again indicated Duke Carlo Emanuele I's wish to settle with Philip IV, and to resolve Savoy's dispute with Genoa over Zuccarello which would be central to improving relations between Turin and Madrid (though France's involvement in a settlement of the issue had been stipulated in the treaty of Monzón).[41] Scaglia was aiming to safeguard Savoyard interests and to entertain the possibility of a Spanish *rapprochement* with his home state. He was calculating that in turn this would increase his credit as a trustworthy mediator in any negotiations between England and Spain, another point of discussion with Mirabel. In any case, the abate's overtures to Mirabel could also indicate to Richelieu in no uncertain terms that the duke of Savoy was capable of detaching himself from the alignment with France. For his part Mirabel seemed equally forthcoming, blaming the difficulties between Spain and Savoy on the past ill-will of Spanish ministers. The Spanish ambassador moreover played on Savoyard territorial aspirations, a guaranteed way to make diplomatic overtures to Duke Carlo Emanuele I, driven as he was by the politics of dynasticism. Scaglia reported back to Turin Mirabel's hints that as part of a drive towards closer relations between the Habsburg and Savoyard

---

[39] Savoy was indeed becoming increasingly cautious about being drawn into further action against Spain, preferring 'to remain spectators until necessity shall draw them to be actors'. BL Add. MS 34,311, f. 68, Wake to Conway, 31 January 1627.

[40] AST LMF m. 27, fasc. 4, Scaglia to Carlo Emanuele I, 1626; AGS Est. K1480, 122, Mirabel to Juan de Villela, 24 August 1626; 128, Mirabel to Villela, 1 September 1626; K1433, consulta of council of state, 17 September 1626.

[41] Though the Spanish regime in Madrid eventually responded with caution to the negotiations over Zuccarello and to endorsing Carlo Emanuele's wider ambitions. AGS Est. K1434, 52, consulta of council of state, 27 February 1627; K1457, 34, Philip IV to Mirabel, 12 March 1627; 57, Philip IV to Mirabel, 23 April 1627.

courts a member of the House of Savoy might be given the governorship of the Spanish Netherlands in the highly probable event of the Infanta Isabella dying without direct heirs, although there was no indication as to whether Savoy would in addition retain the Spanish Netherlands as a heritable possession. As a further token of warmer relations, Mirabel hinted that Prince Tommaso Francesco, Duke Carlo Emanuele I's youngest son, might assume the role that had been taken by his elder brother, Filiberto Emanuele, as a prince favoured by Spain with a military command, as he eventually did in the 1630s.[42]

The subtle and complex development in the abate's diplomacy did not pass unnoticed in Paris. The potential threat posed by Scaglia was given what seemed to be a definite shape in the summer of 1626 when the so-called Chalais conspiracy was broken, the second major aristocratic plot Richelieu faced as cardinal-minister. Focusing on opposition to the marriage between Gaston and madame de Montpensier, the conspiracy aimed to change the direction of French domestic and foreign policies by at the least debilitating Richelieu – the cardinal feared that its true purpose was to remove Louis XIII in favour of his younger brother. In itself the Chalais conspiracy had fundamental political consequences, perhaps more than the better-known Day of Dupes (11 November 1630), marking out irreconcilable divisions between Richelieu and members of the high French nobility, among them Gaston d'Orléans and the count of Soissons.[43] The conspiracy also affected Richelieu's relationship with Scaglia. As soon as Chalais was arrested and had made a confession, Alessandro Scaglia was suspected of complicity in the plot. The cardinal's rather circumstantial evidence, which was later laid down in his *Mémoires*, made reference to the abate's 'dislike of the Spanish peace', the treaty of Monzón.[44] Evidence of wider Savoyard involvement, however, seemed to come from a claim of the cardinal to the papal nuncio that Gaston himself had admitted to contacting Spain, England, Savoy and even the Dutch Republic for help against Richelieu, pinning his hopes on a Spanish military intervention in Picardy (presumably through the Spanish Netherlands), with continuing English support for the Huguenots at La Rochelle. The duke of Savoy, so it was claimed, was willing to offer his own military aid for the project, a claim corroborated by Chalais' confession that Carlo

---

[42] AST LMF m. 28, fasc. 6, 14, Scaglia to Carlo Emanuele I, 13 January 1627.

[43] There are a number of contemporary and secondary accounts of the conspiracies. See, for instance, Richelieu, *Mémoires*, VI; Dethan, *Gaston d'Orléans*, part I, chapter 5; Constant, *Les conjurateurs*, chapter 1. Scaglia's account of Ornano's arrest can be followed in AST LMF m. 27, fasc. 3, 47, Scaglia to Carlo Emanuele I, 7 May 1626.

[44] Richelieu, *Mémoires*, VI, pp. 29, 182.

Emanuele I had promised 10,000 troops in support of a revolt against the cardinal-minister.[45]

It is impossible to know for certain if Scaglia participated in the conspiracy, or even if the cardinal genuinely believed that the abate was at all involved. The evidence given by Gaston on the one hand and Chalais on the other may well have been invented or imagined, either out of political convenience or because it seemed credible that Duke Carlo Emanuele I and his ambassador in Paris were capable of being involved. The abate's own despatches, even his ciphered correspondence to his sovereign where he might have been expected to write more freely, gave no information, not even a hint, of any collusion. Yet perhaps importantly Scaglia was believed to have been capable of complicity, playing into a perception of how Savoy was operating as a diplomatic power after Monzón. After all, Duke Carlo Emanuele I had a reputation for changing his international interests and switching sides when he felt it necessary or advantageous (or, more correctly, as dynastic opportunities arose). Moreover, the possibility of Scaglia's involvement was perhaps too convenient a political opportunity to let pass since it allowed Richelieu to present himself as the wronged party and to move towards a position of moral and political superiority over Scaglia at a time when he and indeed the duke of Savoy were still publicly unhappy with the treaty of Monzón. Richelieu certainly gave the impression that the matter was very serious. The duke of Rohan's *Mémoires* suggested that he held Scaglia, acting on behalf of Duke Carlo Emanuele I, personally responsible for the conspiracies against him, forcing Scaglia on the defensive.[46]

The abate predictably argued that he was innocent.[47] At the end of 1626 he wrote a detailed account for Duke Carlo Emanuele I of the principal events of his diplomatic mission to Paris starting from his arrival at the French court in 1624, possibly so that it would be passed on to the French ambassador in Turin. In his wide-ranging report he discussed among other things the background to France's position with her international allies and the impact of the Huguenot problem. He also provided a narration of the Chalais conspiracy, setting out his own innocence and ignorance of it, both opening and closing with an effective

---

[45] *Ibid.*, VII, pp. 2–4; AST LMF m. 27, fasc. 3, 135, Scaglia to Carlo Emanuele I, 13 August 1626.

[46] Henri de Rohan, *Mémoires du Duc de Rohan sur les choses qui se sont passées en France depuis la mort de Henri le Grand jusqu'à la Paix faite avec les Réformés* (Amsterdam, 1646), pp. 262, 266.

[47] For example, AST LMF m. 27, fasc. 3, 166, Scaglia to Carlo Emanuele I, 15 September 1626; 240, Scaglia to Carlo Emanuele I, 7 December 1626; m. 28 fasc. 6, 68, Scaglia to Carlo Emanuele I, 22 March 1627.

denial of any direct involvement, 'not speaking about these matters with any knowledge, as I have said, but with a great deal of conjecture'.[48] In another revealing letter Scaglia defended himself by arguing that 'God alone judges hearts and from His view it is sufficient to have a good intention to merit His grace; princes want, and ought, likewise to be served with the same candidness, but this does not show itself other than by external actions and what follows from them.' He continued by outlining the length of his service to Carlo Emanuele I and how in fifteen years of service he had always been utterly loyal and trustworthy.[49] Scaglia enjoyed at least some support. The count of Moretta, sent to Paris by Carlo Emanuele I, returned saying that the papal nuncio Bernardino Spada had voiced his belief that abate was innocent, given the absence of any incriminating evidence. The duke also publicly sided with his ambassador. When Marini, the French ordinary ambassador in Turin, claimed that Scaglia, acting against the wishes of Carlo Emanuele I, was behind the intrigues in France, the duke took the unusual measure of producing a letter to the abate where he was explicitly instructed not to become involved in French domestic affairs beyond promoting good offices with Louis XIII for the 'peace of the kingdom'.[50]

Scaglia's meetings with the Spanish ambassador also had the effect of provoking Richelieu at a time when there was also a growing whispering campaign of unnamed French ministers that the abate did not actually want the Anglo-French peace he was publicly advocating.[51] From Turin, Marini maintained his personal campaign to have him withdrawn from the Savoyard embassy in Paris, and, as before, his incessant claim was that the abate was untrustworthy and that it was in Carlo Emanuele I's interests to remove him.[52] Scaglia's position was delicate. While he was undoubtedly looking to weaken Richelieu's position, he still wished to maintain some level of credibility in Paris. After all, despite his deteriorating relationship with the cardinal he continued to advocate a peace settlement between England and France, which on balance was what he wanted in the long term. At the beginning of 1627, not long after the French extraordinary ambassador François de Bassompierre had returned

---

[48] A copy of this long and important document can be found in PRO SP 92/12/217–37. Another version can be found in AST LMF m. 27, fasc. 3, 238, Scaglia to Carlo Emanuele I, 7 December 1626.

[49] AST LMF m. 27, fasc. 1, 169, Scaglia to Carlo Emanuele I, 15 September 1626.

[50] AAE CP Sardaigne, 7, f. 373, Marini to Herbault, 26 December 1626; BL Add. MSS 34,311, ff. 9–v, Wake to Conway, 11 September 1626.

[51] Scaglia did not name these ministers. AST LMF m. 28, fasc. 6, 37, Scaglia to Carlo Emanuele I, 18 February 1627.

[52] AAE CP Sardaigne, 8, f. 2, Marini to ?, 8 January 1627; f. 10, Marini to ?, 26 January 1627.

to Paris from London with high hopes of reaching a settlement, Scaglia publicly reiterated his wish to broker a suspension of hostilities while at the same time defending his personal integrity, so important for his freedom to act as a trustworthy diplomat.[53] Meanwhile in Turin Duke Carlo Emanuele I proved reluctant to accept Marini's arguments that the abate was a hindrance to Franco-Savoyard relations and that he should be removed from Paris, and even when the French ambassador said that he had finally persuaded the duke to recall Scaglia, Carlo Emanuele I was slow to issue the instruction. The duke later added that he had given permission to the abate to pursue a settlement of the English problem and significantly that he wished to make use of his dynastic connections, through his daughter-in-law, Marie Christine, to her mother, Marie de' Medici. Duke Carlo Emanuele I also informed the English ambassador in Turin of his wish to avoid a rupture between the two crowns that would only lead to the 'utter oppression of public liberty'.[54] The choice of words was no doubt deliberate, playing on the familiar rhetoric of anti-Habsburg politics in opposition to the perceived danger of a Habsburg universal tyranny.

Alessandro Scaglia's most powerful political card remained his reputation as an intimate political friend of the duke of Buckingham. In the words of the Venetian ambassador in England, he was Buckingham's prime confidant in France, and it is ironic that in the face of incessant criticism, particularly from Marini, Scaglia could maintain some hold over Richelieu precisely because of what was seen as a friendship with the English favourite. The French cardinal was at once suspicious of Buckingham but also aware that he held the key to much of English foreign policy, probably the most complicating factor in dealing with Scaglia. As a consequence of a widely perceived special relationship between the duke and the abate, Richelieu could not simply disregard, or equally importantly be seen to disregard, Scaglia, whatever he might have thought of his trustworthiness. At the same time, the cardinal might have thought that by entertaining the abate's diplomacy he could also minimise the threat of a separate Scaglia–Buckingham political initiative that would obviously stand against his own interests. During Bassompierre's peace mission to London late in 1626, the count of Verrua concluded that Richelieu was showing favour to his younger brother because he wanted to use him to mediate a complete settlement between the two

---

[53] BL Add. MS 34,311, ff. 22–3v, Wake to Conway, 5 October 1626; PRO SP 78/80/219–21v, Scaglia to ?, 1 January 1627; AST LMF m. 28, fasc. 6, 31, Scaglia to Carlo Emanuele I, 16 February 1627.

[54] AAE CP Sardaigne, 7, f. 355, Marini to Herbaut, 4 December 1626; 8, ff. 10–v, Marini to ?, 26 January 1627; BL Add. MS 34, 311, f. 22, Wake to Conway, 5 October 1626.

crowns. When at the beginning of 1627 Buckingham wrote to the abate that the cardinal privately did not want to include parties other than the duke in the final conclusion of the settlement, the cardinal was implicitly recognising the influence enjoyed by Scaglia.[55] This form of dependence indeed underpinned Scaglia's pragmatic diplomatic strategy after Monzón. The abate was attempting to manoeuvre himself into a position where Richelieu would be forced to acknowledge his political value and thus the wider interests of Savoy.[56] Scaglia's diplomatic method of combining threats with offers therefore seemed at least to have had some effect. Richelieu oscillated between openly expressed hostility towards the abate and very overt displays of affection, although these displays did not necessarily imply any genuine trust.

The cardinal's calculated shows of affection were, moreover, accompanied by other French ministers showing their confidence in the abate. Scaglia informed Duke Carlo Emanuele I of conversations he had with Henri de Schomberg and Secretary of State Antoine d'Effiat during which he had complained that he himself was being blamed for the difficulties in Franco-Savoyard relations, and that he had heard a rumour that those problems would be resolved only on his departure from Paris. Schomberg countered this, adding that Louis XIII thought that Scaglia would never be 'Spanish [spagnuolo]' – a reductive description that encapsulated a much wider set of political allegiances and messages. Elsewhere, Effiat said that the French wanted the same good relations with the abate as there had been with his brother, the count of Verrua, during his mission to Paris. He was in effect informing Alessandro of the well-established connection between the Scaglia di Verrua, as a francophile clan, and Paris, from which the abate was not exlcuded.[57]

Even when Alessandro Scaglia eventually left the Savoyard embassy in Paris in March 1627, against an audible chorus of suspicion, some leading figures in France continued the show of confidence. On his departure it was reported that Scaglia was favourably treated by Louis XIII and

---

[55] PRO SP 78/81/1–3, Buckingham to Scaglia, 17 January 1627; CSPV 1626–8, pp. 54, 88 and 156, where the Venetian ambassador added that Richelieu wanted to use Marie Christine to mediate between her brother, Louis XIII, and her brother-in-law, Charles I. Carlo Emanuele I reportedly came to a less optimistic interpretation of Richelieu's show of affection, saying that he wanted to set Scaglia up to be blamed by the English in the event of the Anglo-French peace talks failing. CSPV 1626–8, pp. 94–5.

[56] CSPV 1626–8, pp. 37, 54. The abate described the state of Anglo-French affairs and his wish to mediate between them in a document written for an unknown English correspondent. PRO SP 78/80/219–21v, Scaglia to ?, on his dealings with Richelieu, 1 January 1627.

[57] AST LMF m. 28, fasc. 6, 68, Scaglia to Carlo Emanuele I, 22 March 1627.

the queen mother, Marie de' Medici. As was the ceremonial custom with parting ambassadors, the abate received gifts from the sovereign, in this case 3,000 écus, though also a diamond from the queen mother. Although Scaglia recognised that their favour might have been little more than a smokescreen of dissimulation, he underlined the point that they themselves harboured no ill feeling towards him. The abate departed enjoying a curious combination of lingering suspicion, which he himself had been instrumental in generating, and almost exaggerated favour from the French regime.[58] This was more than fitting given his own double approach to the French regime that had come to define his pragmatic diplomacy after the treaty of Monzón and that had in turn shaped Savoy's diplomatic position in Europe.

---

[58] AAE CP Sardaigne, 8, f. 62, Marini to Herbaut, 4 May 1627; AST LMF m. 28, fasc. 6, 93, Scaglia to Carlo Emanuele I, 21 April 1627.

4

PRAGMATIC DIPLOMACY: ENGLAND, FRANCE AND SPAIN

The year 1627 was critical, though transitional, for the duchy of Savoy. The duchy's commitment to the anti-Habsburg alliance with France and Venice had effectively come to an end, in no small part because of the treaty of Monzón. But if the alliance was by then doomed, Carlo Emanuele I had not as yet settled on a clear diplomatic position, whether in the simplest terms that meant aligning with either France or Spain. The reasons for his calculated uncertainty lay to a considerable degree with his principal ambassadorial agent. Alessandro Scaglia, whose diplomatic career in Paris had been established through family connections and his prince's dynastic and diplomatic affiliations, had through his own initiatives and in a very short time come to enjoy a powerful position in directing Savoyard international strategies. It was Scaglia's political pragmatism, defined by what he saw as his prince's interests, that constructed a complex and delicate diplomatic approach to the Stuarts, Bourbons and Spanish Habsburgs.

After leaving Paris, Alessandro Scaglia went, without official instructions or formal ambassadorial status, to the Spanish Netherlands. His arrival in Brussels early in May 1627 marked the end of one phase of his diplomatic career and the start of a new one, and though rumours abounded of a return to the French court he was never to do so again. But he did not simply break all contact with the Bourbon regime – that would have been at odds with his brand of pragmatic diplomacy. When he left Paris his overarching strategy probably remained unchanged, to persuade the French back towards a policy that took notice of their allies and alliances, and, as had become clearly established since 1626, the prime means for achieving this was through England. The deterioration in Anglo-French relations, however, continued with an apparent relentlessness during 1627. François de Bassompierre's mission to London on Louis XIII's behalf, which at the end of 1626 had temporarily raised hopes of a peaceful solution to the international crisis, failed to secure any lasting achievements as his negotiations were effectively rejected by the French regime even before his return to Paris.[1] Nor did Scaglia's key friendship with Buckingham yield much of substance for the peace process. Yet the threat of impending war, and indeed the eventual outbreak of military conflict itself when in July 1627 a naval force under Buckingham was dispatched to La Rochelle, did not mark a total cessation of diplomacy between the Stuart and Bourbon crowns. Both continued to entertain terms for a settlement of their grievances, even if they gave no clear indication as to whether or not they thought a settlement at that point was at all possible. This should hardly be surprising. Preparations for war and negotiations for peace invariably took place side by side; it was typically necessary for states to be seen by domestic and foreign audiences alike to be negotiating for mutual concord, perhaps most especially in Catholic Europe where the rhetoric of power politics saw peace as a primary goal.

Abate Scaglia's own use of diplomatic contingency and his application of political pragmatism provides the key for understanding his continuing approach to the French regime during the critical year of 1627 when so much remained in the balance across Europe. Soon after arriving in Brussels, the abate visited the watchful French representative at the court to explain that in going to the Spanish Netherlands he intended nothing more than to pay a complimentary visit to the Infanta Isabella, adding that his true hopes, as before, rested on securing an Anglo-French settlement. This was the story Scaglia had indeed maintained to answer his critics while preparing to leave the embassy in Paris, and was a position furthermore shared by his sovereign prince.[2] To preserve the amicable relationship with France it would be necessary for his trusted representative, the abate, to act with 'complete prudence' in Brussels. Duke Carlo Emanuele I, so he elaborated in a series of letters to his son and heir Vittorio Amedeo, still mistrusted the Spanish, believing their international policies to be at odds with his own interests, adding that an English agent was travelling to Turin with news about the Anglo-French discussions. By inference the duke, like his favoured ambassador, still inclined out of pragmatism and preference to France as the better ally of the two leading Catholic powers.[3]

---

[1] Lockyer, *Buckingham*, p. 352.
[2] AAE CP Pays-Bas Espagnols, 7, f. 160v, Bougy to Herbaut, 9 April 1627; ff. 198–200, Bougy to Hotman, 14 May 1627; ff. 210-12v, Bougy to Herbaut, 21 May 1627. See also AST LMI m. 4, 15, Scaglia to Carlo Emanuele I, 12 July 1627.
[3] AST LDS m. 33, fasc. 11, 4620, Carlo Emanuele I to Vittorio Amedeo, 10 April 1627; 4627, Carlo Emanuele I to Vittorio Amedeo, 18 April 1627; AST LDS m. 46, fasc. 16, 1437, Vittorio Amedeo to Carlo Emanuele I, April 1627.

Although no longer in Paris, Alessandro Scaglia could still exert some influence over the Savoyard embassy there. Following his departure the abate was not immediately replaced with another representative of ambassadorial status, as the secretary of state Pietro Biandrà was effectively left in control. Marini, the French ambassador in Turin, reported Carlo Emanuele I's determination to be involved in the Anglo-French talks through the abate, and that to pursue this Scaglia might indeed return to the embassy in France.[4] Even in the abate's absence there were avenues for informal contact with Paris. In 1626 Scaglia, in his capacity as a diplomatic broker between third parties and Turin, had acted as an intermediary on behalf of an individual named Salmatoris who had wished to offer his military services to Duke Carlo Emanuele I with a levy of troops and cavalry which he personally commanded. There is little biographical information about Salmatoris, save that he was from Saluzzo, the marquisate to the south of the province of Savoie that had been ceded by Henry IV to Carlo Emanuele I in 1601 following the treaty of Lyons. Born in a border province that had only recently changed control from France to Savoy, Salmatoris was ideally suited to passing between the two states and to spreading his service as his personal interests demanded and as patronage allowed. His career highlighted the potential flexibility of service and loyalty to different states at the margins of the Savoyard duchy.[5] Salmatoris was also a client of the duke of Angoulême, one of the abate's personal friends and contacts when he had been in France earlier in the 1620s – in his identity as a cultural patron and broker, Alessandro had already drawn on his friendship with the duke to purchases goods for Carlo Emanuele I, acquiring some of Angoulême's hunting dogs and horses for his sovereign prince.

The potential diplomatic value of Scaglia's informal association became evident when Salmatoris served as a point of contact between the abate and the French court. In July 1627 Scaglia contacted Salmatoris, reiterating his desire to resolve his own lingering differences with members of the French regime and, more broadly, to mediate an Anglo-French settlement. Salmatoris immediately went to the duke of Angoulême to show him the abate's letter and the duke in turn went to Richelieu. According to the Savoyard secretary of state in Paris there followed a long meeting between the two, indicating the seriousness with which

[4] AAE CP Sardaigne, 8, f. 78v, Marini to ?, 22 May 1627; f. 71v, Marini to ?, 18 May 1627. On Biandrà consult Rosso, *Una burocrazia*, p. 369.
[5] CSPV 1626–8, p. 284. Salmatoris had in fact acted as a courier for Carlo Emanuele I in 1618. ASV SS Savoia, 16, f. 323,? to Borghese, 15 July 1618, and in 1624 Scaglia described him as 'very well known to your highness [Carlo Emanuele I]'. AST LMF m. 26, 196, Scaglia to Carlo Emanuele I, 23 August 1625.

the cardinal-minister wished to be seen to be treating Scaglia's overture.[6] Richelieu responded with a calculated show of interest, though he requested further detail to clarify Scaglia's position. The Venetians later reported that Scaglia and Salmatoris planned to meet in The Hague to discuss the conditions for an English peace and the future of Franco-Savoyard relations, and though little practically came out of this, it was also reported that the French were even delaying another channel of peace negotiations via the Dutch ambassador in France to await Scaglia's response.[7]

While the Salmatoris connection eventually closed, other avenues for informal negotiation opened. In the spring of 1627 Walter Montagu (c. 1603–77), the youngest son of the earl of Manchester, arrived at the Savoyard court in Turin. Montagu, already known to Alessandro Scaglia from the complimentary visit he had paid Louis XIII in 1626, fitted into a distinctive typology of an early seventeenth-century courtier-diplomat like two other of Buckingham's agents, Balthasar Gerbier and Endymion Porter. Montagu did not share the hard-line English Protestant outlook of his father, something that undoubtedly enabled him to move around different courts and, importantly, to cross confessional boundaries with relative ease, raising at least parallels with Salmatoris' flexible loyalties between Savoy and France. And as Alessandro Scaglia was to cultivate an international identity as an expert in English diplomacy during the 1620s, so Montagu developed a reputation as a specialist in Franco-Savoyard affairs, primarily because he was a favourite of Queen Henrietta Maria whose sister was of course Marie Christine, consort of Vittorio Amedeo. When Walter Montagu was forced into exile in 1647, having taken holy orders in the Catholic church, it was perhaps no surprise that he settled in France as commendatory abbé of Pontoise and a member of Anne of Austria's regency council.[8]

Carlo Emanuele I informed the French ambassador in Turin, Marini, that Walter Montagu had come to confirm Charles I's wish for him to mediate a peace between the Stuarts and Bourbons. The documents Montagu carried to Turin explained the English king's position, that

---

[6] AST LMI m. 4, 21, Scaglia to Carlo Emanuele I, 4 August 1627.

[7] AST LMI m. 4, 21, Scaglia to Carlo Emanuele I, 4 August 1627; CSPV 1626–8, pp. 284–5, 331.

[8] CSPV 1626–8, p. 198. Montagu had been to Paris ostensibly to congratulate Gaston d'Orléans on his marriage to Montpensier. AST LMF m. 27, fasc. 3, 161, Scaglia to Carlo Emanuele I, 10 September 1626. Curiously Walter Montagu has not attracted much detailed study. The only detailed biographical information on Montagu can be found in the *Dictionary of National Biography*, though consult Caroline Hibbard, *Charles I and the Popish Plot* (Chapel Hill, 1983); Georges Dethan, *Mazarin: un homme de paix à l'âge baroque* (Paris, 1981); G. Albion, *Charles I and the Court of Rome* (London, 1935).

while the French had wronged him he nevertheless still inclined towards a settlement, reiterating his aspiration that the two crowns should maintain 'their common interests [leurs affaires communes]', defined, presumably, in opposition to the Spanish Habsburgs. To stake his place in the process, Duke Carlo Emanuele I in turn emphasised Scaglia's exceptional personal credit with his friend the duke of Buckingham, the abate's best diplomatic credential in any peace talks involving the English.[9] That Montagu was lodged in the Palazzo Verrua and entertained by the count of Verrua, Scaglia's elder brother, also transmitted diplomatic signals to reinforce the abate's mediatory role. Quite plausibly Verrua was employed because he was the leading Turinese courtier at a time when the Savoyard court did not have a formal office of Master of Ceremonies – the first evidence of its existence dated from 1632 when Duke Vittorio Amedeo I embarked on his determined policy of publicising his own royal status, the so-called *trattamento reale*. Verrua might simply have been the most appropriate person to entertain the English agent on behalf of Carlo Emanuele I, and he was certainly reimbursed by the duke for the financial outlay of entertaining Montagu.[10] The count was nevertheless widely known as a prominent francophile and, as Abate Scaglia's elder brother (said by the Venetian ambassador in Savoy to have been behind Montagu's mission to Turin), his involvement could have been a pertinent means of emphasising and legitimising the abate's own position as a mediator.[11]

The motives behind Montagu's mission seem baffling. Why did both Richelieu and Scaglia, backed by Duke Carlo Emanuele I, entertain the possibility of an Anglo-French peace mediated by Savoy, given the all too evident deterioration in their political relationship after the treaty of Monzón? In short they were temporising with different diplomatic and rhetorical tools in a period of enormous diplomatic uncertainty. For Richelieu it seems possible, if not completely probable, that Scaglia did indeed hold a potential key to a settlement. If the abate were in a position to mediate between England and France, primarily through his personal credit with Buckingham, then it would perhaps be no bad thing, especially if the differences between the two kingdoms were consequently resolved. Yet for Richelieu there was also much political profit to be

[9] AST NI m. 3, fasc. 14, 'sujet de la venue du sieur de Montaigu vers S. A.', April 1627; 'Propositions faittes a S. A. par le sieur de Montaigu', April 1627; CSPV 1626–8, pp. 208–10. See also HMC Eleventh Report, appendix, part I, pp. 123–4.

[10] AST Sezione Riunite PCF 1627, f. 78, 20 October 1627.

[11] AAE CP Angleterre, 42, f. 113, paper regarding Montagu, 18 July 1627; ff. 137v–8, Marini to ?, 17 July 1627; ASV SS Savoia, 44, ff. 128v–9, Albertini to Barberini, 24 April 1627. I am grateful to Robert Oresko for advice about the office of Master of Ceremonies at the Turinese court.

gained by appearing, at least in public, to support Savoy's mediation. In a broad sense it was expected that he should seek friendship rather than conflict with Savoy. Since the treaty of Monzón the cardinal had claimed that Duke Carlo Emanuele I was still a trusted ally, even though he also accused Scaglia of involvement in the Chalais conspiracy. For Richelieu to have dropped his rhetorical position would have been to contradict his image as a defender of Italian liberty against so-called Habsburg tyranny, and furthermore to alienate Savoy as a counter-balance to Spanish power in the peninsula.[12] But entertaining the possibility of a settlement mediated by Savoy was also a means of exercising restraint on both English and Savoyard diplomatic and military activity at this crucial time. If the French were to give the impression that they were genuinely interested in a peace mediated by Savoy – however true that was – then England and Savoy would perhaps be more reluctant to turn to Spain.

By making it known through public displays of affection towards Alessandro Scaglia and even through controlled information leaks that he and Carlo Emanuele I were in fact mediating a settlement with England, Richelieu could make further gain by discrediting the concurrent negotiations for an Anglo-Spanish peace. This was what the abate himself later suspected in July 1627 when a politically embarrassing letter written by Marini, the French ordinary ambassador in Turin, was leaked in Brussels by Peter Paul Rubens and shown to the Infanta Isabella and her leading adviser, the veteran Genoese commander Ambrogio Spínola (1569–1630). In the letter Marini reported that Carlo Emanuele I had allowed him to hide behind a tapestry at court while Walter Montagu spoke freely, presumably unaware of the concealed presence of the French ambassador, about Charles I's genuine wish for Savoy to mediate an Anglo-French peace. While this may well have been true given the Savoyard duke's efforts to prove his credentials as the key mediator between England and France and the sensitivity of English and French ambassadors meeting directly in time of war, this 'artifice' was not by coincidence leaked by the French precisely at the time when Scaglia was discussing the preliminaries for an Anglo-Spanish peace with Buckingham's agent, Balthasar Gerbier, and Rubens. The abate believed that the French wanted 'to give credence to the idea that England wants a settlement with France, and that in conveying this to stall your talks with the Spanish, moreover to sour your highness's [Carlo Emanuele I] relations with Spain, that

---

[12] Indeed, in January 1627 the French had dispatched an extraordinary ambassador to Savoy and Mantua in an attempt to settle the future of Mantua and Monferrato to both parties' satisfaction, not least so that Franco-Savoyard relations could be restored from the battering taken by the treaty of Monzón. Parrott, 'The Mantuan Succession', 42–3.

undoubtedly will not please the Spanish, while they want to resolve your dispute with the Genoese [over Zuccarello]'.[13]

But Richelieu was not the only person capable of this kind of political pragmatism. As the cardinal had motives other than just obtaining a peace settlement in dealing with Scaglia, so the abate used this contact as one element in his pursuit of wider interests, pressurising Richelieu without forcing a definitive break with the French regime. Venice's representative in The Hague for one believed Scaglia was following a fine line between unsettling the French and alienating them entirely; even his departure from Paris was interpreted as a deliberate gesture to increase their tensions by implying that he was actively participating in secret talks between England and Spain, whether or not that was actually true. According to this interpretation, Alessandro Scaglia intended to trouble Richelieu, perhaps even to force his removal, but that ultimately he wanted to coerce the French into constancy rather than opposition towards their spurned allies – Montagu's visit to Turin after all had underlined Savoy's wish to bring England and France to a peaceful settlement.[14] Yet even this constituted only half of Montagu's mission.

Although Walter Montagu was to acquire a reputation as a francophile courtier during the 1630s, his mission across Europe in 1627 was not simply one of mediation between England and France. While in Paris, the English envoy had met with Scaglia, and in a ciphered despatch to Turin the abate wrote that Montagu confirmed that the English regime was considering a peace with Spain (as will be seen, Scaglia already knew of the peace preliminaries when Balthasar Gerbier passed through Paris in January 1627). After leaving France for Savoy in April 1627, Montagu entered Lorraine where he contacted Marie de Rohan (1600–79), the duchess of Chevreuse, exiled from the French court following her involvement in the Chalais conspiracy. The duchess, a colourful character in the history of the Bourbon court, was of central importance as an opponent of Richelieu, not least because of her close relationship with the French queen as her first lady-in-waiting, though also because of her blood ties with the sovereign House of Lorraine whose own relations with France remained constantly ambiguous.[15] Walter Montagu then

---

[13] AST LMI m. 4, 17, Scaglia to Carlo Emanuele I, 26 July 1627; BL Eg. MS 2597, f. 29, Gerbier to Carlisle, 6 August 1627. It should be added that Scaglia blamed Bullion for the letter and in a remarkable piece of mental gymnastics claimed that the counsellors of such a great kingdom as France could never be involved in such an artifice.

[14] CSPV 1626–8, p. 317.

[15] Two inadequate biographies of the duchess are Louis Batiffol, *La duchesse de Chevreuse: une vie d'aventures et d'intrigues sous Louis XIII* (Paris, 1913), and Michael Prawdin, *Marie de Rohan, Duchesse de Chevreuse* (London, 1971). See also CSPV 1626–8, pp. 168, 196; L. J. Reeve, *Charles I and the Road to Personal Rule* (Cambridge, 1989), pp. 44–5.

passed through Languedoc, one of the heartlands of the Huguenot community in France, and there he met with the Huguenot duke of Rohan, who was in principle interested in an alliance against Richelieu, if not definitively committed at that moment to action.[16] Turin was Montagu's final destination, and despite lacking clear ambassadorial authority, he committed Charles I to an important written diplomatic pledge. The English king would not come to any settlement with Louis XIII or any of his ministers, so the pledge stated, without first informing and consulting the duke of Savoy. Any agreement would, furthermore, be with the consent of the count of Soissons, himself in self-imposed exile in Savoy following his participation in the Chalais conspiracy. For his part, Soissons, whose status as a French prince of the blood underscored his exceptional political importance, consented to an almost identical pledge in which he likewise agreed not to settle with his home state without Savoy's prior approval. That Charles I was apparently willing to link his diplomatic fortunes so closely to those of Carlo Emanuele I is striking. Both written pledges crucially gave the Savoyard duke a more certain place in England's diplomacy, either to act as mediator or on a lesser level to be involved in any peace deal. At a time when the duchy of Savoy was still viewed with suspicion by both France and Spain, this valuable assurance would have served as diplomatic security. Equally, the pledge demonstrated Charles I's desire to operate according to dynastic affinity, allowing him to cement his goodwill towards his Sabaudian relatives.[17]

Alessandro Scaglia was the linchpin of Savoyard diplomacy during the pivotal year of 1627. From his arrival in Paris in 1624 he had successfully fashioned his identity as an expert in English affairs, strengthened by a deepening knowledge of French domestic politics. By remaining involved in the Anglo-French peace negotiations, Scaglia could ensure the protection of Savoyard interests; by seeking to damage Richelieu, he could attempt to draw the cardinal (or even France without the cardinal) back into a wider and more reliable settlement with Duke Carlo Emanuele I.[18] But this formed only one part of the abate's diplomatic calculations. While mediating in the Anglo-French war, he simultaneously pursued informal talks with the Spanish in Brussels and, more indirectly, in Madrid, partly, it should be added, to put pressure on France. In this,

---

[16] J. A. Clarke, *Huguenot Warrior: The Life and Times of Henri de Rohan, 1579–1638* (The Hague, 1966), p. 142; CSPV 1626–8, pp. 153–4; Lockyer, *Buckingham*, pp. 369–70.

[17] AST NF m. 8, fasc. 33, declaration of Montagu in the name of Charles I, 13 June 1627; declaration of Soissons, 13 June 1627; CSPV 1626–8, pp. 388, 453, 442.

[18] AST LMI m. 4, 7, Scaglia to Carlo Emanuele I, 13 May 1627; BL Add. MS 36,778, ff. 12–v, Carleton to Killutagh, 27 June 1627.

the abate was not acting purely according to a bi-polar conception of international relations that saw France and Spain as the only effective forces in Europe – that would have been to assume that there were no other influential or politically active states other than those leading powers. As a mirror of his French policy, central to the abate's approach to Spain was England and how the English might themselves respond to the possibility of a peace with the Spanish Habsburgs. Of course, in turn he wished to see how this might benefit his own sovereign prince. Alessandro Scaglia knew that the way in which the English reacted to France and Spain – whether by offering peace or by pursuing war with either of them – would have wider implications for their willingness to operate elsewhere in Europe. That obviously encompassed Savoy's immediate sphere of territorial interest in north Italy. Scaglia also understood that the actions of all three royal favourites (his term), Richelieu, Olivares and Buckingham, would directly affect the policies of their home states and subsequently influence the balance of European power. In a period aptly characterised by S. R. Gardiner as one of 'unreal diplomacy', the actual and *possible* outcomes of whatever negotiations involving any of these powers were important since they could all have tangible political effects.[19] This complex set of overlapping power relationships, and the permutations of what might be described as both real and contingent diplomacy, profoundly shaped Savoy's own standing with England.

The duke of Buckingham, fervently hostile to France, eventually realised that a peace with Spain might be necessary given the seriousness and expense of simultaneous wars with the two leading Catholic powers, as Alessandro Scaglia in the summer of 1626 had already come to think. Early in 1627 rumours of peace talks between England and Spain began to reach Paris, confirmed when one of Buckingham's clients, the artist, diplomatic agent and political chancer Balthasar Gerbier, arrived at the French capital.[20] The duke of Savoy, represented by Scaglia, clearly could not afford to neglect the possibility of an Anglo-Spanish peace, and it was Gerbier's informal mission to Brussels from Paris that in all probability prompted the abate himself to leave for the Spanish Netherlands. From Turin a few months later, Walter Montagu reported to London that if the Anglo-Spanish negotiations moved towards a peaceful conclusion then Carlo Emanuele I would shape his cause according to Charles I's aspirations, even though Scaglia had not at this stage put his unequivocal trust in the Spanish. If anything, when he first arrived in Brussels in the spring of 1627 he still inclined to an Anglo-French peace before one with Spain,

---

[19] Gardiner, *History*, VI, p. 163.   [20] CSPV 1626–8, pp. 115–17.

as he outlined to Carlo Emanuele I. In all likelihood negotiating for an Anglo-Spanish settlement was primarily a means of exercising influence over this potentially important line of English diplomacy and of ensuring that Savoyard interests were accordingly maintained.[21]

Under the pretence of buying art for his political patron Buckingham, Balthasar Gerbier had gone from Paris to Brussels, and in February 1627 he met the Infanta Isabella's agent, Peter Paul Rubens – the two already known to each other when Gerbier had visited Paris in 1625 with his patron Buckingham and Rubens was decorating the Luxembourg Palace for Marie de' Medici. The more secret reason for their meeting was to begin informal parleys for a suspension of the Anglo-Spanish war.[22] On 10 May 1627 Alessandro Scaglia himself arrived in Brussels, like Gerbier for an ostensibly non-political reason, to pay compliments to Isabella on behalf of her brother-in-law, Carlo Emanuele I, a story, as it has been seen, the abate maintained to defend himself from critical French observers. Again, his words masked the complete truth. He was looking to stake his own place in the Gerbier–Rubens talks, seemingly in keeping with Carlo Emanuele I's wishes, who had confided as much to the English secretary in Turin.[23] The abate was certainly well placed to work with the two artist-diplomats. Each shared a distinctive diplomatic style. Seeking to interpret the character of Charles I's court, which was arguably alien to many 'orthodox' Protestant Englishmen at a time of increasing political tensions within England, L. J. Reeve has set this firmly in a negative light:

> In addition, the Caroline court was remarkable for attracting capricious and quite bizarre characters from the world where international high politics merged with the arts and Roman religion. The abbé Scaglia and in particular Balthazar Gerbier are examples of this breed ... [W]hat might be termed the Caroline 'lunatic factor' is significant. Individuals such as these were but the more exotic fruit of an overall atmosphere which

---

[21] PRO SP 92/13/55v, Montagu to Conway, 30 May 1627; AST LMI m. 4, 9, Scaglia to Carlo Emanuele I, 11 June 1627. Shortly before, the duke of Savoy had written to Charles I to underline his wish to act in tandem with him in international affairs. PRO SP 92/13/29, Carlo Emanuele I to Charles I, 1 April 1627.

[22] Gerbier, like Porter, deserves an up-to-date study. The best biographical introduction for Gerbier is Hugh Ross Williamson, *Four Stuart Portraits* (London, 1949), pp. 26–60. Rubens' intertwined career as a painter-diplomat has been discussed but it too deserves a new study. The existing studies are G. Cruzada Villaamil, *Rubens, diplomático español: sus viajes a España y noticia de sus cuadros, segun los inventarios de las casas reales de Austria y de Borbón* (Madrid, 1874), and L. P. Gachard, *Histoire politique et diplomatique de Pierre-Paul Rubens* (Brussels, 1877). See also Hugh Trevor-Roper's *Princes and Artists: Patronage and Ideology at Four Habsburg Courts, 1517–1633* (London, 1991), chapter 4.

[23] AST LMI m. 4, 7, Scaglia to Carlo Emanuele I, 13 May 1627; PRO SP 92/13/30v–1, Hales to Killutagh, 12 April 1627.

still distinguishes Charles's regime. That atmosphere was continental, cosmopolitan and avant-garde.[24]

Gardiner's eloquent description of Balthasar Gerbier as 'a man at home in every nation and specially attached to none' reflected not only a willing-ness potentially to change service from one sovereign prince to another but perhaps also his cosmopolitan character, something shared by Rubens and Scaglia alike.[25] All three were agents experienced at court life, in an environment where formal and informal diplomacy intersected. They were multi-lingual, able to converse freely with one another and indeed with like-minded courtiers across Europe. More to the point, they were all involved in unofficial talks that reflected the particular delicacy of their negotiations, and also the particular identities of their home states. Gerbier was secretly representing Buckingham in meetings with Catholic Spain, publicly at war with Protestant England; Rubens was representing the Infanta Isabella, rather than Philip IV, in negotiations that in early 1627 were not clearly endorsed by the court in Madrid; and Scaglia, without being formally accredited as a diplomatic representative to Brussels by his sovereign prince, had on his initiative staked his own place at the negotiating table (though it should be added that Savoy never seems to have sent an ambassador to the archducal court). This was in fact the first sustained contact between Rubens and Scaglia, though their paths had crossed twice before, at the beginning of 1623 and in May–June 1625, when they were both in Paris (Rubens because of his commissions from Marie de' Medici). Perhaps surprisingly, there is also no evidence that Scaglia, the refined patron and collector who was to draw on Van Dyck's artistic expertise, commissioned or bought paintings from Rubens, apart from at the very end of Rubens' life when in the late 1630s the abate brokered the decoration of the Queen's House at Greenwich and sug-gested that Rubens should be involved. Nor indeed had Rubens much prior contact with the Turinese court. During his stays in the Italian peninsula between 1600 and 1608, Rubens had spent most of his time in Mantua, Genoa and Rome, with brief spells in Venice, Verona, Milan and Florence. The 1635 inventory of the Sabaudian collection mentions only one original work by Rubens, a Madonna and Child with Joseph.[26] But the enthusiasm at the meeting of Gerbier, Rubens and Scaglia was quickly in evidence, and without hesitation all three made shows of trust in one another. It was in essence diplomacy among friends. Rubens for his part fully endorsed Scaglia's involvement, and encouraged him to meet and talk with the Marquis Spínola. As he wrote in a now well-known

[24] Reeve, *Charles I*, p. 201.   [25] Gardiner, *History*, VI, p. 161.
[26] Baudi di Vesme, 'La regia pinacoteca', 46.

letter to Gerbier after the abate's visit to Brussels, 'it is clear that we find 2X [the code employed by Rubens alone to designate Scaglia] capable of such important matters'. The abate was equally generous in his assessment of Rubens, recorded several weeks later. 'Rubens has finally arived here [The Hague], the celebrated painter from Antwerp', Scaglia wrote. 'He is a person capable of much more than producing pictures.'[27]

In Brussels Abate Scaglia became interested in more than the progress of the Gerbier–Rubens talks alone. In meetings with the Infanta Isabella and her leading ministers, Scaglia made it clear that her brother-in-law, Duke Carlo Emanuele I, wished to improve relations with Spain specifically through her direct intercessions with their nephew, Philip IV. This was to be integrated into a strategy of re-forming a power balance in north Italy of which there were two basic elements, to square Savoy's territorial interests in the region, so close to Spanish-protected territory, and Spain's strategic interests there. Scaglia proposed a marriage between Cardinal Maurizio, the second surviving son of the duke of Savoy, and Princess Maria Gonzaga, the sole daughter of the previous but one duke of Mantua and Monferrato and also a grand-daughter of Carlo Emanuele I (and thus Maurizio's niece), whose marital status was crucial to the future of the region. Realising the probability that the Gonzaga dynasty was about to die out because of the frailty of the heirless and aged duke, the abate went on to suggest that Mantua and Monferrato should be partitioned where Spain would obtain Mantua and Savoy the other separable sovereignty which Savoy had long coveted and which a dynastic union between Maurizio and Maria would have gone some way to legitimise. As something of a carrot, Scaglia added that he held the fate of the Anglo-French peace talks in his hands (his own phrase) and that he could delay any settlement for up to two months. However realistic this was, the abate was looking to demonstrate the influence he as an individual could command, while emphasising to his Habsburg audience that Carlo Emanuele I supported an Anglo-Spanish settlement. This crucial link between the fortunes of Anglo-Spanish relations in the Atlantic theatre and Savoyard dynastic and territorial interests in north Italy was to become of vital importance to the European conflict in the following year.[28]

---

[27] PRO SP 77/19/145, Rubens to Gerbier, 19 May 1627; AST LMI m. 4, 17, Scaglia to Carlo Emanuele I, 26 July 1627.

[28] AGR SEG 196, f. 390, Infanta Isabella to Philip IV, 23 May 1627; f. 393, anonymous paper, May 1627; AST LMI m. 4, 9, Scaglia to Carlo Emanuele I, 11 June 1627; Reade, *Sidelights*, III, p. 72; Gachard, *Rubens*, p. 52. It is not clear whether Scaglia's offer would have allowed Spanish control of the fortress of Casale in Monferrato which, according to Parrott, was much more important to Madrid than Monferrato itself. Parrott, 'The Mantuan Succession', 56.

Isabella seemed openly happy about the prospect of improved relations between Spain and Savoy. The childless widow clearly held the sovereign Sabaudian House in high regard and affection, not least because of the dynastic ties between Brussels and Turin, a bond which Scaglia fully appreciated and, in approaching her in the first place, had quite deliberately played upon. Since she had no direct surviving heirs of her own she came to see Carlo Emanuele I's sons – her nephews – effectively as her own, and hoped to bring about a reconciliation between Turin and Madrid. As the abate wrote to Carlo Emanuele I:

> She expresses her feelings about past events, that she wished to seek a remedy, and that it should always be one of the things that she most wants in this world for the esteem in which she holds you, and your sons, who she holds not only as her dear nephews, but as her very sons; one by one she asked me of them, especially of the prince [Vittorio Amedeo], and also of your daughters, speaking of them with tenderness.[29]

The practical and symbolic importance of these dynastic ties must not be underestimated. They constantly hinted at the (admittedly distant) possibility of a Savoyard succession to the Spanish Netherlands, a recurrent theme of Savoy's diplomatic relations with the Spanish Habsburgs after Carlo Emanuele I's marriage to Catalina Michaela and that of Albert and Isabella, even though at least formally the marriage contract between the Archdukes stated that, in the absence of legitimate Catholic heirs, the semi-autonomous region would return to Madrid's direct control. Dynastic affinities moreover afforded ready access to the court in Madrid through the secondary channel of Brussels, a crucial conduit more generally for informal negotiations during the Thirty Years' War. Its ambiguous political status within the broader Spanish composite monarchy gave it a highly valuable diplomatic function available both to the Spanish and to those who wished to approach them, as became clear to the abate during his own exile there in the 1630s. Because Scaglia continued to argue that his visit to the Spanish Netherlands was purely complimentary at a time when diplomatic relations between Savoy and Spain were still, at least publicly, cool, this access provided him with the opportunity to open diplomatic relations beyond the more restrictive domain of formal ambassadorial contact. Alessandro Scaglia, as the cultivated courtier, felt at ease with Gerbier and Rubens, while as Carlo Emanuele I's representative (whether formally or informally) he was able to draw on the equally powerful pull of dynastic affinity between the House of Savoy and the Habsburgs.

---

[29] AST LMI m. 4, 9, Scaglia to Carlo Emanuele I, 11 June 1627. See also, 8, Scaglia to ?, 10 June 1627.

Negotiating with the Spanish through Brussels was, however, but one half of a diplomatic process. The Infanta and her agent Rubens after all had been acting only as unofficial points of diplomatic contact with Gerbier and Scaglia. To pursue what were in essence preliminary negotiations towards a more specific conclusion the Infanta needed explicit instructions from the Spanish regime, and it soon became clear that the policies of Brussels and Madrid, at least at this point, did not entirely coincide. While the dynastic and political ambiguities in the relationship between the Spanish Netherlands and the composite monarchy certainly afforded unique diplomatic advantages, there were also limits to these advantages. They were not a single political entity with identical strategic priorities, and while the regime in Brussels willingly supported a peace initiative with Scaglia's mediation, the reactions and response from the court in Madrid were less favourable. First, the progress of the Anglo-Spanish talks was retarded because of the link made by some in London with the Palatinate question and the conflict in the Low Countries, both highly sensitive issues that touched the Stuarts' dynastic affiliations and the religious sensibilities of English Protestants. The idea of a peace with the United Provinces, given its possible terms, still troubled notions of Spanish reputation, not least because the military successes in northern Europe they had enjoyed since the occupation of the Palatinate in 1621 had raised hopes that a peace with the Dutch might at last be secured on Madrid's terms. Buckingham's motives for seeking a peace were also questioned, while the use of Rubens as a diplomatic agent was itself brought into doubt in a memorable letter. 'I have been taken aback', claimed Philip IV in writing to his aunt, 'that in a matter of such importance a painter should be employed as a minister, a point one might say of great discredit to this monarchy.'[30]

If there were specific problems relating to the Anglo-Spanish negotiations then there were equally difficult issues over Scaglia's own involvement as a Savoyard agent, despite the assurances Mirabel had given in the previous year to the abate in Paris and the fact that some ministers in Brussels showed genuine enthusiasm for a *rapprochement* between Turin and Madrid. At the Spanish capital, members of the council of state lined up to voice their suspicions of Savoy. There were still the territorial differences with Genoa over Zuccarello which the treaty of Monzón had pledged to address but had yet to resolve. And if proof were needed of Duke Carlo Emanuele I's duplicity, his duchy had only recently been involved in an open league with France against Spain. It was moreover

[30] AGS Est. 2041, consulta of council of state, 7 June 1627; AGR SEG 196, f. 45, Philip IV to Infanta Isabella, 16 June 1627.

known that he was advocating an Anglo-French peace settlement through Scaglia, as Philip IV effectively reminded his aunt when he requested that the abate should be instructed to leave Brussels.[31] The abate was attempting to shuffle a number of concurrent diplomatic initiatives, and the reactions of Madrid showed the dangers of playing France and Spain against one another with England as the stake.

Following Philip IV's instruction to his aunt that Scaglia should leave the Spanish Netherlands, and within weeks of reaching Brussels, the abate was on the road northwards to the United Provinces, still without formal diplomatic credentials. This did not however mark an abrupt end to his Anglo-Spanish diplomacy. As Scaglia left Brussels so his friend Gerbier had moved to The Hague, as the pressure was maintained in London to encompass both the Dutch Republic and the Palatinate in any formal settlement with Spain.[32] The triumvirate was again completed when late in July 1627 Rubens joined his friends Gerbier and Scaglia, once more on the pretext of selling some statues and paintings to Buckingham's agent. Although Rubens had difficulties in obtaining the necessary passport to visit the United Provinces because, it was believed, the Spanish regime in Madrid had declined to support his line of mediation, he at least remained upbeat about the prospects for a settlement.[33]

Spain's diplomatic tardiness did not necessarily reflect a definitive political position but something approaching a rhetorical stance. For both the French and the Spanish, negotiating with England also served more general strategies of outmanoeuvring the other in Europe. There were ends beyond, and often contradicting, immediate policies. This was most evidently demonstrated in one of the most peculiar initiatives of this complex period of international relations. In September 1627 Don Diego Mexia, the duke of Leganés and a relative of Olivares, arrived in Brussels on a diplomatic mission to the Infanta, the purpose of which was not widely publicised. As far as Scaglia knew, Leganés was in Brussels to discuss

---

[31] AGR SEG 197, f. 45, Philip IV to Infanta Isabella, 16 June 1627; AGS Est. K1481, 100, consulta of council of state, 31 May 1627. Though see also K1457, 78, instructions to Leganés, 15 June 1627, in which, it should be noted, Leganés was instructed to distance Philip IV from Scaglia not because he was seen as pro-French but ironically for the opposite reason, that the abate was viewed with suspicion by Louis XIII. This apparent contradiction can be explained by the fact that Leganés was being despatched on a mission to warm relations with France as part of the Franco-Spanish alignment and the rejection of Scaglia's overtures could thus serve as a signal to Paris that the Spanish were sincere in their diplomatic intentions.

[32] PRO SP 77/19/147, Scaglia to Buckingham, 17 May 1627; BL Eg. MSS 2597, ff. 27–31, Gerbier to Carlisle (?), 6 August 1627, which contains useful information about these negotiations.

[33] AST LMI m. 4, 17, Scaglia to Carlo Emanuele I, 26 July 1627; PRO SP 84/134/265–v, copy of Rubens to Gerbier, 18 September 1627; Reade, *Sidelights*, III, p. 84.

Dutch–Spanish peace talks and their link to the parallel English negotiations. There was an element of truth in this, and in addition he had
come to discuss Olivares' cherished project for the Union of Arms with
the regime in Brussels.[34] But Leganés more ominously was also under
instruction to discuss a possible Franco-Spanish *rapprochement*, contradicting Rubens' explicit assurances to Gerbier that his mission would
in no way affect the talks with England. The *rapprochement* had in fact
already been considered and reconsidered by the Spanish: Philip IV had
discussed it with the French ambassador in Spain following the treaty
of Monzón, if Richelieu's *Mémoires* are to be believed, while Spain's
ambassador Mirabel had also discussed the project with Father Bérulle,
one of the leading *dévots* in Paris. According to this ambitious design,
the two great Catholic states of France and Spain would unite with both
naval and land forces to invade England and a provisional date for the
invasion was even set for the summer of 1627.[35]

At least superficially the project seems bizarre given the obvious tensions between the two powers when they were also seeking to end their
individual wars with England. Some genuine preparations were indeed
made for a military expedition that included the mobilisation of a number
of sea vessels – it was in all probability necessary on both sides to present a
public face to the Catholic world that the plan was serious. Nevertheless,
there was more to the venture than its appearance suggested. The initiative might have served a double diplomatic purpose. In the first place, it
worked to enhance the reputations of the two crowns as Catholic powers,
so important for domestic and international audiences aware of their failure to co-operate on the European stage. But perhaps more significantly,
by planning an attack on England both powers attempted to embroil
the other in a still deeper conflict with the kingdom, preventing each
other's efforts to close that strategic theatre. Spain in particular might
also have hoped to use a Franco-Spanish alliance to isolate the Dutch at
a time when their three-year military agreement with France, signed in
June 1624 at Compiègne, was due for renewal, thereby increasing the
pressure on the Dutch to settle with Madrid.[36]

---

[34] J. H. Elliott, *The Count-Duke Olivares: The Statesman in an Age of Decline* (New Haven
and London, 1988), pp. 274–7.

[35] Richelieu, *Mémoires*, VI, pp. 272–85; AGS Est. K1457, 78, instructions to Leganés,
15 June 1627; AGR SEG 402/2, Mirabel to Infanta Isabella, 5 March 1627; Elliott,
Olivares, pp. 323–30. Scaglia in fact knew of the possibility of such a *rapprochement*
in the winter of 1626, though he passed little comment on it at the time. ASV SS
Francia 65, ff. 425v–6, Spada to Barberini, 10 November 1626.

[36] The Franco-Dutch alliance was not even welcomed in London; its renewal would
undoubtedly have complicated the Anglo-Spanish negotiations because of England's
wish to link the peace with the Dutch and Palatinate problems. Dudley Carleton

Concerned to sustain the momentum of Anglo-Spanish talks, Rubens was quick to dismiss the venture as an artifice of Richelieu, as a league of 'thunder without lightning' between two states who agree like 'fire and water'. The notion that France and Spain might actively co-operate for no selfish reason was difficult for the artist-diplomat to accept.[37] By late August, however, Gerbier was becoming impatient with the delays in the Anglo-Spanish talks and warned that he might return from The Hague to London.[38] Curiously Scaglia, who remained in the Low Countries, still seemed ambivalent about unequivocally supporting Spain, even if he did not show this to Rubens and Gerbier. While he had little desire to aid Richelieu's France, and hoped for the continuation of the Huguenot revolt, it seems that he also wanted to avoid dragging the French irreversibly into a protracted war. That would in itself have given too much political advantage to Spain. But nor did he necessarily want the Franco-Spanish *rapprochement* to come to any point of reality, whether that meant a more serious conflict for either side against England, or to an actual invasion (admittedly, unlikely in itself). The abate needed both France and Spain to remain in balanced opposition to one another, reflecting one calculation implicit in early modern Savoyard power politics. An alliance of interests between the two leading Catholic powers was probably the last thing a second-rank state like Savoy would wish, for while the strategy of playing France and Spain against each other was inherently risky, it at least increased Savoy's leverage in north Italy. Dudley Carleton certainly seems to have understood this danger when he wrote that 'the duke of Savoy adviseth, that either England should pacify with Spain or by seeming so to do, to divert further treaty between Spain and France not doubting but that Spain will prefer the amity of England before France'.[39]

Leganés' diplomatic initiative understandably slowed the progress of the Anglo-Spanish peace talks over the summer of 1627, especially as the regime in Madrid seemingly put obstacles in the way of Gerbier, Rubens

was under secret instruction to prevent the renewal treaty while reassuring the Dutch that they would not be excluded from the Anglo-Spanish talks. AST LMI m. 4, 29, Scaglia to Carlo Emanuele I, 13 September 1627; 41, Scaglia to Carlo Emanuele I, 26 September 1627; 43, Scaglia to Carlo Emanuele I, 27 September 1627; BL Add. MS 36,778, ff. 3v–6v, copy of secret instructions for Carleton, May 1627; CSPV 1626–8, pp. 405–6, 414–15.

[37] AST LMI m. 4, 41, Scaglia to Carlo Emanuele I, 26 September 1627; Max Rooses and C. Ruelens (eds.), *Correspondance de Rubens et documents épistolaires concernant sa vie et ses œuvres*, 6 vols. (Antwerp, 1887–1909), IV, pp. 130–1; William Noel Sainsbury (ed.), *Original Unpublished Papers Illustrative of the Life of Sir Peter Paul Rubens, as an Artist and a Diplomat* (London, 1859), p. 98.

[38] Gachard, *Histoire politique*, p. 62.

[39] AST LMI m. 4, 41, Scaglia to Carlo Emanuele I, 26 September 1627; PRO SP 84/134/224, Carleton to Conway, 17 September 1627.

and Scaglia, effectively ejecting the abate from the Spanish Netherlands, while failing to acknowledge Rubens as a viable mediator. But equally, the English naval expedition to La Rochelle at the same time delayed the parallel French discussions. Scaglia knew that he would have to return to London in person to press for either an Anglo-French or an Anglo-Spanish peace, whichever was more expedient. A diplomatic mission to England had in fact been expected for some time. In a flattering assessment of his character, the Venetian secretary in Turin wrote in July 1627 that Scaglia's mission was being hastened because he was excellently informed of current affairs, that he was sagacious, adroit and esteemed for his virtues, and most importantly that he enjoyed the greatest credit with Charles I and Buckingham.[40] The mission was deliberately delayed. While the English were willing to provide Scaglia with a vessel for his journey across the Channel, publicly signalling the esteem in which he was held in London, the abate chose not to make use of it and instead remained in The Hague, still without any formal diplomatic credentials from Carlo Emanuele I (though it would have been difficult for a Catholic prince like Carlo Emanuele I to have accredited Scaglia to the United Provinces). He himself claimed that he needed to remain in the Low Countries to sustain England's various peace talks there, even though they had lost their forward momentum – apparently, if he were to leave too hastily then those talks, or at least his involvement in them, would be jeopardised. The Venetian ambassador in London had a different interpretation. Scaglia was delaying his journey to thwart all other peace initiatives in London save those of his 'master', the duke of Savoy. Buckingham, after all, was with the English fleet at La Rochelle, and his absence from London would correspondingly have weakened Scaglia's own hand in England's diplomacy. It was not until late 1627 that the abate finally arrived at the Caroline court.[41]

An important question behind Savoyard diplomacy after Monzón, embodied in Scaglia's missions, concerns the point at which its overarching aim shifted from seeking to regain France's support (on Savoy's terms) by coercion and increasing diplomatic contact with Spain to positively endorsing an Anglo-Spanish settlement as an end in itself. The abate's experience before Monzón of working solely with France and its anti-Habsburg allies, in the context of his family's established francophile reputation, would certainly have made the shift towards the Habsburgs all the more significant for him as an individual courtier. It is true that there

---

[40] CSPV 1626–8, pp. 274–5.
[41] CSPD 1627–8, p. 324; CSPV 1626–8, p. 342. See also HMC Eleventh Report, appendix, part I, pp. 125, 128.

was a gradual change in emphasis through this period. The treaty of Monzón provided the initial impetus for a shift away from France, while Alessandro Scaglia's increasing contact with the Spanish during 1627, which ironically began as part of a policy of improving relations with France, further affected his diplomatic perceptions and the way he was himself perceived in the courts of London, Paris and Madrid. But also, the Anglo-French and the Anglo-Spanish negotiations were intimately bound with one another, and Scaglia showed an equal interest in both. At such an uncertain and finely balanced political moment, Scaglia could not afford to neglect either set of discussions, even if it was not entirely clear as to which war he wanted settled.

Scaglia arrived at the English court in November 1627 on the pretext of returning Walter Montagu's visit to Turin, and with open instructions to encourage English merchants to use the Savoyard port of Nice-Villafranca, a policy he had been pursuing throughout 1627 with merchants in both France and the Dutch Republic as well.[42] Once again these were nothing more than secondary issues to the main question of the concurrent Anglo-French and Spanish peace negotiations. By travelling to London, the abate aimed to reinforce both his connections with various influential courtiers and his own political standing with the Caroline court as a viable diplomatic mediator. Since the time of his first – and very brief – visit to London in January 1626, the abate had cultivated and preserved a very favoured status with the English. This was of first importance to the style of diplomacy he embodied. It was largely through his relationship with the English regime under the direction of Buckingham that Scaglia sought to stake his claim to involvement in negotiations with France and Spain. This special status was publicly maintained when he reached the English capital. On the day of his arrival in London the abate was met first by Lord North and then by the earl of Carlisle, who voluntarily fetched him for a dinner at court that evening. John Finet, with his incessant concern for 'correct' diplomatic procedure, was led to comment on this 'supererogatory courtesy of his lordship, and an irregularity of all precedent (when a baron, not an earl should have discharged that part for a duke's ambassador)'.[43] The Venetian ambassador in London, Alvise Contarini, later reported that Scaglia was granted access to the private apartments of the king, as a private gentleman rather than a public

[42] For example PRO SP 92/13/25–7v, copy of instructions to Scaglia regarding free trade at Nice, Villafranca and S. Ospitio, 26 March 1627; AST LMI m. 4, 50, Scaglia to Carlo Emanuele I, 7 November 1627; CSPV 1626–8, pp. 473, 498. The projects to encourage maritime trade of course reflected Carlo Emanuele I's long-standing ambition to overcome the limitations of his essentially land-locked patrimony.
[43] John Finet, *Finetti Philoxenis* (London, 1656), p. 231; CSPV 1626–8, pp. 445–6.

minister, favouritism that went far beyond the usual custom for all foreign diplomats.[44]

As ever, the abate's principal ally – his closest political friend – was the duke of Buckingham. Scaglia's ability to affect in any way the course of English diplomacy was to a great extent dependent on his personal relationship with the duke. Soon after arriving in the English capital Scaglia wrote to Buckingham, knowing full well that in the duke's absence his own influence in London was considerably diminished.[45] Buckingham returned to London in the winter of 1627, and although relations between the two were later put under pressure when in January 1628 Scaglia was involved in the Purbeck incident, the friendship remained firm. An English correspondent sympathetic to France remarked in a letter to Richelieu that the dukes of Savoy and Lorraine had a high standing in London, 'especially Savoy, who has an expert diplomat here; to tell the truth he is too well established and wins all arguments... he has a great amount of credit with the duke'.[46] Alessandro Scaglia also looked to another of his English friends, the earl of Carlisle, for diplomatic support – in a letter to the earl, Rubens later described the abate as his 'great friend and servant'.[47] It had been Carlisle, to whom the abate had been introduced on his arrival at the French court in 1624, who had invited Scaglia to London for his first mission in 1626, and who had accompanied the abate to the court on his second mission. In turn the abate hoped to exploit this friendship by encouraging Carlisle to undertake a mission to Savoy. The earl had already been planning a trip to Lorraine in the autumn of 1627, and Scaglia hoped that he might go from there to Turin with necessary powers to treat for a peace with France or Spain, even though he was less than sympathetic to Spain, if the Venetian ambassador Contarini is to be believed. Whatever Carlisle's affiliations, if he were to obtain the authority in journeying to Turin then Savoy's role in the peace process would clearly be enhanced, and at the very least the mission would create more suspicion and fear in Paris.[48]

---

[44] Finet, *Finetti Philoxenis*, p. 231; CSPV 1626–8, pp. 445, 545. Contarini added here that this informal access to the royal apartments was eventually restricted to the antechamber.

[45] PRO SP 78/82/175, Scaglia to Buckingham, 16 November 1627; CSPV 1626–8, pp. 446–7, 499. Salvetti described Buckingham as Scaglia's 'oracle'. HMC Eleventh Report, appendix, part I, p. 132.

[46] AAE CP Angleterre 42, f. 269, Forster to Richelieu, 17 May 1628.

[47] Rooses and Ruelens (eds.), *Correspondance*, V, p. 24.

[48] AST LMI m. 4, 64, Scaglia to Carlo Emanuele I, 14 December 1627; CSPV 1626–8, pp. 353, 520–1, 531.

While the abate had devoted most of the summer of 1627 to the Spanish element of his diplomatic strategy – the aim of which was clearly to exert pressure on Richelieu – the possibility of a French peace before one with Spain continued to demand at least some of his attention in London. There was always the need for the abate to remain vigilant about Anglo-French relations, and furthermore to remain publicly supportive of a settlement, not least because ambassadors from the Venetian Republic and Denmark were themselves trying to take control of the mediation process. Scaglia could not let the peace talks pass into the hands of other representatives driven by their own diplomatic agendas.[49] But Anglo-French diplomatic relations had in effect been sidelined during the English naval expedition to La Rochelle through the summer and autumn of that year. Even the ignominious retreat from the Isle of Rhé in late October 1627 and Buckingham's return to London ostensibly did little to clarify the state of confused uncertainty. The news of the French victory was greeted in the Savoyard capital of Turin with formal public rejoicing, as was no doubt expected from a Catholic court that had dynastic relations with the Bourbons. Cannons were fired from the city's fortress while fireworks were discharged from Cardinal Maurizio's residence at the Vigna; the courier who bore the news was handsomely rewarded by Marie Christine and a *Te Deum* was appropriately celebrated in the cathedral. In his consternation the English ambassador Isaac Wake, who had generally viewed Carlo Emanuele I positively, wrote back to London that the duke has 'hitherto outgone all the princes of Italy in their expressions of joy for our loss'. He added, '[L]et Abate Scaglia put what colours he can upon it in England. I shall always hold it as an excess of preposterous flattery.'[50] In the face of such celebrations, the wider diplomatic effect of England's military setback was, however, far from clear. The defeat certainly might have entailed a withdrawal of direct English support from the beleaguered Huguenots and a settlement with France, a possibility that Scaglia understood and Rubens, looking on from the Spanish Netherlands, feared. Significantly however both Charles I and the duke of Buckingham continued to express a commitment to supporting the duke of Rohan and the besieged Protestant community at La Rochelle, and almost immediately after the retreat plans were in place for yet another naval expedition. In language that mirrored Scaglia's own, the king and favourite made clear their aspiration to uphold the 'common

---

[49] For example, AST LMI m. 4, 45, Scaglia to Carlo Emanuele I, 7 November 1627; 63, Scaglia to Carlo Emanuele I, 29 November 1627.

[50] BL Add. MS 34,311, f. 135v, Wake to Conway, 3 December 1627; ff. 136v–7, Wake to Conway, 16 December 1627; CSPV 1626–8, p. 513.

cause', but that it was necessary to apply force against France to do so. As 1627 drew to a close the prospect of a definite Anglo-French peace seemed as distant as ever.[51]

This did little to deter the abate. He indeed continued to play his public role as a willing mediator between the two crowns, though he could afford to do so precisely because he knew that a settlement was not close at hand so long as the Huguenot revolt continued and Buckingham was willing to support it.[52] Late in 1627, Scaglia became involved in yet another initiative to broker a peace between the two crowns.[53] The pretext for the renewal of informal talks was the release of the French secretary and confidant of Richelieu, Launay-Rasilly, who had been imprisoned in London in 1626 as peace between England and France had broken down. Late in December 1627 both Buckingham and Scaglia had meetings with him in which they spoke of the state of relations between the two crowns.[54] On 1 February 1628, Launay-Rasilly returned to Paris with messages from Scaglia to the king of France and Richelieu, where the abate expressed his hope that the French were not implacably opposed to him, and his wish (and that of the duke of Savoy) to serve them in the interests of so-called 'public affairs'. Playing upon his perceived importance as a mediator, Scaglia added that he knew the true state of English affairs from confidants close to Buckingham and that the Anglo-French war could be resolved quickly once the Huguenot problem was settled. The response from Paris was not unfavourable. Perhaps surprisingly Richelieu allowed the possibility of the talks to continue by not rejecting them out of hand, while Scaglia heard from his francophile brother, Augusto Manfredo Scaglia, that the French seemed willing for him to operate as a mediator.[55]

Alessandro Scaglia's continuing involvement in peace talks with France was by no means universally supported in London. The Venetian and Danish representatives there were from the start less impressed by the

---

[51] AST LMI m. 4, 56, Scaglia to Carlo Emanuele I, 21 November 1627; 80, Scaglia to Carlo Emanuele I, 5 February 1628; Sainsbury, *Unpublished Papers,* p. 106; Gardiner, *History*, VI, pp. 220–2; Lockyer, *Buckingham*, p. 404.

[52] As Scaglia wrote in discussing his offers to Charles I for a Savoyard mediated suspension of arms, 'I find the king full of affection and esteem towards you, but very far from conceding this suspension.' AST LMI m. 4, 56, Scaglia to Carlo Emanuele I, 21 November 1627.

[53] AAE CP Angleterre, 42, f. 221, memorial of Launay-Rasilly, 1 February 1628; f. 223v, Scaglia to ?, 1628.

[54] AST LMI m. 4, 70, Scaglia to Carlo Emanuele I, 28 December 1627.

[55] AAE CP Angleterre, 42, ff. 219–21v, memorial of Launay-Rasilly, 1 February 1628; ff. 222–v, Scaglia to Verrua, 1628; ff. 223–4, Scaglia to ?, February 1628; f. 225, Scaglia to ?, 1628; ff. 226–7, Scaglia to 'monsieur', 5 April 1628; Richelieu, *Mémoires,* VI, pp. 44–7.

abate's declared wish to mediate. Like Scaglia, they too were seeking to mediate a peace involving England, no doubt to further the interests of their home states who were certainly more unequivocal in their hostility to Spain. But given his known involvement with the concurrent Spanish negotiations, Scaglia seemed more of a threat, despite his claims that his sovereign prince still inclined to a settlement.[56] The Venetian ordinary ambassador, Alvise Contarini, thought that in coming to England the abate was in actuality set on creating trouble for Cardinal Richelieu – Scaglia had brought 'fire rather than water' to the French peace negotiations, and the Venetian added that the service rendered by the abate to Charles I and Buckingham was no less great than the disservice rendered to the 'common cause'.[57] Contarini believed that Carlo Emanuele I was willing to fight France if England wished, but that correspondingly he did not want to be excluded from their peace talks. The Venetian's revealing conclusion was that Scaglia believed that the time for the 'public cause' – the anti-Habsburg coalition – had come and gone. The abate was no longer concerned with opposing Spain as a policy in itself because the opportunity to do so had been squandered with the treaty of Monzón. The Venetian representatives in Turin and Paris went further, claiming that Scaglia wanted to prolong the Anglo-French war specifically to improve Savoy's diplomatic hand in any negotiation for peace.[58]

If proof were needed that Scaglia, and the duke of Savoy by association, were covertly undermining Richelieu then it was revealed following Montagu's dramatic seizure by the French in November 1627 as he was returning from Turin. The arrest of an accredited ambassador travelling to or from a formally recognised embassy was rare, even where the ambassador was known to be hostile to the state through which he was passing. However, Montagu had travelled not as an officially accredited ambassador but only as a courier, making him vulnerable despite the facts that in theory he still had some 'legal' protection and that he had even been apprehended outside French sovereign territory proper, in the duchy of

---

[56] AST LMI m. 4, 64, Scaglia to Carlo Emanuele I, 14 December 1627. There is a relevant contemporary parallel to the diplomatic rivalry between Scaglia and the Venetian and Dutch representatives; when the English ambassador Thomas Roe was despatched in 1629 to mediate between Gustavus Adolphus and the Poles in part to free the Swedish king so that he could intervene in Europe, Roe found that the French ambassador to Sweden, Hercule de Charnacé, had already begun mediating. The subsequent friction between the two ambassadors was no doubt because each felt that he was better placed to negotiate and because each was attentive to his particular state's interests. Strachan, *Sir Thomas Roe*, chapter 12.

[57] CSPV 1626–8, pp. 445–7.

[58] CSPV 1626–8, pp. 473, 334–5. What is noticeably absent from Scaglia's comment is any willingness to state that Savoy would fight against Spain.

Lorraine. Following his capture and the seizure of his correspondence Walter Montagu was taken to the Bastille, where only the personal intercessions of Marie de' Medici were said to have saved him from torture. Quite understandably he had been suspected of being involved in some cabal against Richelieu. It had, after all, become one of Scaglia's aims to put the cardinal under pressure through his mission. Remarkably, the abate seems to have underplayed the significance of Montagu's arrest when he wrote to Carlo Emanuele I that it concerned him only to the extent that there would be a delay in the movement of correspondence between London and Turin. But nevertheless it provided Richelieu with a powerful means of seeking the truth behind Scaglia's 'fair words' and of embarrassing those powers who had been involved in his negotiations – Savoy, England, Lorraine and the duke of Rohan.[59]

Among the documents seized by the French was a letter from Duke Carlo Emanuele I to Scaglia, ciphers from the count of Verrua to his brother and, importantly, a copy of Montagu's written pledge regarding Savoy's involvement in the Anglo-French talks. Evidence was also produced that Montagu had discussed a project for uniting the exiled count of Soissons, Rohan (as leader of the Huguenots), the duke of Savoy and the duke of Lorraine in a concerted effort against Cardinal Richelieu. Troops would be raised to mount an attack on different fronts against France, with Soissons invading from Savoy through the Dauphiné in the south-east. Meanwhile, Duke Carlo Emanuele I would continue to support English diplomatic efforts for reducing Richelieu's power. In his intercepted letter to the abate, Carlo Emanuele I instructed Scaglia to discuss a French peace if the English wanted one, but also to declare Savoy's support if the English wished to pursue war. It is equally telling that he was also instructed to indicate that there would be no Savoyard military action in conjunction with England against Spain. The duke would provide nothing more than a financial subsidy in the event of the continuation of the Anglo-Spanish war.[60]

Alessandro Scaglia was as usual involved in simultaneous diplomacy with both major powers, as he had been since the treaty of Monzón

[59] CSPV 1626–8, pp. 489, 529; AST LMI m. 4, 70, Scaglia to Carlo Emanuele I, 28 December 1627; AST LMF m. 27, fasc. 5, 9, Moretta to Carlo Emanuele I, September 1627; Gardiner, *History*, VI, p. 218. The legal status of both diplomatic representatives and couriers during the period before the writers Hugo Grotius and Abraham de Wicquefort (which was by no means clear) deserves an up-to-date study. The only existing work seems to be E. R. Adair, *The Extraterritoriality of Ambasssadors in the Sixteenth and Seventeenth Centuries* (London, 1929).

[60] AAE CP Angleterre, 42, ff. 116–7, Carlo Emanuele I to Scaglia, 5 November 1627, 'prise avec Montagu'; f. 119v, copy of a promise made by Charles I to Carlo Emanuele I; CSPV 1626–8, pp. 526–7.

in March 1626. Drawing conclusions from the period between Monzón and 1628 indeed seems far from easy. Savoy had been let down by France, and the abate seems to have believed that France, under the direction of Richelieu, had even let itself down. But rather than standing back as a passive observer, Scaglia sought to reverse the damage that he thought had been done by Monzón by embarking on a subtle strategy of altering the direction of French foreign policy. He could not necessarily achieve this by direct means but he could significantly increase his political influence by drawing on the power of his English friends. It was England that represented the key to much of his diplomacy because of the certainty that London would eventually sue for peace with either Paris or Madrid. If there was consistency anywhere then it was here. Throughout his mission in London the abate acted according to his signature style of pragmatic diplomacy. He advocated an Anglo-French peace, knowing that on one level it was not very likely given the continuation of the Huguenot revolt and the willingness of the English, under Buckingham's guidance, to support it. At the same time he tried to revitalise negotiations for a Spanish settlement, even though some ministers in Madrid seemed reluctant to endorse Savoy's mediation (to which even he himself was not then entirely committed). That neither of the negotiations was concluded during 1627 was arguably of less importance to the abate than the very fact that he was involved in the concurrent talks. Through his mediation, Scaglia could work to secure the interests of the duke of Savoy as the fortunes of international relations changed.

This two-year period of intense negotiations raises a wider question about the way in which diplomatic history is generally considered. In retrospect the immediate and understandable temptation is to focus on the measurable products of diplomatic negotiations, such as treaties and alliances, while giving less weight to the kinds of dead-end discussions engaged by Scaglia. The period between the treaty of Monzón and the Gonzaga succession dispute does not however fit neatly into this conception, and what makes the period so intriguing and important in equal measure is that there were few concrete results in relation to the sheer intensity of diplomatic activity. The fluidity of international affairs in the two years after Monzón meant that policy-makers had to respond to events and take a variety of diplomatic precautions without necessarily staking all their interests on them. Indeed, Scaglia's participation in two contradictory sets of peace negotiations allowed him to retain a high degree of flexibility precisely so that he could act as circumstances demanded. It would nevertheless be wrong to conclude that this was the sum total of his diplomacy. Behind the obfuscating smoke screen of dissimulation and contradictory discussions was a more coherent conception of what should be done in relation to France and Spain. There was an implicit understanding that Scaglia, operating with the complete support of the duke of Savoy and in turn affecting the direction of Savoyard policies, could influence the shape of events by attaching himself to England. France and Spain were quite evidently the most powerful states in Europe, but they were not the only ones, and given that their affairs were so vulnerable to change in a period of great uncertainty, the influence of the secondary states of England and Savoy was magnified.

Scaglia initially sought to revive an alliance with the French, though one that would prove more reliable for Savoy. He did not simply drop all commitments to France in favour of whatever alternative option appeared, but initially sought to coax Richelieu into constancy towards his allies. But the methods Scaglia employed, of combining threats with offers, had in turn a curious effect. His involvement in anti-Richelieu activity understandably influenced their relationship, making the abate's participation in Anglo-French talks all the more complicated, while his contact with the Spanish Habsburgs in Brussels also changed the way in which he thought Savoy should operate in the international arena. As the Spanish enjoyed military successes in Europe so the need for his home state to stand well with Madrid took on greater importance, even if Philip IV's ministers were initially less forthcoming. More strongly, the effect of contacting and maintaining a contact with the Spanish, in conjunction with the abate's changing attitudes to Richelieu, also began to draw the abate away from unequivocal support of France towards a pro-Habsburg position. This subtle shift did not take place at a uniform speed; as circumstances and pragmatism required, the abate oscillated from one side to the other and it is this that makes understanding the period of intense diplomacy after Monzón ostensibly so difficult. The transition of Scaglia's political affinities away from unequivocal support of France was not fully resolved until the beginning of 1628. What finally untangled the ambiguities in his diplomacy and those of his home state were the dynastic politics of north Italy. On the 26 December 1627 Duke Vincenzo II of Mantua and Monferrato died and Savoy once again embarked on a war to satisfy unresolved territorial ambitions in the region.

PART III

THE WAR FOR MANTUA AND MONFERRATO, 1628–1632

5

THE WAR, 1628–1631

The treaty of Monzón forced a reconsideration of Savoy's strategic priorities and its relations with the two leading powers of France and Spain. With the scaling down of Carlo Emanuele I's immediate ambitions on Zuccarello, linked as it was to an alignment with France, the duke shifted his attention to another potential source of unfulfilled territorial gain, Monferrato. As ever, if one set of territorial or dynastic interests stalled then the duke of Savoy could always replace it with another legitimate claim, thanks to the sheer variety of claims and the fact that so many were still open to juridical dispute. The fundamental importance of dynastic interest to Savoy was that it could be reactivated when appropriate opportunities arose (something that itself has contributed to Carlo Emanuele's reputation for political inconstancy). The confluence of circumstance and dynastic accident had brought the issue of the duchies of Mantua and Monferrato back onto the international agenda after Monzón, and at the instigation of Savoy and with the involvement of the leading powers, the issue of succession to the duchies rapidly became a critically important problem of European dimensions.

Well before 1627 the linked duchies of Mantua and Monferrato showed that they had an explosive political power that could resonate not only within the peninsula but also throughout Europe. In 1615 France and Spain came close to open war over the territories when Duke Carlo Emanuele I had invaded Monferrato following the death of his son-in-law.[1] Crucial to the problem of the twin duchies - one might say to many

---

[1] The most detailed guide to the complexities of Mantua and Monferrato before the war is still Quazza, *Mantova e Monferrato*. For the period of the war itself Quazza, *La guerra per la successione* is absolutely essential, although it relies almost entirely on Mantuan archives. One dated and limited study that does employ some Italian and non-Italian archives is Reade, *Sidelights*, III. David Parrott has completed two important articles that clarify a number of issues about Mantua and Monferrato and their traditions of succession, especially for Anglophone audiences, 'The Mantuan Succession', and, with

regional disputes in early modern Europe – was the contested issue of dynastic succession, even though each had its own customs of inheritance. Primogeniture has come to be seen as the most obvious method of passing on hereditary territorial possessions, but this was by no means universally true in early modern Europe, and north Italy in particular. Successive rulers of the duchy of Mantua (rather than Monferrato) exercised partible inheritance where land was apportioned among a number of legitimate offspring rather than passed to the eldest male individual alone. By the end of the sixteenth century the practical consequences of partible inheritance in Mantua were clear, with the existence of several smaller sovereign territories, among them the duchy of Guastalla, the principality of Bozzolo and the principality of Sabbionetta, each one ruled by cadet branches of the main House of Gonzaga.[2] By its nature partible inheritance excluded clear-cut single claims to entire hereditary possessions, favouring instead multiple claims to parcels of land, and there were consequently good opportunities for a variety of claimants to obtain recompense, whether territorial or financial, at the moments of dynastic succession, more obviously so in the event of successions that were contested. North Italy, like other regions juridically encompassed by the Holy Roman Empire, was marked by the relative fluidity of territorial possessions. Different claimants with varying arguments could increase their holdings and change the extent of their states, not necessarily by blatant military conquest which in any case was generally frowned upon, but within more acceptable (but in practice no less divisive) legal and dynastic frameworks.[3]

As a result of the custom of partible inheritance in Mantua alone, there were two significant claimants to the duchy from cadet branches of the Gonzaga House. Of the two, the better placed was Carlo Gonzaga, the duke of Nevers (1580–1637). He was descended from the younger son of Federico II (1500–40) and Margherita, through which he could claim a right to the hereditary possessions of both Mantua and Monferrato in the

---

Robert Oresko, 'The sovereignty of Monferrato', in Ferari and Quondam (eds.), *Stefano Guazzo*. See also David Parrott, 'The Mantuan Succession and the Thirty Years' War', in Bussmann and Schilling (eds.), *1648*.

[2] Parrott, 'The Mantuan Succession', 26–7.

[3] On the persistence of partible inheritance in the Holy Roman Empire see P. S. Fichtner, *Protestantism and Primogeniture in Early Modern Germany* (New Haven and London, 1989), and for some examples of comparable noble dynastic strategies within Savoy see Woolf, *Studi sulla nobiltà*. For some case studies of territorial acquisition by sovereigns within legal frameworks in early modern Europe see Mark Greengrass (ed.), *Conquest and Coalescence: The Shaping of the State in Early Modern Europe* (London, 1991).

absence of a direct male heir. His position was undoubtedly complicated by the facts not only that he was a sovereign prince in his own right but that he was also a fief holder of the king of France. His ducal title and that of his son Charles (1609–31) the duke of Rethel were inherited from his parents, Ludovico Gonzaga (1539–85), a *prince étranger* at the French court, and Henriette de Clèves. Many historians (and perhaps some contemporaries too) have tended to take this French connection at face value, assuming that the duke of Nevers was automatically submissive to Louis XIII, and explaining his subsequent alignment with France during the succession war at a stroke. His relationship with the French had in truth been marked by friction. He had been involved in the disputes between Marie de' Medici and Louis XIII during the king's minority, and up to the very point of the war for the succession of Mantua and Monferrato it was to a degree unclear as to whether he would actually work with or against Richelieu, especially given the uncertainty over France's relations with his prime dynastic rival, Savoy, prior to 1628.[4] The other main claimant to Mantua was Ferrante II (d. 1630), duke of Guastalla, who came from a different cadet branch of the Gonzaga. He was the son of Cesare (1533–75), prince of Guastalla and descendant of the brother of Federico II, and who was himself the sovereign of what had been a portion of the Mantuan patrimony divided at the end of the sixteenth century.[5]

Monferrato, in contrast to Mantua, had the status of a *feudo feminino*, and this provided the basis for the claim of the House of Savoy to that duchy alone. Duke Carlo Emanuele I repeatedly argued that female succession was by historical precedent permissible in Monferrato, underpinned by the marriages of Aimone, count of Savoy, to Iolanda, daughter of Teodoro Paleologo, marquis of Monferrato, in 1330 and Duke Carlo I to Bianca, daughter of Guglielmo VI Paleologo, in 1485. Savoy's claim to Monferrato, or portions of the duchy, was never clearly settled either way, something that was complicated still further by the fact that the dowry from Carlo I's marriage (with the growing interest that accrued from it), was not paid. Emperor Charles V, as overlord, did not fully settle the matter, leaving the duchy with a claim that could be reactivated, and in 1587 Emperor Rudolf indeed judged that Savoy's claim was still valid. Moreover, Savoy's interest in Monferrato was bolstered by the marriage in 1608

---

[4] For a detailed study of the political affinities of Nevers see David Parrott, 'A *Prince Souverain* and the French crown: Carlo de Nevers, 1580–1637', in Gibbs, Oresko and Scott (eds.), *Royal and Republican Sovereignty*; Parrott, 'The Mantuan Succession', 32.

[5] *Ibid.*, 30, for some background information to Guastalla's dynastic interests.

of Margherita, one of Carlo Emanuele I's daughters, to Francesco IV, who ruled as duke of Mantua and Monferrato in 1612 until his untimely death in the same year.[6] However, the possibility of female succession in Monferrato which provided Carlo Emanuele I with his interest also opened the way to other claimants. Both the Holy Roman Empress Eleonora Gonzaga (1598–1655) and Margherita Gonzaga (1591–1632), duchess of Lorraine, were themselves sisters of Francesco IV of Mantua and Monferrato with their own potential claims and concerns, as members of the Gonzaga House, to keep the inheritance of both Mantua and Monferrato intact.[7]

While Mantua and Monferrato, with their different patterns of succession, had the potential to destabilise north Italy there was also a European dimension to the territorial problem. The two Catholic super powers of France and Spain had long considered Mantua and Monferrato, like much of northern Italy, to be of crucial strategic and symbolic significance to their own ruling dynasties. In the first place both duchies were situated in a geographically sensitive position, between the Italian peninsula and the rest of Europe. The fortresses of the ducal capital of Mantua and Casale (in Monferrato) were strongpoints upon which movement through the region depended.[8] Secondly and more broadly, the long-standing dynastic and strategic rivalries between the House of France and the Habsburgs over the Italian peninsula that dated back to the late fifteenth century meant that neither side felt able to stand back during moments of tension between Italian states. Mantua and Monferrato, like indeed Savoy, had the inherent potential of drawing the leading Catholic powers into a general war precisely because of the region's traditional position as the battlefield between the Houses of France and Spain, even if at given times they were reluctant to do so. Indeed, the ever-present danger that north Italy as a region might cause a major European conflagration had already been demonstrated twice in the seventeenth century, in the dispute between France and Savoy over Saluzzo in 1600 and in the previous Mantuan succession crisis following the death of

---

[6] Litta, *Celebri famiglie Italiane*, 'Duchi di Savoia', table VII (Milan, 1841), and 'Paleologo, Marchesi di Monferrato', tables I–II (Milan, 1847). Guichenon, *Histoire généalogique*, I, p. 645; Capriata, *Wars of Italy*, pp. 7–9. See also Parrott, 'The Mantuan Succession', 32–3, and footnote 14 in Parrott and Oresko, 'The sovereignty of Monferrato', in Ferari and Quondam (eds.), *Stefano Guazzo*.

[7] Litta, *Celebri famiglie Italiane*, 'Gonzaga, Duchi di Mantova', table VI (Milan, 1835); Capriata, *Wars of Italy*, p. 352.

[8] On the importance of Casale consult Parrott and Oresko, 'The sovereignty of Monferrato', in Ferari and Quondam (eds.), *Stefano Guazzo*.

Francesco IV[9]. The problem was moreover explicitly addressed in a secret clause of the treaty of Monzón where both France and Spain agreed not to give support to any Italian state in a regional dispute without prior mutual consultation.[10] Last, though by no means least, Mantua and Monferrato were both under the legal jurisdiction of the Emperor as Imperial fiefs. The practical consequences of this were not always made clear, not least because the actual extent of his jurisdiction in the Italian peninsula remained ill-defined into the seventeenth century, but the Emperor was in a position to intervene in dynastic and territorial disputes as feudal overlord, a power that was more than theoretical as rival claimants could and did turn to Vienna for arbitration or action if they felt aggrieved.[11]

These dynastic, strategic and legal issues were brought together into sharp focus by the unexpected accession of Duke Vincenzo II (d. 1627) to the two duchies in October 1626, hardly the ideal candidate to assume the throne. When he succeeded his heirless brother Ferdinando I, Vincenzo II was himself childless despite the fact that he had been married to Isabella of Novellara-Bozzolo since 1616. Isabella was able to bear children – she had had five by her previous marriage – but the failure of the ducal couple to produce a legitimate heir after ten years of marriage was deeply alarming, more so because Isabella herself was already in her forties when she had married Vincenzo II.[12] Increasingly desperate to secure his line's succession, Vincenzo II had already tried in vain to have his marriage annulled even before he came into possession of the two duchies, so that he could take another bride. His challenge to the legitimacy of his own marriage, added to the fact that Isabella had fled to Rome in the wake of her estranged husband's actions, opened the way to a predictable succession dispute and an equally predictable international crisis.[13] To make matters worse, the health of the new but aging duke was all too frail from the very outset of his reign. As early as April 1627 the English secretary in Turin wrote an alarming report back to London that 'notwithstanding that the duke of Mantua doth seem outwardly to recover his health, yet is the inward state of his body so decayed, as much time cannot pass, but that out of necessity he must yield'. He added

[9] Quazza, *Mantova e Monferrato*, chapter 1.

[10] Dumont (ed.), *Corps universel diplomatique*, V, part II, p. 489.

[11] For some examples see Parrott, 'The Mantuan Succession', 29–30.   [12] *Ibid.*, 37.

[13] See the comments by Isaac Wake, BL Add. MS 34,311, ff. 79v–81v, Wake to Conway, 12 March 1627. It should be added that Duke Vincenzo II had in fact fathered a number of illegitimate offspring, though they were barred from the succession. Quazza, *Mantova e Monferrato*, chapter 4; Litta, *Celebri famiglie Italiane*, 'Duchi di Mantova', table VI (Milan, 1835).

ominously that Carlo Emanuele I was readying his troops for a possible dynastic war.[14] For their parts, the dukes of both Guastalla and Nevers, two principal claimants, began to angle for their own settlements to the impending dispute as 1627 wore on. Guastalla, whose Habsburg connections were already well established, repeatedly sent envoys to the courts in Madrid and Vienna to win the support of the twin Habsburg Houses. The ambitious duke of Nevers also began to make his own preparations by opening discussions in Paris with Alessandro Scaglia, as Duke Carlo Emanuele I's accredited representative there. In December 1626 Nevers had already implied that he was willing to resolve the potential succession question with Carlo Emanuele I, and possibly without the involvement of other parties, referring in all probability to Guastalla.[15]

The genuineness of Nevers' diplomatic advances must be questioned. His apparent willingness to acknowledge the Savoyard interest did not lead to any settlement of the issue, and if anything he soon began to retreat from his earlier position of advocating an accommodation with his powerful dynastic rival, Carlo Emanuele I.[16] The duke of Savoy on the other hand was adamantly unwilling to let the matter of a disputed succession pass without some claim to Monferrato, as was no doubt his responsibility to his own family's interests as a dynastic claimant. Abate Scaglia had already made an offer in March 1627 to the Spanish through the Infanta Isabella for a separate arrangement to divide Mantua and Monferrato during the Anglo-Spanish negotiations between Gerbier and Rubens in Brussels. Even if in itself this might have been an extravagant suggestion, possibly with an eye to improving relations between Turin and Madrid as part of Scaglia's post-Mónzon diplomatic strategy, it was not made without a genuine belief that his sovereign prince should obtain something from a disputed succession given his dynasty's legitimate claims for either territorial or financial compensation. This conviction was eventually put to paper on Christmas Day 1627, marking the extent to which Savoy and

---

[14] PRO SP 92/13/30–v, Hales to Conway, 12 April 1627. Indeed, within two months of the accession of Vincenzo II, the Florentine agent in Paris stated that the new duke was not expected to live long. AST LMF m. 27, fasc. 1, 278, Scaglia to Carlo Emanuele I, late December 1626. See also LMF m. 28, fasc. 6, 60, Scaglia to Carlo Emanuele I, 8 March 1627.

[15] Quazza, *Mantova e Monferrato*, chapter 5; AST LMF m. 27, 257, Scaglia to Carlo Emanuele I, 18 December 1626. On Guastalla's Habsburg connections see the footnote in Elliott and de la Peña (eds.), *Memoriales y cartas*, II, p. 27, and Parrott, 'The Mantuan Succession', 44. In fact, a year before the talks with Scaglia, Nevers had sent his son to Mantua to secure a stronger bargaining position in the event of a succession crisis. Parrott, 'A *prince souverain*', in Oresko, Gibbs and Scott (eds.), *Royal and Republican Sovereignty*, p. 172.

[16] AST LMF m. 28, fasc. 6, 25, Scaglia to Carlo Emanuele I, 11 February 1627; 60, Scaglia to Carlo Emanuele I, 8 March 1627.

Spain had realigned themselves from positions of distant hostility over the course of 1627. Carlo Emanuele I signed a military agreement with Don Gonzalo de Córdoba, the governor of Milan, where Savoy would occupy portions of Monferrato while Córdoba would take control of Mantua and the fortress of Casale in Monferrato.[17] The alliance was a clear indication that force would be used to obtain at least some of the dynastic claim (if not its entirety) while at the same time maintaining Spain's regional influence.

While Carlo Emanuele I prepared for a possible military solution to the dynastic crisis, the duke of Nevers sought to strengthen his bargaining position. Only hours before the death of Vincenzo II, Nevers' son and heir, the duke of Rethel, married Maria (1609–60), daughter of the last-but-one duke of Mantua and Monferrato, effectively initiating a *coup d'état*. On the future of the princess and her marital status a considerable part of the dynastic problem turned. She was a member of the main branch of the Gonzaga family, the granddaughter of the duke of Savoy and the niece of the Holy Roman Empress Eleonora Gonzaga, as well as a leading claimant in her own right to Monferrato because of its individual custom of female succession. Her importance had indeed been recognised for some time; before her marriage to Rethel her hand had already been sought by Vincenzo II, Guastalla, and three of Carlo Emanuele I's sons – Filiberto prince of Oneglia, whose portrait of 1624 by Van Dyck may indeed have been commissioned to underscore the marital negotiations, Tommaso Francesco, and even Cardinal Maurizio.[18] However, Maria's marriage to Rethel brought the prospect of direct conflict to the point of certainty, taking place without the essential consent of the Emperor Ferdinand II as feudal overlord, and with no deference to the other claimants to the two duchies – control of the princess had become a political issue as far back as 1612 after her father's death. The marriage gave Carlo Emanuele I and Spain not merely the excuse but also the motivation to move into action against the duke of Nevers with a strong sense of juridical legitimacy. As the wronged parties they had to intervene, so they argued, to preserve their respective reputations and to ensure a legally acceptable outcome to the succession dispute that also gave due recognition to Imperial arbitration.[19]

The decision by Spain, under the immediate direction of Olivares much more than the reluctant Philip IV, to become involved in an Italian inheritance dispute has unsurprisingly been the subject of close

---

[17] Quazza, *La guerra per la successione*, I, p. 37.
[18] Brown and Vlieghe (eds.), *Van Dyck*, p. 172.
[19] Quazza, *La guerra per la successione*, I, pp. 22–4, 28; Parrott, 'The Mantuan Succession', 26–8.

scrutiny. It was a turning point in Spain's involvement in European conflict, precipitating the eventual slide to total war with the Bourbons – 1627 and 1628 were, according to J. H. Elliott, the two most critical years in Olivares' twenty-two-year ministry as he, rather than Philip IV, became personally responsible for the war's outcome.[20] By aligning with Carlo Emanuele I, the count-duke was no doubt hoping both to sour Franco-Savoyard relations and to undercut the possibility of the seemingly francophile duke of Nevers obtaining both Mantua and Monferrato, something that threatened to close the duchies to Spanish influence. An alliance with the Savoyard duke would additionally have served to protect Spanish interests in north Italy, implicitly recognising the duchy's wider strategic importance. The capture of the fortress of Casale (in Monferrato) would furthermore have improved enormously the reputation of Spanish arms while strengthening their grip over north Italy and its logistical routes.[21] Certainly then, the temptation to view the war over Mantua and Monferrato from this great power perspective is considerable, not least because it seems to confirm the historiographical tradition of Franco-Spanish rivalry alone at the expense of helpless Italian sovereigns. But such a view does little justice to the rulers of the peninsula as discrete powers. Nevers had forced the issue to a crisis by his reluctance to listen to other claimants like Carlo Emanuele I and Guastalla and, crucially, by the political coup of his son's marriage to Maria Gonzaga. And it was largely Carlo Emanuele I who, driven by his dynastic responsibility and reluctance to drop the issue, drew Spain, and by extension France, into a very dangerous regional conflict.[22] While Guido di Bagno, the papal nuncio in Paris, was reluctant to become overtly involved in a conflict between Catholic princes, he indeed went so far as to suggest that Carlo Emanuele I was undoubtedly the 'greatest cause of the war', who 'under the cover of peace has always pushed for conflict'.[23] How,

---

[20] Elliott, *Olivares*, p. 359; R. A. Stradling, 'Olivares and the origins of the Franco-Spanish War, 1627–35', *English Historical Review*, 101 (1986), reprinted in his collection, *Spain's Struggle for Europe, 1598–1668* (London and Rio Grande, 1994).

[21] On Spanish policy-making see for instance R. A. Stradling, 'Prelude to Disaster: The Precipitation of the War of the Mantuan Succession, 1627–29', and 'Olivares and the Origins of the Franco-Spanish War', reprinted in *Spain's Struggle for Europe*; Elliott, *Richelieu and Olivares*, chapter 4; R. Ródenas Vilar, *La política europea de España durante la Guerra de Treinta Años, 1624–30* (Madrid, 1967), pp. 171–7; Elliott and de la Peña (eds.), *Memoriales y cartas*, II, pp. 5–59. This collection of documents clearly demonstrates the strain on relations between Philip IV, attempting to take a greater control of government, and Olivares as a consequence of the war.

[22] I am grateful to David Parrott for advice on this. His article, 'The Mantuan Succession' expands this argument, though with a slightly different interpretation.

[23] ASV SS Francia, 73, ff. 148v–9, Bagno to Barberini, 22 April 1630; 71, f. 89v, Bagno to Barberini, 26 December 1629.

then, should Duke Carlo Emanuele I's ready willingness to make a pact with Spain and advocate the use of force be interpreted? Much of the answer lies with the fortunes of Savoyard diplomacy outside the Italian peninsula.

Alessandro Scaglia's diplomatic strategy after the treaty of Monzón, of cultivating a role in England's parallel peace negotiations with France and Spain, had provided political flexibility for Savoy at a time of great fluidity in international relations. In turn this had given Carlo Emanuele I a degree of political security so that he felt he could intervene in the succession dispute without the threat of immediate French reprisals. In the first place, the abate's contact with the Spanish Habsburgs in Brussels over the course of 1627 had helped to reinforce Savoy's diplomatic connections with England, while at the same time improving previously strained relations with Madrid (even though they had been put on hold during the summer of 1627). Through his friendship with the duke of Buckingham, Scaglia had manoeuvred himself into a position where he could mediate in the negotiations for an Anglo-Spanish settlement. Second, Alessandro Scaglia's concurrent involvement in the talks between the Stuart and Bourbon courts provided Duke Carlo Emanuele I with what seemed to be the means of influencing the extent of direct French military activity in the Italian peninsula. What had begun after Monzón as a strategy of coercing Richelieu into constancy had evolved into a policy first of containment and then more markedly of opposition to the cardinal. During his mission to London at the end of 1627 Scaglia had moreover made it clear to his duke that the prospect of a cessation of aid to the Huguenots was not immediate, and almost as soon as Buckingham returned to the English capital preparations for a further naval expedition in defence of La Rochelle were begun. At least for the foreseeable future, then, the duke of Savoy could hope, or perhaps even expect, France to remain preoccupied with internal affairs and with England, especially given Richelieu's reluctance at that point to be drawn into a 'total war' with Spain on multiple fronts. Even if the English made moves towards a settlement Carlo Emanuele I still had Charles I's written pledge delivered by Walter Montagu that seemed to guarantee Savoy's involvement in any peace proposals, with the potential to influence or perhaps even to stall a settlement between the Stuart and Bourbon crowns. For Scaglia and his home state of Savoy, events in what can be described as the Atlantic theatre had a direct relationship with the fortunes of north Italy.

In March 1628 Monferrato was invaded as Savoyard troops captured the fortresses of Alba and Trino in quick succession, while Spanish forces under the governor of Milan, Don Gonzalo de Córdoba, occupied other portions of the duchy; in April 1628 Córdoba began besieging the strate-gically crucial fortress of Casale in the duchy, the fate of which potentially governed the military outcome of the entire conflict.[24] The invasion cut through the diplomatic equivocation of the previous year. Alvise Contarini, the Venetian ordinary ambassador in London, reported a definitive change in the direction of Scaglia's diplomacy, recording that the abate had openly declared that Carlo Emanuele I was hoping to gain from a territorial partition of Mantua and Monferrato, while also injur-ing the French in retaliation for the treaty of Monzón.[25] He added that Scaglia was pushing for an Anglo-Spanish peace settlement and opposing a parallel Anglo-French peace; the abate, so Contarini believed, knew that the only way for the French to help the duke of Nevers was by a military incursion into north Italy which they would be unable or unwilling to execute so long as the Huguenot problem remained unresolved. Most interestingly, Scaglia justified his prince's actions by arguing that the po-litical insensitivity of France had forced Savoy to turn to an alliance with Spain, adding that while this was clearly a gamble it was better to have the noose of servitude in one's own hand than to be throttled by somebody else. This is a telling statement. Scaglia was revealing not only a level of distrust in both the leading Catholic powers, even as his prince was in a military alliance with Spain, but also a firm conviction that the duchy of Savoy was able to take an active rather than a passive role on the stage of European power politics. Savoy, the abate was implicitly suggesting, was not totally powerless before the two great powers.[26]

Yet whatever his own diplomatic skills, Scaglia could not control the mutability of events. From the outbreak of open hostilities in north Italy, the abate continued to focus on England's relations with France and Spain as the best means of influencing the course of the dynastic conflict. As second-rank states with dynastic affinities, England and Savoy had dur-ing the 1620s repeatedly co-operated on the European stage. This pattern had underscored the diplomacy of Scaglia, who, while offering himself as a mediator, always looked to cultivate and preserve his friendships with courtiers in England to gain support for his diplomatic initiatives. The delicacy of his strategy, of indirectly influencing the military and political freedom of France and Spain through their diplomatic rela-tions with England, nevertheless remained heavily dependent on each link in London, Turin, Brussels and Madrid working together. In

---

[24] Vittorio Siri recorded, with perhaps more than a little justification, that upon the future of Casale 'the destiny of Italy depended'. *Memorie recondite*, VI, p. 452. The success of the siege would also have greatly improved the domestic position of Olivares within Spain, given the pressure he had come under. Elliott, *Olivares*, p. 342.

[25] CSPV 1628–9, pp. 48–9, 431. See also p. 51. [26] CSPV 1628–9, pp. 56, 57.

September 1628 the abate had left England for the continent, no doubt in the belief that his strategy was still intact. Later in the month his diplomatic calculations were suddenly thrown into doubt by the devastating news of Buckingham's murder as the duke had returned to take command once again of the English fleet at Portsmouth.[27]

At least initially the English regime stressed that there would be continuity in foreign policy, and in a letter explaining what had happened Secretary of State Dorchester (whom Scaglia had met in The Hague in 1627) added that 'his majesty has instructed me to assure you that he is resolved to follow the same policies based on the same advice without any change . . . and he has likewise pressed me to assure you of the warmth he feels towards you'.[28] Charles I himself wrote to the abate reiterating his personal commitment to the peace with Spain while pointing out that the fleet which Buckingham had been preparing to command was ready to set sail for the French coast in support of the besieged Huguenots. The king's wish to ensure that it would be business as usual, according to L. J. Reeve, in part reflected his need to prove that he himself could take control of foreign policy following the sudden death of his highly unpopular favourite.[29] A hopeful Scaglia, not wishing to lose time, for his part sought to emphasise diplomatic continuity with his Spanish contacts, assuring Cardinal de la Cueva, the abate's chief correspondent in Brussels in the absence of Ambrogio Spínola, that the progress of the Anglo-Spanish peace talks would not be hindered.[30]

Such optimism however could not hide the fact that Buckingham's untimely death was a stunning blow to Alessandro Scaglia, as it was a critically important political event more generally. The potential weakness of the style of personalised diplomacy upon which Alessandro Scaglia had depended during the 1620s was severely exposed: the most important individual in his network of informal contacts and friends was lost. It had been primarily through his friendship with the duke as both ambassador and cultivated courtier that Scaglia had been able to exert any significant influence on English diplomacy. Without him the abate faced the danger of becoming isolated from the political affairs of England. Buckingham had furthermore been the political patron of another two of

---

[27] Reeve, *Charles I*, pp. 35, 54.
[28] PRO SP 92/14/37–v, Dorchester to Scaglia, 2 September 1628; Reeve, *Charles I*, pp. 36–7. A letter from Scaglia, presumably a reply to Dorchester's letter, with an assessment of Buckingham's character can be found in PRO SP 92/14/62–v, Scaglia to Dorchester, 29 October 1628.
[29] Reeve, *Charles I*, pp. 52–5.
[30] AGS Est. 2042, Scaglia to Cueva, 29 October 1628; PRO SP 92/14/37–v, Dorchester to Scaglia, 23 August 1628; AST LPD m. 46, Scaglia to Tommaso Francesco, 2 October 1628.

Scaglia's friends, Balthasar Gerbier and Endymion Porter, raising doubts about their own futures at the Caroline court. The political vacuum left by Buckingham had indeed created uncertainty over the future direction of English foreign policies, despite Charles I's apparent willingness to renew a military campaign in France. Without Buckingham there were understandable concerns about whether Charles I would find a new favourite with a different set of priorities and with different clients, whether the war with France, so strongly motivated by a personalised dispute involving the duke, would come to a more speedy end, and finally whether the seemingly close diplomatic relationship between England and Savoy would be damaged.[31] To make matters worse, in late October 1628 reports reached the abate of the fall of the Huguenot enclave at La Rochelle which the impotent presence of the English fleet offshore had failed to prevent. Richelieu's success in reducing his domestic problems accordingly paved the way for direct French intervention in north Italy, the very thing Scaglia's diplomatic strategy had been working to avoid.

Alessandro Scaglia had to respond to the changing political circumstances to preserve the delicate diplomatic strategy he had spent the 1620s cultivating. In the first place he needed to reaffirm his own role as a mediator in the Anglo-Spanish peace talks, which continued to depend on his personal influence and friendships with particular courtiers and ministers in London. That had indeed been fundamental to his style of conducting diplomacy throughout his career, reflecting one important way in which a second-rank state like Savoy could enjoy increased influence on the stage of European power politics. While he was no longer personally present in the English capital, Scaglia still hoped to draw on alternative sources of informal power for negotiating an end to the Anglo-Spanish war. He could perhaps hope to have the support of pro-Spanish ministers such as Richard Weston and Francis Cottington, establishing their credentials as important political figures in their own right after Buckingham's death.[32] With more certainty the abate could also draw on the support of his remaining friends and allies at the English court who were themselves emerging from Buckingham's shadow. Among them was the earl of

---

[31] AST LMI m. 4, Barozzio to Carlo Emanuele I, 25 January 1629: AGS Est. 2517, 47, Juan van Male to Olivares, 20 September 1628; CSPV 1628–9, pp. 283, 306, 361.

[32] Michael Alexander, *Charles I's Lord Treasurer: Sir Richard Weston, Earl of Portland (1577–1635)* (London, 1975); Havran, *Cottington*, pp. 88–9. On the rivalries within the court see the comments in Kevin Sharpe, *The Personal Rule of Charles I* (New Haven and London, 1992), p. 173. It was in the aftermath of Buckingham's death that ministers associated with a 'Spanish faction' were most influential. Albert Loomie, 'The Spanish faction at the court of Charles I, 1630–38', *Bulletin of the Institute of Historical Research*, 59 (1986).

Carlisle, who had returned to England from a ceremonial mission at the Turinese court in the hope of increasing his influence in the wake of his former political patron.[33] On the earl's return, Scaglia wrote directly to Carlisle expressing his warm affection, while in a letter to Olivares he emphasised Carlisle's affection for the Spanish *valido*, possibly confirming the earl's conversion over the course of 1628 to the merits of an alliance with Spain that his biographer Roy Schreiber has discerned.[34] Henry Rich, the earl of Holland, was a second candidate to replace Buckingham as the leading favourite of Charles I, and as with Carlisle, Scaglia also claimed his friendship; the abate went so far as to describe him as 'well-disposed to the negotiation [the Anglo-Spanish talks], and a very great friend of mine'.[35]

That Alessandro Scaglia was hoping to draw on both Carlisle and Holland while looking to Cottington and Weston as potential allies indicated the range of the network of friends and contacts in London he had acquired since the mid-1620s, and, possibly, the flexibility of the court Spanish and French 'factions' as terms for designating individuals who were defined by rigid differences over policy priorities. While Carlisle and Holland vied for the now vacant position of favourite (indeed assuming that it would be filled) and also disagreed over policy issues with more overtly pro-Spanish ministers like Weston and Cottington, it evidently did not mean that Scaglia could not maintain contact with all of them. Carlisle had, it seems, been won over to a pro-Savoyard position through his friendship with Scaglia that dated back to the mid-1620s; after Buckingham's demise the earl continued to advocate a war policy against France while seeking to end the Anglo-Spanish war, in line with Scaglia's strategy. As for Holland, while there is no explicit evidence to explain his friendship with the abate, their contact does seem to conform to the pattern of courtier–diplomat relationship that had been evident in Scaglia's relationships with other courtiers, including Buckingham. The earl had first encountered Scaglia in 1625 when they were both in

---

[33] The earl had gone to Turin on a purely complimentary visit, leaving in January 1629. The abate had in part organised the mission of his friend, hoping that it would further his influence in London. AST LMI m. 4, 64, Scaglia to Carlo Emanuele I, 14 December 1627; CSPV 1626–8, pp. 353, 520–1, 531; Bell, *Handlist*, p. 231.

[34] Schreiber, 'James Hay', p. 111. Prior to this, Schreiber argues that Carlisle was more interested in the possibility of organising an alliance of states independent of an unreliable France but which nevertheless were opposed to Spain. *Ibid.*, pp. 103–10.

[35] PRO SP 92/14/160–v, Scaglia to Carlisle, 3 December 1628, in which Scaglia wrote of the warmth of his feelings for Carlisle; PRO SP 94/34/73, Scaglia to Olivares, 22 April 1629; AGS Est. 2517, 71 Scaglia to Cueva, late 1628; AST LMI m. 4, Barozzio to Carlo Emanuele I, 25 January 1629; CSPV 1628–9, pp. 262, 341, which report the possibilities of Holland or Carlisle becoming the new favourite.

Paris during the negotiations for the marriage between Charles Stuart and Henrietta Maria. Holland, as one of the leading connoisseurs in the English court, was in many respects a natural friend of the abate, given his own well-defined cultural identity. It had, perhaps unsurprisingly, been the earl of Holland, along with Carlisle, who had reconciled Scaglia to Buckingham following the bizarre dispute over the attempted arrest of Buckingham's sister-in-law Lady Purbeck early in 1628.[36]

As Scaglia needed to re-form his network of contacts at the English court so he also had to sustain the forward momentum of his talks via Brussels to Madrid, which L. J. Reeve has claimed had been halted by Buckingham's death.[37] At the beginning of December 1628 Duke Carlo Emanuele I despatched the abate to Spain on the pretext of seeking the release of an English vessel captured by the Spanish. He arrived on 3 January 1629, bringing a series of diplomatic initiatives concerning both England and north Italy, again recognising the crucial link between the Atlantic and Italian theatres of war and diplomacy.[38] In the first place Scaglia was to stall the negotiations for a temporary settlement of the Italian question brought to Madrid by the French extraordinary ambassador Guillaume Bautru, who had suggested that the succession issue should be resolved through a neutral third party, to the probable exclusion of Carlo Emanuele I.[39] While preventing an unfavourable settlement to the Italian succession dispute, the abate was also to advance the Anglo-Spanish peace talks for which he and the duke of Savoy reportedly had a 'religious care'. The possibility of reaching an agreement certainly did not seem unrealistic; Olivares continued to support Scaglia's mediatory role, and with the arrival at the Spanish court in July 1629 of the hispanophile Francis Cottington, hopes were further raised that an Anglo-Spanish peace was at last close at hand.[40]

---

[36] The earl of Holland has been portrayed as a bitter opponent of Weston and Cottington. Havran, *Cottington*, p. 94; Sharpe, *Personal Rule*, pp. 173–9, where Sharpe none the less argues that factions were not always associated with hard-line ideological positions. For another viewpoint see R. Malcolm Smuts, 'The Puritan followers of Henrietta Maria during the 1630s', *English Historical Review*, 93 (1983).

[37] Reeve, *Charles I*, p. 54.

[38] AST LMS m. 21, fasc. 1, 8, Scaglia to Carlo Emanuele I, 3 January 1629; 9, Scaglia to Carlo Emanuele I, 7 January 1629.

[39] CSPV 1628–9, p. 402; AST LMI m. 5, 1, Carlo Emanuele I to Scaglia, 9 January 1629; Quazza, *La guerra per la successione*, I, pp. 285–90. Bautru eventually left Madrid with a reply but not total satisfaction. AST LMS m. 21, fasc. 1, 62, Scaglia to Carlo Emanuele I, 12 February 1629; 72, Scaglia to Barozzio, 16 February 1629.

[40] BL Add. MS 34,311, f. 252v, Wake to Carlisle, 6 December 1628, in which Wake without any apparent irony quite generously complimented Scaglia, 'in whom I have as much faith as I can in a man that is cardinable'; AST LMS m. 21, fasc. 1, 84, Scaglia to Carlo Emanuele I, 22 February 1629.

While the abate was negotiating at the Spanish court, Pietro Barozzio travelled to London via Brussels to act as a diplomatic agent of Duke Carlo Emanuele I in the absence of an accredited Savoyard ambassador.[41] Barozzio, the client of the Scaglia di Verrua clan who owed his position as a secretary of state to his patrons, was understandably on close terms with the abate. His selection as an informal representative to Charles I was calculated to promote Scaglia's involvement in the Anglo-Savoyard diplomacy, a recognition in Turin that the abate was their best means of influencing the shape of English foreign policies and, by extension, the war in north Italy. On his arrival in the English capital Barozzio was warmly welcomed by Scaglia's friend, the earl of Carlisle, and later introduced to the king. For Barozzio, it was important to ensure not only that Savoy's interests were maintained but, equally importantly, that they were filtered through Scaglia, with whom Barozzio remained in close written contact.[42] This involved pressing the English about the progress of talks with France, in a state of forward momentum following the low-key mission of Walter Montagu in October 1628 to Paris, while operating as a point of contact between the Huguenot leaders and Scaglia at a time when one of the leaders, Soubise, was negotiating for a possible resumption of aid from the English.[43] Shortly after arriving in London he submitted a diplomatic initiative to Charles I outlining his suggestions, first requesting that there should be no innovations in the negotiations without Scaglia and secondly that his patron should be provided with an English vessel to carry him from Spain to England, not only for safe passage but also to demonstrate London's goodwill.[44]

Despite his best efforts to maintain a three-way process of negotiation between Madrid, London and Turin, Scaglia's efforts nevertheless did not bear the longed-for fruits. The duke of Buckingham had been of prime importance in prolonging the Anglo-French war because of his personalised dispute with Richelieu and the extent of his control over English foreign policy. Following his death there were few compelling reasons for the war to continue, and in April 1629 news reached Spain that England and France had finally negotiated a suspension of hostilities.

---

[41] Barozzio's letter of introduction can be found in PRO SP 92/14/233, Carlo Emanuele I to Charles I, December 1628. See also PRO SP 92/15/29, Scaglia to Dorchester, 28 January 1629. The relative informality of Barozzio's diplomatic status can also be inferred from John Finet's remarks. Loomie (ed.), *Notebooks*, pp. 52–3.

[42] For example, AST LMS m. 21, fasc. 1, 98, Scaglia to Barozzio, 2 March 1629.

[43] AST LMI m. 4, Barozzio to Carlo Emanuele I, 31 January 1629; Barozzio to Carlo Emanuele I, 24 February 1629; Barozzio to Carlo Emanuele I, 6 June 1629.

[44] CSPV 1628–9, p. 459; AST LMI m. 4, Barozzio to Carlo Emanuele I, 28 January 1629; PRO SP 92/15/82, Dorchester to Wake, 2 February 1629; HMC Eleventh Report, appendix, part I, p. 152.

Quite understandably Scaglia was shocked: 'the Abate of Scaglia doth in his last letters tax us [the English] for our sudden concluding the peace with France who as he writeth doth seek a peace with Spain'.[45] When the news reached the Savoyard court in Turin, Duke Carlo Emanuele I was himself quick to express the extent of his displeasure to Isaac Wake, the English ordinary ambassador. As the duke pointed out, both he and the abate had given credit to the pledge obtained in the name of Charles I from Walter Montagu two years earlier and which the king of England had only recently written to Carlo Emanuele I to reiterate.[46] When he complained to Wake that the suspension of arms had been concluded without prior consultation or indeed his consent, contrary to the written agreement obtained from Montagu in 1627, the ambassador responded that a courier had indeed brought the news of the negotiations to Turin and that, since there was no reply whatsoever from the duke, Charles I had assumed that Savoy had tacitly agreed to the settlement. In London the earl of Carlisle, who had advocated war against France, apologised to Scaglia's secretary, Barozzio, for the way in which Savoy had been treated. The pro-Habsburg English treasurer, Richard Weston, somewhat shame-facedly admitted that Duke Carlo Emanuele I had every reason to feel aggrieved with the English. The treasurer's only defence was that a serious want of money and the breakdown of relations with Parliament had forced Charles I to settle with France, out of necessity rather than choice.[47]

What seemed to make matters worse was that the English regime began to distance itself from the abate, marking what could have been inter-preted as a clear break from the special relationship that had been seen to exist so publicly under Buckingham. The Venetian ordinary ambassador in London, Alvise Contarini, wrote that the English boat requested by Barozzio and destined to carry the abate in safety from Spain to England had been detained, along with a passport and letters.[48] There was an in-ference to be drawn from this in a political system where any informal

[45] Rooses and Ruelens (eds.), *Correspondance*, V, p. 61. On the Anglo-French peace treaty see Reeve, *Charles I*, pp. 51–2. S. R. Gardiner emphasises the role played by the Venetian ordinary ambassador Alvise Contarini in the negotiations. *History*, VII, p. 100. As with Scaglia, he had offered himself as a diplomatic mediator so as to promote the interest of his home state.

[46] AST LFI m. 48, Charles I to Carlo Emanuele I, January 1629; LMS m. 22, fasc. 5, 3, Carlo Emanuele I to Scaglia, 20 January 1629; PRO SP 92/15/82, Dorchester to Wake, 1 February 1629; AST LMI m. 4, Barozzio to Carlo Emanuele I, 24 February 1629.

[47] BL Add. MS 34,311, ff. 317–v, Wake to Carleton, 15 May 1628; AST LMI m. 4, Barozzio to Carlo Emanuele I, 20 April 1629; Barozzio to Carlo Emanuele I, 25 April 1629.

[48] CSPV 1628–9, p. 600; 1629–32, p. 19.

or ceremonial act by a state or sovereign towards a foreign representative could be understood as a diplomatic signal in its own right, as much as any 'formal' statement of policy. During 1627 Alessandro Scaglia had gradually come to represent a diplomatic position understood throughout the courts of Europe. He effectively signified a pro-Habsburg and anti-French approach to international relations. The cool treatment meted out to Scaglia on this mission was to be interpreted by contemporary observers as an informal declaration of foreign policy priorities; by deliberately exploiting their ceremonial treatment of the abate to serve as a diplomatic signal, the English could emphasise to the French that they were genuine about the suspension of hostilities.

In private at least there still appeared to be room for manoeuvre. Seeking to clarify England's modified diplomatic position, Barozzio presented a written memorial to Charles I in which he suggested that the settlement with France is 'nothing other than a suspension of arms which can be broken at any moment, if Spain satisfies you concerning your relatives, that is to say over the Palatinate'. Barozzio added that the French settlement would in no way hinder a Spanish agreement but that in the event of an Anglo-Spanish peace the one with France could be broken. It seems that these were not merely empty words, or the aspirations of a minister desperately clutching at straws. The centrally important phrase that the French peace was nothing more than a breakable suspension of arms was one Barozzio claimed had been employed not only by Weston but also by Charles I himself.[49] But even this verbal assurance did not provide any binding diplomatic guarantees at a time when the politically fluid English court lacked a dominant voice on foreign affairs, as there had been under Buckingham.[50] Barozzio presented the document to the earl of Dorchester on the 11 August. After pestering him for a written response, the English secretary of state quite remarkably claimed that Barozzio's memorial had been lost. When it eventually reappeared nine days later, with the written response of Charles I added in the margin, there were a number of emendations possibly made by the pro-French Dorchester which presented a very different picture of English foreign policy objectives. The altered memorial in effect retracted any notion that the peace was a suspension of arms that could be broken, claiming among other things that 'the settlement with France is the renewal of the ancient friendship between the two crowns'. This could of course have been seen as standard rhetoric associated with any peace agreement, but Barozzio

[49] Or so Pietro Barozzio claimed. AST LMI m. 4, Barozzio to Carlo Emanuele I, 14 May 1629; 'Memoire du Sieur Barozzi', with response from Charles I, 20 August 1629.
[50] On differing foreign policy priorities among the ministers and courtiers of Charles I see Reeve, *Charles I*, chapter 7.

for one was stunned and immediately complained to Dorchester, though to little effect.[51]

The diplomatic and military complications were mounting at what seemed to Scaglia an alarming rate. Even before the conclusion of the Anglo-French peace, in March 1629, French forces under the direct leadership of Louis XIII passed without significant opposition through the Alpine valley of Susa into the heart of the Savoyard state. Quite what had happened was not entirely clear, and rumours predictably spread that the French regime had signed a secret agreement with Carlo Emanuele I, despite his military pact with the Spanish, allowing them entry into the Italian peninsula in return for a more favourable outcome to Savoy's dynastic claim to Monferrato. The abate's reaction when he heard the reports was understandably one of surprise; initially he proved reluctant to believe the news and soon wrote back to Turin for specific information, perhaps implying that at this crucial moment he had for once been left in the dark by his prince.[52] Scaglia's strategy of minimising French involvement in Italy by carefully exploiting the war with England seemed to be shattered. His prime political ally, the duke of Buckingham, was dead, the Anglo-Spanish war had yet to be resolved, and the English had settled with Paris and were appearing to reject the possibility of breaking the peace. To make matters worse for the abate, French troops had entered the patrimony of Savoy.

Alessandro Scaglia's options, while clearly reduced, nevertheless still gave him some room for hope, as he persevered not only with the Huguenot problem but, much more importantly from this point, also with the Anglo-Spanish peace talks. Implicit in his thinking was that the flow of events in the Atlantic theatre could still have a critical effect on what happened in Italy, especially given that there were still unresolved problems facing France, and that England was not necessarily neutralised as an active European power. If the French could enter the war by settling their domestic problems then conversely they could be diverted from north Italy by renewed difficulties within their kingdom. First, the abate continued to press both the English and the Spanish to provide aid for

---

[51] AST LMI m. 4, 'Memoire du Sieur Barozzi', 20 August 1629; Barozzio to Carlo Emanuele I, 12 September 1629. Dorchester's actions can be contrasted with his effusive words of praise for Scaglia earlier in the year. PRO SP 92/15/7–v, Dorchester to Scaglia, 21 January 1629.

[52] AST LMS m. 22, fasc. 5, 41, Carlo Emanuele I to Scaglia, 8 March 1629; m. 21, fasc. 1, 164, Scaglia to Pasero, 14 April 1629; 167, Scaglia to Vittorio Amedeo, 21 April 1629; Hanotaux and de la Force, *Richelieu*, III, book 3. France and Savoy did indeed sign a treaty at Bossoino on 10 May 1629 where Savoy would keep the disputed portion of Monferrato and have the support of France in any settlement. Dumont, *Corps universel diplomatique*, V, part II, pp. 583–4; Parrott, 'The Mantuan Succession', 62.

Soubise and Rohan, whose envoy was sent to Madrid to secure their support. In May 1629, seven months after the fall of La Rochelle, the Spanish consented to a formal agreement to provide money for Rohan so that he could continue his revolt, despite the predictable concern that supporting heretics ran contrary to Spanish reputation as a Catholic power.[53] Scaglia also believed, with perhaps greater ambition, that further pressure could be exerted on Richelieu by providing aid for aristocratic malcontents within France and by organising a military diversion into the kingdom. Olivares himself had raised both of these as possible means of pinning the French down in their own state. In January 1629 the count-duke, surely with more fancy than reality, suggested that the Spanish, in conjunction with the Emperor, the bishop of Verdun and the duke of Lorraine, should organise a campaign in Burgundy.[54] This aggressive rhetoric was sustained by Olivares after news arrived of the entry of Louis XIII in north Italy with a show of confidence that was intended as much to display Habsburg power.[55]

While attempts were made to pin the French down outside north Italy, the abate persisted with his efforts to increase the scope of Spanish involvement in the peninsula by mediating with England. The general strategic principle of the war again held, that the capability of a power to intervene in one region could be improved if its commitments in other theatres were reduced, all the more so for Spain given the enormous scale of its military commitments around Europe from the Low Countries to the Mediterranean. It certainly seemed that the possibility of reducing Spanish commitments outside the Italian peninsula was improved by the presence in Madrid of Ambrogio Spínola, who earnestly wished to bring peace to the war-torn Low Countries and whose inclination towards an Anglo-Spanish peace was already known to the abate. From Madrid, Olivares and Philip IV took the decision to despatch Spínola, a commander with exceptional experience, to north Italy to

---

[53] AST LMS m. 21, fasc. 1, 98, Scaglia to Barozzio, 2 March 1629; LMI m. 4, Soubise to Scaglia, *c.* May 1629; Soubise to Rohan, *c.* May 1629; Siri, *Memorie recondite*, VI, pp. 642–8; Clarke, *Henri de Rohan*, pp. 174–5. It is worth noting that an earlier attempt in 1625 by Rohan to secure aid from Spain had been discussed by a meeting of Spanish theologians and accepted, ironically to prevent another French incursion into north Italy, albeit in conjunction with Savoy. Olivares denied to the papal nuncio in Madrid that any help was given. Elliott, *Olivares*, p. 227.

[54] AGS Est. K1437, 14, voto of Olivares, January 1629; AST LMS m. 21, fasc. 1, 18, Scaglia to Carlo Emanuele I, 8 January 1629; 19, Scaglia to Carlo Emanuele I, 7 January 1629. As Scaglia noted, the count-duke's plans were as much intended to downplay the loss in 1628 of the Spanish silver fleet to a Dutch attack – he wished to signal to Scaglia that Spanish aid to Savoy would not as a consequence diminish.

[55] AST LMS m. 21, fasc. 1, 152, Scaglia to Carlo Emanuele I, 31 March 1629.

assume control of the Spanish war effort, possibly to inject a new lease of life into the faltering siege at Casale (though the decision might also have been influenced by Olivares' concern to remove him as a potential rival at the Spanish court). Perhaps to assuage Spínola's overriding desire for a peace in northern Europe, he was also to oversee any diplomatic negotiations as the new governor of Milan, with full powers to pursue the war or to settle the succession dispute, and, more strikingly, the necessary authority to discuss peace with England.[56] The importance of Spínola's commission for the military and political fortunes of north Italy was abundantly clear. The potential importance of his commission to Anglo-Spanish relations was equally evident, reiterating the connections between England and the dynastic conflict in north Italy, evident even before its outbreak and which had been instrumental in Carlo Emanuele I's gamble to pursue his dynastic claim to Monferrato with violence. In July 1629 Spínola left the Iberian peninsula for north Italy. Scaglia travelled with him, aware that the marquis had the authority to satisfy many of Savoy's diplomatic objectives within the Italian peninsula and further afield.[57]

The military progress of the war in north Italy in the year between the outbreak of hostilities and the spring of 1629 had almost entirely favoured the duke of Savoy and his Spanish allies at the expense of the duke of Nevers. Carlo Emanuele I and Córdoba had succeeded in gaining control of much of Monferrato, though the fortress of Casale still held out against the governor of Milan who had planned for its quick capture. However, the entry of French troops into north Italy in March 1629, under the direct command of Louis XIII, following the fall of La Rochelle and the suppression of the Huguenot revolt, fundamentally changed the character of the war, to Carlo Emanuele I's obvious detriment. At least Savoy and Spain obtained one hitherto unfulfilled 'objective'. Part of the initial justification for taking action against the duke of Nevers by invading Mantua and Monferrato – even if with hindsight it might seem to have been a legal fiction – had been to ensure that the reputation and juridical rights of the Holy Roman Emperor as feudal overlord were maintained, with recognition that both Carlo Emanuele I and the duke of Guastalla

---

[56] AST LMS m. 21, fasc. 5, 176, Scaglia to Carlo Emanuele I, 4 May 1629; BL Add. MS 34,311, ff. 326v–7, Wake to Dorchester, 13 June 1629; AST LMI m. 5, Carlo Emanuele I to Barozzio, 12 June 1629.

[57] Among the other passengers travelling to the Italian peninsula was the painter to the Spanish court, Diego Velázquez (1599–1660). The tantalising possibility that Alessandro Scaglia had substantial contact with the artist cannot unfortunately be gleaned from any known archival evidence.

had legitimate claims to financial or territorial compensation.[58] Before France's intervention Emperor Ferdinand II had, if anything, remained tacitly sympathetic to Nevers and unwilling to commit troops in favour of Savoy and Spain, exposing differences between the Habsburg courts in Madrid and Vienna over the Gonzaga succession dispute. The only significant action taken by Ferdinand, under pressure from Guastalla and his vocal supporters at the Imperial court, had been in March 1628 to issue a sequestration of Nevers' property pending a juridical resolution of the dispute.[59] France's intervention, enabled by the conclusion of the Anglo-French war and Huguenot revolt, and triggered by Nevers' own military operations against Savoy, forced an alteration in Imperial policy to the succession dispute. The issue of the emperor's reputation had been brought into question by military aggression within his feudal jurisdiction, and equally seriously by the willingness of Nevers to seek military aid from a prince outside the Empire without seeking consent.[60] In response to what were arguably challenges to his authority, the emperor intervened. Late in May 1629 the first Imperial contingents were in the Swiss cantons; by June Imperial troops made their destructive entry into the duchy of Mantua under the command of Rombaldo, the count of Collalto (1575–1630), totalling 30,000 infantry and 6,000 cavalry by August.

From this point on, the character of the war was set, confronting Savoy with some unpalatable choices. Carlo Emanuele I's agreement with Louis XIII, signed as French forces had passed through the Val di Susa, did little to prevent the duke returning to his Spanish alignment. But while Carlo Emanuele tried to find a balanced position between France and Spain, French troops continued to menace his patrimony, entering the duchy for a second time in March 1630 and occupying the fortress of Pinerolo in Piemonte. In the meantime Imperial troops ravaged the duchy of Mantua, culminating with the capture and sacking of the ducal capital and fortress of Mantua in July of the same year.[61] Meanwhile, the crucial

---

[58] This may well have formed a component of Savoyard rhetoric, though David Parrott has argued that Carlo Emanuele I did not in fact want the Emperor to arbitrate, since this would not necessarily secure a favourable outcome. Parrott, 'The Mantuan Succession', 52.

[59] Ibid., 50–1.

[60] AST LMS m. 22, fasc. 5, 15, Scaglia to Carlo Emanuele I, 15 September 1629; Siri, Memorie recondite, VI, pp. 657, 680–1; Capriata, Wars of Italy, p. 394; Elliott, Olivares, pp. 375–6; Manuel Fernández Álvarez, Don Gonzalo Fernández de Córdoba y la guerra de sucesión de Mantova y del Monferrato, 1627–1629 (Madrid, 1955), pp. 68–70.

[61] Quazza, La guerra per la successione, I, chapters 4 and 5; II, chapters 6 and 7. For biographical information on Collalto see Ventura Ginate González, El conde de la Roca, 1583–1658: un diplomatico estremeño en Italia (Madrid, undated), p. 167. For a detailed

fortress of Casale remained in possession of its French garrison and lay besieged, apart from a brief respite, by the Spanish, under the command of Córdoba first and then of his successor as governor of Milan, Ambrogio Spínola.

While France, Spain and the Emperor jostled for military superiority in north Italy, Alessandro Scaglia continued to fix his attention on what could be achieved by combining diplomacy and the application of force outside the peninsula. When he returned to the Italian peninsula, the Anglo-Spanish peace talks were advancing through Francis Cottington in Madrid, at the Spanish court from July 1629. That their outcome might influence the war in north Italy was clear enough – as Olivares appreciated, the conclusion of Spain's conflict with England would free Spanish resources, stretched as they were by the heavy demands in north Italy and the Netherlands. Perhaps given their importance to Savoy, the abate attempted to move the Anglo-Spanish talks closer to his home state, where Spínola, already invested with the necessary authority, might be able to bring them to a conclusion. Accordingly, Scaglia asked Isaac Wake, Charles I's ambassador in Turin, to obtain the powers to treat, and even before his return to the peninsula with Spínola, Scaglia had reportedly written to England to ask that an authorised English representative might be sent to Savoy.[62] When nothing came of this, Scaglia tried to persuade the English regime to send Cottington from Spain to north Italy to conclude his negotiations with Spínola, though Cottington proved reluctant to cede his diplomatic powers to anyone, including Scaglia who, in seeking to resolve the impasse, himself offered to return to Spain.[63] If diplomacy represented one lever that Scaglia hoped to use against France then force was another. As the abate worked to bring the Anglo-Spanish war to an end he looked to exert military pressure directly on France. In his letters he wrote that the Spanish might send an army through Catalonia to enter Provence; alternatively, Imperial troops, either under the command of Wallenstein or under Collalto, might attack the French by passing into Burgundy via the duchy of Lorraine, a diversion Spínola repeatedly requested to enable him finally to capture Casale.[64]

---

narrative of the French military campaigns see Jacques Humbert, *Une grande entreprise oubliée: les Français en Savoie sous Louis XIII* (Paris, 1960).

[62] BL Add. MS 34,311, f. 327, Wake to Dorchester, 13 June 1629; On Savoy's wish to settle the Anglo-Spanish war see also PRO SP 92/18/219–v, Wake to Dorchester, 30 May 1630.

[63] BL Add. MS 34,311, f. 340, Wake to Dorchester, 31 August 1629; f. 413–v, Wake to Dorchester, 29 April 1630.

[64] See for example AST LMM m. 17, fasc. 2, Scaglia to Carlo Emanuele I, 26 August 1629; Scaglia to Carlo Emanuele I, 27 August 1629; Scaglia to Carlo Emanuele I, decipher, *c.* September 1629. Collalto's reluctance to aid Spínola by a diversion reflected the barely concealed animosities between the two Habsburg commanders.

The year 1629 was a busy one in the war. It saw not only an esca-
lation in the conflict with both French and Imperial involvement, but
also a concurrent emphasis on seeking a diplomatic solution to the crisis. Scaglia's attempts to influence the course of the conflict by pursuing
both political and military policies outside the peninsula demonstrated
both the extent to which disputes in different European strategic theatres were mutually dependent and the fact that war and diplomacy
were inextricably linked in the dynastic conflict. The connection between military and political action was underlined still further by the
repeated attempts by all participants to negotiate a diplomatic solution
to the Gonzaga succession dispute while simultaneously pursuing their
military actions. This was hardly surprising given, more generally, the
closeness of war and diplomacy in early modern international affairs;
where necessary, states negotiated for peace in order to gain time for military preparations and likewise delayed negotiations to conduct military
operations with the end of obtaining greater diplomatic bargaining power.
Both tactics were employed by the participants in the war for Mantua
and Monferrato, depending on the relative strengths of their military
and political positions at given times.[65] After all, the war in north Italy
had been legitimised by competing arguments of juridical and dynastic
rights, which by their nature were receptive to diplomatic bargaining and
negotiation.

Spínola, as the commander of Spanish forces in the Italian peninsula,
had of course arrived in north Italy with full powers either to prosecute or
to settle the war, and it was because of the extensive range of his powers
that Scaglia had returned there, while the Imperial commander in the
Italian peninsula, Collalto, had likewise obtained full powers to treat for
peace on behalf of the emperor. The year 1629 also marked the point at
which Pope Urban VIII Barberini became directly involved in the peace
process. While the pope generally had an ambiguous political role in early
modern Europe given his identity as a secular sovereign Italian prince,
often wary of the extent of Spanish power within the peninsula, he was
also the spiritual head of the Catholic world with a moral public duty
to preserve peace and unity among potentially fractious Catholic princes
and states. Since his election to the papal throne in 1623 Urban VIII
Barberini, and his representatives, had more than once exposed their
suspicions of Spain by tacitly and even openly supporting France.
Following the entry of French troops into the duchy of Savoy, Cardinal
Bagno, the nuncio in France, was reportedly ecstatic, seriously damaging
his credibility in the opinion of Philip IV's ambassadorial representative

---

[65] For example, Quazza, *La guerra per la successione*, II, p. 17.

in Paris.[66] In public however the pope's role throughout the conflict was to mediate between the warring Catholic powers, and from the start of the Gonzaga succession dispute Urban VIII Barberini remained officially neutral so that at least publicly he could fulfil his moral duty as a peacemaker.[67] While he had given the impression to the French that he was prepared to enter a defensive league with them and the Venetian Republic in favour of the duke of Nevers, the entry of French troops into the peninsula led Urban VIII to change course. The pope wished to demonstrate publicly (albeit pointedly against the Spanish with loaded rhetoric) that he was the 'common lord [padrone comune] who deserves a reputation of honour and decency for opposing the unjust oppression of neighbouring princes, and for staking his authority to establish a good peace in Italy'.[68] During the summer of 1629 the pope finally despatched envoys, Giacomo Panciroli and Giulio Mazzarini, the future Cardinal Mazarin, to north Italy to mediate between the different parties.[69]

As with the other participants in the war, the Savoyard duke always expressed his wish that the conflict should be brought to a mediated settlement, and it was Abate Scaglia, described by Romolo Quazza as 'the most astute of those shrewd ministers in service to Carlo Emanuele I', who took the leading role in negotiations between the duke, the Habsburg commanders and the papal representatives.[70] The quest for a negotiated

---

[66] Quintín Aldea Vaquero, 'La neutralidad de Urbano VIII durante los años decisivos de la guerra de los treinta años', *Hispania Sacra*, 139 (1968), which is, admittedly, sympathetic to the Spanish; Siri, *Memorie recondite*, VI, pp. 367, 786. On the papal nuncio Bagno see Georg Lutz, *Kardinal Giovanni Francesco Guido di Bagno: Politik und Religion im zeitalter Richelieus und Urbans VIII* (Tübingen, 1971). The Francophile bias of the pope, or the suspicion of his bias, was also evident after the Gonzaga succession dispute and before the outbreak of open hostilities between France and Spain, as seen for instance in a letter of Saavedra Fajardo to Philip IV from July 1633. Quintín Aldea Vaquero (ed.), *España y Europa en el siglo XVII. Correspondencia de Saavedra Fajardo: 1631–1633*, 2 vols. (Madrid, 1986), I, pp. 77–8.

[67] Quazza, *La guerra per la successione*, I, p. 216; Auguste Leman, *Urbain VIII et la rivalité de la France et de la maison d'Autriche de 1631 à 1635* (Lille, 1920), pp. 1–2.

[68] Siri, *Memorie recondite*, VI, pp. 612–3. On Pope Urban VIII Barberini's growing reluctance to offer open support for Nevers see Quazza, *La guerra per la successione*, I, pp. 124–5, and a text of the putative treaty between France, the papacy, Nevers, Savoy and Venice can be found in Dumont (ed.), *Corps universel diplomatique*, V, part II, pp. 572–3, dated 11 March 1629.

[69] The best biography of Mazzarini, which also deals with his early career, is Georges Dethan, *Mazarin*, a revised edition of an earlier work, *Mazarin et ses amis* (Paris, 1968). There are twelve volumes of correspondence in the Archivio Segreto Vaticano, Paci directly relating to papal mediation in the war.

[70] Quazza, *La guerra per la successione*, II, p. 28. See also p. 33: 'on the other hand, Carlo Emanuele I and his representatives, principally Scaglia, never ceased to state in their discussions that universal peace was at the top of their agenda'. The near daily course of Scaglia's negotiations can be followed in great detail in AST LMM m. 17, fasc. 2, and LMS m. 23, fasc. 5.

settlement to the Gonzaga dispute continued to depend to a great extent on the duke of Savoy. It had been the duke who had forced the war in the first place and any settlement would have to take into account his dynastic claim to Monferrato and settle the issue permanently so as to prevent the dispute being reactivated in the future. What is more, prior to the capture of the Piedmontese fortress of Pinerolo by the French, Savoy still enjoyed some considerable strategic influence. So long as the Spanish were determined to besiege Casale, Savoy had an important tactical bargaining tool that could be used to extract political advantages from either France or Spain. On the one hand, Carlo Emanuele I could actually allow the French passage through his territories in order to relieve Casale. The importance to France of access to north Italy through Savoy had been recognised in the secret treaty of Susa which had been signed with Savoy when Louis XIII had entered the Italian peninsula in March 1629.[71] But Carlo Emanuele I could alternatively refuse, or at least obstruct, passage to help the Spanish with their siege of the fortress, as he opted to do soon after agreeing to his treaty with the French and something that Scaglia recognised when he wrote to Carlo Emanuele I that ' you hold the outcome of peace or war in your hands'.[72]

On 26 July 1630 Duke Carlo Emanuele I of Savoy died, bringing to an end a tumultuous reign that had lasted fifty years. Few commentators, either contemporary or in the light of historical retrospection, have viewed his involvement in the Gonzaga succession dispute positively – even patriotic Italian historians treated the conflict with a sense of ambivalence.[73] Carlo Emanuele I had entered the war – perhaps he had been compelled to do so – to pursue his family's centuries-old dynastic interests in Monferrato. But on his death, the patrimonial territories of the House of Savoy were once again suffering the ravages of war at the hands of foreign troops, just as they had suffered a century before as Charles V and Francis I had vied for influence in north Italy. But what effect did the death of Carlo Emanuele I have on the shape of Savoyard diplomacy? The accession of a new ruler was always a critical political juncture in states which depended on personal rule since it potentially brought changes in policy priorities and changes within the court, raising new favourites or ministers. Abate Scaglia for one had obviously devoted

---

[71] For a text of the agreement see Dumont (ed.), *Corps universel diplomatique*, V, part II, pp. 571–2; Siri, *Memorie recondite*, VI, pp. 608–11.

[72] AST LMS m. 23, fasc. 5, 42, Scaglia to Carlo Emanuele I, 20 March 1630; Capriata, *Wars of Italy*, pp. 395, 416–17. It should be added that the duke of Savoy did not necessarily want the Spanish to capture Casale – that would have given the Spanish too much of a strategic advantage, again to the detriment of Savoy.

[73] Siri, *Memorie recondite*, VII, pp. 197–8; Capriata, *Wars of Italy*, pp. 436–7; Salvatore Foa, *Vittorio Amedeo I, 1587–1637* (Turin, 1930), pp. 65–6.

his entire public career up to that point to serving Carlo Emanuele I,
like indeed the Scaglia di Verrua as a family clan, and for much of that
period he had been treated by the duke and viewed by contemporaries
as his most influential diplomat.[74] It was certainly possible that the accession of Vittorio Amedeo I would not result in many significant changes
in the direction of foreign policy; after all, when he succeeded his father Vittorio Amedeo I was far from inexperienced in matters of state
as he had during the 1620s been closely involved in decision-making
with the aging Carlo Emanuele I.[75] But the changes nevertheless came.
The accession of Vittorio Amedeo I immediately entailed a more pacific
policy regarding the Gonzaga succession dispute. The Savoyard state had
been severely ravaged by the war and the new duke badly wished to ex-
tricate himself from a conflict in the course of which Savoy's supposed
ally, England, had withdrawn from her war with France. Moreover, the
French had shown in the treaty of Susa, signed as French troops had first
entered Savoy in 1629, that they were willing to listen to Savoy's claims
to Monferrato – the origin of the dispute with the duke of Nevers –
and the fact that Vittorio Amedeo I was himself married to a sister of
the king of France itself encouraged prospects for peace.[76] In any case,
it had become clear to Vittorio Amedeo I that the war for Mantua and
Monferrato in alliance with Spain was bearing few tangible fruits. The
alliance with the Spanish always promised much but equally failed to
deliver those promises in full.[77]

The gap between the rhetoric and reality of Spanish power had certainly been widened by Alessandro Scaglia's own claims, themselves based
on Olivares' typically bold pronouncements, and by the amount of faith
placed in Spínola's capacity to succeed either at war or at peace by negotiating a settlement that satisfied both Spanish and Savoyard reputation.
Clear differences between the Spanish commander and Savoy had already
emerged in the course of 1629 and 1630, in part because of Spínola's
growing suspicions of the fidelity of Carlo Emanuele I as the duke had
played the French and the Spanish off against one another, though also
because of Savoy's inherent lack of faith in a commander of Genoese
origins. Spínola's reluctance to render sufficient military aid to protect

---

[74] As was no doubt expected from somebody of his standing at the Savoyard court, Scaglia
immediately wrote a letter expressing his loyalty to the new duke. AST LMS m. 23,
fasc. 5, 70, Scaglia to Vittorio Amedeo I, 19 August 1630.
[75] Capriata, *Wars of Italy*, p. 439.   [76] Siri, *Memorie recondite*, VII, p. 198.
[77] As Spínola noted, 'the duke of Savoy desperately wants peace'. AGS Est. 3437, 156,
Spínola to Philip IV, 21 August 1630. See also Siri, *Memorie recondite*, VII, p. 198;
Quazza, *La guerra per la successione*, II, pp. 186–7, which suggests that on the accession
of Vittorio Amedeo I 'the probability of peace greatly increased'; Foa, *Vittorio Amedeo
I*, pp. 65–7; Hanotaux and de la Force, *Richelieu*, III, p. 264.

the duchy of Savoy from marauding French troops and his willingness to consider a suspension of arms which seemingly paid little interest to Savoy had infuriated Carlo Emanuele I, something that emerged when Scaglia returned to Madrid as extraordinary ambassador in February 1630. Significantly, Savoy's alienation from Spínola also played into long-standing rivalries within the Spanish political world. To Olivares, any criticism of Spínola, one of the count-duke's potential rivals at the Spanish court, was naturally welcome, and almost immediately the full powers that initially had been granted to Spínola to negotiate a settlement were revoked, devastating the morale of the marquis. Peter Paul Rubens implied that his rapid loss of health and his death outside the walls of the still unconquered fortress of Casale in September 1630 was linked to Scaglia's mission to Spain.[78]

Spínola could not be held entirely responsible – he had indeed requested reinforcements and a diversion into France to relieve the situation in north Italy. Spain's inability to provide sufficient aid to Savoy was in part the result of overstretch, the perennial problem of the composite monarchy throughout the sixteenth and seventeenth centuries. Even the Holy Roman Emperor's military involvement and the willingness of his commander, Collalto, to provide reinforcements had done little to ameliorate Savoy's position; the geographical proximity of Savoy to France had highlighted one of the characteristics of Savoyard geo-political and strategic concerns, that it was easier for the French than the Spanish to pour large numbers of troops into the patrimonial territories of the duke of Savoy, not only into Savoie but also into Piemonte, striking at the heart of the duchy. This had been the implicit concern behind Scaglia's diplomatic attempts from the outset of the war to keep Richelieu tied down outside the Italian peninsula. While complete neutrality towards the leading powers was rarely an option for Savoy, the risks of turning against France without adequate support from Spain were exposed. Savoyard military and diplomatic strategies were well served by exploiting differences between the leading powers, and even by taking sides when they were involved in conflicts with other powers, such as during the Anglo-French and Anglo-Spanish wars. But it was evidently more dangerous to take sides when the arena of conflict was as close to home as north Italy. With the presence of both French and Habsburg troops in the duchy, the seventeenth-century historian Pietro Capriata wrote (albeit with some overstatement) that Duke Vittorio Amedeo I

---

[78] Rooses and Ruelens (eds.), *Correspondance*, V, pp. 339–40; Capriata, *Wars of Italy*, pp. 418, 422, 445–7; CSPV 1629–32, p. 334; Elliott, *Olivares*, pp. 399–400; Antonio Rodríguez Villa, *Ambrosio Spínola, primer marqués de los Balbases* (Madrid, 1904), pp. 588–9; Quazza, *La guerra per la successione*, II, p. 185.

had become more of a subject than a sovereign in his own dynastic patrimony.[79]

At the same time the other participants in the conflict had their own reasons for wishing to terminate the Gonzaga succession dispute. If David Parrott is correct in arguing that Richelieu's broad aim in the war was not in fact to support Nevers but to gain Savoy then he was to a degree successful. Having said that, the breakdown of relations with Marie de' Medici and Gaston d'Orléans closer to home threatened his position by, as will be seen, opening the door to Spanish-backed intervention in the kingdom. Yet Spain of course had burdensome commitments elsewhere with the exhausting war against the Dutch. At the same time, Emperor Ferdinand II was faced with a renewed threat from the Turks, the problem of the war in central Europe and the intervention of Gustavus Adolphus (1594–1632), and tensions with the Imperial electors at a time when he was looking to call an Imperial diet.[80] Pressures from the electors had already forced the emperor to cashier the mercenary-general Albrecht Wallenstein (1583–1634) and disband his army, preventing Imperial troops from entering France in support of Spain. It was in this atmosphere that on 13 October 1630 an agreement was concluded between representatives of the king of France and the Holy Roman Emperor at Regensburg, setting the foundations for an end to the succession dispute and, at least on paper, to the presence of French, Spanish and Imperial troops in Savoy and Mantua.[81] According to the treaty, the duke of Nevers would obtain Imperial recognition as duke of Mantua and Monferrato while the duke of Savoy would be granted territorial compensation in Monferrato, that included Trino and land with annual rents worth 18,000 scudi a year, in return for renouncing all outstanding claims to that duchy. Margherita Gonzaga, the duchess of Lorraine, would renounce her claim to Monferrato, while the other main claimant to the twin duchies, the duke of Guastalla, was to be granted financial compensation amounting to 6,000 scudi in annual rent for dropping his claim to both Mantua and Monferrato in favour of Nevers. For their parts, French and Imperial troops would gradually withdraw from all their occupied places.

---

[79] Capriata, *Wars of Italy*, p. 470. Capriata also made the explicit point that Savoy was better served by maintaining peace between Spain and France than by taking sides in a conflict between the two powers. *Ibid.*, p. 437.

[80] Quazza, *La guerra per la successione*, II, p. 241.

[81] For a text of the treaty of Regensburg see Dumont (ed.), *Corps universel diplomatique*, V, part II, pp. 615–18. See also Quazza, *La guerra per la successione*, II, pp. 202–3. For a French account of the negotiations see Hanotaux and de la Force, *Richelieu*, III, pp. 267–74.

In reality, the treaty of Regensburg by no means conclusively ended the Gonzaga succession dispute. The Spanish bitterly resented the fact that they had neither been consulted in the negotiations nor even mentioned in the wording of the treaty, despite their enormous military and financial commitment to the war in north Italy.[82] Even Cardinal Richelieu argued against consenting to its ratification, apparently dismayed at the article forbidding the French to offer aid to the enemies of the Holy Roman Emperor and claiming, in what has been seen as a landmark in the evolution of international law, that the French representative at Regensburg did not have sufficiently defined diplomatic powers to commit Louis XIII to a binding agreement in the first place.[83] The seemingly forlorn duke of Nevers too was left less than satisfied, concerned that Vittorio Amedeo I had been excessively compensated beyond what the treaty of Susa between France and Savoy had stipulated; Nevers was to die in 1637, alienated from Richelieu because of the concessions given to his dynastic rival. He had a point. The extent of Savoy's compensation had reflected Vittorio Amedeo I's greater strategic importance to French interests in the Italian peninsula, as the historian Vittorio Siri indeed implied.[84] It took two more treaties, both signed at Cherasco on 6 April 1631 and 19 June 1631, for a lasting peace to be reached.[85] Even then the theatre of north Italy was not fully neutralised. The French failed to comply with the treaties on the critical issue of leaving the fortress of Pinerolo, and Richelieu soon drew a written agreement from Vittorio Amedeo I which allowed the French to station a garrison in the fortress.[86] The cardinal argued that he wanted to have unrestricted access to the peninsula, to defend the Italian princes from Habsburg tyranny. Vittorio Amedeo I later justified his consent by pointing out that the compensations he obtained offset the loss of a fortress that was in any case not as strategically important as many assumed.

To others, Alessandro Scaglia importantly among them, the presence of French troops in Pinerolo was primarily a means for France to retain a powerful, and fundamentally unacceptable, controlling influence over

---

[82] AST LMS m. 23, fasc. 5, 81, Scaglia to Vittorio Amedeo I, 9 November 1630.

[83] O'Connell, 'A cause célèbre'.   [84] Siri, *Memorie recondite*, VII, pp. 416–17.

[85] On the two treaties of Cherasco see Dumont (ed.), *Corps universel diplomatique*, VI, part I, pp. 9–12, 14–16; Ginate González, *Conde de la Roca*, pp. 189–233. In October 1631 Duke Vittorio Amedeo I signed an additional agreement with Louis XIII allowing the French access to the Italian peninsula, a pact that gave the French effective control of Pinerolo. Dumont (ed.), *Corps universel diplomatique*, VI, part I, pp. 20–1.

[86] *Ibid.*, VI, part I, pp. 20–1, 38–9.

the Savoyard state.[87] Whether Vittorio Amedeo I, as a principal dynastic claimant to Monferrato, had gained or not from the war was to some degree overshadowed by the wider ramifications of aligning with France on what seemed to be Richelieu's terms. The balance of power that had traditionally enabled the duchy to play the leading states against one another in north Italy had, it seemed, been seriously compromised.

---

[87] Even Urban VIII was uneasy about France's retention of Pinerolo. Leman, *Urbain VIII*, book I, chapter 2.

6

AFTER THE WAR, 1631–1632

The desire for peace had, at least rhetorically, been shared by all the participants in the war for Mantua and Monferrato. The Spanish regime under the direction of Olivares had always argued that the primary aim of military intervention in the north Italian conflict was to restore the rule of law to the region; in a set of diplomatic instructions to the count of La Roca, Philip IV spoke of his 'sincere spirit', which hoped 'only for calm, the peace of Italy and the public good of Christendom'.[1] In expressing their desire for peace the Holy Roman Emperor, the French and the pope all tapped into similar language to justify their own military and diplomatic interventions.[2] Within the peninsula itself, armed conflict had brought about a general feeling of war weariness exacerbated by the presence of 'foreign' troops and the concomitant effects of a particularly virulent plague that came with the war. Alessandro Scaglia for one repeatedly expressed his wish for an end to the conflict that had been ravaging north Italy and his home state in particular. In one revealing letter he began with the words, 'Pax nobis', and, in a tone that was almost pleading, added that 'may God bring about the execution of the peace as easily as the treaties suggest, and that all the calamities will cease as everyone wants'.[3] The abate's application of a distinctive language conformed to a recognisable pattern of diplomatic practice. In a broad sense the rhetoric of peace was precisely what a seventeenth-century minister had to articulate to a public audience. According to contemporary political theory and practice, princes, as represented and embodied by their diplomats, were expected to seek peace rather than war with other

---

[1] Ginate González, *Conde de la Roca*, p. 164.
[2] On French attitudes see for instance Siri, *Memorie recondite*, VI, p. 557, and for the papacy see Leman, *Urbain VIII*.
[3] AST LMS m. 23, fasc. 5, 82, Scaglia to Vittorio Amedeo I, 9 November 1630. See also 87, Scaglia to Pasero, 29 November 1630; LMS m. 24, fasc. 1, 45, Scaglia to Vittorio Amedeo I, 20 July 1631.

sovereign rulers. The quest for peace defined the identity of prudent diplomacy.[4]

The rhetoric of reconciliation was not, however, the sum total of diplomacy in the period. Quite apart from the pervasive, and unresolved, problems of whom to trust following the breakdown of European religious unity in the sixteenth century, any commitment to seeking peace invariably had to co-exist with equally compelling notions of reputation in power politics.[5] It was of little value if a sovereign prince consented to an agreement that damaged his territorial or 'moral' state, given his particular responsibilities to his dynasty and, by association, to posterity. This critical point of tension between seeking peace and maintaining reputation, as a shorthand for a variety of political, dynastic, cultural and religious aspirations, could clearly complicate the processes of diplomatic negotiations. It occupied the territory where public ministers, obviously including diplomats, felt justified in advocating the use of force to obtain acceptable conclusions to international disputes, at least in early modern Catholic Europe. It is indeed this moralised political pragmatism that accounts for Alessandro Scaglia's reaction to the treaty of Regensburg and the subsequent two treaties of Cherasco, just as it had accounted for his pursuit of seemingly contradictory diplomatic policies after Monzón. While it is clear that he supported the treaty of Regensburg as it was written, it was equally evident that he could not accept the delay in its full implementation by the French. The abate wanted to see the execution of the treaty in its entirety, with the complete withdrawal of French troops from the fortresses of Pinerolo, Bricherasio, Susa and Avigliana in the Savoyard state, and that of Casale in Monferrato. Without these fundamental conditions Scaglia believed that the peace in the Italian peninsula would have no real substance, and indeed would cut directly against Savoy's interests and fundamental patrimonial integrity. And even after the

---

[4] As Christ said of a prudent king when confronted with a superior force in a passage from Luke 14:32, 'he sendeth an ambassage, and desireth conditions of peace [Legationem mittens rogat ea, quae pacis sunt]'. Bragaccio, *L'Ambasciatore*, p. 36. See also the implicit connection made between Christ and the ambassador in Juan Antonio de Vera y Figueroa, *El enbaxador* (Seville, 1620), p. 106. From this point onwards Scaglia's letters drew increasingly on religious imagery and language, connecting the treaties of Regensburg and Cherasco with notions of prudent public policy. AST LMS m. 23, fasc. 5, 82, Scaglia to Vittorio Amedeo I, 9 November 1630; 87, Scaglia to Pasero, 29 November 1630, for some examples.

[5] On the problems of trust in post-Reformation diplomacy consult Mattingly, *Renaissance Diplomacy*, especially pp. 184–7. The issue of reputation in foreign policy has of course long been recognised in studies of the Spanish Habsburgs, most obviously J. H. Elliott, 'A question of reputation? Spanish foreign policy in the seventeenth century', *Journal of Modern History*, 55 (1983).

French garrisons left Bricherasio, Susa and Avigliana (but, significantly, not Pinerolo) shortly afterwards, he did not back down from this trenchant position. It featured in virtually all of his letters to both Vittorio Amedeo I and the Spanish regime from late 1630 onwards, highlighting a paradox of the kind of diplomacy he represented. Alessandro Scaglia repeatedly expressed his abiding commitment to peace by wishing to continue the conflict, for as the English secretary in Madrid succinctly put it, 'the abate tells me plainly that he hopes not for peace in Italy until the French be called from thence by a divertive war'.[6] There was no clearer expression of Scaglia's sense of diplomatic pragmatism that underpinned his approach to power politics.

This was without doubt an important moment in his political career in service to the House of Savoy. For the first time Alessandro Scaglia was advocating a policy that seemingly ran contrary to his sovereign prince's stated wishes. The abate and his family had always been loyal – and immensely successful - members of the Savoyard court clientele, whether that had meant serving in court offices or diplomatic missions abroad, or indeed operating as cultural patrons and brokers. From his arrival in Paris in 1624 he had rapidly established himself as Carlo Emanuele I's leading ambassador and had done much to shape Savoyard foreign policies over the course of the decade, developing his own idea of what he thought were his home state's best interests. However, circumstances had for the abate and his home state changed following Savoy's realignment with France after Vittorio Amedeo I's accession. Given the problems faced by Savoy in the midst of the conflict, the duke needed to re-evaluate his relationship with the major powers. Duke Vittorio Amedeo I wanted to see peace in the Italian peninsula – any further conflict would only lead to 'our total destruction', as he wrote to Scaglia.[7] But he also wanted to balance his position between the leading powers, which, given the alignment with Spain during the war, entailed an accommodation with his brother-in-law, Louis XIII of France. The peace treaties of Regensburg and later Cherasco had after all provided him with generous territorial compensation for the dynastic claim to Monferrato, even if a French

---

[6] BL Eg. MS 1820, f. 21v, Hopton to Cottington, 14 April 1631. See also AST LMS m. 23, fasc. 5, 89, Scaglia to Vittorio Amedeo I, 7 December 1630; 87, Scaglia to Pasero, 29 November 1630; LMS m. 24, fasc. 1, 3, Scaglia to Vittorio Amedeo I, 10 January 1631; 17, Scaglia to Vittorio Amedeo I, 26 February 1631; AGR SEG 600, Scaglia to Olivares, 20 November 1631.

[7] AST LMM m. 18, 'Registro delle lettere del Duca', Vittorio Amedeo I to Scaglia, 11 April 1631; LMS m. 22, 23, Vittorio Amedeo I to Scaglia, 4 November 1630. The abate in contrast argued that Spain was essentially a more reliable ally than France. AST LMS m. 24, fasc. 1, 27, Scaglia to Vittorio Amedeo I, 26 April 1631.

garrison remained in the key Savoyard fortress of Pinerolo.[8] Driven by his now implacable mistrust of Richelieu, Alessandro Scaglia in contrast believed that his prince should end the conflict with the military and financial aid of Spain to force the complete removal of all French forces from Savoyard patrimonial territory. The acceptability of the settlement with France, which was to become a fundamental sticking point among the Savoyard political elites during the 1630s, was effectively prefigured in Alessandro Scaglia's reactions as an individual minister with the experience and capability to act according to his own initiative. While it may have been either undesirable or impractical actually to force the French out of Pinerolo, the abate could not countenance what he saw as the unacceptable level of their encroachment in the Savoyard state, a position increasingly shared by hispanophile and anti-French subjects of the duke of Savoy as the decade progressed. Therein lay one of the dilemmas of a second-rank state like the duchy of Savoy. It is true that Savoy almost always had enormous opportunities for playing the leading powers against each other, either by itself or in alliance with other second-rank states, most importantly during the 1620s with England. Only rarely did France and Spain find common ground on matters of foreign policy, and the very fact that there was a war in north Italy, one of Europe's powder kegs, involving the House of France and both branches of the Habsburgs between 1628 and 1631 showed how easy it was for a state like Savoy to light the fuse. But in turn this carried the problem for Savoy of competing and inherently conflicting strategic priorities, whether it was better to support France or Spain, given that complete or permanent neutrality was rarely a viable, or indeed desirable, policy.[9]

This did not, however, imply that Savoy was a passive victim of great power rivalry. The process of concluding the war in north Italy also raised difficult questions for the leading powers. Both Spain and France had to clarify where they stood with the House of Savoy and in both cases they were reluctant to hand an alliance with the duchy to the other. The reaction of the Spanish council of state to the peace treaties of Regensburg and Cherasco was understandably mixed.[10] The duke of Feria, reappointed to the governorship of Milan following Spínola's death in 1630, continued to advocate the use of military force to obtain Spanish

---

[8] The duke indeed consented to extending the period of French control of Pinerolo in an agreement dated May 1632. Dumont (ed.), *Corps universel diplomatique*, VI, part I, pp. 38–9.

[9] AST LMS m. 24 fasc. 1, 17, Scaglia to Vittorio Amedeo I, 26 April 1631; C. E. Patrucco, 'L'antifrancesimo sotto il regno di Vittorio Amedeo I', *Bollettino Storico-Bibliografico Subalpino*, 1 (1896).

[10] Capriata, *Wars of Italy*, pp. 452–3; Quazza, *La guerra per la successione*, II, p. 252.

interests in the region. The hawkish Spanish commander was openly dis-
satisfied with Vittorio Amedeo I's decision to settle with Paris at, what
he argued, was the expense of Spain.[11] Olivares was equally angry at the
settlement negotiated at Regensburg, 'the most discreditable peace we
have ever had', as he claimed – it was after all (from Spain's perspective)
primarily his war rather than Philip IV's, and his reputation had as a result
taken a severe battering.[12] But he was also more measured towards the
strategically crucial Savoy. The *valido* said in a meeting of the council
of state that he well understood the need for Vittorio Amedeo I to sue
for peace so that he could restore his territorial possessions, even though
this entailed sacrificing ground to the French. The Savoyard prince had
accordingly taken a pragmatic decision to end his participation in the
hostilities. As the count-duke went on to suggest, Vittorio Amedeo I
was unlikely to turn against the Habsburgs, especially given that it was
arguably more reasonable to obtain the restitution of French-occupied
territory in alliance with Spain than to enter a considerably more risky
French agreement that might lead Savoy to attack the state of Milan.
Behind his conciliatory and somewhat optimistic rhetoric, Olivares nevertheless appreciated the precariousness of Spain's position in the north
Italian theatre. French troops remained within the Italian peninsula and
in possession of Pinerolo and Casale, while the mountain passes through
the Valtelline, so important to the Spanish Road, needed to be restored
to the *status quo ante bellum* according to the treaty of Monzón and as
the treaty of Regensburg had stipulated. The delays by the French in
executing the treaty of Regensburg had moreover necessitated keeping
an army in the field for several months at great financial expense to
Spain.[13]

Both during and after the war the Spanish regime faced perpetu-
ally difficult choices of balancing competing international interests that
drained both the money and manpower of the composite monarchy. On
the one hand, if the war in north Italy were concluded and the region
at last neutralised (even if this meant ceding ground to the French over
the occupation of Pinerolo and Casale) then the Spanish could concentrate their resources on the still unresolved threat posed by the Dutch in

---

[11] See for instance AGS Est. 3336, 139, Feria to Philip IV, 12 April 1631; AST LMS
m. 24, fasc.1, 30, Scaglia to Vittorio Amedeo I, 3 May 1631; 37, Scaglia to Vittorio
Amedeo I, 17 May 1631; Capriata, *Wars of Italy*, pp. 462–3. Feria had first been
appointed governor of Milan in 1618, and was replaced in 1629 by Spínola. Elliott,
Olivares, pp. 62, 370, 400.

[12] Quoted in *ibid.*, p. 401.

[13] AGS Est. 3336, 79, consulta of council of state, 6 May 1631; 3444, 264, Philip IV to
La Roca, 6 October 1631; Ginate González, *Conde de la Roca*, pp. 215–18.

northern Europe.[14] There was however an inherent danger in this policy since Savoy might be lost to an alliance with France, a possibility Olivares was extremely reluctant to countenance even though the alignment with Savoy had only taken shape as recently as 1627. The duchy remained strategically important to Spain in limiting the encroachment of French influence in what could certainly remain a contentious strategic theatre, as it had been since the late fifteenth century, not least because the loss of Savoy's support would entail further insecurity to Spanish dominions in the Italian peninsula, particularly to the duchy of Milan, and also to the ever-sensitive Spanish Road. In one of his rhetorical flourishes Olivares reiterated the need to remain on good terms with Savoy because Vittorio Amedeo I effectively held a balance of power in Europe, and while the count-duke might be discounted for the extravagance of his claims, he repeated the offer to Scaglia, whether realistically or not, for further military and financial aid to force the removal of the French from north Italy.[15] Significantly, he also made advances to Vittorio Amedeo I's younger brothers, Cardinal Maurizio and Prince Tommaso Francesco, in the hope of buying their loyalty to Madrid. Given that before 1632 Duke Vittorio Amedeo I had no male heirs of his own, the two other princes were the best placed to succeed their elder brother to the ducal throne in the event of his death, pre-empting the profound dynastic instability that was to beset the Savoyard House and the duchy as a whole during the 1630s.[16]

In reporting the count-duke's offers and presenting information with a particular slant, Alessandro Scaglia implicitly pushed his own political agenda as an individual minister, or at least what he thought were the best interests of Savoy.[17] If a renewed military alliance with Spain formed one of his projects, then another tried strategy of focusing on what could be achieved in the theatre of north Italy by exploiting circumstances outside the peninsula comprised another. One means of exerting pressure on Richelieu was to continue financing the defeated Huguenot leaders, Soubise and Rohan. A second option was to reactivate

---

[14] BL Eg. MS 1820, f. 104, Hopton to Dorchester, 1 December 1631; Quazza, *La guerra per la successione*, II, p. 261; Ginate González, *Conde de la Roca*, pp. 248–19.

[15] AGS Est. 3336, 79, consulta of council of state 6 May 1631; AST LMS m. 23, fasc. 5, 91, Scaglia to Vittorio Amedeo I, late 1630; 92, Scaglia to Vittorio Amedeo I, 9 December 1630; Ginate González, *Conde de la Roca*, pp. 246–7.

[16] AST LMS m. 23, fasc. 5, 86, Scaglia to Vittorio Amedeo I, 29 November 1630; LMS m. 24, fasc. 1, 3, Scaglia to Vittorio Amedeo I, 10 January 1631; 7, Scaglia to Vittorio Amedeo I, 26 January 1631; 14, Scaglia to Vittorio Amedeo I, 1 February 1631; 19, Scaglia to Vittorio Amedeo I, 15 March 1631; Ginate González, *Conde de la Roca*, pp. 169, 183–4.

[17] AST LMS m. 23, fasc. 5, 16, Scaglia to Vittorio Amedeo I, 30 July 1631.

England as a military lever. Buckingham's death in 1628, the termination of Parliament in 1629, and the settlement of both wars with France and Spain, might have marked a total cessation of active English participation on the continent. But the Anglo-Spanish peace treaty signed in November 1630 in fact seemed to pave the way for a possible offensive alliance with Spain as a clique of hispanophile ministers like Weston and Cottington gradually assumed a degree of influence in London. In January 1631 Francis Cottington, in Madrid for the third and final time, negotiated a secret alliance for joint Anglo-Spanish action against the Dutch, raising Abate Scaglia's hopes that the English might also resume some kind of military action against France, though precisely what kind of action remained unclear. While Charles I might not have been in a position to offer a land force of his own given the tumultuous circumstances surrounding the dissolution of Parliament in 1629, his territories could at the least serve as a source of mercenaries for the Habsburgs to levy for use in central Europe against the Swedes. It was also believed, however correctly, that the English king had a navy at his disposal that was sufficiently powerful to threaten the French in the Channel.[18]

The final settlement of the Anglo-Spanish war after more than three years of diplomacy involving Alessandro Scaglia provided the pretext for a mission to the English court, though one that from its very inception lacked any clearly stated purpose.[19] The peculiarity of the mission was doubled by the remarkable fact that Scaglia was despatched as both extraordinary ambassador of the duke of Savoy and diplomatic agent of the king of Spain. Vittorio Amedeo I had, it seems, given the go-ahead for Scaglia's mission at the beginning of 1631; in May 1631, Philip IV granted the abate his formal credential from Spain, in which Scaglia was described as *Ducis Sabaudiae Orator*, together with a personal Spanish cipher and a generous financial payment of 8,000 ducats, in addition to monthly payments for expenses.[20] A simultaneous mission by one diplomat on behalf

[18] On Cottington's secret treaty see Reeve, *Charles I*, pp. 256–9; Sharpe, *Personal Rule*, pp. 70–2; AGR SEG 600, Scaglia to Olivares, November 1631. Charles I of course gave permission for troops to be levied on behalf of Gustavus Adolphus as well. Reeve, *Charles I*, pp. 266–7.

[19] Scaglia was explicitly named in the treaty of Madrid for his part in the negotiations. Dumont (ed.), *Corps universel diplomatique*, V, part II, p. 620. See also AST LDS, m. 48, Charles I to Vittorio Amedeo I, 15 December 1630. It is possible that he was being sent by the Savoyard duke to offer congratulations to Charles I on the end of the war with Spain.

[20] PRO SP 92/19/3, Vittorio Amedeo I to Charles I, 13 February 1631; PRO SP 94/35/221, Philip IV to Charles I, 22 May 1631; AGS Est. 2519, 124, Philip IV to Rocas, 19 April 1631; 128, Rocas to Olivares, 12 June 1631; CSPV 1629–32, p. 507.

of two sovereign princes seems to have been unique for the period of the Thirty Years' War, contradicting the first principle of loyalty and service to a single sovereign prince that was assumed in all contemporary diplomatic practice. If a diplomat embodied and represented his sovereign, as was generally accepted, how could he serve more than one at the same time?[21] Curiously the question was never explicitly raised, let alone answered, though the simplest explanation for the double mission might be one of expediency, that in essence it was convenient for Spain to make use of an acceptable diplomat who had in any case already planned to visit London for his own prince. This was the position outlined in a document for Scaglia signed by Philip IV.[22] Having said that, by 1631 the abate was without doubt one of the most well-known diplomats in Europe. He was clearly identified by his sympathies to Spain. By employing him, the Spanish (if not Vittorio Amedeo I) were in all likelihood seeking to give the impression that relations with the Savoyard court were as strong as ever, whatever was happening 'officially', and that there was a new, anti-French, diplomatic initiative afoot. As if to underline Spain's confidence in the abate, Scaglia was granted the gift of an abbey at Mandanici in Sicily, and when he set out to Lisbon to take a ship for the mission it was even reported by a French observer that he was treated as if he were 'an Infante of Castile'.[23] The Spanish moreover were clearly hoping that Scaglia would draw on his reputation with his friends and contacts in London to secure their interests, despite the fact that his closest friend, Buckingham, was dead. The abate also hoped to achieve something tangible from the mission. As Arthur Hopton (c. 1588–1650), the English agent in Madrid, put it, recording the special relationship that Scaglia enjoyed as a go-between:

> This gentleman the Abate of Scaglia is doubtless his Majesty's [Charles I] servant, and there is as little doubt but that he is a well-willer to this crown [Spain], having received many favours from this king, and some very lately, in which indifferent disposition here is gone, that both sides may hope of good from him, and I have a hope that he will endeavour to bring things to such a passing as the kings may continue good friend each with other and

---

[21] For example, Bragaccio, *L'Ambasciatore*, p. 26.

[22] AGS Est. 2574, 'Lo que se ofrece de mi servicio de que vos el Abad Don Alessandro Cesar Scaglia embajador extraordinario del duque de Saboya mi primo, y de su consejo de estado haveis de ir advertido en vuestra jornada a Inglaterra es lo siguente', c. spring 1631.

[23] AAE CP Espagne, 16, f. 275, de Perry to Hotman, 26 July 1631. The abbey of Mandanici was apparently worth 2,300 ducats a year. AST LMS m. 24, fasc. 1, 40, Scaglia to Vittorio Amedeo I, 3 June 1631; CSPV 1629–32, p. 521.

both to him, for I am informed from a very good hand, that he hath told the conde of Olivares that since they have made choice of him, among many servants the king hath, to negotiate with the king of England, because they take notice that his Majesty hath a good opinion of him, he is resolved to deceive neither, and hath desired him not to employ him in anything but what they purpose . . . to perform, which the conde hath promised him.[24]

Vittorio Amedeo I's reaction to renewing an international military alliance against France was ambiguous to say the least, as was his reason for consenting to Scaglia's double mission in the first place – he fully knew that the abate's mission would generate sharp hostility in Paris. This ambiguity certainly emerged in the contradictory messages he transmitted to Scaglia. While Vittorio Amedeo I had already played down the possibility of a renewed alliance with Spain, he had also hinted that the war against France could in fact be continued outside the Italian peninsula where there would obviously be much less damage to his Savoyard patrimony. The duke seemed to suggest that if the war in north Italy were settled then he himself might be free to support the restless, and exiled, Gaston d'Orléans in a confrontation with Richelieu.[25] But it is difficult to conclude that this was a preferred or firmly set policy. The Savoyard duke also claimed that he specifically did not want a resumption of the war close to home in north Italy so soon after its conclusion, especially as the war had resulted in the occupation of his patrimony by foreign troops. Indeed, the closer Scaglia came to beginning his mission to London the more uneasy Vittorio Amedeo I became, writing to Alessandro Scaglia that the duke of Feria's aggressive rhetoric ran contrary to his desire for peace. By June 1631, when the abate was on the point of leaving the Iberian peninsula for London, the Savoyard duke had at least in public instructed Scaglia to postpone the mission and to refrain from talk of resumed military co-operation with Spain. The Spanish could not be relied upon to keep their promises, so Duke Vittorio Amedeo I reasoned, adding in a letter to Scaglia that 'as you have seen in the current affairs, the execution of the peace is taking place at a pace, and it is better for us

---

[24] PRO SP 94/35/244–v, Hopton to Dorchester, 15 June 1631. See also PRO SP 94/35/246, Hopton to Weston, 18 June 1631, in which Hopton wrote, without any discernible sense of irony, that, 'he hath drawn all business upon himself, by the reputation he hath gotten of square dealing'; Ginate González, *Conde de la Roca*, p. 254. The mission certainly generated speculation and suspicion from Giovanni Soranzo, the Venetian ambassador in London. For example CSPV 1629–32, pp. 527, 530, 537.

[25] AST LMM m. 18, 'Registro delle lettere del Duca', Vittorio Amedeo I to Scaglia, 11 April 1631; Vittorio Amedeo I to Scaglia, 16 April 1631.

to avoid anything that might destabilise it, especially since we see no clear evidence that Spain will definitely break with France. They are sending no help to Gaston.'[26]

Vittorio Amedeo I did not want to be drawn into yet more costly military action given that the Spanish had themselves shown that they were incapable of sustaining heavy commitments in north Italy, but nor did he necessarily want to antagonise the regime in Madrid. The impression of Duke Vittorio Amedeo I at this point is of equivocation, or perhaps more realistically of uncertainty. He was avoiding too strong a position over Scaglia's mission that might have alienated either Spain or France, and puzzlingly Alessandro Scaglia's mission to the English court still went ahead; he arrived in London in September 1631 and remained until March 1632. But even if Vittorio Amedeo I wanted a sustainable peace close to home, the stability of the French state seemed far from secure with the internal crisis faced by the Bourbon court. Marie de' Medici's complicity in the Day of Dupes, the failed attempt to have Cardinal Richelieu removed from office, split the royal family. In the wake of the débâcle, the queen mother fled France for the refuge of the Spanish Netherlands at a time when the king's younger brother, Gaston d'Orléans, was himself again at odds with Richelieu over the unresolved question of the prince's marital status – in early January 1632 the prince had married Marguérite de Lorraine, a sister of the duke of Lorraine, whose family's own relations with the Bourbons could hardly be described as stable. While attention around Europe was understandably drawn to the spectacular advances through central Europe of the Swedish king Gustavus Adolphus, the problems within the House of France in the aftermath of the Day of Dupes were potentially dangerous for continental stability. True enough, Marie de' Medici was a source of embarrassment and financial cost to whatever state accepted her as a refugee, given her political position and the fact that her household expenses as a dowager queen-consort had to be defrayed.[27] Both she and Gaston nevertheless presented the Spanish regime and Scaglia with political opportunities to create enormous domestic trouble for Cardinal Richelieu; they could serve as legitimate focal

---

[26] AST LMM m. 18, 'Registro delle lettere del Duca', Vittorio Amedeo I to Scaglia, 28 July 1631. See also AGS Est. 3646, 30, Vittorio Amedeo I to Philip IV, 14 April 1631; Ginate González, *Conde de la Roca*, pp. 186–7.

[27] Certainly Charles I was extremely reluctant to accept her as a refugee in England throughout the 1630s because of the political and financial costs that she would generate. See for example CSPV 1636–9, pp. 445–6. She nevertheless went to her son-in-law's court in 1638 as her position in the Spanish Netherlands became untenable. For a detailed, if somewhat coloured, account of the journey by her official polemicist see Jean Puget de la Serre, *Histoire de l'entree de la reine Mere dans la Grande Bretagne* (London, 1639).

points for mobilising military opposition to the cardinal, even though he could claim that their exile was a matter for Louis XIII alone as their blood relatives and not for him as a mere minister.[28] In public at least the Habsburg regime offered to mediate between the queen mother and Louis XIII, through Scaglia in London. That no doubt was what they were expected to do, given the double dynastic context of Philip IV's marriage to a daughter of Marie de' Medici, Elisabeth de Bourbon, and Louis XIII's marriage to Anne of Austria. However, behind the public rhetoric of reconciliation, Spain hoped to extract as much political capital as possible from the double exile of the queen mother of France and the heir to the kingdom. As Scaglia's secret instructions elaborated, she and Gaston were to be used to lead a new military and political front against the cardinal involving an alliance between England, Savoy and Lorraine, yet again in the belief that pressure could be exerted in north Italy by exploiting events outside the peninsula.[29]

The divisions within the French royal family were understandably of concern to Richelieu, more so because of the threat posed to his domestic security by Scaglia's mission to London. Even before the abate had left the Iberian peninsula for England it was clear that his mission was going to prove controversial. As the English secretary in Turin put it, 'the going of the Abate Scaglia into England is much eyd by the French here and they do believe that that active and stirring minister, will bring forth some dangerous and disadvantageous fruit to the French crown'.[30] Vittorio Amedeo I, too, knew that the French would be more than suspicious about the mission, concerned as he was that they would use it as an excuse to avoid executing the peace treaties in full, and he informed Scaglia that his 'journey could certainly not have come at a worse time for our interests, for coming at the point when the fortresses should be returned you ought to be aware that every small incident or pretext for suspicion is enough to disturb what has been agreed'.[31] The duke's

---

[28] See the comments in Michel Carmona, *Marie de Médicis* (Paris, 1981), p. 464.

[29] AGS Est. 2574, 'Lo que se offrece', *c.* spring 1631; K1415, 57, consulta of council of state, 13 June 1631; 2045, 45, consulta of council of state, 5 August 1631; K1665, 50, secret instructions for Scaglia, spring 1631; Quazza, *La guerra per la succesione*, II, p. 317. See also AST LMS m. 24, fasc. 1, 17, Scaglia to Vittorio Amedeo I, 26 February 1631; Ginate González, *Conde de la Roca*, pp. 184–5; Reeve, *Charles I*, pp. 264–5. The profound fears generated by the split in the French royal family were also felt in Rome, where Saavedra Fajardo reported the concern that the Habsburgs would exploit the problems faced by France and make a move into Germany. Aldea Vaquero (ed.), *Correspondencia*, I, p. 22.

[30] PRO SP 92/19/71, Hales to Dorchester, 10 July 1631.

[31] AST LMM m. 18, 'Registro delle Lettere del Duca', Vittorio Amedeo I to Scaglia, 28 July 1631, another of the same date.

fears proved to be justified. In September 1631 Cardinal Maurizio, the middle of the Savoyard princes and next in line of succession to the duchy of Savoy, arrived in Paris, offering to mediate in the Bourbon dispute with the aid of Marie Christine's confessor, Pietro Monod.[32] When they reached the French court, Maurizio and Monod were met with openly expressed anger over Scaglia's mission, coupled with implicit threats that it might complicate relations between the courts of Paris and Turin. Richelieu claimed that the security of Franco-Savoyard relations, and by implication the future restitution of Pinerolo, was in direct jeopardy precisely because of the abate's double mission, a complaint the French ordinary ambassador in Turin was under instruction to repeat.[33]

Richelieu soon began to turn the diplomatic screw. Early in 1632 Giulio Mazzarini was in Paris, in an unofficial capacity to secure an alliance between France and Savoy, believing that it would provide the foundations for a powerful, and indeed strategically vital, anti-Habsburg powerbase in the Italian peninsula. On Mazzarini's arrival, the cardinal-minister's criticisms of Scaglia became more extreme, asserting that his 'number one enemy [enemigo capital]', the abate, had hired a number of Spaniards in the name of Philip IV to kill him. Richelieu's startling claim is important. It naturally begs the wider question about the correlation between rhetoric and reality, whether he genuinely thought he was in mortal danger from Alessandro Scaglia. Without alienating the Turinese regime completely, the cardinal may well have deliberately exaggerated the threat posed by Scaglia, just as he may have done after the Chalais conspiracy in 1626, to serve as a bargaining tool both to exert diplomatic pressure on the Savoyard court and to nip in the bud any potential alliance with Marie de' Medici and Gaston. Mazzarini was certainly alert to the fact that Richelieu's accusations preceded any discussion about the future of Franco-Savoyard relations.[34] But at the very least, whether deliberately invented or not, the claim revealed the narrowness between personal

---

[32] Vittorio Amedeo I had instructed Cardinal Maurizio to assure Richelieu that Savoy would not offer any assistance to Marie de' Medici or to Gaston d'Orléans. Capriata, *Wars of Italy*, p. 467; Quazza, *La guerra per la successione*, II, p. 316.

[33] For instance, AAE CP Sardaigne, 18, f. 510, Richelieu to Servien, 5 December 1631; f. 180, Louis XIII to Servien, 9 September 1631. Servien reported on several occasions that he requested the recall of Scaglia, 'that deeply pernicious minister'. AAE CP Sardaigne, 18, f. 319v, Servien to Louis XIII, 11 September 1631. See also Capriata, *Wars of Italy*, p. 466.

[34] AST LMF m. 31, fasc. 3, 2, Mazzarini to Vittorio Amedeo I, 17 May 1632; LMS m. 20, fasc. 1, Ventimiglia to Vittorio Amedeo I, 25 September 1632. The bishop of Ventimiglia negatively described Scaglia as a 'man with little fear of God [hombre poco temoroso de Dios]', while a near contemporary historian, Vittorio Siri, also described the abate as an 'open enemy of the cardinal'. Siri, *Memorie recondite*, VII, p. 500.

politics and state diplomacy. In effect Richelieu was once again merging his widely known and personalised animosity towards Scaglia with the progress of Franco-Savoyard diplomatic relations. By implication he was also crediting the abate with an enormous amount of political influence, fearing that his negotiations would threaten his own mortal safety.

Richelieu had a more than receptive audience. Father Monod and, more importantly, Cardinal Maurizio viewed the abate with a mixture of dislike and resentment, adding a further layer of complexity to the relationship between the Savoyard House and the Scaglia di Verrua. Pietro Monod was known as an ambitious cleric and he had quickly emerged following the accession of Vittorio Amedeo I and Marie Christine, with whom he enjoyed particular favour. Following the declaration of Savoy's royal status in 1632, the *trattamento reale*, it was Monod who spearheaded the official propaganda campaign to justify the royal status, and he continued to be a loyal supporter of the ducal couple.[35] Yet as Vittorio Amedeo I and his consort had assumed power, Monod had also emerged as an opponent of the Scaglia di Verrua family clan within the Turinese court, and a significant rival to the abate. An anonymous document drawn up in Paris acknowledged with a note of brevity, though unfortunately no further detail, that 'Monod has a great plan for ruining the count of Verrua'.[36]

The cardinal-prince Maurizio had equally poor relations with Alessandro Scaglia dating back to the mutual animosities that had emerged when the abate had served as his secretary in Rome. At least initially, the abate and the cardinal had been closely identified with one another. Alessandro's role as his family's point of contact with the church mirrored that played by Maurizio for the ruling House, and the abate had of course served early in his career as a gentleman in Maurizio's household, emphasising his significance to his family's fortunes as a client of the cardinal-prince. As a skilled cultural broker, Alessandro Scaglia had furthermore done much to add to the cardinal's artistic collection while serving as ambassador to the papal court, so important not only to Maurizio as an individual but to the House of Savoy in its campaign to assert its cultural authority in Europe. But in Rome the abate had also supported Alessandro Tassoni at a time when the writer was locked in a series of bitter disputes with Maurizio's clients, and when in 1623 the Savoyard cardinal-prince took

---

[35] Monod, *Trattato del titolo regio*; Oresko, 'House of Savoy', in Oresko, Gibbs and Scott (eds.), *Royal and Republican Sovereignty*, p. 326, footnote 91.

[36] AAE CP Sardaigne 18, f. 471, memoire, 14 November 1631; ff. 517v–8, memoire, 14 December 1631. Richelieu, who deeply mistrusted Monod, advised the French ordinary ambassador in Turin to watch him 'like a poisonous snake'. Dethan, *Mazarin*, p. 151. Eventually he persuaded Marie Christine to have him arrested.

part in the papal conclave that elevated Urban VIII Barberini, the tensions with Scaglia had increased still further. Much to the abate's irritation, and indeed that of Duke Carlo Emanuele I, Maurizio had deliberately excluded Scaglia from the conclave, taking two of his own clients instead. The cardinal had then tried to press his advantage by having his favourite, Balìo Delescherene, transferred to Rome as Savoy's extraordinary ambassador, vilified by (the somewhat biased) Tassoni as a 'vain man, inexperienced in the ways of Rome, ill-informed of Carlo Emanuele I's interests, and in service to the cardinal, his patron, out of personal ambition and his own aspirations'.[37] Carlo Emanuele I finally intervened after Scaglia wrote to him and Vittorio Amedeo. The cardinal's request was refused on the pretext that Delescherene was to be sent on a mission to Bavaria. Instead, Count Guido Aldobrandino S. Giorgio was sent as a diplomat of a much more suitable social status to congratulate the Barberini pope on his elevation, so Carlo Emanuele I stated. The Savoyard duke indeed made clear his displeasure at Maurizio's handling of the papal conclave and of Scaglia's exclusion.[38] According to Tassoni, Maurizio loathed the abate as a person 'too eminent among his vassals', adding that it was Maurizio who 'forced him to leave Rome out of envy of his ability'.[39] While therefore the Savoyard cardinal was sceptical about the veracity of Richelieu's claims, his persistent antipathy to the abate came to bear over his judgement as he reported Richelieu's hostility to his ducal brother.[40] As a member of the sovereign family of Savoy, Maurizio was undeniably a more dangerous opponent to Scaglia than Monod (essentially a court rival, albeit one who enjoyed the special favour of Vittorio Amedeo I and Marie Christine). Responding to Richelieu's pressure, Maurizio decided to despatch his treasurer, Masserati, to instruct the abate to leave England for France.[41]

    While Vittorio Amedeo I was seeking, at the least, to avoid alienating the French regime, Scaglia's mission provided Richelieu with a diplomatic

---

[37] Tassoni, *Manifesto*, p. 406.
[38] Delescherene died, according to contemporary accounts, a forlorn figure in Turin soon after. Adriani, *Memorie*, pp. 214–18; Tassoni, *Manifesto*, p. 411.
[39] *Ibid.*, p. 408.
[40] For instance, AST LPD m. 15, Maurizio to Vittorio Amedeo I, 25 October 1631; Maurizio to Vittorio Amedeo I, 10 November 1631; Maurizio to Vittorio Amedeo I, 12 November 1631.
[41] AST LPD m. 15, Maurizio to Vittorio Amedeo I, 14 September 1631; CSPV 1629–32, p. 542. When Masserati arrived in England, Scaglia side-stepped the instruction by writing to Maurizio complaining about his ill-health. AST LMI m. 4, 103, Scaglia to Maurizio, 23 September 1631, while in a letter to Duke Vittorio Amedeo I he elaborated the reasons as to why he should remain in London. AST LMI m. 4, 104, Scaglia to Vittorio Amedeo I, 6 October 1631.

bargaining tool to use against the duke. Yet the volume of Richelieu's criticism of the abate was also a measure of the concerns felt in Paris over the future of relations with Savoy, and the rhetorical campaign directed against Scaglia itself implied that the political influence of Paris over Turin (despite the French occupation of Pinerolo) was not as strong as it appeared. Carlo Emanuele I's death in July 1630 and the end of the war in north Italy had precipitated a period of uncertainty in equal measure to political opportunity for the regime in Paris, just as it had done for the Spanish. As Olivares was reluctant to lose a Savoyard alliance so Richelieu understood the strategic necessity of winning over Duke Vittorio Amedeo I. Savoy's willing support was essential if Richelieu were to organise a league of Italian states to counter Habsburg power in the peninsula, a plan that had existed throughout the course of the Gonzaga succession dispute and earlier and which played into the established anti-Habsburg ideal of Italian liberty. The cardinal's strategy, however, faced a double threat. In the first place Scaglia, under instruction from the Spanish regime, was pushing for Duke Vittorio Amedeo I to become involved in a new international project that directly threatened Richelieu's security within France. At the same time, Pietro Monod's arrival in Paris unequivocally informed the cardinal of the danger that Duke Vittorio Amedeo I or his French consort might favour unreliable or ambitious courtiers who were at best indifferent to Richelieu. His fear was that Monod might seek to influence Savoyard policy-making to his detriment, even though Marie Christine's blood ties with Louis XIII implied a closer alignment with France and Richelieu himself was ironically using Monod as a tool against Scaglia. The potential fragility of Franco-Savoyard relations was all the more acute because of the fact that at this point the ducal couple did not have a male child and heir. If Vittorio Amedeo I were suddenly to die, the succession would very probably pass to Cardinal Maurizio as the next eldest brother, or possibly to the youngest of the brothers, Tommaso Francesco (whom Olivares was trying to win over), bypassing Vittorio Amedeo I's wife, Marie Christine, and thus possibly jeopardising French influence still further.

The potential threat posed by Monod and any other anti-French ministers or courtiers could at least be offset by supporting established francophiles in Turin. But this too presented problems to Richelieu since the best placed of all the francophile subjects of the duke of Savoy was the count of Verrua, Alessandro Scaglia's elder brother. By seeking to discredit Alessandro through his rhetorical campaign, Richelieu was potentially endangering Verrua's own position at the Savoyard court, a fact not lost on the cardinal. His response was twofold. In the first place he sought to distinguish the two brothers as political figures in their own rights, playing down the significance of their filial affinity, even though it had invariably been a defining point of the Scaglia di Verrua as a court clan up to that point. The cardinal went on to assure Verrua that his favour in France was secure, despite the very public attacks on his younger brother; with an eye on the uncertain Savoyard succession, Richelieu added that the count would be provided with a safe haven in the event of any sudden change of political fortune in Turin that might threaten Verrua's own safety. 'You should assure the count of Verrua', Richelieu instructed the French ambassador in Turin, 'that he has protection, a pension and a retreat if he needs them, in the event of the duke of Savoy dying without children.'[42] Given that co-operation between family members had up to this point been central to maintaining the collective power of the Scaglia di Verrua as a court clan, quite what Augusto Manfredo Scaglia made of these offers remains tantalisingly unknown.

While Richelieu sought to strike a very delicate balance between attacking Alessandro Scaglia and protecting his elder brother, Vittorio Amedeo I had to respond to the hostile signals coming from Paris. When Cardinal Maurizio's treasurer failed to persuade Scaglia to leave England, the duke decided to send Carlo Vittorio Scaglia, the marquis of Caluso, to Alessandro. The choice of envoy was by no means thoughtless; the marquis was the abate's eldest nephew and heir to the Scaglia di Verrua's patrimony. Caluso's instructions are more than revealing about the way in which the Savoyard duke thought a member of the Scaglia di Verrua family clan might influence the abate and also on the perceptions of Alessandro Scaglia as a politically important figure capable of operating on his own initiative. Carlo Vittorio was in the first place instructed to express how highly his uncle was esteemed by Duke Vittorio Amedeo I. He was then to explain the reasons why the Savoyard duke had consented to the peace treaties of Regensburg and Cherasco while ultimately declining the possibility of resuming the war with Spanish aid. Finally, the abate was to be informed about the suspicion his mission was generating and how in turn that was actually delaying the execution of the peace treaties which the abate himself had said that he so earnestly wanted.[43] But rather than persuading Alessandro of the threat posed to his sovereign's interests by his mission, his nephew's arrival only confirmed his fears of the

---

[42] AAE CP Sardaigne 18, f. 471, draft of a letter to Servien, late 1631;

[43] AST NI m. 1, instructions to the marquis of Caluso, c. September 1631; AAE CP Sardaigne, 18, f. 186, Vittorio Amedeo I to Richelieu, 3 September 1631; f. 237, Cardinal Maurizio to Richelieu, 18 September 1631. It seems that Caluso also had some verbal instructions, though their content remains unknown. PRO SP 92/19/ 92–v, Hales to Dorchester, 4 September 1631; ff. 96–v, Hales to Dorchester, 6 September 1631.

pernicious influence of the French over Vittorio Amedeo I. Scaglia was slow to react to the ducal instruction, claiming in one of his characteristic delaying tactics that he was unable to leave because he was physically unwell.[44] A state of diplomatic stalemate had emerged where the abate had become a contentious political issue in Savoy's relations with both the French and Spanish. Vittorio Amedeo I's treatment of Alessandro Scaglia as an individual courtier and diplomat with a known political position would, from the wider perspective of international relations, signal to both France and Spain his own political preferences. On the one hand, the French continued to insist that Scaglia personally jeopardised the future of their relations with Turin, while Richelieu believed that his own position was under threat because of the breakdown of the French royal family and the possibility that Scaglia was in London to organise an international coalition around Marie de' Medici and Gaston d'Orléans. But the Spanish on the other hand argued that the abate's stay in London was absolutely essential for the integrity of their diplomatic interests. From their perspective, the fortunes of international relations remained very much in the balance at the close of 1631. The Swedes were advancing through central Europe at a frightening speed while the peace in north Italy had given Spain few favours. But, as Scaglia was dispatched to London, England seemed to be in position to intervene militarily on the side of the Habsburgs, and Marie de' Medici and Gaston d'Orléans had gone into exile, bitterly disaffected from Richelieu. With a typical sense of drama, it seemed to Olivares that 'the critical moment in current affairs has arrived'.[45]

It was at this point that both the political and personal stakes for Alessandro Scaglia were increased. From Paris, Cardinal Maurizio threatened that if he did not leave London and return to Savoy via France then he would lose all of his Savoyard benefices comprising his three commendatory abbeys and ecclesiastical pensions. In one obvious sense this was intended as an ultimatum in response to the diplomatic pressure being brought to bear by Richelieu. The abate also suspected however that the cardinal, who had always had an eye on his valuable ecclesiastical benefices, not least the wealthy abbey of Staffarda, wished to take control of them for himself, once again merging their lingering personal rivalries with wider political problems. In Madrid the matter was seen as serious enough to

---

[44] AGS Est. 3647, 177, Scaglia to Olivares, 15 October 1631; AST LMI m. 4, Scaglia to Vittorio Amedeo I, late 1631.

[45] AGS Est. 2519, 139, consulta of council of state, 20 November 1631. See also, 2045, 78, consulta of council of state, 30 November 1631. J. H. Elliott wrote that Scaglia had made a deep impression on the count-duke, who had been interested in winning him over to Spanish service for some time. Elliott, *Olivares*, pp. 399–400.

warrant discussion in the council of state. Since the twin issues of ser-
vice and loyalty had been forced by Cardinal Maurizio, the nature of
Scaglia's increasingly peculiar diplomatic position between the courts of
Savoy and Spain came under scrutiny. Initially two council members, the
duke of Alva and the marquis of Gelves, argued that simultaneous service
to Philip IV and to Vittorio Amedeo I was incompatible and that since
Scaglia had proved himself an able diplomat he should be tempted over to
Spanish service. Philip IV himself added in a marginal note to a consulta
that information should be withheld from the abate because he might
return to Savoy with too much secret knowledge about Spain's strategic
plans. When the matter was raised again early in 1632, Olivares' opinion
was shared by all the members of the council when he said that the king
of Spain should 'give thanks to the abate for his care and diligence in
service to His Majesty', adding that while it was desirable for Scaglia to
stay in Savoyard employment, he should work for Spain and be assured
of Philip IV's protection. Olivares added that he should not be exposed
to the danger implied by travelling to France. After all, Richelieu, so the
count-duke claimed, was Scaglia's 'leading enemy [mayor enemigo]'.[46]

The position of the Spanish regime was set. While hoping to retain
Abate Scaglia as a valuable diplomatic link between the courts of Madrid
and Turin, Olivares would not abandon him to political isolation and
disgrace, or to the personal danger implied by the ducal instruction to
return to Savoy via France. Philip IV wrote to Vittorio Amedeo I, *Señor
Hermano*, emphasising the importance of Scaglia's mission in England and
requesting that he should not be recalled. At the same time he instructed
the Spanish agent in London, Juan de Necolalde, to assure the abate that
he would have his protection, a promise Philip IV repeated directly to
the abate while adding that 'I have never allowed anyone in my service
to lose anything.'[47] By choosing to support Scaglia in public, the Spanish
were demonstrating that as a matter of reputation they did not abandon
their allies or subjects. In a wider sense the regime was also expressing its
policy regarding Savoy, clearly framed in opposition to France. Vittorio
Amedeo I was being pushed into declaring his hand, whether he wished
to opt for a French alignment which ostensibly implied peace in north
Italy or whether he wanted a position more sympathetic to Spain which
probably entailed an alliance against Richelieu, possibly with England and
the exiled Bourbons. Perhaps unsurprisingly he gave no clear answer, no
doubt because he did not want to alienate either of the major powers in

---

[46] AGS Est. 2520, consulta of the council of state, 9 January 1632. See also AGS Est.
2519, consulta of council of state, 30 November 1631.
[47] AGS Est. 3445, 12, Philip IV to Vittorio Amedeo I, 22 January 1632; 2574, Philip IV
to Necolalde, 25 January 1632; Philip IV to Scaglia, 25 January 1632.

Europe, or even Scaglia's own family, given its record of loyalty to the ducal House and its continuing political importance within Savoy. As something of a compromise Alessandro Scaglia was instructed to return to Savoy via the Spanish Netherlands and Lorraine, rather than France.

In March 1632 the abate finally departed from London against a backdrop of diplomatic confusion and uncertainty about his future in the service of Savoy. His mission had achieved little in real terms, and, as John Finet caustically remarked, 'he left many men ill satisfied after their hopes and trust given of his nobler proceeding'.[48] The abate had become a subject of controversy because of his Habsburg sympathies and his perceived political influence, and his impact on Savoy's relations with France and Spain was magnified by Vittorio Amedeo I's efforts to readjust his relationships with the leading powers. Complicating his position still further, Savoyard diplomacy had completely merged with Scaglia's antagonistic relationship with Richelieu, Cardinal Maurizio and Father Monod. At this critical diplomatic juncture wider 'state' interests could not be separated from private interests and personalised animosities. Later in the month the abate arrived in the Spanish Netherlands to a warm welcome from the Infanta Isabella. While he put on the pretence that he would return to Turin once he was physically able, he was never to return to his home state of Savoy, contravening Vittorio Amedeo I's instruction. Abate Scaglia had entered self-imposed exile, where he was to spend his remaining years.

The years 1628–32, encompassed by the conflict over Mantua and Monferrato, witnessed what seemed to be a transformation of Savoy's political landscape. The duke of Buckingham's murder precipitated the withdrawal of England from active participation in the European conflicts; the death of Duke Carlo Emanuele I in July 1630 in turn resulted in a redirection of Savoy's alignment away from Spain towards neutrality. For Scaglia these changes seriously damaged his international influence, given that his brand of personalised diplomacy had come to depend on a chain of friends and contacts across Europe and, more specifically, on active co-operation between Savoy, England and Spain. This became all the more apparent as Duke Vittorio Amedeo I's strategic priorities took a different direction, while the duke and his French consort favoured courtiers opposed both to the abate and, perhaps also, to his family clan. By the time of his last mission to London the abate was in evident

---

[48] Loomie (ed.), *Notebooks*, p. 123. See also CSPV 1629–31, pp. 562, 566. Writing in December 1631, the papal nuncio in Paris gave the impression that because of the failure of his negotiations the abate 'may have fallen into a deep depression, and needs a cure being in danger of losing his mind'. ASV SS Francia, 74A, f. 229v, Spada to Barberini, 5 December 1631.

difficulty, assaulted both by Richelieu's sniping campaign and the envy of Cardinal Maurizio and Father Monod. Yet there was more to Scaglia's position than the dilemmas of an individual minister. With his own idea of what Savoy's interests were, the abate encapsulated the kinds of political problems faced on a wider level by his home state. The war for the succession of Mantua and Monferrato had raised critical questions for Savoy as a second-rank state, particularly about its strategic relationships with France and Spain. Carlo Emanuele I's crucial decision at the end of 1627 to force a war in north Italy over the disputed succession had come on the crest of a wave of fortuitous political circumstances. With the French pinned down by events outside the peninsula, Carlo Emanuele I had gambled on an offensive alliance with Spain to pursue his dynastic claim to Monferrato, encouraged not least by Alessandro Scaglia's own diplomatic initiatives beyond the Italian peninsula. The subsequent difficulties of translating warm diplomatic relations with England into positive action to restrict French freedom of manoeuvre, the failure to capture Casale by force of Spanish arms, and the eventual occupation of Pinerolo, transformed the military and political dynamics of the dynastic war. The entry into the war of French troops, and later of Imperial forces in 1629, had escalated the conflict into something both Scaglia and his sovereign prince had by no means intended.

It would be wrong however to assume that the events of the war demonstrate Savoy's fundamental unimportance or impotence in European power politics. True enough, Charles I retreated from his commitment to joint diplomacy with Savoy following the Anglo-French peace in the spring of 1629, while the occupation of Pinerolo, whether by tacit agreement or not, further reduced Vittorio Amedeo I's bargaining power with France, even though to Richelieu he was more important to French interests than the duke of Nevers. But the strategic importance to both Richelieu and Olivares of Savoy, as the key to influencing north Italy, was clearly demonstrated in the drawn-out process of ending the Gonzaga dispute. Neither the cardinal-minister nor the Spanish favourite was willing, or more correctly able, to neutralise Savoy once and for all. In turn, the 1630s were to see the continuation of this rivalry played out through the political and factional divisions within the duchy, and the worsening dynastic problems of Savoy's sovereign House. Nor was Alessandro Scaglia's diplomatic career finished. He too was to spend the 1630s actively involved in Savoyard political and dynastic problems and his own family's responses to crisis, linked as before to the rivalries between the leading powers over influence in north Italy.

PART IV

ALESSANDRO SCAGLIA: EXILE AND SAVOY DURING THE 1630S

7

POWER AND PATRONAGE: ALESSANDRO
SCAGLIA IN EXILE

In a revealing letter to the papal nephew Antonio Barberini, Rome's inter-nuncio in the Spanish Netherlands set out the reasons for Alessandro Scaglia's unexpected arrival in the capital city of Brussels:

> Abate Scaglia is here, and although it is said that he has come to take the waters of Spa, he is evidently out of favour with the duke of Savoy, given that he handed Pinerolo over to the king of France. He found himself in Spain well-liked by Olivares, and after being sent to England Cardinal Maurizio recalled him. Scaglia did not wish to go, fearing Cardinal Richelieu who is said to be his enemy. Now it is thought that he has been sent by the count-duke to offer his advice to ministers in the Spanish Netherlands, and the marquis of Aytona does nothing without his opinion; since his prince [Vittorio Amedeo I] is at the moment pro-French, Scaglia is totally in favour of Spain, and has decided to pin his hopes on them so long as the duke remains French.[1]

This was a stark interpretation of Scaglia's position, but it was essentially correct. His retreat to the Spanish Netherlands in March 1632 was not the act of a minister retiring from an increasingly frustrating political career with the consent of his sovereign prince. He made the journey against Vittorio Amedeo I's orders to return to Savoy, something that may well have signalled the end of his diplomatic career in service to the House of Savoy. As he was one of the two senior members of the Scaglia di Verrua clan it may also have spelt disaster for his family's fortunes at the Turinese court. Behind Scaglia's decision to disobey the order to return to Savoy was a deep suspicion of what seemed to be strengthening French influence at the court of Turin. Between the treaty of Monzón in 1626

---

[1] ASV SS Fiandra, 21, ff. 5–v, Lagonissa to Barberini, 6 July 1632. A partial transcription and translation into French of this letter can be found in Lucienne van Meerbeeck (ed.), *Correspondance du nonce Fabio de Lagonissa, archevêque de Sonza, 1627–1634* (Brussels and Rome, 1966), pp. 355–6, which also contains transcriptions, generally incomplete, of other letters.

and the definitive conclusion of the Gonzaga succession dispute in 1632 he had become identifed by his pro-Habsburg approach to diplomacy. But the change in Savoy's international alignment following the death of Carlo Emanuele I and the end of the war for Mantua and Monferrato, coupled with England's retreat into neutrality after Buckingham's murder, had clearly weakened the abate's position to the point that exile seemed to be his only viable option.

Yet Alessandro Scaglia for one did not consider his political career to be over, and for good reason. His refuge in the Spanish Netherlands with its particular, perhaps unique, identity in European power politics was a calculated move, allowing him to remain active on the diplomatic stage, if unofficially and in relative safety. The Spanish Netherlands was a nerve-centre of the Habsburg dynastic system and Brussels, the archducal capital, was the 'true heart of seventeenth-century Spanish espionage', as the Spanish historian Alcalá-Zamora has suggested.[2] The reasons for this are not hard to find. The Low Countries was a border region, the point of contact between different but crucial theatres of European power politics and trade, and this remained true for the Spanish Netherlands in the early seventeenth century under the archdukes. The rebellious Dutch provinces that comprised the United Provinces were of course to the north, while England and the North Sea to the west represented a second political and economic arena. To the south lay France, with the Holy Roman Empire to the east, though juridically the Low Countries remained related to the Empire through the Pragmatic Sanction of 1548.

A geo-strategic interpretation of the Spanish Netherlands affords only a partial understanding of its identity in early modern Europe and why it was such a useful refuge for the abate. The marriage in 1598 joining the Infanta Isabella and Archduke Albert, a brother of the Holy Roman Emperor Rudolf (1552–1612), transformed the region, both politically and culturally. Between the death of Don Carlos in 1568 and the birth of the future Philip III in 1578, Isabella was an heiress presumptive of the Spanish sovereign, acutely concerned with the fragility of his family line. Isabella's marriage twenty years after the birth of Philip served as compensation, albeit much delayed compensation, since she no longer appeared likely to transmit her father's patrimony. Philip II stipulated in the act governing the marriage that if the archdukes were to have a Catholic child of their own then the Spanish Netherlands would devolve by primogeniture to their family; correspondingly, if they had no legitimate heirs then authority would by the act return to the male head of the main branch of the Spanish Habsburgs, though the union also raised the

<hr />

[2] José Alcalá-Zamora y Quiepo de Llano, *España, Flandes y el mar del norte, 1618–1639* (Barcelona, 1975), p. 191.

possibility of a Savoyard succession because of Carlo Emanuele I's own marriage to the younger of Philip II's two daughters (even though this was not explicitly specified in any marriage contract, and in any case the Spanish would have wished to avoid this outcome).[3]

Albert and Isabella's marriage complicated the status of the Spanish Netherlands as a potentially independent sovereignty. After 1598 the court of Madrid was careful to ensure some administrative influence over the region.[4] The Spanish regime also maintained direct control of the army of Flanders, together with the appointment of the army's captain-general – the arrival of Ambrogio Spínola in the Low Countries in 1604 and his eventual assumption of the command of the army of Flanders following Albert's failure to recapture Ostend served as a clear indication of Spain's continuing military power in the region beyond the command of the Brussels court.[5] Moreover, while Isabella enjoyed the title of duchess of Burgundy, the ducal title itself did not pass to Albert as her husband but instead continued in the main branch of the Spanish Habsburgs, ensuring that Philip II and his own heirs retained control of the sovereign Burgundian order of the *Toison d'Or*.[6]

These were admittedly limitations on the full independent sovereignty of the archdukes. Yet for the first time since Philip II had left the Low Countries in 1556, the provinces of the Spanish Netherlands enjoyed effective resident sovereigns. Household institutions associated with a functioning Burgundian court were activated and placed under their control, and the so-called Collateral Councils, principally the Conseil des Finances, the Conseil Privé and the Conseil d'Etat, came under archducal authority.[7] The Spanish Netherlands also enjoyed a form of diplomatic recognition, an attribute of discrete sovereignty that distinguished it from other areas within the Spanish composite monarchy. The English crown had begun to send accredited representatives to the archducal court from 1600, among them Scaglia's friends, Balthasar Gerbier, the earl of Carlisle and Endymion Porter, and in turn representatives were sent from Brussels

---

[3] Dumont (ed.), *Corps universel diplomatique*, V, part I, pp 573–4, 'conditions sous lesquelles les Pays-Bas sont cedez à Isabelle-Claire-Eugenie d'Autriche par Philipe II', 6 May 1598.

[4] Hugo de Schepper, 'Les archiducs et les institutions du gouvernement au Pays-Bas espagnols, 1596–1621', in Werner Thomas and Luc Duerloo (eds.), *Albert and Isabella: Essays* (Brussels, 1998), pp. 224, 228.

[5] Asunción Retortillo Atienza, 'Poder e influencia de Ambrogio Spinola en la corte de los archiduques (1602–1607)', in Thomas and Duerloo (eds.), *Albert and Isabella*, pp. 233–40.

[6] Dumont (ed.), *Corps universel diplomatique*, V, part I, p. 574.

[7] G. Parker, 'The decision-making process in the government of the Catholic Netherlands under the "Archdukes", 1596–1621', in his collection *Spain and the Netherlands* (Glasgow, 1990); de Schepper, 'Les archiducs', in Thomas and Duerloo (eds.), *Albert and Isabella*, pp. 221–31; Charles H. Carter, 'Belgian "autonomy" under the archdukes, 1598–1621', *Journal of Modern History*, 36 (1964).

to London (albeit not of a full ambassadorial status). Indeed, the court at Brussels retained its diplomatic autonomy even after the death of Albert in 1621 when, according to the marriage act, effective sovereign control of the Spanish Netherlands should have returned to the main branch of the Spanish Habsburgs and Isabella's freedom to operate on her own initiative was correspondingly reduced.[8]

The Spanish Netherlands remained integral to the Spanish composite monarchy after 1598, yet it simultaneously emerged as a semi-independent sovereignty in its own right, with important consequences for its role in European power politics. In the first instance the strategic priorities of Brussels and Madrid did not always coincide, implying that the relationship between the two courts during the reign of the archdukes was at times like that between Madrid and the Austrian branch of the Habsburg dynasty in Vienna. After succeeding his father, Philip III repeatedly tested the limitations of archducal power by aggravating the relationship between his court and that in Brussels, even though he had formally accepted the provisions of the marriage act prior to Philip II's death.[9] For their part the archdukes seemed more than capable of pursuing diplomatic initiatives without the immediate permission of Madrid. As Pauline Croft has observed, 'the increasing confidence of Albert and Isabella in conducting their own foreign policies was all too apparent' during the preliminary negotiations for the Anglo-Spanish peace of 1604.[10] Only a few years later, the Twelve Years' Truce of 1609 with the Dutch was willingly signed in Antwerp by the archdukes representing Spain. The Spanish Netherlands, after all, was on the front line of the gruelling war of attrition between the United Provinces and Spain, and Albert and Isabella (and eventually Spínola too) were far more conscious than policy-makers in Madrid of the acute difficulty of militarily defeating the Dutch, and consequently more willing to negotiate with them.[11]

---

[8] Bell, *Handlist*, pp. 265–71. Accredited Spanish ambassadors were also despatched to Brussels in this period. Joseph Lefèvre, 'Les ambassadeurs d'Espagne à Bruxelles sous le règne de l'archiduc Albert (1598–1621)', *Revue Belge de Philologie et d'Histoire*, 2 (1923).

[9] Werner Thomas, 'The reign of Albert and Isabella in the Southern Netherlands, 1598–1621', in Thomas and Duerloo (eds.), *Albert and Isabella*, p. 6; Dumont (ed.), *Corps universel diplomatique*, V, part I, pp. 575–6.

[10] Pauline Croft, 'Brussels and London: the Archdukes, Robert Cecil and James I', in Thomas and Duerloo (eds.), *Albert and Isabella*, p. 82, See also J. Cuvelier, 'Les préliminaires du traité de Londres (29 août 1604)', *Revue Belge de Philologie et d'Histoire*, 2 (1923).

[11] The timing of the truce also had much to do with the fortuitous arrival of two silver fleets in Spain, raising fears among the Dutch that Spínola would build on his military successes of 1604. I am grateful to Professor Patrick Williams for this point.

It would probably be wrong however to overstate the differences between Brussels and Madrid, and the dominant impression of the twin Habsburg courts during the archducal period is of dynastic and political intimacy. In itself this could afford significant diplomatic possibilities both to the Spanish and to other European powers, as informal negotiations with Spain could be pursued through Brussels without necessarily attracting unwelcome attention or criticism. The first tentative steps in the Anglo-Spanish peace negotiations of 1627 that had involved Gerbier, Rubens and Scaglia had taken place through the court in Brussels rather than Madrid, in part because the war between England and Spain made any direct negotiations between London and Madrid politically sensitive. The double identity of the Spanish Netherlands as a semi-independent sovereignty and a Habsburg territory likewise facilitated informal peace negotiations between the Spanish and Dutch after the resumption of conflict in 1621. Again, Alessandro Scaglia found himself involved as a peace mediator while operating informally for the Spanish during the 1630s. In the middle years of the decade he opened a private line of communication with Frederick Henry (1584–1647) Prince of Orange and his secretary Constantijn Huygens (1596–1687), though without any clear-cut outcome, and without seeking the participation of the Estates-General at The Hague where any formal negotiations ultimately had to take place.[12]

While the Spanish Netherlands emerged as an arena for informal negotiations during the early seventeenth century it was also an attractive destination for religious and political exiles, probably the most important in Europe. In fact well before the archducal marriage, following the accession of Elizabeth I in 1558, the Catholic Low Countries was established as a principal refuge for recusants fleeing England, and English and Scottish colleges were founded at Douai.[13] At the same time there was a comparable traffic of exiles between Ireland and the Spanish Netherlands, and they too had a college at the university town of Louvain which enjoyed a particularly fruitful period at the end of the sixteenth century.[14]

---

[12] For example Jonathan Israel, *The Dutch Republic and the Hispanic World, 1601–1661* (Oxford, 1989), pp. 299–314. On Scaglia's mediation see for instance AGR SEG 598, ff. 16–19, Scaglia to Olivares, 5 June 1636; f. 171–v, Scaglia to Huygens, 7 June 1636; ff. 199–v, Scaglia to Huygens, 27 December 1636, though Echevarría Bacigalupe has suggested that the Dutch Republic was not in fact an area of the abate's political expertise. Echevarría Bacigalupe, *Diplomacia secreta*, p. 216.

[13] On English exiles see Albert Loomie, *The Spanish Elizabethans: The English Exiles at the Court of Philip II* (Fordham, 1963); Robert Lechat, *Les réfugiés anglais dans les Pays-Bas espagnols durant le règne d'Elisabeth, 1558–1603* (Louvain, 1914).

[14] See for example T. J. Walsh, *The Irish Continental College Movement: The Colleges at Bordeaux, Lille and Toulouse* (Dublin and Cork, 1973), pp. 61–70. I am grateful to Professor Alan Ford of Nottingham University for advice on this topic.

The attractions of the Spanish Netherlands to Catholic exiles from the British Isles, at least after 1598, were fairly clear. Not only did the region enjoy its advantageous geographical position on the North Sea, but it also afforded a relatively warm welcome to those fleeing persecution for their faith. The confessional sensibilities of Albert and Isabella placed them at the vanguard of the Catholic revival in northern Europe; during their reign they oversaw the revitalisation of the church in the Spanish Netherlands, and they also lent their support to the English and Irish colleges, as well as to specific recusants who had taken residence at their court.[15]

Given its geo-strategic significance and its semi-separation from the Spanish composite monarchy, the Spanish Netherlands was ideally placed for exiles who wished to remain in contact with their home states while negotiating a settlement or encouraging disorder within those states. The proximity of the Spanish Netherlands to France certainly made the region an accessible destination for French political refugees in particular. The border was within easy reach of Paris and the French court during moments of internal crisis, a point made by Marie de' Medici when she fled France after the Day of Dupes: 'I regarded this place as nearby haven, where I could flee the storm that was unsettling me.'[16] Moreover, as a semi-separate sovereignty, it could, at least while France and Spain were formally at peace, be viewed as a neutral refuge where an exile could enjoy the backing of Spain without arguably being in Spanish territory proper, a factor that presents a further explanation as to why Scaglia settled there.[17]

Early modern historians have been surprisingly slow to integrate the subject of exile into general accounts of political or court history, apart from the considerable research on the Stuarts after their flight from

---

[15] Paul Arblaster, 'The archdukes and the northern Counter-Reformation', in Thomas and Duerloo (eds.), *Albert and Isabella*, pp. 90–1. However, T. J. Walsh suggests that the financial plight of the Irish colleges in the Spanish Netherlands during the seventeenth century was in fact precarious. Walsh, *Continental College Movement*, pp. 66–7.

[16] *Declaration de la Reyne Mere du Roy tres-Chrestien contenant les raisons de sa sortie des pays-bas* (London, 1638), p. 3. See also 'Tres-humble, tres-veritable et tres-importante remonstrance au Roy', in Abbé de Saint-Germain (ed.), *Diverses Pièces faictes pour la défense de la Royne Mére et de Monseigneur, Frère unique du Roy tres-chrestien Louys XIII., contre les violences et calomnies du Cardinal Richelieu* (Antwerp, 1632 edn), p. 64, and Ernest Gossart, *L'auberge des princes en exil: anecdotes de la cour de Bruxelles aux XVIIe siècle* (Brussels, 1905), pp. 9–10. It should be added that the queen mother also made it clear that she did not intend remaining in the Spanish Netherlands.

[17] This was certainly a point made by another exile, Marie de' Medici's advisor Père Chanteloupe. 'Lettre de Chanteloupe aux nouvelles chambres de justice', in Saint-Germain, *Diverses Pièces* (Antwerp, 1644 edn), p. 5.

England in 1689.[18] Exile as both a state and a process was far from straightforward, and covered different categories, subtly shaded by a range of meanings. A person could enter self-imposed exile, as Scaglia did. Alternatively a person could suffer internal exile within his or her home state, or be disgraced from court or, in more extreme instances, be exiled abroad. All of these implied varying levels of disgrace or disfavour, that accordingly entailed different political dynamics. Crucially, exile was reversible, like the punishment of execution in effigy, and did not necessarily imply the end of a public career or alternatively total isolation from a home state. Lines of communication could remain open between exiles and their political allies or families remaining in their home states; sovereigns themselves could employ exiles to maintain informal diplomatic channels with other states, raising the possibility that an exile could return to favour by showing loyalty or by operating on behalf of his or her home state while in exile. Exile undoubtedly had the potential to be an important element of court politics. Ministers, courtiers and their families could employ exile as a tool to serve their own interests in times of crisis. Cardinal Mazarin's spectacular departure from the French court on two occasions into self-imposed exile to the Imperial city of Cologne succeeded in undermining his Frondeur opponents, and he only returned the second time, by Louis XIV's invitation in October 1652, when his enemies had effectively torn themselves apart.[19] In two comparable examples, the Epernon and Condé families seemingly employed exile to safeguard their collective interests at times of internal crisis in France during the first half of the seventeenth century. Bernard (1592–1661) duke of la Valette, a son of Epernon and a nephew of Richelieu by marriage, fled France and the threat of execution for the safety of England in 1638, while following the collapse of the Frondes, Louis II Condé (1621–86), the so-called 'Grand Condé', went into exile in the Spanish Netherlands at the head of his personal army; exile allowed the prince not only to escape from political crisis but also to strengthen his position from which he could bargain for a favourable settlement.[20]

---

[18] For example Eveline Cruikshanks and Edward Corp (eds.), *The Stuart Court in Exile and the Jacobites* (London, 1995); Edward Gregg, 'Monarchs without a crown', in Oresko, Gibbs and Scott (eds.), *Royal and Republican Sovereignty*. One recent exception is Christine Shaw, *The Politics of Exile in Renaissance Italy* (Cambridge, 2000), dealing with the widespread incidence of exile from the city-states of the fifteenth century.

[19] For a recent account of Mazarin's exiles during the Frondes consult Orest Ranum, *The Fronde: A French Revolution, 1648–1652* (New York and London, 1993), especially pp. 335–41 on his second exile.

[20] During the ministry of Richelieu, the third son of the duke of Epernon remained faithful to the cardinal while the second son was consistently opposed to Richelieu during the 1630s. Vicomte de Noailles, *Le Cardinal de la Valette, général des armées du*

It is this fundamental sense of ambiguity, both in the special identity of the Spanish Netherlands and in the state of exile itself, that may well have appealed to the abate when in the spring of 1632 he made his decision not to return to Savoy. From the relative safety and semi-neutrality of Brussels he could hope to continue as an active political figure, if not on the centre stage of international relations then at least from the sidelight, and ostensibly away from his pro-French prince. But since exile was inherently ambiguous, Alessandro Scaglia's refuge in the Spanish Netherlands nevertheless raised searching questions about the nature of his loyalty to his home state of Savoy. For the abate, exile encapsulated the elements that had up to that point given definition to his diplomatic profile, of the connections between service and interest, of the interaction between state and family power, and of the role played by a powerful individual driven by his own political agenda.

Because of his record of unbroken fidelity to the House of Savoy prior to his exile there were certainly expectations at the Turinese court, and indeed further afield, that Alessandro Scaglia would continue to serve Duke Vittorio Amedeo I even while he had deliberately disobeyed him and seemed to be in disgrace. While some observers used the term 'disgrace' to define his standing with the Savoyard court and his sovereign prince, it is striking that there was never a formal declaration by the duke that Scaglia was officially in a state of either disgrace or even exile.[21] That Alessandro's commendatory benefices and pensions held in Savoy were not ultimately sequestered by the duke, as he had feared might happen when he considered disobeying Vittorio Amedeo I in 1631 and as Cardinal Maurizio had wanted (not least so that he might obtain them), certainly did not pass unnoticed in Paris where the abate was still a figure of concern.[22] Quite possibly the Savoyard duke did not wish to offend Alessandro's elder brother, Augusto Manfredo, count of Verrua. If the abate's possessions were seized, the duke would deny the count, one of his most consistent and trusted courtiers, the opportunity to negotiate their transfer to his own second son, Filiberto Scaglia, himself marked out for a

---

roi, 1635 à 1639 (Paris, 1906). For the parallel example of the Condé during the ministry of Cardinal Mazarin see J. J. Inglis-Jones, 'The Grand Condé: power politics in France, Spain and the Spanish Netherlands, 1652–9', (DPhil thesis, University of Oxford, 1994).

[21] AGS Est. 2051, 104, summary of Piochet to Prince Tommaso Francesco, February 1636; CSPV 1632–6, pp. 109, 113.

[22] When the abate arrived in Brussels, Richelieu, still distinguishing the abate from his francophile elder brother, clearly expected him to be declared a rebel by Vittorio Amedeo I ('Quand M. de Savoye declare ledit abbé rebelle selon la forme et la pratique d'Italie'). AAE CP Sardaigne 20, f. 159v, memorial of Richelieu, 18 June 1632. Precisely what this means is unclear.

career that combined benefice holding and service to the ducal family.[23] Because of the ambiguousness of Alessandro Scaglia's relationship with Savoy throughout the years of exile, it was also credible that on some level he was acting in conjunction with Duke Vittorio Amedeo I in order to maintain a covert contact with Spain while the Turinese court was ostensibly aligned with France. Although the Savoyard duke had withdrawn from alliance with Spain after 1632 and had agreed to the occupation of Pinerolo by French troops, it might still have been to his advantage to retain at least some political flexibility, something the abate's Habsburg affinities could very possibly provide. If therefore Vittorio Amedeo were to sever relations completely with Abate Scaglia it would have had the double effect of closing a potential avenue for mediation with Spain and discouraging other people or courts from approaching Scaglia as a way to the duke of Savoy. In short, if the abate's exile retained a deliberate, albeit low-key, level of ambiguity then it could serve as a useful diplomatic tool for the duke. The surviving documentary evidence again offers no clear-cut explanation for this ambiguity, nor, given the nature of such a relationship if it had existed, should it be expected.

The Spanish, not least Olivares, had also hoped that Scaglia might stay in some form of contact with Duke Vittorio Amedeo I when he had thought about switching to their service early in 1632.[24] It was clearly believed that the abate enjoyed a special relationship as a mediator between Savoy and Spain which potentially could be utilised at an appropriate time in either formal or informal negotiations between the two.[25] A year after the abate's arrival in Brussels, Spain and Savoy finally came to a settlement over their long-running negotiation concerning the disputed territory of Zuccarello in the Genoese republic which had so closely involved Alessandro Scaglia during his mission in 1630–1 to Philip IV's court, and which was completed afterwards by his nephew Filiberto.[26] The English agent Arthur Hopton reported from Madrid that this might actually have signalled a reconciliation between the two courts:

> upon which ground the Abate of Scaglia's friends . . . begin to speak of his return to serve as ambassador in this court, whereunto it would be no

[23] AST LMF m. 33, fasc. 5, 34, Vittorio Amedeo I to S. Maurizio, 1 May 1634.

[24] AGS Est. 2520, consulta of council of state, 9 January 1632.

[25] Echevarría Bacigalupe has suggested that Philip IV and Olivares saw Scaglia as a means of inserting a pro-Spanish regime in Turin. Echevarría Bacigalupe, *Diplomacia secreta*, p. 214.

[26] According to a document dated 27 November 1631 Savoy was to drop the claim to Zuccarello in return for generous financial compensation. Dumont (ed.), *Corps universel diplomatique*, VI, part I, pp. 23–4.

hard matter to persuade them [Savoy], but that it would not well stand with their purpose to temporize with the French, whose good opinion the abate hath so much lost, as wheresoever he be they think they smell gunpowder.[27]

Beyond contemporary rumour and retrospective speculation there is however no unequivocal evidence that Scaglia ever continued to operate even informally for Vittorio Amedeo I, or even that he wished to return to official service while the duke gave precedence to relations with Richelieu over those with Spain.[28] Alessandro Scaglia's status remained a highly sensitive political issue in Turin, not only because of his apparent disobedience to Vittorio Amedeo I but also because of his overt Habsburg sympathies. If moreover there had been the suggestion that he was representing the duke of Savoy in any capacity, then Franco-Savoyard relations would almost certainly have been soured, as Hopton's telling comment above clearly implied, presenting Richelieu with a potential lever to exert further pressure on Vittorio Amedeo I (just as Scaglia's mission to London in 1631–2 had done).[29] While there are no indications that Vittorio Amedeo I personally wished to terminate relations with one of his most important ambassadorial agents who was also a member of a leading court clan, diplomatic pressure prevented direct or regular contact with the abate. The last documented occasion when the Savoyard duke wrote directly to Scaglia and described him as his ambassador was in a letter from May 1632, written within weeks of the abate's arrival in the Spanish Netherlands. When the abate fell seriously ill in 1635 the Savoyard duke stated in a despatch to his ordinary ambassador in Paris, probably in the expectation that he would inform Richelieu, that the abate had not contacted him for more than two years.[30]

Whatever the precise state of Alessandro's relations with the Turinese court, it is probable that he himself had decided to wait for the mutable

---

[27] PRO SP 94/36/240–v, Hopton to Coke, 17 February 1633. However, Hopton continued by setting out the problems involved in a Spanish-Savoyard reconciliation.

[28] But some thought that in 1633 Scaglia wanted to be reconciled to the duke of Savoy. CSPV 1632–6, p. 171.

[29] AGR SEG 597, f. 182, Scaglia to Olivares, 13 November 1634; AAE CP Sardaigne 21, f. 339, copy of Mazzarini to Servien, 8 May 1632; ff. 396v–7, Servien to Richelieu, 9 June 1632; f. 416, Servien to Richelieu, 14 June 1632.

[30] AGR SEG 600, Vittorio Amedeo I to Scaglia, 5 May 1632, in which the duke described Scaglia as 'most illustrious and reverend councillor of state and our most dear extraordinary ambassador [Ilustrissimo et molto reverendissimo consigliere di stato et ambasciatore straordinario nostro carissimo]'. AST LMF m. 33, fasc. 4, 14, Vittorio Amedeo I to S. Maurizio, 24 February 1635. It is worth adding that this description probably refers back to the abate's status as Savoy's extraordinary ambassador in London, as it seems that no ambassadors were dispatched from Turin to Brussels.

nature of Savoy's international policies to swing back in his favour, away from Vittorio Amedeo I's alignment with France and possibly to one that favoured Spain. The abate still believed that the political position of his home state was open to change, whether or not Duke Vittorio Amedeo I was in practice better served by allying with the regime in Madrid. He was careful to show no bitterness towards Vittorio Amedeo I as if he pointedly did not wish to antagonise him. If Scaglia blamed anyone for what he saw as Savoy's troubled predicament then it was Richelieu, though also to a lesser extent Cardinal Maurizio who had been so pliant while in Paris in 1631–2. As the papal inter-nuncio in Brussels Fabio Lagonissa put it, 'he [Scaglia] expresses his antipathy to Cardinal Richelieu, and also to the cardinal of Savoy for having taken a contrary position [by believing] that the duke of Savoy should align with France'[31] Scaglia's last surviving letter to Vittorio Amedeo I, dated 20 October 1632, was actually a letter of congratulations on the birth at the beginning of the month of a ducal son and heir, Francesco Giacinto. The content of the letter, while strongly rhetorical, was obviously not one of alienation or anger: 'and although many others will be saying the same thing', Scaglia wrote, 'may I assure you that the joyous pleasure I take in this ought to distinguish me from them, as I distinguish myself from all in devotion and debt to your highness'.[32] Scaglia's tone was characteristic of the language and etiquette associated with formal expressions of rejoicing which sovereign princes throughout Europe expected from their leading subjects at great dynastic moments. His failure to have written would have been a clear demonstration of a definitive break from Vittorio Amedeo I as his sovereign prince.

The point might be pushed further. Alessandro Scaglia seems to have viewed his exile in the Spanish Netherlands as a means for securing political advantages for Savoy, albeit indirectly by applying pressure on Cardinal Richelieu. The abate continued to view international relations as an inter-connected web of issues where events in one area could directly affect circumstances elsewhere, just as he had done after the treaty of Monzón in 1626. The withdrawal from France in 1631 of Marie de' Medici and Gaston d'Orléans with a large number of followers and some significant opponents of Richelieu was not, as many secondary accounts too readily assume, a straightforward victory for the cardinal. The exiled Bourbons raised a serious, though at that moment uncoordinated,

---

[31] ASV SS Fiandra 21, f. 17, Lagonissa to Barberini, 10 August 1632.

[32] Van Meerbeeck (ed.), *Correspondance*, p. 363; AST LMS, m. 23, Scaglia to Vittorio Amedeo I, 20 October 1632. News of the birth of Francesco Giacinto reached Brussels by 12 October from a gentleman sent by Vittorio Amedeo I. ASV SS Fiandra, 19, f. 253v, Lagonissa to Barberini, 12 October 1632.

threat to Richelieu.[33] While Marie de' Medici was long established as a figurehead of opposition to the cardinal, she was of probably greater importance as the mother of the queen of England and the duchess of Savoy. It was certainly possible that her senior dynastic position could be used to reconcile the Habsburgs and Bourbons as part of a broader European peace among the Catholic powers, one of her longed-for aspirations. More seriously, her exile presented opportunities for Spain to improve diplomatic relations with England and Savoy and detach them from alliance with France. That would have proved a considerable defeat for Richelieu, restricting French access to the Italian peninsula – one of Richelieu's principal objectives for intervening in the Gonzaga crisis in the first place – and perhaps drawing England back into the European conflict against France.[34] For his part, Gaston, as the next in line to the French throne, was ideally placed to head a revolt against Richelieu's ministry.[35] His military potential was certainly reflected in the fact that the Spanish regime in Madrid was willing to pay Gaston to command a military incursion into France, even though members of the council of state suspected (with some justice) that he could not be trusted to lead consistent opposition to Richelieu, and also in the fact that he had returned in November 1632 to Brussels following the dismal failure of the Montmorency revolt and the duke of Montmorency's execution at the end of October.[36]

But Scaglia's hopes of exploiting the Bourbon divisions did not have a favourable outcome. The abate had travelled to London in 1631 with secret instructions from Madrid that something might be made of the Bourbon split, and between 1632 and Gaston's reconciliation with his elder brother in October 1634 Scaglia concentrated much of his energy in the Spanish Netherlands on securing their co-operation to oppose Richelieu. Marie de' Medici's and Gaston's exile, however, proved to be nothing short of a fiasco for all concerned; they were both much more

---

[33] For an indication of who travelled with the queen mother and Gaston see AGS Est. 2051, 142, 'Memorial de los mas principales de la Casa de la Reina Madre y de las damas del seguito, como de los criados que tiene cada uno por sí', undated; PRO SP 77/22/268, 'Liste de ceux de qualité de la suitte de Monsieur de Duc d'Orléans', 21 November 1632.

[34] AGR SEG 221, ff. 161–v, Cardinal-Infante to Philip IV, 24 February 1639.

[35] As soon as he arrived in Brussels, D'Orléans was expressing his interest in organising another revolt. AGR SEG 600, Scaglia to Olivares, 29 December 1632.

[36] ASV SS Fiandra, 18, ff. 289–v, Consa to Barberini, 16 August 1631; H. Lonchay and J. Cuvelier. (eds.), *Correspondance de la cour d'Espagne sur les affaires des Pays-Bas au XVIIe siècle*, 6 vols. (Brussels, 1923–37), II, p. 617; AGR SEG 597, f. 83, Scaglia to Philip IV, 16 May 1634.

concerned with securing their own interests as competing individuals, and D'Orléans indeed eventually negotiated the return of his appanages and the acquisition of the governorship of Auvergne as part of his reconciliation package, while leaving his mother and his forlorn Lorraine bride (herself forced into exile) in the Spanish Netherlands.[37] Writing in 1635, after Gaston's return to France, Balthasar Gerbier astutely observed that 'in a world of Chimeres, Monopoles and Stratagemes [*sic*] these poor exiled are involved, all seeming to long for a deliverance, and all contributing to the contrary'.[38] There is no better summary of the intense political disorder, squabbles and private duels that bitterly divided the community of French exiles and prevented them from organising into a coherent force while in the Spanish Netherlands.[39]

On his arrival in the Spanish Netherlands in the spring of 1632, Alessandro Scaglia had unsuccessfully attempted to secure a position as a formal Spanish representative to Marie de' Medici because of the doubts over the nature of her sovereignty. But Olivares nevertheless employed him as the informal point of contact between the French exiles and the Spanish regime in Madrid, at least until 1636 when the abate entered semi-retirement.[40] The fact that he was not provided with any formal office was certainly not an indication of fragile relations with the Spanish Habsburgs. On the contrary, he continued to enjoy a special relationship with the regimes in Brussels and Madrid as an important diplomatic agent, even after his favour with the Spanish gradually waned, in clear contrast to the remaining French exiles in Brussels who came under increasing suspicion as Franco-Spanish relations deteriorated to the point

---

[37] Dumont (ed.), *Corps universel diplomatique*, VI, part I, pp. 73–4.

[38] PRO SP 77/25/338v, Gerbier to Coke, 21 December 1635. With similar eloquence Scaglia claimed that 'I am writing to your majesty [Philip IV] ... a history that in the future will seem like a ballad ... and what we see is no less amazing than what the history books tell us of the times of the Roman Emperors.' AGR SEG 596, f. 277, Scaglia to Philip IV, 12 September 1633. See also AGR SEG 597, f. 75, Scaglia to Olivares, 11 May 1634.

[39] PRO SP 77/23/38v, Gerbier to Coke, 12 February 1633. See also AGR SEG 596, f. 176, Scaglia to Olivares, 19 March 1633; 597, f. 75, Scaglia to Olivares, 11 May 1634. The papal inter-nuncio in Brussels commented on the incessant duelling among followers of Gaston, for instance ASV SS Fiandra, 19, f. 105, Consa to Berberini, 11 May 1632. For further information consult Toby Osborne, ' "Chimères, monopoles and stratagèmes": French exiles in the Spanish Netherlands during the Thirty Years' War', *The Seventeenth Century*, 15 (2000), esp. 162–4.

[40] Lonchay and Cuvelier (eds.), *Correspondance*, II, p. 631; AGR SEG 600, Scaglia to Philip IV, June 1632. The issue of the queen mother's diplomatic status in the Spanish Netherlands and whether she could either send or receive formal ambassadors was a matter of some delicacy for the Spanish. Osborne, 'French exiles', 157–8.

of war in 1635. The papal inter-nuncio Fabio Lagonissa commented that he 'took care to know what abate Scaglia is up to, and found that he has been sent here by the count-duke, as someone very well-informed about the interests of Italian princes and also the Spanish crown; he should enjoy the same position with those ministers in service to His Catholic Majesty'.[41] When some of the French exiles in the retinues of Marie de' Medici and Gaston attempted to destroy the abate's favour with Spain out of jealousy of a political rival, Olivares himself came to Scaglia's defence in the Spanish council of state.

> I cannot hesitate to underline to your majesty [Philip IV] the way in which the matter shown in these documents is being treated in Flanders, more so since neither you nor the Infanta nor any other minister had been given account of what these papers claim, nor of the suspicion . . . that [it is said] the Infanta and the marquis of Aytona have of the abate; it would be a strange and very extravagant thing if it were true.[42]

The informality in the relations between Scaglia and Spain might furthermore be explained by the fact that he was still seen as a Savoyard subject who would return to the official service of the duke of Savoy if diplomatic relations between the courts in Madrid and Turin were to become more favourable. By not formalising his position, Olivares could retain the option of using the abate as an acceptable mediator with Turin in the event of any future settlement with Savoy. Political exile was rarely viewed as permanent, and the person in exile could hope under the right circumstances to return to favour. It might also have been thought that the abate could potentially enjoy increased political flexibility if he remained nothing more than an unofficial diplomatic agent. He could be of greater value to the count-duke by operating without an explicit connection with Madrid yet at the same time enjoying a high level of informal access to the Spanish regimes, both there and in Brussels.

Alessandro Scaglia's unofficial role as a Spanish agent in turn had another dimension. From 1632 the abate was presented with small financial gifts and later with a monthly stipend that accounted for the services of a Spanish secretary, Juan Antonio Canapero, together with informal payments, presumably to pay for acquiring information that could be sent either to the regime in Brussels or more probably back to the

---

[41] ASV SS Fiandra, 21, f. 17, Lagonissa to Barberini, 10 August 1632, translated in van Meerbeeck (ed.), *Correspondance*, p. 363. See also CSPV 1632–6, p. 109.

[42] AGS Est. K1424, 110, report of Olivares concerning the count of Maure, 4 August 1633. See also, 89, report of Olivares to Philip IV, April 1633; 111, report concerning the Lingendes' paper, 4 August 1633.

count-duke in Spain.[43] According to Echevarría Bacigalupe he was the
'last great seventeenth-century spy-master in the Spanish Netherlands',
though this significant claim should not be taken to imply the existence
of an organised intelligence system in a modern sense – even the global
Spanish monarchy, with its enormous resources, had its logistical limitations.[44] To aid the flow of sensitive information specifically to Olivares,
the abate was also given a personal cipher. Since the customary practice
of the Spanish regime was to employ general ciphers in governmen-
tal correspondence, with individual ones reserved for correspondents of
high political or social status, including viceroys and members of the
sovereign House, this was in itself a clear indication of the regard in
which the abate was held by the count-duke.[45] The abate also retained
something of the international network of contacts and friends that he
had established during his years of formal service to Savoy during the
1620s, though perhaps on a reduced level. From his base in the Spanish
Netherlands, he remained in touch with Alessandro Tassoni in Rome until the writer's death in 1635. His correspondence with Prince Frederick
Henry of Orange and his secretary shows a level of contact with the
Dutch Republic, and, as will be seen, he still had friends and contacts of
varying levels of formality and informality in London and Turin.[46]

The practical value of Scaglia's network of friends and contacts as a
source of intelligence was demonstrated most powerfully when in 1633 he
was instrumental in uncovering a noble plot in the Spanish Netherlands,
the best known of all his political achievements and the high point of

[43] AGS Est. 2051, 106, junta of council of state, February 1636; AGS Est. 2246, Philip IV
to Cardinal-Infante, 20 September 1639; AGR SEG 222, f. 322, Cardinal-Infante to
Philip IV, 17 October 1639. On Scaglia's secretary see AGR SEG 597, f. 195, Scaglia
to Olivares, late 1634; f. 215, Scaglia to Philip IV, 30 May 1635. (Both of these letters
in fact were petitions resulting from delays in payments to the secretary.) The Cardinal-
Infante wrote that 'this secretary of the abate knows all of the secrets and intelligence
reports he has had'. AGR SEG 212, f. 551, Cardinal-Infante to Philip IV, 15 May
1635. The level of closeness between Scaglia and his secretary is furthermore indicated
by the fact that the abate included him in his will. ASB, Archivio Scaglia di Verrua,
Testamenti, XCVI, 2537, will of Alessandro Scaglia, 10 May 1641.

[44] Echevarría Bacigalupe, *Diplomacia secreta*, p. 238.

[45] Scaglia's access to a personal cipher can be inferred from AGS Est. 2047, 'Lo que
presupuesta la entrada del Duque de Orleans en francia', 1632. On the use of codes
by the Spanish and the importance attached to personal codes see Hildegard Ernst,
'Geheimschriften im diplomatischen Briefwechsel zwischen Wien, Madrid und
Brüssel 1635–1642', *Mitteilungen des Österreichischen Staatsarchivs*, 42 (1992). I am grate-
ful to Professor R. J. W. Evans for indicating this article to me. See also Jérôme P. Devos,
Les Chiffres de Phillipe II, 1555–1598, et du despacho universal durant le XVIIe siècle
(Brussels, 1950).

[46] On his value to Olivares as a source of information see the comments in Echevarría
Bacigalupe, *Diplomacia secreta*, p. 203.

his informal service to Spain in the 1630s.[47] The plot – described as the 'aristocratic fronde' of the Spanish Netherlands – centred on a group of leading Walloon noblemen, among whom were the prince of Epinoy (1580–1635), the count of Egmont (1596–1654) and (probably by implication rather than direct involvement) the duke of Aerschot (1587–1640), who planned to disconnect the Spanish Netherlands with French and Dutch support from the direct control of Spain to create a neutral territory at peace. Without seeking permission from London, the English agent had offered his residence in Brussels as a safe house for the conspirators to meet and organise their plan. But Gerbier had his own personal interests to consider at this time as delays in payments of diplomatic expenses from London had led him to a state of financial ruin. Looking to make some money, he approached his friend Scaglia with the offer of information in return for the enormous sum of 20,000 escudos. The abate immediately contacted Madrid and negotiations followed between the abate and Gerbier, with parallel discussions in the Spanish council of state. The plot was fully broken and the conspirators either were arrested or fled from the Spanish Netherlands; the duke of Aerschot, who was also implicated, spent the rest of his life imprisoned in Spain until his death there in 1640. For supplying the information the somewhat over-reaching and impecunious Gerbier was duly paid by the Spanish, although less than he originally hoped.[48]

That Alessandro Scaglia operated informally as a Spanish agent certainly until his semi-retirement to Antwerp in 1636 indicated the remarkable wealth of his experience and also the level of his political credit with the Habsburg courts in Brussels and Madrid. Having said that, there were no compelling financial reasons to continue his career, and he certainly did not need any further sources of income that more formal service with the Spanish might offer – 'Scaglia was no beggar', as Echevarría Bacigalupe has put it.[49] At the point of going into exile Alessandro retained control of all three of his commendatory abbeys and pensions held in Savoy, in addition to the abbey of Mandanici in Sicily that had been granted by the

---

[47] Echevarría Bacigalupe, *Diplomacia secreta*, pp. 223–34; Paul Janssens, 'La Fronde de l'aristocratie belge en 1632', in Werner Thomas and Bart de Groof (eds.), *Rebelión y resistencia en el mundo Hispánico del siglo XVII* (Louvain, 1992); A. Waddington, *la République des Provinces-Unies, la France et les Pays-Bas Espagnols de 1630 à 1650*, 2 vols. (Brussels, 1895–7), I, pp. 145–180.

[48] AGS Est. 2240, Philip IV to Scaglia, 12 December 1633. This letter was marked, 'most secret reply'. It is worth adding that Scaglia also used another cipher with Olivares, albeit a simplistic one that styled Gerbier as 'el amigo' and the count-duke, appropriately enough, as 'padre grande'.

[49] Echevarría Bacigalupe, *Diplomacia secreta*, p. 237.

Spanish in 1631 as a gift for his services (before leaving official Savoyard service). Although, in the absence of the abate's personal papers, it remains difficult to quantify with precision the extent of his resources, whether as income from ecclesiastical holdings or as money held through investments including objects of art, or to trace how the income from his abbeys was transferred to him in exile, it is more than clear from indirect evidence that he enjoyed a comfortable existence in the Spanish Netherlands.[50] Writing from London, the Venetian ordinary ambassador there noted that despite the abate's supposed disgrace he continued to live well because of the money he had deposited with Peter Ricaut, a Brabanter merchant based in England whose sympathies lay with the Spanish and who had well-established connections with the Caroline court.[51] Scaglia probably knew Ricaut from his diplomatic missions to London and may well have employed the merchant because of his Habsburg affinities and contacts with the court, and because the English capital was a safe place for the abate to deposit his resources. It is once again unfortunate that there are no known documents detailing Ricaut's financial transactions, but in 1633 it was reported that 10,000 crowns in remittances had been transferred to Scaglia from the banker. He further reported that the abate received a remittance from Baronis, a merchant attached to the court at Savoy, while he was passing through Brussels back to Turin in 1633, perhaps implying a continuing level of informal contact with his home state.[52]

Alessandro Scaglia also remained sufficiently prominent to attract attention from the Turinese court, above and beyond the involvement he was to have with the increasingly disgruntled younger brothers of the Savoyard duke during the course of the 1630s. Savoy never had a resident diplomat at the semi-autonomous court of Brussels, but Vittorio Amedeo I's ambassador to Charles I recorded that the abate had one of the best houses in Brussels, full of sumptuous furnishings. In a letter written in 1636 to the duke, he provided further insights into Scaglia's lavish manner of life, writing that at the same time each day the abate took a drive in his four coaches, each with six horses and each with two servants

---

[50] The papal nuncio in Turin wrote that the abbey of Staffarda was worth 7,000 ducats, the abbey of Muleggio 2,000 ducats and Susa 500. These figures probably do not signify the actual value of the abbeys, but possibly the entry payments made to the Roman church by an individual granted a benefice. ASV SS Savoia, 44, f. 365, Albertini to Barberini, 6 September 1625.

[51] CSPV 1632–6, pp. 106, 109. Secondary evidence is scant, but see *Dictionary of National Biography* for Ricaut's son. Ricaut was involved, with Francis Windebank, the earl of Arundel and the Spanish ambassador in London in an aborted West Indies venture to rival the Dutch.

[52] CSPV 1632–6, pp. 140, 171.

dressed in black livery. The ambassador went on to comment on the generosity of his hospitality at home, where he had a well-stocked table with beer and Spanish wine, while the papal inter-nuncio recorded one particular dinner Scaglia held in honour of Prince Tommaso Francesco and the marquis of Aytona, the leading minister in Brussels between the death of the Infanta Isabella in December 1633 and the Cardinal-Infante's arrival in the following year.[53] When he later moved to semi-retirement in Antwerp, Scaglia settled in the *Keizerstraat*, the most prestigious street for private residences in the city.[54] It could count among its other residents at the time Nicolaas Rockox (1560–1640), nine times burgermaster of Antwerp and one of the city's leading citizens. Rockox was himself a patron and collector of exceptional importance, a learned numismatist and bibliophile, and a close friend and early patron of Peter Paul Rubens, responsible most spectacularly for Rubens' *Deposition from the Cross* (1611–14) that he commissioned for the city's cathedral. His extensive collection of paintings contained works not only by Rubens, but also by Van Dyck and earlier masters from the Low Countries including Quintin Metsijs (1466–1530), Jan van Eyck (1395–1441) and Pieter Bruegel the Elder (*c.* 1525/30–69), though unfortunately there is no known evidence that Scaglia and Rockox knew each other directly despite their clear cultural affinities.

On 10 May 1641 Alessandro Scaglia composed his will, only eleven days before his death. This will, which was drawn up in the Franciscan convent of the Recollects in Antwerp, existed in two copies, one deposited in the city and the other returned at some point by the abate's Franciscan confessor, Peter Stunbergen (also of the convent), to the Scaglia di Verrua's family archive in the Piedmontese town of Biella. As Arabella Cifani and Franco Monetti have rightly argued, the will affords the most detailed information into the extent of his wealth and also of the lavishness of the abate's life in exile. It included references to at least some of his possessions, indicating that in his Antwerp residence Scaglia had gold clocks, tapestries, ornate furnishings and wines from the Rhineland, Moselle and France.[55] More importantly still, the will also reveals something of his habits as an artistic patron and collector, especially through his 'Gratificationes', personal gifts to named friends,

[53] AST LMI m. 5, Ciza to Vittorio Amedeo I, 26 June 1637.

[54] AST LMI m. 5, Ciza to Vittorio Amedeo I, 3 July 1636; L. Schlugleit, 'L'abbé de Scaglia, Jordaens et "l'Histoire de Pysche" de Greenwich-House (1639–1642)', *Revue Belge d'Archéologie et d'Histoire de l'Art*, 7 (1937), 143; Augustin Thys, *Historiques des rues et places publiques de la ville d'Anvers* (Antwerp, 1873), pp. 222–5.

[55] ASB Archivio Scaglia, Testamenti, XCVI, 2537, will of Alessandro Scaglia, 11 May 1641.

though it should be added not necessarily the full extent of his pictorial collection – once again, there are unfortunately no personal papers detailing his possessions. To Henriette de Vaudemont (*c.* 1605–60), princess of Phalsbourg and the sister of the duke of Lorraine, who had entered exile in the Spanish Netherlands following the occupation by French troops of Lorraine in 1634 (with her sister, Marguérite de Lorraine, Gaston's bride from 1632), the abate left a flower painting on a panel. It was described as being by someone from the Jesuits and thought to be the work of Daniel Seghers (1590–1661), a member of the order based in Antwerp who specialised in floral pictures. An inventory drawn up by the artist of his floral works, which survives only in an eighteenth-century copy, described the painting as being of a spray of roses. This was one of at least two works by Seghers in Scaglia's collection, the other being a painting of a vase of flowers, also recorded in the artist's inventory.[56] To one of the executors of his will, Andreas Pikanotti, the abate left a painting of fruits by the still-life and animal painter Frans Snyders (1579–1657), who was also a regular collaborator in Antwerp with Rubens; the association between Scaglia and Snyders was all the stronger because, like the abate, he had a house on the *Keizerstraat*, and the artist later recorded that Scaglia was a regular visitor to his residence there.[57]

By far the most spectacular of Scaglia's artistic commissions dating from his exile are those by Anthony van Dyck. In the spring of 1634 Van Dyck returned to his native city of Antwerp, having been in London since 1632, and it was in his year-long spell in the Spanish Netherlands that he began painting for the abate. During the next six years Van Dyck completed up to ten commissions for Alessandro Scaglia, not all of them included in the will, establishing Scaglia as one of the most significant individual patrons of the Brabanter artist and underlining the abate's wider importance in the history of collecting. While Scaglia's will represents an important document detailing his possessions, several of the Van Dyck works were not included. Without doubt the most significant absence was the full-length portrait donated in 1999 to the National Gallery in

---

[56] Cifani and Monetti, 'New light', 511. The paintings are listed consecutively in the inventory as: 'een feston van Roosen voor Le Abata Lescalli d [deleted] Savoyaer die het heeft for testament aen de Princesse van Saelsboorch [Phalsbourg]', and 'nog een klijn bloempottjen voor den zelven Heer'. Walter Couvreur, 'Daniël Seghers' Inventaris van door hem geschilderde bloemstukken', *Gentse Bijdragen tot de Kunstgeschiedenis en de Oudheidkunde*, 20 (1967), 105–6. The inventory also records paintings by the artist for Cardinal Maurizio, probably painted, so Couvreur suggests, when Seghers was in Rome between 1625 and 1627, and Tommaso Francesco, which comprised flowers and a picture of the Virgin by Cornelis Schut (1597–1655), a collaborator of Seghers. *Ibid.*, 95, 109.

[57] Schlugleit, 'L'abbé de Scaglia', 146, 155.

London by the Camrose family in lieu of death duties, with a copy also by the artist which is now in the Koninklijk Museum voor Schone Kunsten in Antwerp, both probably painted in 1635 during the artist's time there (Figs. 6 and 7). An inscription on the copy, which also dates the abate's death, indicates that the portrait was given to the convent where he was buried, the inscription having been added to the painting after Van Dyck's own death.[58] Another work not mentioned in the will is a religious composition, *The Lamentation* or *Mater Dolorosa* (Fig. 8). It was commissioned, possibly after Van Dyck's return to London, to hang as the predella to the altar he planned for the convent of the Franciscan Recollects in Antwerp, already established as one of Antwerp's premier places for interment. The tomb itself was removed during the French Revolution, but an eighteenth-century description gives some ideas as to how the painting was set, together with the Van Dyck portrait of the abate. Extending the theme of the *Mater Dolorosa*, the tomb referred to the Seven Sorrows of the Virgin, a focal point of Marian devotion that was not in fact formally endorsed by the church at this point. At the top of the altar was a statue of Mary, Mother of Sorrows, itself above a rich marble setting of the *Mater Dolorosa*, which was in turn flanked by statues depicting the flight of Mary and Joseph to Egypt, one of the Seven Sorrows.[59] The *Mater Dolorosa*, a dramatic composition, shows the limp body of the dead Christ with Mary mourning on the left and two angels emerging from clouds to the right, serving 'to render the harrowing scene unforgettable', according to Christopher Brown. After Scaglia's death, the convent had a copy made of the picture and sold the original, which is currently in the city's Koninklijk Museum.[60]

The remaining Van Dyck works were recorded in Scaglia's 'Gratificationes'. In the first place was a second half-length portrait in an oval frame, depicting Scaglia adoring the Virgin and Child, and which is

[58] The inscription reads: 'Caes. Alexander Scaglia ex. Comitib. Verrucae marchionib. Caluxii Abbas Staphardae et Mandanices. Legationem et rer. gestar. Fama inclitus. Fratribus pro aeterna memoria hoc altare erexit. Obiit XXI mai MDCXLI.'

[59] The convent was founded under the direction of Duke Philip the Good (1396–1467) in the mid-fifteenth century. In the year before Scaglia's burial there, Rockox was interred in a tomb in the convent, above which was a triptych by Rubens. Thys, *Historiques*, pp. 182–4, 224. For details on the tomb see A. Monballieu, 'Cesare Alesandro Scaglia en de "Bewening van Christus" door A. van Dijk', *Jaarboek van het Koninklijk Museum voor Schone Kunsten* (1973), 267, and 256–60 on its fate.

[60] Christopher Brown, *Virgin and Child by Anthony van Dyck* (London, 1971). The tomb is now gone, along with the convent which was demolished in the early nineteenth century when it was replaced by the Académie des Beaux-Arts, but a description of it can be found in *Inscriptions funéraries et monumentales de la province d'Anvers*, VI. (Antwerp, 1871), p. 185.

Fig. 6 Anthony van Dyck, *Alessandro Cesare Scaglia* (*c.* 1635). The 'Camrose' portrait, that in 1999 was acquired by the National Gallery in London, in lieu of death duties. Together with the other portraits of the abate, it establishes an 'iconography' of Scaglia, as a cultivated patron, courtier and ecclesiastic.

Fig. 7   Anthony van Dyck, *Alessandro Cesare Scaglia* (*c.* 1635). A copy of the
'Camrose' portrait by Van Dyck. Clearly, the inscription was added after the
abate's death, and the portrait itself was planned to hang on Scaglia's tomb in
the Franciscan Recollects' Convent in Antwerp. Beneath the inscription is the
abate's coat of arms, based on his family's arms and incorporating a black hat
and Scaglia's personal motto, *Quiescendo Sapimus*, a motto that may have had
resonances of political and stoical self-control.

Fig. 8 Anthony van Dyck, *The Mater Dolorosa* (c. 1635). Intended as a predella to Scaglia's tomb in the Franciscan Recollects' Convent, Antwerp, the painting may have been commissioned as a result of Scaglia's illness of 1635, when he came close to death. This original was sold after his death and replaced by a copy. The work, together with the abate's tomb to Our Lady of the Seven Sorrows, reinforces the importance to Scaglia of Marian devotion, most evident in his later years when he began to retire from the political limelight.

Fig. 9   Anthony van Dyck, *Alessandro Scaglia adoring the Virgin and Child*
(*c.* 1635). An intriguing portrait, not least because the identity of the Virgin
has been subject to considerable speculation. The portrait also reiterated the
abate's veneration of Mary, a quite typical expression of piety in early modern
Catholic culture.

also in the National Gallery in London, mentioned in the will as 'a round
picture of an image of the Blessed Mary with the Boy Jesus and the figure
of the illustrious master [Imago Beatae Mariae rotunda cum puero Jesulo
et figura Illustrissimi Domini]' (Fig. 9). The other Van Dyck pictures
owned by Scaglia are indeed mentioned only in the will and the works
themselves have yet to come to light. It is not even certain that the abate
himself commissioned them. These included what would be a unique
quadruple portrait of Charles I and Henrietta Maria together, it seems,
with the painter and his wife [effigies Regis et Reginae Angliae de manu
Van Diik cum imagine eiusdem pictoris et uxoris eius]. Unlike the portraits and possibly the *Lamentation*, the quadruple portrait was certainly
painted at a later date, between Van Dyck's marriage in 1639 to Mary

Ruthven and his death in 1641, strongly suggesting that contact between Van Dyck and Scaglia continued after the artist returned to London in June 1635. There was also a mythological picture of Thetis, the nymph mother of Achilles, and another Virgin and Child ('Imago Beatae Mariae cum puero Jesulo ex artificio Van Diik'), though when they were painted remains unclear. All three works were left to Alexander Poliagus, a canon of Antwerp cathedral and one of the executors of Scaglia's will. The Franciscan convent where the abate was interred also received a Crucifixion with angels collecting Christ's blood ('Crucifixi et Angelorum in calicibus sanguinem Domini Jesu suscipientium'), while Paul Dorkius, another of Scaglia's executors, was given a portrait of Queen Henrietta Maria ('Imago Reginae Angliae maior').[61]

The two known portraits of Alessandro Scaglia (with Van Dyck's second version of the full-length portrait) have been subjected to detailed scrutiny, placing them in different contexts – artistic, historical and religious. The full-length 'Camrose' portrait has been described as a penetrating study of a subtle though physically frail diplomat: 'to judge from the weary eyes of his handsome face, he, like Van Dyck, possessed a sensitivity that left him vulnerable to the opinion of others', so Arthur Wheelock has written, while Judy Egerton has suggested that the painting was 'monumental yet understated, deeply perceptive yet entirely uningratiating'.[62] Interpretations of the oval portrait of Alessandro in devotion to the Virgin have been still more suggestive. A mountain range sets the backdrop to the picture, seen by Christopher Brown as a reference to the Alps and thus indicating the abate's home state of Savoy. The Virgin, so he adds, was painted according to the conventions of seventeenth-century portraiture and taken from an actual subject. One long-standing tradition has in fact identified her as the duchess of Arenberg, though precisely who this was is not clear – presumably, it was a mis-identification of Countess Maria Cleopha von Hohenzollern-Sigmaringen (1599–1685), the third wife of Duke Philippe Charles of Aerschot, who gave birth in 1633 to Charles Eugene, the future duke of Arenberg (d. 1681).[63] To Brown, however,

---

[61] ASB Archivio Scaglia, Testamenti, XCVI, 2537, will of Alessandro Scaglia, 11 May 1641, partially printed in Cifani and Monetti, 'New light', 514. A short version of the will exists in the Staatsarchief in Antwerp, Notarissen Rousseau, 1641, f. 163.

[62] Arthur Wheelock *et al.* (eds.), *Van Dyck Paintings* (London, 1991), pp. 272–3. Egerton's assessment can be found in Brown and Vlieghe (eds.), *Van Dyck*, p. 272. Oliver Millar similarly described Van Dyck's 'Camrose' portrait as 'one of the finest he ever produced, with its combination of splendour and restraint, of monumentality and latent movement.' Oliver Millar, *Van Dyck in England* (London, 1982), pp. 58–9.

[63] H. Granville Fell, 'Some topics of the moment', *The Connoisseur*, 101 (February 1938). Presumably, Granville Fell's mistake has arisen from the fact that Charles Eugene was to become duke of Arenberg as an adult.

the Virgin was none other than Duchess Marie Christine, with her young son and heir to the duchy, Francesco Giacinto (born 1632), as the Christ child. For a Savoyard subject in exile, the painting has accordingly been interpreted as a demonstration of loyalty, even though ultimately Scaglia never returned to north Italy, remaining instead in the Spanish Netherlands until his death.[64] Another perhaps more intriguing interpretation has concluded that the Virgin may in fact have been modelled on the princess of Phalsbourg. This attribution has been based on the apparent likeness of the Virgin and Phalsbourg, who Van Dyck also painted during his stay in Antwerp, and Scaglia's supposedly close relationship with the princess, though mainly because the painting was left to the princess in Scaglia's will.[65]

Even if Van Dyck modelled his Mary on a specific individual, speculation about her identity is tantalising but ultimately fruitless, not least because of the lack of specific archival evidence. The majority of the abate's private papers have yet to be found, if they still exist, and there is indeed very little at all in contemporary accounts about Scaglia's commissions from Van Dyck beyond the will. Frustratingly, his surviving correspondence in the archives of Brussels and Simancas, written primarily to Olivares and Philip IV, yields nothing. Yet there seems to be no compelling reason as to why the abate should want a portrait of the Savoyard duchess as the Virgin, apart from the fact that while in exile he avoided antagonising Duke Vittorio Amedeo I and his French consort. Nor is it clear who would definitely have seen the picture other than the abate, raising further questions about its effectiveness as an overt demonstration of loyalty to the Sabaudian dynasty. In any case Van Dyck had probably only seen her once, when he visited Turin in 1622–3, at which time she was aged seventeen – not the image of the more mature woman he painted for Alessandro.[66] As for the principal alternatives, if the portrait was of the duke of Aerschot's wife, then it would be of considerable irony given that the abate had been indirectly responsible for the duke's imprisonment in Spain following the collapse of the noble plot in the Spanish Netherlands. On the other hand, the 'Gratificationes' of Scaglia's will certainly record that he left the painting to Phalsbourg, together with the Seghers floral panel, and the abate indeed considered her as another

---

[64] Brown, *Virgin and Child*.

[65] Cifani and Monetti, 'New light', 512–13. The portrait of the princess of Phalsbourg is now in the Iveagh Bequest at Kenwood. Brown and Vlieghe (eds.), *Van Dyck*, pp. 264–5.

[66] Aware of this problem, Brown suggested that Van Dyck 'would have worked from an engraving, a drawing by another artist or even from Scaglia's description'. Brown, *Virgin and Child*.

important link in the international chain of opponents of Richelieu, not least because of the fact that her sister was married to Gaston d'Orléans. But this is the only clear evidence of a connection between the painting and the princess.[67]

Although the difficulties in attributing the Virgin to any particular individual are evident, the Van Dyck commissions, both the full-length portrait and the devotional portrait, can still be taken in a broader sense as visual records of Alessandro's social and political fortunes, even though he was in exile. The importance of the Scaglia di Verrua as a court clan with the skill and experience to commission works of art and literature was already well established, as was the abate's particular expertise, and the Van Dyck commissions reiterated his social position as an individual with substantial financial resources and a high level of cultural sophistica-tion. The portraits of Alessandro Scaglia moreover recorded a distinctive iconography of an individual who was both a member of the church and an aristocratic diplomat located in a system of early modern Catholic court culture. His black cloak and swirling silk soutane in the full-length 'Camrose' portrait immediately mark him out as an ecclesiastic. The por-trait of Scaglia and the Virgin, together with his tomb to Our Lady of the Seven Sorrows, more clearly illuminate Alessandro's religious sensi-bilities, in keeping with the refound confidence of the Catholic church that after the Council of Trent had successfully reincorporated venera-tion to the Virgin and depictions of Marian devotion into its religious system. Finding other evidence for Scaglia's religiosity, particularly from surviving written evidence is, however, tricky. Again his will presents some information, recording his financial gifts to lay and ecclesiastical institutions in the city where he was eventually buried. In the first place he set aside money for the completion of his own tomb in the Franciscan convent in Antwerp and for the saying of masses, and he also had a Franciscan confessor and was ultimately buried in the order's habit. It is unclear as to why he seemed so attached to the order, though according to his funeral oration given by A. van Oudenhoven of the Franciscan convent, before his death the abate took its third rule, 'Of Penitence', that is to say he lived as a lay member of the Franciscans. Indeed, Van Oudenhoven's eulogistic oration gave details of Scaglia's deepening piety at the convent, taking his meals on the ground with penitent brothers and protesting that 'he never was fed with such enjoyment in the halls of

---

[67] Phalsbourg, as the sister-in-law of Gaston d'Orléans, was a potentially important means of influencing the heir to the French throne through Gaston's wife. Phalsbourg herself was anxious not only to secure the independence from France of Lorraine for her family, but also the future of her own principality. Osborne, 'French exiles', 162.

the great as he now found in the food which came from begging'. On Holy Thursday, the day when the superior washed the feet of mourning brethren, the oration recorded that Scaglia willingly undertook the task, while he also asked for a cell to be built from which he could see and meditate on the high altar.[68] Scaglia's donations were not limited to the Franciscans. To the Sisters of the Annunciation in Antwerp he left 3,000 florins for an act of perpetual devotion in honour of the Franciscan St Anthony of Padua, the 'Hammer of Heretics', who enjoyed particular favour in reformed Catholic devotion as a hero figure defined against Protestantism, and who had connections with the Piedmontese town of Vercelli. To other ecclesiastical institutions and groups in Antwerp associated with reformed Catholicism, among them the Jesuits, the Discalced Carmelites and the sodality of the Holy Sacrament, money was given for the saying of requiem masses and divine offices for his soul's repose.[69]

The abate's copious correspondence from across his career affords further, if somewhat occasional, insights into his religious sensibilities. It remains difficult to establish any of the churches or sites of pilgrimage at which he worshipped, aside from the information given by his will. It is known however that he visited Loreto on at least two pilgrimages, first in 1617 and then in 1623, while returning to Turin from his diplomatic missions to the papal court.[70] Loreto, sited near Ancona on the Adriatic coast of the Italian peninsula, had long been established as one of Europe's most important centres of Marian devotion, claiming to be the miraculous site of the stable where Christ was born and that had moved to the peninsula at the end of the thirteenth century. Its importance became all the greater in the sixteenth and seventeenth centuries as the church

---

[68] The oration, printed by the Plantin Press in 1641, has been partially transcribed in Monballieu, 'Cesare Alesandro Scaglia', 267.

[69] ASB Archivio Scaglia, Testamenti, XCVI, 2537, will of Alessandro Scaglia, 11 May 1641. The Discalced Carmelites, reformed by St Theresa of Avila (1515–82), enjoyed particular favour in the Spanish Netherlands under the direction of the Infanta Isabella, who founded their first convent in Brussels between 1607 and 1615. Luc Duerloo and Werner Thomas (eds.), *Albert et Isabelle, 1598–1621* (Brussels, 1998), p. 266. On the importance of the sodalities in Antwerp and early modern Catholicism more generally consult Louis Chatellier, *The Europe of the Devout: The Catholic Reformation and Formation of a New Society* (Cambridge, 1989).

[70] AST LMR m. 28, fasc. 1, 165, Scaglia to Carlo Emanuele I, 4 December 1617; 167, Scaglia to Carlo Emanuele I, 15 December 1617; ASV Avvisi, 9, f. 17v, 21 January 1623. He was not the only member of the Scaglia di Verrua to make the pilgrimage. As Tassoni's letters had recorded, his nephews and brother paid visits to the shrine. Filiberto Scaglia also intended to visit Loreto again in 1635, though his journey was diverted. AST LP 'S' m. 48, 'Relazione del viaggio intrapreso dall'abate Filiberto Gherardo Scaglia'.

validated devotion to the Virgin.[71] For obvious reasons Scaglia was also familiar with the written text of the Catholic church, the Vulgate Bible. In an intriguing letter to Duke Vittorio Amedeo I written shortly before he went into exile, a crucial moment in his political career when his loyalty was being brought directly into question, the abate compared himself to St Paul, the suffering (and obviously loyal) servant sent to do God's bidding, paraphrasing directly from the Latin Vulgate: 'I can say to your highness what Saint Paul said to God. I have finished my course, I have kept the faith. Henceforth there is laid up for me a crown of righteousness, which the righteous judge shall give me [Cursum consumavi fidem servavi, in reliquo reposita est mihi corona iustitiae quam reddit mihi iustus iudex]'. If the abate saw himself as Paul then God, by clear and obvious inference, was to be understood as his sovereign prince.[72]

An insight into Alessandro Scaglia's mental world might be opened still further by examining the engraving made of the top half of the full-length 'Camrose' portrait by Paul Pontius (1603–58) and included posthumously in Martin van den Enden's second edition of Van Dyck's so-called *Iconographia* (1641) (Fig. 10). The purpose of the collection is implied by the full title of the next and larger edition, published under the direction of Gilles Hendricx; the *Icones principium virorum doctorum, pictorum, chalcographorum, statuariorum nec non Amatorum Pictoriae artis numero centum* (1645–6) comprised engravings of his portraits of leading figures of the age – sovereigns, nobles, artists, writers and political figures. It was in short a *Who's Who* of the early seventeenth century. The *Iconographia* had a complex editorial history and was published in several major editions in the first half of the seventeenth century, the most complete being Hendricx's 1645–6 version, and it included mostly portraits executed by Van Dyck himself, no doubt to emphasise his success as a court artist while also playing to an international consumer market interested in acquiring portraits, or at least more affordable engravings, of the famous.[73] Alessandro Scaglia's inclusion in the collection immediately indicated his own importance in the world of early seventeenth-century court culture. The engraving by Paul Pontius, probably the ablest and most important

---

[71] Indeed, there was a specific culture of devotion to 'Our Lady of Loreto'. Chatellier, *Europe of the Devout*, pp. 152–5.

[72] AGR SEG 600, Scaglia to Vittorio Amedeo I, December 1631. The (mis)quotation is from 2 Timothy 4:7–8. See also AGR SEG 600, Scaglia to Vittorio Amedeo I, 14 November 1631; Scaglia to Vittorio Amedeo I, 28 December 1631.

[73] On the complex history of its publication see Marie Mauquoy-Hendrickx, *L'iconographie d'Antoine van Dyck*, 2 vols. (2nd edition, Brussels, 1991), I, chapter 3. See also Alfred Moir, Francine de Nave and Carl Depauw (eds.), *Antoon van Dyck & Antwerpen* (Antwerp, 1991).

CÆSAR ALEXANDER SCAGLIA ABBAS STAPHARDÆ ET MANDANICES

Hic, quem tacentem nobilis finxit manus,
Nuper diserta Principes linguâ movens.
Momenta rebus magna perplexis dedit.

Sibi nunc silendo uiuit : actotum procul
Vndare Mundum tacitus . e Portu intuens
Animum ad futura. doctus ex uiis, parat.

P. Pontius sculp.   Ant van Dyck pinxit   cum privilegio

Fig. 10   Paul Pontius, *Alessandro Cesare Scaglia* (engraved after 1641). The engraving of Scaglia in the *Iconographia* is a reverse of the full-length portrait by Van Dyck. The fact that it was included in the collection marked the abate's importance in the world of early seventeenth-century court culture, while the accompanying inscription, unusual for the *Iconographia*, recorded the links between the abate's religiosity and his political career.

of Van Dyck's collaborators in the production of the *Iconographia*, was in fact marked out from all but two of the other engravings in the Hendricx version (those of the artist Gerard Seghers (1591–1651) and of Nicolaas Rockox) because it was accompanied by a Latin verse inscription at its bottom:

> This man, whom now in silence a noble hand has fashioned,
> Lately stirred leaders with his eloquent tongue
> And gave great import to complex affairs.
>
> Now saying nothing he lives for himself: in silence gazing from his haven
> Upon the whole world far off in turmoil,
> He prepares his mind for the future, having learnt from what he has seen.[74]

Like an emblem book, the accompanying inscription provided a key to interpreting the image and to interpreting Scaglia himself. The verse distilled the ideals of Alessandro's career as an ambassador, of diplomacy as a moral vocation underpinned (if not explicitly) by Catholic sensibilities. The full-length portrait was executed at a time when Alessandro was seriously ill, and the text, composed with hindsight after his death, can also be taken as a reference to the abate's physical frailty from 1635, 'hinting at the Franciscan spirituality to which he was increasingly drawn', so Cifani and Monetti have suggested.[75] Through introspection and personal devotion the abate was preparing not only for his own death but also for eternal life.

Reformed Catholicism was a defining parameter of Alessandro's life, encompassing his conception of his role as a minister in the service of the duke of Savoy and borne out in his artistic commissions, even in exile. So far as the *Iconographia* was concerned, Alessandro Scaglia was identified implicitly through the association of peace and diplomacy, one of the recurrent themes of early modern diplomatic rhetoric. Such clear allusions to the duties of the diplomat had already been made in another text praising the abate among other members of the Scaglia di Verrua,

---

[74] The Latin original is:

> Hic, quem tacentem nobilis finxit manus,
> Nuper diserta Principes lingua movens
> Momenta rebus magna perplexis dedit.
>
> Sibi nunc silendo vivit: actotum procul
> Undare Mundum tacitus, e Portu intuens
> Animum ad futura, doctus ex visis parat.

Anthony van Dyck, *Icones principium virorum doctorum, pictorum, chalcographorum, statuariorum nec non amatorum pictoriae artis numero centum* (Antwerp, 1646), p. 28. For further information see Moir *et al.* (eds.), *Antoon van Dyck*, pp. 370–1.

[75] Cifani and Monetti, 'New light', 508.

the *Elogia* composed by the Piedmontese Jesuit and historian Emanuele Tesauro, it seems, for Filiberto Scaglia's *laureato* in 1634, ironically after the abate had entered exile:

Uncle Alexander lives on, truly the Great
Who never stands still, in the manner of some divine power active everywhere,
Always sent off to every leader, so that political freedom may stand firm[76]

In both texts the abate was therefore defined according to an ideal of diplomatic rhetoric, operating, as he did, at the point of contact between religion and politics. It was his duty to bring peace between Catholic princes, though as his reactions to the treaties of Monzón, Regensburg and Cherasco had all too clearly shown, for him it had to be peace that fulfilled his particular criteria about Savoy's interests. More direct evidence about Alessandro's political assumptions is, like evidence for his religious sensibilities, difficult to find. This is not helped by the fact that in the absence of his personal papers no evidence has come to light of any books or treatises he owned, and equally importantly, which books he would have read and annotated. Only occasionally are there hints of what literature he might have known, such as a comparison he made of the siege by Spanish troops of the fortress of Verrua in 1625 with an example from an unspecified work of Francesco Guicciardini (1483–1540), or a series of classical allusions in a Latin poem criticising the entry of French troops into Savoy during the war for Mantua and Monferrato which seems to have been co-written by the abate and Hernando de Salazar, the Jesuit confessor of Olivares.[77] Alessandro Scaglia nevertheless came from a particular generation of political figures that had grown up in the atmosphere of revitalised Catholicism. He himself, along with his brother, may well have been educated by one of the principal exponents of what might be

---

[76] The play on words in this verse, with the tacit comparison of Scaglia with Alexander the Great and the references to public liberty, can best be understood from the Latin original:

> Vivit Alexander Patruus, vere Magnus
> Qui Numinis more ubique agentis
> Ad Principes omnes semper ablegatus
> Ut politica stet libertas, numquam stat.

Tesauro, *Inscriptiones*, pp. 221–3, 232–3. According to this collection, the *elogia* was written to mark Filiberto's *laureato*, though there is no evidence to suggest where he was educated. The fact that Tesauro was a Jesuit suggests that Filiberto might have been a pupil of the order, in which case the poem would have been a standard work to mark the graduation of a student. In the defence of his *laureato*, Filiberto would in any case have had personal sponsors who would have served to indicate the student's particular social status, though again there are no indications as to whom they might have been. I am grateful to Professor Louise Rice of Duke University for advice.

[77] ASV SS Francia, 65, f. 405, Bagno to Barberini, 23 October 1626; BN Nouvelles Acquisitions Français, 3109, ff. 70–v, 'Diergeticon ad Italiam', 1630.

described as Catholic power politics, Giovanni Botero, though no direct evidence confirms this possibility. More definitely, the abate knew either directly or through correspondence individuals who are now established as significant political figures in their own rights, among them Diego de Saavedra y Fajardo, described by Robert Bireley as representing the climax of the anti-Machiavellian tradition in Catholic statecraft, Philip IV's official historian Virgilio Malvezzi, the poet, polemicist and diplomat Fulvio Testi, and Peter Paul Rubens, whose own political world has been reconstructed with reference to his artistic output.[78] Through the accumulation of indirect evidence and the evidence of his own career it would not be unreasonable to view Alessandro Scaglia as a representative public figure of early seventeenth-century Catholic Europe, where confessional sensibilities, practical politics (encompassing what has been described as moralised political pragmatisim) and court culture overlapped. In this sense, the abate used his wealth to project an image that placed him within a distinctive court system, and the Van Dyck commissions were themselves integral to the abate's self-fashioned identity as a widely known diplomat and collector, although it also remains difficult to assess where they would have been hung (other than the works intended for his funerary monument) and who indeed might have seen them.

Prior to executing the full-length 'Camrose' portrait, Anthony van Dyck is known to have made at least four preparatory sketches in chalk of the abate, two of which are in the British Museum. Another of the sketches, in the Institut Néerlandais in Paris, has been described by Judy Egerton as 'conversational in spirit, as if he [Scaglia] were enjoying the encounter', a pose that showed the abate seated and holding a document, rather than standing and leaning on a ledge as he was eventually depicted (Fig. 11).[79] It is quite possible that Scaglia and Van Dyck may have met as early as 1623, when the artist was in Turin on his two-year journey around the peninsula from his base in Genoa and the abate was back in the Savoyard capital during a brief gap from the Savoyard embassy in Rome.[80] Yet again no direct evidence exists to corroborate the connection, though the existence of a friendship struck up between the two during the 1630s and borne out by the chalk sketches is obviously more credible, especially in the light of their shared interests and the fact that they had other friends in common, among them Endymion Porter and Balthasar Gerbier. But as has been seen, friendship was

---

[78] For Saavedra see Fernández-Santamaría, *Reason of State*; M. Fraga Irabarne, *Don Diego de Saavedra y Fajado y la diplomacia de su época* (Madrid, 1955); Bireley, *Counter-Reformation Prince*, chapter 8. For Peter Paul Rubens consult Morford, *Stoics and Neostoics*.
[79] Brown and Vlieghe (eds.), *Van Dyck*, p. 272.
[80] *Ibid.*, p. 272; Cifani and Monetti, 'New light', 513.

Fig. 11 Anthony van Dyck, *Alessandro Cesare Scaglia* (*c.* 1635). One of two line drawings (the other is in the British Museum on the reverse of a drawn portrait of Johann of Nassau-Siegen) that served as a study for the full-length portrait, although there are some differences, as Scaglia is shown here seated and clasping a document.

multi-dimensional and could be strongly politicised, signifying more than just 'private' affinities between individuals. Friendships cultivated through the visual arts can and should be viewed in different contexts, beyond that between the sitter and the artist as in the example of Scaglia and Van Dyck. In his analysis of Bacon's concept of friendship, Wootton suggests that Bacon's views encompassed not only the horizontal relations that existed primarily among social equals but also vertical relations between patrons and clients. If he is correct then the intriguing quadruple portrait of the English king and queen with Van Dyck and his wife owned by the abate can be taken as a record of a type of friendship where it expressed patronage and favour between the artist and his royal patrons. For the abate the commission, together with that of the portrait of Henrietta Maria, may also have served to record the special relationship he enjoyed with the Caroline court that dated back to the mid-1620s. Charles I had so favourably treated the abate during the 1620s and had evidently taken a liking to him, in part for who he represented, though also for what, as a cultivated individual, he embodied, even though their relationship was still essentially one of social unequals.[81]

By commissioning pictures from an established artist such as Anthony van Dyck, Alessandro Scaglia could signal his continuing membership in a distinctive international political and cultural world that extended to the ruling dynasties in Savoy and England. Van Dyck was by the 1630s already established as a portrait painter in London, while the Sabaudian dynasty had also employed him to mark significant political and dynastic occasions. According to Baudi di Vesme, Van Dyck had first visited Turin in 1622 in the entourage of Aletheia (d. 1654) countess of Arundel, wife of one the major patrons at the Stuart court. While this argument is not entirely certain, it is more probable that Van Dyck spent a brief amount of time in Turin in 1623, when he might have painted portraits for several members of the ruling House (though none of them survives).[82] In the following year, when in Palermo, he painted Prince Filiberto Emanuele as viceroy of Sicily. In 1635, the year of Alessandro's major commissions, Queen Henrietta Maria had her children painted by the artist and sent as a gift to her sister Marie Christine in Turin to mark the dynastic affinity that

---

[81] While this view of friendship is problematic, Antonio Feros has argued that the sovereign could have a special friend from a lower social group – his favourite. Antonio Feros, 'Images of evil, images of kings: the contrasting faces of the royal favourite and the prime minister in early modern European literature, *c.* 1580–*c.* 1650', in Elliott and Brockliss (eds.), *The World of the Favourite*.

[82] Baudi di Vesme, *L'arte negli stati sabaudi*, pp. 522–5; M. Vaes, 'Il soggiorno di Antonio Van Dyck alla Corte di Torino: 4 Dicembre 1622–Febbraio 1623', *Bollettino Storico-Bibliografico Subalpino*, 43 (1942).

Fig. 12   Anthony van Dyck, *The Children of Charles I* (1635). From left to right, the children are Charles (later Charles II), Mary and James (later James II). The painting served as a diplomatic gift from Henrietta Maria to her sister Marie Christine, consort of Vittorio Amedeo I, who reciprocated with a painting of her own children, though the return gift is now lost. Even though Caroline foreign policy was conducted at a lower rate of intensity during the Personal Rule of the 1630s when compared with the 1620s, the gift, a work of a painter employed by both the Stuarts and the Savoyards, could serve to reiterate the dynastic and cultural links between London and Turin.

still linked London and Turin despite the relative cooling of diplomatic relations (Fig. 12); and in the same year Tommaso Francesco, the prince of Carignano, had his equestrian portrait painted, depicting him in his role as a commander in the army of Flanders (Fig. 13).[83] Given this

[83] Ferrero (ed.), *Lettres*, p. 40; Brown and Vlieghe (eds.), *Van Dyck*, pp. 295–7. The painting from Henrietta Maria, now in the Galleria Sabauda, Turin was reciprocated by Marie Christine, though this return gift no longer seems to exist.

Fig. 13   Anthony van Dyck, *Prince Tommaso Francesco of Carignano* (*c.* 1635).
The equestrian portrait was commissioned by the prince during the same
period as the Scaglia commissions. The work marked Tommaso Francesco's
assumption of a command in the Army of Flanders following his self-imposed
exile to the Spanish Netherlands from Savoy in 1634, depicting the prince in
armour, with the *Annunziata* around his neck, the supreme chivalric order of
the House of Savoy.

patronage conferred on Van Dyck by members of the Sabaudian House, Scaglia's own commissions from Van Dyck thus allowed him to identify himself with the ruling dynasty.

Equally significant were the contacts and frendships the exiled Scaglia maintained with fellow diplomats, courtiers and political figures on his social level, including those from England, despite reduced contact with London following the murder in 1628 of his closest friend, the duke of Buckingham, and the fact that Scaglia never returned to England in person. In November 1632, William Boswell (d. 1649), the resident agent in The Hague, was instructed to open contact with Scaglia as a means of communicating with Spain.[84] Meanwhile, the Venetian ambassador in London claimed that Scaglia still had many friends who had access to the English court, most notably the Brabanter merchant Peter Ricaut, while Scaglia wrote that he received news from 'a correspondent very close to the treasurer [Weston] and Carlisle'. Antonio Barberini, the younger of Urban VIII Barberini's nephews and the Protector of English Catholics, suggested in a letter to the papal inter-nuncio in Brussels that Scaglia and Aytona should take particular responsibility for the 'English nuns' resident in Brussels, though who they were and whether they acted as another line of informal contact with their home state of England, as was so often the case with religious exiles, remains unclear.[85]

One of the more intriguing and long lasting of Scaglia's friendships was with the English diplomatic agent, artist, architect and political chancer Balthasar Gerbier. Like that with Endymion Porter, the friendship pro-vides a clear example of how an interest in the visual arts could overlap with court politics. The abate and Gerbier had first met in 1627, dur-ing the informal negotiations for an Anglo-Spanish peace when Gerbier was part of that network of clients operating under the direction of Buckingham, mixing diplomacy with the patronage and brokering of the arts, the point at which Alessandro Scaglia's credit at the Caroline court was at its highest. Balthasar Gerbier remained in Brussels between 1631 and 1641 as an accredited diplomatic agent of England and was also the most significant point of contact available to the abate during the 1630s, especially as the abate's friendships with other English courtiers gradually waned – the earl of Carlisle remained sporadically in contact until his death in 1636, while the earl of Holland appears no longer to have written to the abate after his final departure from England.[86] In

[84] Rooses and Ruelens (eds.), *Correspondance*, VI, p. 26.
[85] CSPV 1632–6, p. 106; AGR SEG 596, f. 263, Scaglia to Olivares, 26 August 1633.
[86] The abate's last letter to Carlisle seems to have been as a letter of recommendation for the prince of Chimay as he was travelling to Charles I's coronation in Scotland. BL Eg. MS 2597, f. 126, Scaglia to Carlisle, 28 May 1633.

contrast, not only did Gerbier regularly inform Scaglia of news from London but he also sought to include him in the various informal negotiations during the 1630s for closer political ties between the English and the Spanish. The agent reported back to London his discussions with Scaglia about the thorny problem of the Palatinate and of the abate's hope that Charles I might be able to broker a peace treaty between the Dutch and the Spanish. As John Taylor, an English diplomatic agent passing through Brussels, wrote, 'the Abate of Scaglia with great protestations told me the other day that there is nothing upon earth he desireth more than to see the amity between England and Spain drawn into an indissoluble knot'.[87] Two years later in 1634, after Gerbier had sold information to Scaglia about the noble plot in the Spanish Netherlands, the agent once again suggested that Scaglia might be employed to mediate between England and Spain. Endymion Porter, Van Dyck's friend depicted in 1635 in a double portrait by the artist and who can be counted as another member of Scaglia's network of friends, travelled as Charles I's agent from London to Brussels. His mission was ostensibly to congratulate the Cardinal-Infante Ferdinand on his assumption of the governor-generalship of the Spanish Netherlands following Isabella Clara Eugenia's death in December 1633, though Porter also took suggestions about strengthening diplomatic relations between London and Madrid over the Palatinate question. Scaglia was seen as an obvious agent to organise such negotiations, following the informal discussions involving the abate and the marquis of Aytona.[88] Even after Scaglia's semi-retirement in 1636 Gerbier continued to involve him in secret and informal negotiations. The duchess of Chevreuse and the princess of Phalsbourg, both of whom were themselves in exile in the Spanish Netherlands and also personally known to the abate (Chevreuse from after her involvement in the Chalais conspiracy), undertook their own initiatives with Charles I. Their aim was to secure closer co-operation with Spain following a renewed interest in Anglo-Habsburg relations after the breakdown of a series of negotiations with the French regime.[89] Once again, Scaglia was involved. The princess of Phalsbourg, whose association with the abate was later confirmed by Scaglia's bequests in his will, specifically asked for

[87] PRO SP 77/22/209, Taylor to unknown, 31 October 1632.
[88] Bodleian Library, Clarendon State Papers, 15, ff. 71–v, Secret instructions for Porter 11 November 1634 (o.s.?), in which Windebank expressed his concern that Scaglia and Aytona had first spoken with Gerbier on such an important matter, rather than contacting London directly.
[89] The death in March 1635 of the pro-Habsburg minister Richard Weston seriously damaged the strength of the 'Spanish faction' in London. In turn, this encouraged talk of an alliance with the French. On this (underdiscussed) diplomacy and the aftermath see Sharpe, *The Personal Rule*, chapters 8 and 14.

him, 'a man of trust and habilities', to be used as a confidant in her talks, rather than any Spanish subjects, because of her trust in him, 'against the almost inscrutable ways of these strange people'.[90]

With their common diplomatic interests and cultural compatibility it was entirely fitting that the last occasion when Scaglia and Gerbier worked together was to secure an artistic commission. Following the completion in 1635 of Inigo Jones' Queen's House in Greenwich, the hunting lodge originally intended for James I's queen consort Anne of Denmark (1574–1619) but taken over by Henrietta Maria, Scaglia was approached by Gerbier to broker the commission for the decoration of her apartments. As the instructions to the signet clerk Edward Norgate put it, 'the said Abate, living at Antwerp, and having good skill in handling such mercenary men, was by sieur B. Gerbier, thought the fittest hand to guide the said business', a task Scaglia took on 'very willingly and cheerfully'.[91] While both Rubens and Van Dyck had been considered for the project, they were both deemed to be too expensive to a king lacking in ready financial resources. Instead, Jacob Jordaens, whose workshop was based in Antwerp, was approached by Scaglia, acting on behalf of the English king; the abate himself suggested that Frans Snyders should be employed to paint details, reinforcing the impression of a close association between the two, and despite Gerbier's opposition Rubens was also consulted, if mainly for the sofito (the only documented occasion, it seems, when Scaglia and Rubens discussed an artistic commission).[92] Scaglia was in addition asked to keep the identity of the royal patron secret, no doubt to keep the cost of the commission to a minimum. Jordaens planned a cycle of twenty-two works depicting the mythological history of Psyche. However when in May 1641 Alessandro Scaglia died only seven of the works had been completed and five other had been started; indeed, it was never completed, as Charles I's attention was diverted by civil war. Jordaens eventually took a lawsuit out against the abate's executors, seeking payment for both the completed and the uncompleted paintings, evidently in the belief that he had been the patron.[93]

With Alessandro Scaglia's long-established expertise as a patron of the arts, this was an entirely justifiable assumption and serves as a fitting end to this aspect of his life. From the outset of his first diplomatic mission to the papal court in 1614 until his death in 1641 the abate had fashioned

---

[90] PRO SP 77/28/549–50v, Gerbier to Windebank, 6 November 1638; ff. 563–5, Gerbier to Windebank, 13 November 1638.

[91] Sainsbury (ed.), *Unpublished Papers*, p. 212.

[92] See for instance *ibid.*, pp. 222, 225–6, which is particularly revealing as to Scaglia's own knowledge of the commission and his keen eye for painting.

[93] Schlugleit, 'L'abbé de Scaglia', 139–65.

an image that placed him in a distinctive system of court culture and dynastic politics, confirmed by the spectacular series of commissions from Anthony van Dyck. But looking back over the years of his exile, it would be tempting to conclude that his career was at an end, whether or not the move to the Spanish Netherlands represented a decision to retire from political life. Exile, however, was not that straightforward. It was a process rather than a definitive event. Moreover, Scaglia, with his wide-ranging experience and powerful reputation as a courtier and diplomat, did not think that he had retired, whether this meant trying to co-ordinate the French exiles or maintaining his friendship with Gerbier, or, indeed, attempting to secure his return to Savoy and the end of what he saw as Richelieu's hold over his sovereign prince and home state.

8

THE HOUSE OF SAVOY AND THE SCAGLIA DI VERRUA: DYNASTIC INSTABILITY AND CIVIL WAR, 1632–1642

If the exiled Alessandro Scaglia wished to remain actively engaged in Savoyard politics, then he did not have to wait for long. While he persevered with the French political refugees in Brussels to force Richelieu out of power as a means of redefining Savoy's relationship with France, circumstances in his home state soon drew the abate's attention more directly back to north Italy. Marie Christine was only thirteen, the so-called *sposa-bambina*, at the time of her marriage in 1619 to Vittorio Amedeo, prince of Piemonte.[1] Although she had managed a successful pregnancy in 1629 when she gave birth to a daughter, Ludovica Cristina, the child was barred from succession to the inheritance of the duchy of Savoy by the application of Salic Law, and was furthermore rumoured to have been illegitimate through her mother's relationship with a French courtier named Pommeuse.[2] The new duke and duchess had thus ascended to power in July 1630 without a direct male heir after eleven years of marriage. But in September 1632 the political world in Turin was transformed. Marie Christine at last gave birth to a legitimate son and heir, Francesco Giacinto.

The tone of the court was quickly set by the Savoyard duke following this crucial dynastic and political event. Vittorio Amedeo I's decision to assert what he believed were his House's rights to royal honours and to regulate court protocol, the *trattamento reale*, at precisely this time indicated that both he and his Bourbon consort attached great importance to the arrival of the longed-for male heir. From Turin a court-sponsored propaganda campaign was initiated to reiterate the dynasty's royal claims to Cyprus that included not only the publication of erudite scholarship such as Pietro Monod's royalist treatise but also the manipulation of visual iconography through the closing of the Savoyard crown to imply a

---

[1] Merlin, *Guerre e tornei*, p. 25.
[2] Pommeuse was exiled from the court following the appearance of the rumour. Dethan, *Mazarin*, p. 154.

raised status, and the addition of the Cypriot arms of a red lion with a gold crown.[3] At the same time Savoyard ambassadors serving in different European courts were expected to seek diplomatic recognition of the royal claim from other ruling sovereigns, among them the marquis of S. Germano who was sent to London as extraordinary ambassador in August 1634. John Finet, by then the Master of Ceremonies at the Caroline court, was initially uncertain as to what to do on his arrival.

> The said ambassador having it for his chief negotiation in charge to him to procure for the duke his master the title of king of Cyprus, which his master had assumed not long before and which the pope, the emperor, the kings of France and Spain, had refused to give him, and assisting to that purpose all of the formality of a king's ambassador, I had been put to a straight in what style to have treated him.[4]

Finet's notebooks – both published and unpublished – reveal the great care to which he went to ensure correct diplomatic procedure was kept with all visiting ambassadors to England at a time when issues of diplomatic protocol were still being codified. However, his particular uncertainty as to what to do with S. Germano reflected the general reluctance around Europe to accept Savoy's contentious claim. Issues of court protocol involving the states of the Italian peninsula were extremely sensitive, and those surrounding Savoy's self-proclaimed royalty after 1632 were certainly no exception. Recognition of the claim would undoubtedly have encouraged disputes over status among Savoy's ever-vigilant rivals in the peninsula, the grand-duchy of Tuscany, the republic of Genoa, and, perhaps most of all, Venice. As soon as Vittorio Amedeo I's ordinary ambassador at the papal court requested a change of his official ceremonial title, the Florentine and Genoese ambassadors there instantly demanded equal treatment, Florence no doubt because of its grand-ducal status, and Genoa possibly because of the republic's own contentious claim to the royal crown of Corsica.[5] As Finet observed above, the leading Catholic

[3] Domenico Valle, 'Il Padre Pietro Monod della Compagnia di Gesù, consigliere di stato e istoriografo della Casa di Savoia, e le sue relazioni col Cardinale Richelieu', *Miscellanea di Storia Italiana*, 14 (1910), 59; Siri, *Memorie recondite*, VII, p. 734. On the closing of the crown and its royal connotations see Oresko, 'The House of Savoy', in Oresko, Gibbs and Scott (eds.), *Royal and Republican Sovereignty*, pp. 279–80.

[4] Loomie (ed.), *Ceremonies*, p. 163. On the reactions to the *trattamento reale* in France consult Foa, *Vittorio Amedeo I*, pp. 214, 278. Monod returned to Paris in 1636 in order to renew the campaign for recognition of the claim and there were similar negotiations in London, Vienna and Rome. CSPV 1632–6, pp. 113, 126, 207, 269, 272; Testi, *Lettere*, I, p. 435, where Fulvio Testi recorded that the claim 'was unacceptable, leading many to laugh and many to murmur'.

[5] Testi, *Lettere*, II, pp. 295, 324. Genoa's claim to royalty through Corsica was fragile, though in 1637 the republic tried to bolster its status as a 'royal republic' by declaring

powers had already shown their reluctance to give formal recognition to Savoy's *titolo reale*, even though, as Robert Oresko has argued, the French implied a willingness to recognise a resurrected kingdom of Lombardy in Savoy's favour if the Spanish-controlled duchy of Milan were duly conquered.[6] For his part Charles I, clearly distancing himself from the dynastic intimacy that had marked Anglo-Savoyard relations with his 'father', Duke Carlo Emanuele I, when England was actively engaged in wars against France and Spain, was always more guarded with Vittorio Amedeo I. The English king repeatedly dodged formal recognition, much to the pleasure of the watchful Venetian ambassadors in London.[7]

The successful pregnancy of the ducal couple was not even universally welcomed in Savoy, whatever the level of support for the ruling dynasty's royal ambitions (which was in any case unquestioned from Savoyard subjects). The lingering doubts about the fecundity and faithfulness of Marie Christine had created an atmosphere in which some thought that the future of the duchy might lie with the cadets of the ruling House, Cardinal Maurizio and Prince Tommaso Francesco. When Francesco Giacinto was born, the youngest of Vittorio Amedeo I's brothers, Prince Tommaso Francesco Carignano, was already the father of three legitimate sons through his marriage to Marie de Bourbon-Soissons.[8] The birth of a male heir to the ruling duke not only distanced still further the prince and his own sons from the Savoyard succession but also strengthened Marie Christine's position at the court of Turin, much to the relief of her brother Louis XIII and Cardinal Richelieu, who were extremely anxious to retain close relations with Savoy (despite, it should be added, their evident reluctance to recognise formally Savoy's royal claim). Tommaso Francesco indeed seemed genuinely troubled by what he saw as the excessive influence of Paris in his home state, coupled with the continuing presence of French troops in the Savoyard fortress of Pinerolo (just as Alessandro Scaglia was). In 1634 the prince of Carignano was asked by

the Virgin Mary as its queen. Oresko, 'The House of Savoy', in Oresko, Gibbs and Scott (eds.), *Royal and Republican Sovereignty*, p. 294.

[6] Robert Oresko, 'The House of Savoy and the Thirty Years' War', in Bussmann and Schilling (eds.), *1648*, I, p. 147.

[7] Venetian ambassadors in England indeed noted the derision with which Savoy's claims were met in London, though they were no doubt keen to downplay the Savoyard claim to the kingdom of Cyprus which the republic of Venice contested. CSPV 1632–6, pp. 116, 126. It should be added that diplomatic relations between Savoy and Venice remained icy throughout this period, and regular contact was not re-established until 1662. C. E. Patrucco, 'Sulle relazioni della Casa di Savoia colla Republica di Venezia durante la reggenza di Maria Cristina', *Bollettino Storico-Bibliografico Subalpino*, 1 (1896), 212.

[8] For the genealogical table of the House of Carignano see Litta, *Celebri famiglie Italiane*, 'Duchi di Savoia', table XXII (Milan, 1841).

his ducal brother to represent him as a plenipotentiary at the French court to secure an alliance against Spain. He refused and journeyed instead to the Spanish Netherlands, a decision that was undoubtedly influenced by news that Marie Christine was once again pregnant – she gave birth in June 1634 to a second son, the future Duke Carlo Emanuele II.[9] Tommaso Francesco was leaving a court at which his dynastic prospects and his influence had quite clearly diminished.

The arrival of Prince Tommaso Francesco in the Spanish Netherlands added a new complication to Scaglia's already ambiguous exile. Certainly, the presence of a member of the sovereign House of Savoy provided the abate with the chance of reassuming an active political role in the affairs of his home state after two years in exile. It was as if to mark this important event for posterity that the abate commissioned the full-length 'Camrose' portrait from Van Dyck in the following year, as Carignano himself commissioned an enormous equestrian portrait from the artist to mark his assumption of a command in the Army of Flanders.[10] Perhaps predictably, rumours soon circulated that Scaglia himself had contrived Prince Tommaso Francesco's flight to Brussels through a secret correspondence with Savoy and Spain, so convenient did it seem for his aspirations. Writing from Rome, Fulvio Testi reported Giulio Mazzarini's claim that since entering exile in 1632 Scaglia had been working to persuade Tommaso Francesco to leave north Italy for Spanish service, without Duke Vittorio Amedeo I's knowledge. The papal nuncio in Turin went still further and reported a rumour that the duke himself was covertly involved in the exile of his younger brother. 'Whatever Prince Tommaso may have done', the nuncio wrote, 'the involvement of President Costa, and the continuing presence of Abate Scaglia in Flanders adds to the suspicions of Vittorio Amedeo's complicity.'[11] The last member of the Savoyard dynasty to serve with the Spanish army in an official command had been Prince Filiberto, the third of Duke Carlo Emanuele I's sons to survive into adulthood. Filiberto, prince of Oneglia and viceroy

---

[9] Quazza, *Tommaso*, pp. 25–7; Capriata, *Wars of Italy*, pp. 629–30; Patrucco, 'L'antifrancesismo', 165–8. Guido Quazza dates Tommaso Francesco's suspicions of Richelieu's Italian ambitions to September 1632 when he met the cardinal in Lyons. Guido Quazza, 'Guerra civile in Piemonte, 1637–1642 (nuove ricerche)', *Bollettino Storico-Bibliografico Subalpino*, 57 (1959), 298–9.

[10] The equestrian portrait of Tommaso Francesco is now in the Galleria Sabauda in Turin. Brown and Vlieghe (eds.), *Van Dyck*, pp. 275–6.

[11] CSPV 1632–6, p. 222; Testi, *Lettere*, II, p. 190; ASV SS Savoia, 60, f. 72, Nicastra to Barberini, 15 April 1634; Foa, *Vittorio Amedeo I*, p. 216. However, in a conversation with Balthasar Gerbier, Scaglia denied any particular knowledge of why Tommaso Francesco was coming to Brussels, adding quite correctly that he was not his minister. PRO SP 77/24/143–4, Gerbier to Coke, 19 April 1634.

of Sicily, had performed an important function in strengthening Savoy's relations with Spain, and his untimely death in 1624 had been a factor in the duchy's shift back towards an alignment with France and the military incursion into the Genoese republic. Scaglia for one was aware of the potential parallels between Tommaso Francesco and Filiberto, and his sense of expectation, if not excitement, spilled into his correspondence with Olivares. 'He is a very pliant prince of good standing and Christian morals', a prince who was 'no less than Prince Filiberto'. Scaglia pushed the comparison with the prince's dead elder brother in another letter, enthusiastically adding that Tommaso Francesco was a capable and experienced soldier looking for employment in the service of Spain.[12]

In one sense Tommaso Francesco was therefore fulfilling a particular role that had previously been filled by an elder brother, and indeed by his grandfather Emanuele Filiberto in the mid-sixteenth century, underlining the long-standing dynastic affinities between the Habsburgs and Savoyards. High-level military service with the Habsburgs was both a convenient source of employment for younger sons of the Savoyard House in particular and a potential means for bringing Madrid and Turin together. But he also had the potential to create new political problems within France by mobilising opposition to Cardinal Richelieu. Tommaso Francesco's marriage in January 1625 to Marie de Bourbon-Soissons connected him to the French nobility and the princes of the blood; his brother-in-law, the count of Soissons, not only was in line to the French throne as a member of a cadet branch of the Bourbons but had also been implacably opposed to Richelieu since 1626 when he had been denied the hand of Madame de Montpensier earlier promised to him by the cardinal. Soissons' subsequent refusal to marry one of Richelieu's 'nieces' was followed by his implication in the failed Chalais conspiracy, and then exile until 1641 when after instigating a revolt in France he was eventually killed in suspicious circumstances following his victory at the battle of La Marfée.[13] There was a strong expectation that the prince of Carignano would be able to exploit the connections that ran between opponents of Richelieu in Brussels, France and Spain and draw Savoy away from its alignment with France, a possibility the abate himself repeatedly emphasised in his correspondence with Madrid.[14]

---

[12] AGR SEG 597, f. 67, Scaglia to Olivares, 24 April 1634; f. 70, Scaglia to Philip IV, 24 April 1634; ff. 94–5v, Scaglia to Olivares, 20 June 1634. In this last letter the abate said that of all the brothers of the House of Savoy, Tommaso Francesco was the least 'French [francese]'.

[13] For some brief remarks see Hanotaux and de la Force, *Richelieu*, IV, pp. 449–50.

[14] Quazza, *Tommaso*, pp. 30–1. Tommaso Francesco's wife did not join her husband but went instead to Madrid, from where she maintained a correspondence with her mother

Carignano was obviously important to Scaglia's political calculations for destabilising Richelieu and possibly realigning Savoy towards Spain. The abate was in turn of value to the prince as a point of contact with the Habsburg courts in Brussels and Madrid. True, Alessandro Scaglia was never attached to the prince's household in any formal capacity – the abate after all had no official function of any sort throughout his exile during the 1630s. But he did have a near daily correspondence with Olivares and Philip IV as well as his semi-official role as a mediator between the Spanish regime and the French exiles in Brussels (at least until 1636). Moreover, beyond their particular self-interests there was evident warmth between the abate and the prince, who may well have known each other since childhood (Scaglia was only four years older than Carignano). The Venetian ambassador in London concluded that Scaglia was first among Tommaso Francesco's personal advisers, while Balthasar Gerbier wrote that while many pretenders sought to gain the attention of Tommaso Francesco, the abate was his 'leading star'.[15] Their affinity was understandable. Both were away from their home state pursuing a similar political objective of reducing France's influence over the Savoyard duke and duchy. Prince Tommaso Francesco furthermore had only a small number of Savoyard clients with him in the Spanish Netherlands. In part this was because when the prince had left Savoy in 1634 no more than a handful of followers travelled with him, though also because the regime in Madrid sought to control the nationalities of the prince's advisers and military commanders to minimise any potential security threats. Following the declaration of war with France in the following year, the Spanish regimes in Brussels and Madrid quickly increased controls on French nationals or their allies under their jurisdiction, among them the French exiles who still resided in the Spanish Netherlands with Marie de' Medici.[16] In a similar move, Philip IV instructed his brother the

in France, reiterating the fact that exile rarely spelt total isolation for individuals and their families. C. E. Patrucco, 'Intorno alle relazioni del conte di Soissons col principe di Carignano (1636–1641)', *Bollettino Storico-Bibliografico Subalpino*, 1 (1896), 313–7. One of Scaglia's letters reported a rumour of possible coalitions of *Grands* against the cardinal if Tommaso Francesco were to encourage noble opposition. For example, AGR SEG 597, f. 67v, Scaglia to Olivares, 24 April 1634; f. 96, Scaglia to Olivares, 20 June 1634; ff. 122–4v, Scaglia to Olivares, 9 July 1634.

[15] PRO SP 77/24/164, Gerbier to Coke, 28 April 1634; CSPV 1632–6, p. 220. There was one report, originating from the Savoyard ordinary ambassador in Rome, that Scaglia was actually in disgrace with Tommaso Francesco. Philip IV gave little weight to the story, though, claiming that it was merely a piece of misinformation, a type of diplomatic tactic commonly employed by his own ambassadors. AGS Est. 2049, draft of Philip IV to the Cardinal-Infante, 19 January 1635.

[16] AGR SEG 213, f. 269, Philip IV to the Cardinal-Infante, 30 November 1635; Lonchay and Cuvelier (eds.), *Correspondance*, III, pp. 77, 79.

Cardinal-Infante, as governor-general of the Spanish Netherlands, that Tommaso Francesco should have no servants other than those of Spanish, Neapolitan or Sicilian origins, all subjects within the Spanish composite monarchy. The letter added in an interesting comment that 'although the Milanese are trustworthy as those in my service, one should exclude those who are not reliable and not from the elites, as [potential] sympathisers of Piemonte', revealing a clear level of distrust from which importantly Scaglia as a highly favoured individual was excluded.[17]

Tommaso Francesco was not the only member of the House of Savoy to drift towards the Habsburg camp after the accession of Vittorio Amedeo I. Of his four legitimate sisters, Margherita, the widowed consort of Duke Francesco IV of Mantua and Monferrato whose death in 1612 had led to the first Gonzaga dynastic crisis, was openly supportive of the Habsburgs. In 1634 she left Mantua for the Iberian peninsula where she was subsequently appointed as the governess and vice-regentess of Portugal, the last before the revolt there in 1640.[18] When Tommaso Francesco went into exile, the middle of the three Savoyard brothers, Maurizio, was the Cardinal Protector of France, a position which carried a pension and which established him as the main advocate of French interests at the papal court of Rome. Yet despite his semi-formal attachment to France, the rapacious cardinal too had decided that it was time to consider offers from the Habsburgs. The death in 1634 of Cardinal Ludovico Ludovisi, ironically a patron of the writer Alessandro Tassoni whose relations with Maurizio had in the 1620s proved so difficult, left the valuable Imperial Protectorate vacant. Although there was a plan at one stage to transfer the Protectorate to one of the pope's nephews, Antonio Barberini, Maurizio set his sights on obtaining it.[19] And like his younger brother, Cardinal Maurizio looked on Alessandro Scaglia as the means to establish informal contact with the Habsburgs in Madrid, despite the open animosities that previously had troubled relations between the cardinal and the abate. In 1634 the abate reported to Olivares that Cardinal Maurizio had been writing to him via his nephew Abate Filiberto Scaglia to raise the possibility of entering Spanish service. Alessandro Scaglia explained

---

[17] AGR SEG 214, f. 224, Philip IV to the Cardinal-Infante, 9 April 1636. For an indication of who followed Tommaso Francesco see Quazza, *Tommaso*, p. 26.

[18] In an effort to disabuse the French, Vittorio Amedeo I eventually confiscated his brothers' appanages. Randi, *Maurizio*, p. 63. On Margherita and her Spanish loyalties see Quazza, *Margherita di Savoia*. The duke of Savoy certainly connected the actions of Margherita with the ambitions of his brothers. AST LMF m. 33, fasc. 5, 59, Vittorio Amedeo I to S. Maurizio, 3 October 1634. See also ASV SS Savoia, 60, f. 177, Nicastra to Barberini, 2 September 1634.

[19] Dethan, *Mazarin*, p. 59; Testi, *Lettere*, II, p. 62.

that he had replied to these letters by advising the cardinal either to send a representative or to write directly to Spain.[20]

Maurizio left Turin for Rome to negotiate the transfer of his allegiance, disregarding the warnings from his elder brother Vittorio Amedeo I who was himself under increasing pressure from Paris to control the actions of his siblings. The cardinal explained his journey by arguing that he actually wished to promote French interests at the papal court, though clearly he was more concerned with his own future in the Habsburg camp, hinting to Tommaso Francesco that if he were to go to Rome he might be able to talk more freely with the Spanish about his prospects. In October 1635, after considerable negotiation, he relinquished the French Protectorate and was granted the title of Protector of the Empire together with a large pension, adding to the uncertainty in Savoy.[21] Despite his status as a cardinal of the church without a spouse and sons, Maurizio was still the second of the Savoyard brothers and technically closer to the ducal throne than Prince Tommaso Francesco, and his switch to the Habsburgs may have further strengthened the abate's hopes for a change in the allegiance of the duke of Savoy. However, Alessandro Scaglia for one remained sceptical, a fact that should be placed in the context of the long-running friction between the two that dated back to Scaglia's diplomatic mission to the papal court. True enough, the abate viewed all three brothers of the House of Savoy as *non francese* in their political affinities, but he still believed Cardinal Maurizio to be fickle and potentially untrustworthy. When Duke Vittorio Amedeo I fell violently ill in 1636, Scaglia reported that Duchess Marie Christine, planning to retain power in the event of the death of her husband, had made an informal offer to share control of the duchy with the cardinal. Although Maurizio was officially attached to the Habsburgs from 1635 as Cardinal-Protector of the Empire, the abate said that the cardinal was indeed willing to discuss the possibility of a secret deal over the future of the duchy to the exclusion of his younger brother, Tommaso Francesco.[22] Hardly the actions, the abate was implying, of a trustworthy person.

Nevertheless, the willingness of three members of the House of Savoy, including the two brothers of the duke who were both potential claimants

---

[20] AGR SEG 597, ff. 94–v, Scaglia to Olivares, 20 June 1634. In 1632 the papal nuncio in Turin, Gallo, wrote that 'the cardinal of Savoy is being assaulted with great offers from the French and Spanish to follow them'. ASV SS Savoia, 55, f. 63, Gallo to Barberini, 11 September 1632.

[21] Randi, *Maurizio*, pp. 53–62; Testi, *Lettere*, I, p. 221; II, pp. 15, 62; Capriata, *Wars of Italy*, p. 630.

[22] 'I say that none of his [Prince Tommaso Francesco's] brothers were pro-French.' AGR SEG 597, f. 94, Scaglia to Olivares, 20 June 1634; 598, f. 131, Scaglia to Olivares, 13 September 1636.

to his throne, to offer their services to the Habsburgs, whatever their trustworthiness, was an indication of the continuing lure of Spanish patronage
and of the concerns felt over the extent of French influence in their
home state. This understandably presented grave problems for the court in
Turin, not least because of the lingering suspicions of a secret arrangement
between Vittorio Amedeo I and his brothers to ally with Spain, or at
least to ensure that there were members of the sovereign dynasty openly
supporting both the Bourbons and the Habsburgs.[23] Even if the French
regime was genuinely suspicious, the very expression of these doubts
could be used as a diplomatic lever to force Vittorio Amedeo I into
still closer alliance with Paris, just as Richelieu had used Scaglia's double
mission to London in 1631–2 to gain an advantage in his negotiations
with Savoy.

For his part, Alessandro Scaglia remained hopeful that Vittorio
Amedeo I might yield to pressure from his younger brothers and become more favourable to his entrenched opposition to Richelieu, especially after the outbreak of formal hostilities between France and Spain
in 1635. Writing to Olivares, the abate argued that the grip of France
over Savoy could be loosened if action were taken to persuade Duke
Vittorio Amedeo I of the benefits of alliance with Spain, despite the fact
that France and Savoy signed a treaty at Rivoli in July 1635 committing the duchy to offensive military action against the Spanish in north
Italy, and the Milanese state in particular.[24] Scaglia claimed that Marie
Christine would never align with Spain. Moreover he added that she
could not even serve the interests of her sons or Savoy, for despite having
allies and clients within the court the duchess lacked a natural basis of
support among the subjects and towns of the duchy. He wrote however
that Vittorio Amedeo I could be encouraged to change his political affiliation. To achieve this, the abate suggested a simple policy: 'there is only
one solution. His Majesty [Philip IV] should put himself in a position to
negotiate with the duke of Savoy as the French negotiate.'[25] He explained

---

[23] Writing from Rome, Fulvio Testi said that when Tommaso Francesco went to Brussels
there were suspicions of a secret arrangement with Vittorio Amedeo I, 'but this is a sure
way to place himself at total odds with the French'. Testi, *Lettere*, II, p. 185. However,
the nuncio in Turin reported in the spring of 1635 that the duke may have had a secret
contact with Spanish representatives and that he was inclined to align with Spain. ASV
SS Savoia, 59, f. 130, S. Severina to Barberini, 10 May 1635. Emanuele Tesauro also
suspected this. Emanuele Tesauro, *Origine delle guerre civili del Piemonte, in seguimento de'
Campeggiamenti del principe Tomaso di Savoia* (Cologne, 1673), p. 7.

[24] For further information on the treaty see S. Foa, 'Il trattato di Rivoli', *Bollettino Storico-
Bibliografico Subalpino*, 28 (1926), and Dumont (ed.), *Corps universel diplomatique*, VI,
part I, pp. 109–10 for a text.

[25] AGR SEG 597, ff. 227v–8, Scaglia to Olivares, 15 November 1635.

that Madrid should argue that there could be no future security for the duchy of Savoy without Spanish assistance and that Spain was a more reliable ally than France, more or less a repetition of the argument Scaglia had used immediately after the treaty of Regensburg in 1630. This was something the abate reiterated following the outbreak of open hostilities between France and Spain. He wanted to take advantage of the ineptitude of the French war effort under the direction of the duke of Créquy to counter the claim that France was the most reliable ally for Savoy, elaborating that Spain should exploit the weakness of France and strike out in the military theatre of north Italy. He went on to suggest that this should be co-ordinated with both action in the Holy Roman Empire and disorder in Provence and Languedoc, ever a favoured policy of the abate and one that rested in a context of Savoyard ambitions dating back to the time when Carlo Emanuele I had attempted to seize Provence and recreate the kingdom of Arles during the last stages of the French Wars of Religion.

Given that Alessandro Scaglia always retained the strong, and perhaps realistic, aspiration that Duke Vittorio Amedeo I would consider turning from alliance with France, his exile could not equal simple retirement from politics. The abate may well have believed that going to the Spanish Netherlands was a pragmatic decision for the best interests of the duke, and also for himself if Vittorio Amedeo I were to switch sides. While serving Savoy during the 1620s Scaglia had already shown his willingness and ability to act according to a form of moralised political pragmatism for what he saw as greater strategic objectives, most evidently after the treaty of Monzón when he had sought to play France and Spain against one another through their negotiations with England. From exile, Scaglia continued to apply his brand of political pragmatism by attempting to co-ordinate the community of French exiles against Richelieu while at the same time working with the restless siblings of Duke Vittorio Amedeo I. Added to this, the content and rhetoric of Scaglia's letters did not substantially change because of exile, although his correspondence was understandably shaped for his Spanish recipients. The abate continued to express the same views about the political relationship between Savoy and France as he had done during the Gonzaga succession dispute prior to his exile. His underlying diplomatic premise was that the Italian states, and indeed Europe, needed to retain something approaching a political balance and that this balance had been disrupted by France's retention of the fortress of Pinerolo. At the very least, the French regime under the direction of Richelieu had to be contained in Europe and their forces ejected from the territories of Savoy, and, like a moral Catholic diplomat, the abate stated with rhetoric typical of the early seventeenth century that his wish was to obtain a European Christian peace. Obviously this was to be one that satisfied his own political criteria. 'I hope to see Christendom', he wrote in a telling letter, 'restored from the damage inflicted by France's heresies and machinations, and that we can enjoy peace and quiet.'[26]

While exile had marked implications for the nature of the abate's service to his prince and to the sovereign House of Savoy at a time of general dynastic uncertainty, the parallel effect on his own family was equally significant. This was all the more so because of the family's exceptionally high profile both at the Turinese court and on the stage of international politics. At least until Alessandro's controversial mission to London in 1631 when Richelieu had tried to divide him from his more francophile elder brother, the Scaglia di Verrua had always remained aware of shared family responsibilities and had acted on them. While different members of the family cultivated their own careers in service to Savoy, collective power as a court clan had always been of paramount importance. When for instance the abate's elder brother had returned to the Turinese court in 1624, Alessandro Scaglia had assumed responsibility for educating his nephews in diplomatic service. In turn the abate's domestic legal and financial interests arising from his properties and pensions were in part organised by Augusto Manfredo Scaglia from the family Palazzo Verrua in Turin.[27] Yet how should the abate's disobedience and exile be considered in the context of what had been a close familial relationship? Where Alessandro Scaglia had been seen as the leading diplomat of Savoy before his exile, his elder brother, the count of Verrua, was described as the minister closest to the duke in Turin. Carlo Emanuele I and Vittorio Amedeo I attached great value to Augusto Manfredo after he succeeded his father as head of the family House in 1619. During the 1628–31 war for Mantua and Monferrato not only had the count taken commands in the ducal army but he had also been one of Vittorio Amedeo I's representatives in negotiating a settlement with the French. Following the declaration of war between France and Spain in 1635, as an experienced

---

[26] AGR SEG 598, f. 97, Scaglia to Olivares, 22 August 1636. See also f. 104–v, Scaglia to Olivares, 30 August 1636; ff. 105v–6, Scaglia to Philip IV, 6 September 1636. Shortly before the declaration of the Franco-Spanish conflict Scaglia presented a series of arguments to Olivares in favour of a just war against France. AGS Est. 2153, 'Razones que pueden mover a su Magestad con francia', February 1635; Echevarría Bacigalupe, *Diplomacia secreta*, pp. 209–11.

[27] For example AST Sezione Riunite, Insinuazione di Torino 1627, book 3, ff. 641–5; 1627, book 10, ff. 29–33; 1629, book 12, ff. 451–v, 457–9; 1630, book 1, f. 13. These documents were legal records by which Verrua represented his brother in problems of sub-tenancies and pensions arising from Scaglia's ecclesiastical holdings held 'in commendam'.

and aristocratic military commander, Verrua was appointed general of Savoy's infantry.[28] Such a close association with the ducal regime from the 1620s and through the 1630s pointed to the fact that Augusto Manfredo had his own future to consider in service to the duke of Savoy, as well as the future needs of the family as a court clan. It was hardly surprising, then, that he remained in Turin despite the actions of his exiled brother. The differences in political allegiance between the two were apparently greater still. A summarised letter from Girolamo Piochet, secretary of Prince Tommaso Francesco, put it with a succinctness that verged on the blunt: 'the count of Verrua was always French, and received from that king [Louis XIII] twelve thousand ducats in gold with diamonds. The abate is Spanish because Cardinal Richelieu is French'.[29]

Verrua remained the most powerful and, from Richelieu's perspective, the most reliable member of what was seen as the French faction in Turin. As has been seen, successive members of the family served in numerous diplomatic missions to the French court (of course ironically including the abate himself). In one sense the abate's overt Habsburg sympathies were a striking exception to what seems to have been the rule of the family's international affinities established earlier in the seventeenth century by his father. For Richelieu, the count of Verrua was crucial as a counterbalance to the volatility of the Turinese court and the unreliability of Marie Christine's Jesuit confessor Pietro Monod, whom the cardinal had already learnt to hold in suspicion. Monod was known to be deeply ambitious, influential as the duchess's confessor and moreover ambivalent about the value of the Savoyard alignment with France, as Richelieu had concluded in 1631 when the Jesuit had represented Vittorio Amedeo I in Paris. His position in Turin also seemed secure, for despite sustained pressure the duke and duchess of Savoy had shown that they were reluctant to dispense with his services as a confessor and loyal apologist for their royal ambitions. All too aware of the potential threat from Monod and the difficulty in dislodging him from Turin, the cardinal understood Verrua's importance as a political asset and consequently treated him as a valued ally, as he had done since Alessandro's alienation from Savoy in 1631.[30] Richelieu willingly overlooked the fact that Scaglia had left the service

---

[28] Writing in 1627 the papal nuncio in Turin described Verrua as 'the leading noble of this court'. ASV SS Savoia, 46, f. 128v, Albertini to Barberini, 24 April 1627. At the point of his death in 1637, the count of Verrua was the commander of the duke of Savoy's infantry. Capriata, *Wars of Italy*, p. 630.

[29] AGS Est. 2051, 104, summary of Piochet to Prince Tommaso Francesco to Costa, February 1636.

[30] On Richelieu's dislike of Monod and his supposed involvement in the Caussin Affair of 1637 see Valle, 'Il Padre Pietro Monod'; G. Claretta, *Storia della reggenza di Cristina di Francia, duchessa di Savoia*, 3 vols. (Turin, 1868–9), I, pp. 249–70.

of the duke of Savoy and had switched service to the Spanish regime. Augusto Manfredo was nevertheless more than aware that his brother's actions were politically embarrassing. While Scaglia's loyalty to Spain was never considered to be compromised because of Verrua's francophilia, his elder brother was in a potentially more difficult position at the Savoyard court because of the abate's consistent Habsburg affinities.[31]

Like most early modern courts, Turin had overlapping political and family factions and rivalries. The rivalry between Savoie and the principality of Piemonte, the two core components of the Savoyard state that were separated by the Alps, meant that in effect there were two distinct groups of nobility, one predominantly Francophone and the other Italian-speaking, though the Italian nobles had gradually assumed pre-eminence in the seventeenth century. Such broad differences between the elites of competing provinces were not the only faultlines running through the Savoyard court. The repeated shifts during the reign of Carlo Emanuele I between aligning with France and Spain exposed still further the differences between factional groups vying for influence over the direction of Savoy's foreign policy. While the alliances with France after Vittorio Amedeo I's marriage and the presence of his Bourbon consort Marie Christine did much to strengthen French influence in Turin, a sizeable element opposed to any strong reliance on France nevertheless remained embedded in the political culture of the court.[32] Intermeshed with these problems were family and personal rivalries that cut across wider factional affiliations which were accentuated after the war over Mantua and Monferrato and Carlo Emanuele I's death as the new duke, with a new set of favoured ministers and courtiers, moved back towards an alliance with France. Giulio Mazzarini observed the sharp tensions within a court that had seemingly lost its natural order when he stopped in Turin on his way to Paris on a papal mission in October 1634. 'I will tell your excellency only that this court is riven by intrigues, with different parties in opposition to one another. It is impossible that something terrible will not happen, since everyone follows his own interests without any regard to the service of his highness [Vittorio Amedeo I].'[33] This was a court, Mazzarini continued, in which ministers were trying to destroy each other with slander and rumour that included most sensationally accusations of

---

[31] AAE CP Sardaigne, 20, f. 159, memorial of Richelieu, 18 June 1632. As an expression of his satisfaction with Verrua, Louis XIII presented him with a diamond ring reportedly worth several thousand écus. AAE CP Sardaigne, 20, ff. 170v–1, Bouthillier to Servien, 30 June 1632.

[32] On the problems of faction see Merlin, *Guerre e tornei*, pp. 89–119.

[33] AAE CP Sardaigne, 22, ff. 595–8v, copy of Mazzarini to Barberini, 4 October 1634; Dethan, *Mazarin*, p. 195.

witchcraft and worship of the devil.[34] In an atmosphere of pervasive political disorder Verrua was understandably vulnerable to attack as a leading political figure and the head of one of the elite court families. Both before and after Scaglia's exile, the duchess' confessor, Father Monod, was hostile to Verrua because of the closeness of the count to Duke Vittorio Amedeo I. The Scaglia di Verrua were also locked in their rivalry with the S. Martino d'Agliè, another Piedmontese aristocratic clan; the need by the Savoyard duke to balance them had already been seen in the promotion of members of both families to the *Annunziata* in 1619. Under Vittorio Amedeo I and Marie Christine, members of the S. Martino d'Agliè had moreover consolidated their position as central members of the court group surrounding the ducal couple (especially the duchess), principal among them the poet Filippo d'Agliè, whose relations with Marie Christine became a notorious source of scandal, and his uncle, Ludovico, who served for much of his career as the Savoyard ordinary ambassador in Rome.[35] Since Abate Scaglia was not only in exile but also firmly associated with Spain, Verrua was vulnerable to criticism from the S. Martino d'Agliè and their ally Monod as well, despite the fact that the count was himself part of the same court circle around the duke and duchess as his opponents.[36]

The sniping campaign over his loyalties forced Augusto Manfredo to take counter-measures to safeguard his own position and that of his family within the court of Turin. He certainly avoided any overt association with his exiled younger brother, confirmed by the total absence of correspondence between them during this period, and he claimed in 1636 that Scaglia wrote to him only in the previous year when the abate was close to death.[37] Placing further distance between himself and Alessandro,

---

[34] Mazzarini's comments about witchcraft might be a reference to the accusation levelled by the secretary of state Giovanni Tommaso Pasero against his bitter ministerial and court rival Lelio Cauda who was president of the council of state. Roberto Bergadini, 'Rivalità tra stato e chiesa per intrighi politici alla corte di Vittorio Amedeo I di Savoia', *Bollettino Storico-Bibliografico Subalpino*, 24 (1922); de Castro, *Fulvio Testi*, pp. 102–4.

[35] In a letter to Mazzarini, Marie Christine wrote of the d'Agliè that 'there is no need to tell you how much I love them'. Dethan, *Mazarin*, p. 156. While in Rome, Ludovico was active in acquiring art for Cardinal Maurizio, just as Alessandro Scaglia had done. Oberli, *Maurizio von Savoyen*, especially chapter 7. On the family during the 1630s see Gallina, 'Le vicende di un grande favorito'.

[36] The closeness between Monod and Filippo d'Agliè was a particular concern to Mazzarini, who wrote in a letter to Rome that 'Monod and count Filippo speak openly against France, striking the king with their ironic darts and preaching the imminent collapse of this kingdom.' Quoted in Giuliana Brugnelli Biraghi and Maria Bianca Denoyé Polonne, *Chrestienne di Francia: duchessa di Savoia, prima Madama Reale* (Turin, 1991), p. 60.

[37] AAE CP Sardaigne, 24, f. 742v, Verrua to Mazzarini, 26 September 1636.

he no longer conducted business and legal affairs from the family palace on behalf of the abate, who instead employed a private agent.[38] Augusto Manfredo was also careful to keep Richelieu on his side, no doubt to out-manoeuvre his political opponents in Turin by pre-empting any grounds for suspicion about his own political loyalties.[39] In this, he was certainly helped by his close association with Giulio Mazzarini, described by Georges Dethan, Mazarin's biographer, as 'one of his closest friends'. The two had met during the Gonzaga succession dispute, and for the papal representative the count of Verrua represented the best means of ensuring the stability of Franco-Savoyard relations (a cornerstone of his conception of security in the Italian peninsula), a belief that was no doubt confirmed when on his way to Paris in 1634 Mazzarini saw for himself the ambitions of Monod and Filippo d'Agliè within the Turinese court.[40] Mazzarini remained in France until 1636, and Verrua ensured that he was kept informed not only of his own movements but also of events in Turin. The benefits, no doubt, were reciprocal as regular contact afforded Mazzarini access to the court of Turin while Verrua could maintain a sympathetic voice in Paris.[41]

Verrua was evidently conscious that he could not maintain any overt written contact with his younger brother. Yet what of their views of one another, given the clear differences their political affiliations implied? No explicit information reveals what Verrua thought of the choices taken by his younger brother, though the fact that the count chose to remain silent should not be taken as a sign of displeasure since his freedom to express his political sentiments was obviously restricted, or rather self-restricted, by wider considerations of family interest and delicate court politics. The abate correspondingly gave little away about what he thought about his brother when he was alive, though he broke his silence following his brother's death on 7 October 1637, only three days before that of the duke of Savoy. Scaglia wrote with some feeling and rhetorical flourish

---

[38] AST Sezione Riunite, Insinuazione di Torino 1634, book 1, ff. 111–v, book 7, ff. 151–2v; 1636, book 6, ff. 219–21v. The last entry is dated 7 March 1639.

[39] For example AAE CP Sardaigne, 22, f. 224, Verrua to Louis XIII; f. 249, D'Hémery to Richelieu, 18 July 1637.

[40] Dethan, *Mazarin*, p. 152, which suggests that Mazzarini had a reputation for being *Savoyardissime*.

[41] See for example AAE CP Sardaigne, 24, f. 743v, Verrua to Mazzarini, 26 September 1636; 25, ff. 20v–1, Verrua to Mazzarini, 23 January 1637. Mazzarini's role in Franco-Savoyard relations between the end of the Gonzaga succession dispute and his death in 1661 was critical, yet it has not been adequately considered. One exception is G. Quazza, 'Giulio Mazzarini mediatore fra Vittorio Amedeo I e il Richelieu, 1635–1636', *Bollettino Storico-Bibliografico Subalpino*, 48 (1950). On his continuing interest in Franco-Savoyard relations during the 1650s see Inglis-Jones, 'The Grand Condé', pp. 307–34.

of self-criticism that 'I consider this to be of such importance that I be-lieve that God called him so that he should not suffer the faults of a brother. There can be no doubt that if he had lived he would have been of great importance in thwarting the designs of the French with the influ-ence he wielded.'[42] This was a revealing statement. By wishful thinking he freely overlooked the French sympathies of Augusto Manfredo. Alessandro Scaglia implied that his brother was politically redeemable in the same way that the duke had been, and that if he were alive then he would have displayed his true fidelity to their home state, as the abate defined it, given the wider dynastic and political crisis provoked by the sudden death of Duke Vittorio Amedeo I.

There remains another important question to answer. As the abate might have gone into exile by tacit agreement with Duke Vittorio Amedeo I so the two Scaglia brothers might have had a strategy relating to their political affiliations to ensure that the family had a degree of flex-ibility. The existence of a family strategy would clearly be of the highest importance. It would raise wider questions about how discrete interest groups like elite court families dealt with acute political uncertainty in early modern Europe, and illuminate further some of the complexities entailed by political exile. But the surviving archival material offers no coherent answer, hardly surprising given that such a plan would not have been committed to paper even if it had existed. It is nevertheless hard to believe that in 1632 Alessandro Scaglia and the count of Verrua shared an explicit agenda by which they agreed to side with opposing factions or with different members of the sovereign House for the good of the family.[43] The actions and reactions of both, at least at the initial point of Alessandro's exile in 1632, suggest that they were genuinely attached to their political views despite the powerful attraction of family bonds. When the abate went to the Spanish Netherlands he was not compelled to do so in the interests of his family because of any overt problems within the court or duchy. The Savoyard state was not suffering from the severe internal crisis that developed in subsequent years, although Scaglia for one argued from the treaty of Regensburg onwards that his home state's alignment with France was unacceptable. He had not acted by pre-meditation with his brother as a response to instability within either the court or the duchy of Savoy, unless his undeniably exceptional political talents were further enhanced by the rare gift of foreknowledge. While the abate had clearly thought about the wider significance of going into

---

[42] AGR SEG 598, f. 239, Scaglia to Philip IV, 30 October 1637.
[43] This may well be the case in spite of the observations of the French ambassador in Turin who for one acknowledged the possibility of a premeditated family plan. AAE CP Sardaigne, 24, f. 209, D'Hémery to Richelieu, 25 August 1636.

exile before travelling to Brussels, he did not operate in conjunction with his elder brother at that point and there was no pressing reason to do so.

But while Alessandro's exile proved to be an embarrassment to Augusto Manfredo as the head of the family House, it could paradoxically secure some political advantages for the Scaglia di Verrua, particularly as the political situation in Savoy worsened over the course of the decade. The dynastic and political divisions within the House of Savoy not only created their own internal problems but also entailed uncertainty for the fortunes of leading court clans linked with particular members of the ruling family. The Scaglia di Verrua were no exception, given the close association of their head with Duke Vittorio Amedeo I at a time when the duke's younger brothers had pointedly left the duchy. It seems that after 1634 at least some junior members of the Scaglia di Verrua clan themselves turned to the exiled Alessandro as one means of dealing with the deepening political crisis at the heart of the Savoyard state.

The count of Verrua had three sons: Carlo Vittorio Scaglia, Abate Filiberto and Maurizio Scaglia, all of whom had already experienced service to the duke of Savoy, either through miliary commands or, in the case of Carlo Vittorio and Abate Filiberto, through diplomatic service.[44] Like his father, the eldest of Verrua's sons, Carlo Vittorio, refrained from communicating with his exiled uncle, even though it was Carlo Vittorio (under instruction from Vittorio Amedeo I) who had tried to persuade the abate to terminate the London mission in 1631. Naturally, as the heir to the count of Verrua and the greater part of the Scaglia di Verrua's patrimony, he was not in a position to act irresponsibly. As with his father, either a covert correspondence with Alessandro or an act of open disobedience to Duke Vittorio Amedeo I may have damaged his own prospects at the court and, equally dangerously, animated his family's watchful political rivals. Accordingly, Carlo Vittorio remained in Turin with his father, ensuring the continuation of the family's physical presence in the ducal court where it had derived much of its power. In this respect he enjoyed some notable success. In 1633 he was made an ordinary gentleman of the ducal chamber in recognition of service to the duke, and he was to receive regular gifts of money and land from Vittorio Amedeo I. Even his marriage reinforced his associations with the ducal court as his wife, Francesca d'Hermance, was established as the first lady-in-waiting to Marie Christine.[45] The corollary of his close association with the ruling family in Turin was a distance from his exiled uncle.

---

[44] Manno, *Patriziato Subalpino*, XXIV, pp. 242–51.
[45] AST Sezione Riunite PCF 1632–3, f. 151, 169, 20 February 1633; Manno, *Patriziato Subalpino*, XXIV, p. 247. Francesca d'Hermance was the daughter of Claudia della Rovere, who was herself a painter. Baudi di Vesme, 'L'arte negli stati sabaudi', p. 229.

There is no evidence that he contacted Scaglia on his own initiative; indeed, when Alessandro himself wrote to his nephew following the death of Verrua in 1637, Carlo Vittorio took care to send a copy of the letter to Marie Christine with a disclaimer to explain that it concerned nothing more than family affairs.[46]

The actions and political alignments of the abate's two other nephews, in contrast, were much more ambiguous. In 1635 Alessandro fell seriously ill.[47] When news of his illness reached Turin, Duke Vittorio Amedeo I despatched the youngest of the nephews, Maurizio Scaglia, to the Spanish Netherlands. The duke informed his ordinary ambassador in Paris that he was anxious about Alessandro's health, adding that the count of Verrua had not heard anything from his brother since he had entered exile, effectively informing the French of the distance between Turin and the abate. But there may also have been a political subtext to the mission. The resounding Habsburg victory in September 1634 at the battle of Nördlingen gave much of the international initiative back to Spain, and the presence of Prince Tommaso Francesco in the Spanish Netherlands calling for his ducal brother to join with Spain might have made Vittorio Amedeo I at least consider a political realignment away from France. Alessandro's illness might therefore have been a convenient pretext for the duke to raise the possibility of a double reconciliation with both Tommaso Francesco and Spain.[48]

By travelling to Brussels as Duke Vittorio Amedeo I's informal courier, Maurizio would have enjoyed ducal protection from the immediate criticisms of the Scaglia di Verrua's rivals in Turin. This seemingly encouraged the nephew to use his journey for both family and personal interest. As a younger son with no immediate prospects of inheriting the family's patrimony, he was arguably less restricted by the kinds of familial considerations that made contact with the exiled Alessandro Scaglia dangerous. In short, if Maurizio, with the help of his exiled uncle, could enter service under Prince Tommaso Francesco's direction then the Scaglia di Verrua could claim loyalty simultaneously to more than one member of the Savoyard House at a time when the sovereign House was openly divided and facing an uncertain future. As the youngest of three brothers with little chance of inheriting his family's patrimony, Maurizio could also establish a socially acceptable career for himself as an army officer. Having

---

[46] AST LP 'S' m. 48, Carlo Vittorio Scaglia to Marie Christine, 28 June 1639.

[47] ASV SS Fiandra, 22, f. 178, Stravius to Barberini, 19 May 1635, transcribed and translated into French in Wilfred Brulez (ed.), *Correspondance de Richard-Pauli Stravius, 1634–42* (Brussels and Rome, 1955), p. 65.

[48] AST LMF m. 33, fasc. 4, 14, Vittorio Amedeo I to S. Maurizio, 24 February 1635. This process can be followed in Quazza, *Tommaso*, pp. 39, 60–2.

fulfilled his original instructions of conveying the letter to Tommaso Francesco and visiting Abate Scaglia, Maurizio Scaglia remained in the Spanish Netherlands. In 1635 he entered the Italian infantry regiment of Andrea Cantelmo as a *maestre de campo* under Tommaso Francesco's command in the Army of Flanders, and he went on to serve in active duty against the French after the declaration of war between the two Catholic powers.[49]

More important still was the Abate Filiberto Scaglia, usually known by contemporaries as the abate di Verrua to distinguish him from his better-known uncle. Of the three nephews, Filiberto was the closest to Alessandro Scaglia. As the two clerical members of the family and second sons to successive counts of Verrua there was understandably a strong affinity between them – in 1631 Filiberto had served in his first formal diplomatic mission to Spain under the watchful guidance of his uncle.[50] The abate also had the family responsibility of ensuring that his commendatory benefices were passed to Filiberto, for like son and father Filiberto was effectively Alessandro's heir. The abbey of S. Giusto di Susa was passed to the nephew when Scaglia was in London in October 1631, and when he was close to death in 1635 he planned the transfer of a second abbey, S. Pietro di Muleggio together with a pension worth 600 écus to his nephew.[51] In contrast to his father, the count of Verrua, Filiberto moreover did not break contact with his exiled uncle in the Spanish Netherlands. It is evident from the above that at least in 1634 for example he wrote letters directly to the abate, though this correspondence remains elusive. In the following year Abate Filiberto undertook a journey from Turin to Rome. Rather than travelling directly south he made his way to the Spanish Netherlands on the pretext of taking an alternative route, a journey subsequently described in great detail by one of the two secretaries who travelled with him. Abate Scaglia clearly enjoyed the fact that a second nephew had come to him, and he made the most of introducing both Maurizio and Filiberto to the court in Brussels.

---

[49] AGR SEG 597, f. 212, Scaglia to Olivares, 29 March 1635; 598, f. 69, Scaglia to Olivares, 7 August 1636. The troops under Cantelmo were Italian and so were organised as a Spanish tercio with the *maestre de campo* as the colonel and first captain of the first company. Parker, *The Army of Flanders*, pp. 274–5.

[50] Filiberto Scaglia took over the negotiations between Savoy and Genoa when Abate Scaglia went to England in the summer of 1631. AST LMS m. 24, fasc. 1, 40, Scaglia to Vittorio Amedeo I, 3 June 1631. Filiberto's ducal correspondence can be followed in AST LMS m. 24, fasc. 2.

[51] AST Materie Ecclesiastiche. Abbazia S. Giusto di Susa, m. 10, Papal Bull of Deposition, 8 October 1631; Brulez (ed.), *Correspondance*, p. 65. Stravius said that the pension, which was held from the diocese of Tarantaise, was worth 300 écus per annum. ASV SS Fiandra, 22, f. 178, Stravius to Barberini, 19 May 1635.

In travelling there Filiberto had quite obviously taken a significant diversion, and it seems, as with Maurizio Scaglia's trip to Brussels, that there was a secret motive behind the visit. Scaglia himself suggested that his nephew had some verbal information that he had been unwilling to put to paper, yet the precise reason for the journey of Abate Filiberto remains unclear.[52] The most detailed source of evidence, the relation of the journey, completely passed over the political content of Filiberto's actions as the writer confined himself to describing whom and what Filiberto saw in the course of his travels.

Quite possibly Filiberto was under informal instruction from Duke Vittorio Amedeo I, and it is certain that the duke's involvement was suspected by some baffled observers. Girolamo Piochet, in service to Prince Tommaso Francesco, confessed that he did not understand what was happening, although he implied that there might have been some secret talks afoot involving the duke of Savoy. The Modenese ambassador in Madrid, Fulvio Testi, wrote to Virgilio Malvezzi that the dukes of both Parma and Savoy, at least formally through the treaty of Rivoli in alliance with France, were seeking to resolve their political differences with Spain. Filiberto's journey to his uncle was accordingly interpreted as an attempt by Vittorio Amedeo I to establish an unofficial diplomatic channel with an eye on a possible settlement with Madrid. Alessandro Scaglia was to act as the informal mediator, in keeping with Testi's assumption that the abate could serve as the means for a reconciliation between Turin and Madrid.[53] Fulvio Testi's interpretation perhaps was not unreasonable. He had, after all, a long-standing relationship with the Turinese court that dated back to his dedication in 1617 of a collection of verse to Duke Carlo Emanuele I, a commission brokered by Scaglia.[54] Following the outbreak of formal hostilities between France and Spain in 1635, Savoy, Parma and France were involved in an offensive military alliance against Spain. At the time of Filiberto's journey the war in the Italian peninsula was not

---

[52] AST LP 'S' m. 48, 'Relazione del viaggio intrapreso dall'abate Filiberto Gherardo Scaglia'. The relation runs to eighty pages of densely written text and covers the period from Filiberto's departure from Turin in 1635 to his journey to Spain in 1637, and back to north Italy in 1638. AGS Est. 2051, 104, summary of Piochet to Tommaso Francesco, 20 February 1636; AGR SEG 598, f. 1, Scaglia to Olivares, 17 February 1636.

[53] AGS Est. 2051, f. 104, summary of letter of Prince Tommaso Francesco to Costa, 20 February 1636; Archivio di Stato Bologna, Archivio Malvezzi-Lupari, 369, m. 6, 3, Testi to Malvezzi, 13 January 1637. I am grateful to José-Luis Colomer for this reference.

[54] Testi's most recent contact with Savoy had been through a diplomatic mission to Turin in 1635. Giovanni de Castro, *Il conte Fulvio Testi e le corte Italiani nella prima metà del Seicento* (Milan, 1875); D. Perrero, *Il conte Fulvio Testi alla corte di Torino negli anni 1628 e 1635* (Milan, 1862).

running to Savoy's advantage, owing in no small part to French military incompetence and Richelieu's seeming lack of commitment to the effort, and it is possible that Vittorio Amedeo I wanted to obtain a suspension of the conflict just as he had extricated himself from the Gonzaga war when Spain's military effort had petered out.[55] Unfortunately no further reports of the diplomatic initiative exist, but at the very least the report suggested something about the difficulties faced by the duke of Savoy, caught, as he felt he was, between the French and the Spanish and also confronted with a divided family House. It also revealed something about Alessandro Scaglia's political image and how he was expected to operate despite being in exile, given his background and reputation as a still powerful diplomat.

It is equally possible however that Filiberto was following through a family strategy at the same time, given the political problems within Savoy and the divisions within the sovereign House. By going to Brussels he could increase the spread of his family's contacts, that is to say that through his uncle's offices he could offer his services to the Spanish regime. Filiberto was certainly well placed to enter some form of service with Spain. Not only did he have a well-connected uncle in Brussels but he was personally known to the Spanish Habsburgs through his diplomatic mission to Madrid in 1631 when he had replaced Scaglia in the negotiations over the future of Zuccarello – the abate later described him as 'a great servant' of Olivares.[56] A year after arriving in Brussels Filiberto indeed seems to have made the transition to Spanish service; Alessandro employed his nephew as a courier to convey messages to the prince of Orange as part of a process of informal negotiations for a settlement of the conflict between the Dutch Republic and Spain.[57]

As with so much of Scaglia's exile, the equivocal archival sources fail to offer a clear answer to the possibility of an organised family response to the dynastic problems faced by the House of Savoy. There is no evidence drawn up by members of his family to suggest that the two nephews had become convinced of the merits of service to Spain as an end in itself, or that they had been instructed by their father, Augusto Manfredo, to join Alessandro. Once again it is impossible to answer the problem definitively and the genuine probability that an explicit (or even tacit) family strategy

---

[55] On the general shortcomings of the French army in the first half of the seventeenth century consult D. A. Parrott, 'The administration of the French army during the ministry of Cardinal Richelieu' (DPhil thesis, Unversity of Oxford, 1985).

[56] AGR SEG 597, f. 94, Scaglia to Olivares, 20 June 1634.

[57] AGR SEG 599, ff. 132–5, Scaglia to Filiberto Scaglia (?), 18 April 1636; AGR SEG 598, ff. 16–9, Scaglia to Olivares, 5 June 1636; ff. 171–v, Scaglia to Constantijn Huygens, 7 June 1636; ff. 199–v, Scaglia to Constantijn Huygens, 27 December 1636.

existed has to be balanced against the fact that Filiberto's actions placed the count of Verrua in a delicate public position, albeit less so than if he himself had contacted his exiled brother. In a letter to his friend, Guilio Mazzarini, the count expressed unequivocal astonishment, emphatically denying any involvement in the actions of his second son Filiberto, and, as if to place further distance between himself and Filiberto's journey, Verrua described the abate not as his brother but as the uncle of his son. At the same time the count made it equally clear to the French representative in Turin, Michel Particelli, the seigneur d'Hémery, that neither he nor the duke of Savoy had any involvement in his son's surprise journey.[58] More realistically, Maurizio and Filiberto Scaglia may have taken their own initiative, possibly with the tacit consent of their father, to spread their family's options by claiming loyalty to different members of the Savoyard ruling House and to both France and Spain, even though their father Augusto Manfredo Scaglia strongly denied any involvement in Abate Filiberto's journey.[59] As a leading figure at Vittorio Amedeo I's court and a central member of the French faction in Turin, he could in all probability have done little else.

The 1630s, like much of the seventeenth century thereafter, have gen-erally been characterised as a period of unbroken French domination of the duchy of Savoy in the context of the great power rivalry, as French forces continued to occupy Pinerolo and the duke and his Bourbon con-sort seemingly came under Richelieu's irrepressible sway. A recent book on early modern Italy has described Savoy as little more than a 'French satellite' from the 1640s with 'its options limited by policies decided in Paris'.[60] While it would be difficult to deny that Vittorio Amedeo I's preference for much of the 1630s was for an alignment with France after the war for Mantua and Monferrato, or that France's occupation of Pinerolo (and Casale in Monferrato) increased Richelieu's leverage over the duchy, the inference that Savoy was little more than a passive puppet was not completely true. The conclusion of the Gonzaga suc-cession dispute did not neutralise Savoy as a politically unstable region that might turn against France, not only because of France's declaration

---

[58] AAE CP Sardaigne, 24, f. 9, Verrua to Mazzarini, 11 January 1636; f. 44, D'Hémery to 'Monsieur', 14 January 1636. Of course, if Filiberto did have a secret negotiation with Scaglia or Tommaso Francesco then Verrua was evidently not telling the truth to the French.

[59] AAE CP Sardaigne, 24, f. 9, Verrua to Mazzarini, 11 January 1636; f. 44, D'Hémery to 'Monsieur', 14 January 1636.

[60] Hanlon, *Early Modern Italy*, p. 273. Biraghi and Pollone similarly wrote that the treaty of Cherasco 'signalled for the Savoyard duchy the end of independence', that was itself to last for fifty years. Biraghi and Pollone, *Chrestienne di Francia*, p. 51.

of war against Spain and the weaknesses of the French military efforts in north Italy immediately after 1635, but more importantly because of the worsening dynastic tensions within the sovereign House and the political dynamics they themselves generated. It was against this backdrop of tension and deepening crisis within Savoy that the self-imposed exile of Abate Alessandro Scaglia functioned as a mechanism of informal diplomacy and as a means of ensuring some flexibility not only for the ruling family but also possibly for the Scaglia di Verrua. Scaglia's diplomatic career certainly did not end with his exile in the Spanish Netherlands. It continued in a different context, all too clearly confirmed by the events that overtook the duchy in 1637, the climax of his career as state history, dynastic power politics and aristocratic family history once again merged.

At the beginning of October 1637 both Duke Vittorio Amedeo I and Augusto Manfredo Scaglia, the count of Verrua, attended a banquet organised by maréchal de Créquy, Charles de Blanchefort, in command of the French forces in north Italy. Within a week of the feast both were dead. The sudden demise of two of the most important political figures in Savoy and the unfortunate coincidence generated instant suspicion of poison. Their deaths also put into doubt the security of Franco-Savoyard relations. Giulio Mazzarini, one of the architects of closer relations between Turin and Paris after the Gonzaga succession dispute, was certainly fearful. Since one of the immediate suspects was Créquy, whose relations with the Piedmontese commanders had beforehand been far from satisfactory, the papal diplomat believed that this might seriously weaken relations between Paris and Turin. The loss of both the duke and Verrua moreover removed what Mazzarini had seen as one of the foundations of a stable pro-French political grouping at the Savoyard court.[61]

Unsurprisingly the crisis also played into the existing concerns felt within the sovereign House and by sections of the political elite that surrounded the ducal court over French military interference in the duchy. Vittorio Amedeo I had died leaving his wife and five legitimate children, Ludovica Cristina (1629–92), Francesco Giacinto (1632–8), the duke of Savoy by the application of Salic Law, the future Carlo Emanuele II (1634–75), Margherita Yolanda (1635–63), Adelaide Enrichetta (1636–76) and Caterina Beatrice (?). Given the youth of the new Savoyard duke, aged

---

[61] Dethan, *Mazarin et ses amis*, p. 188; Foa, *Vittorio Amedeo I*, p. 285; Brulez (ed.), *Correspondance*, p. 244. The circumstances of the deaths of Vittorio Amedeo I and the count of Verrua have been closely discussed since 1637. If poison had been used then we should accept at least two other suspects, the S. Martino d'Agliè family and Marie Christine, as some contemporary rumours suggested. One recent account has suggested that the duke probably died of a virulent bout of malaria. Biraghi and Pollone, *Chrestienne di Francia*, pp. 65–6.

only five at the time of his father's death, there was a genuine opportunity for Prince Tommaso Francesco and Cardinal Maurizio to claim a stake in the control of Savoy as either sole or co-regents on behalf of the heir Francesco Giacinto. The tradition of succession in the duchy of Savoy was primarily through the male line, and although female regencies were not unknown, it was argued by the princes' supporters that they were not customary. To make matters worse, Vittorio Amedeo I had left no legally binding will. The only evidence that his wish was for the regency to be handed to his consort as the tutrix came from a reported deathbed whisper to his Dominican confessor, P. Giacinto Broglia, a story recorded in the following year in a published description of the duke's funeral (and later by the genealogical historian Samuel Guichenon, whose reliability must be doubted given his position as a client and polemicist of Marie Christine).[62]

In theory, the regency was therefore open to dispute, though before committing himself to action Prince Tommaso Francesco wanted information, not least about his remaining brother, Cardinal Maurizio, given that Maurizio was of course older than him and technically closer to the succession. It would indeed be misleading to assume that the two princes were necessarily united over the issue of succession to the duchy of Savoy. Tommaso Francesco, no doubt with his eye on the possible elevation of his cadet family line to the ducal inheritance, was markedly cautious about what his elder brother might do to secure a role for himself in a regency, and concerned about Maurizio's customary fickleness and rapaciousness.[63] Fulvio Pergamo, one of the prince's captains who had journeyed into exile with him in 1634, was sent to Madrid to consult the Spanish, while Piochet, another of his clients, set about publicising the case for Tommaso Francesco to assume a leading role in the regency. In the meantime the prince sent the Piedmontese Jesuit and writer Emanuele Tesauro, who had been in Brussels since 1636, to north Italy to sound

---

[62] P. Luigi Giuglaris, *Funerale fatto nel duomo di Torino alla gloriosa memoria dell'invittissimo, e potentissimo prencipe Vittorio Amedeo I Duca di Savoia Prencipe di Piemonte Rè di Cipri, &c.* (Turin, 1638), p. 8; Guichenon, *Histoire généalogique*, I, pp. 209–10. Examples of female regencies can be found in Capriata, *Wars of Italy*, p. 629; Randi, *Maurizio*, p. 66. See also ASV SS Savoia, 59, f. 339, S. Severina to Barberini, 8 October 1637. Samuel Guichenon was also responsible for a sympathetic (though unpublished) account of Marie Christine, his *Soleil en sou apogeé ou la vie de Christine de France*, a copy of which can be found in the Biblioteca Reale in Turin. Claretta, *Storia della reggenza*, vol. I, part VII. For a contrary view of the issue of regencies see Tesauro, *Origine delle guerre*, pp. 9–20, which was written explicitly to defend Tommaso Francesco's position, taking as its premise the argument that the prince did not initiate the war in Savoy, but 'found it there'.

[63] Quazza, 'Guerra civile', 301.

out the intentions of Cardinal Maurizio and the marquis of Leganés, the Spanish governor of Milan.[64]

Perhaps surprisingly, Alessandro Scaglia responded with caution to his brother's death. While he acknowledged the possibility of human treachery he concluded that Augusto Manfredo at least had not been assassinated. He also remained silent over the fate of Vittorio Amedeo I, no doubt to avoid endorsing an interpretation that could be seen as directly hostile to Marie Christine at a moment of such political uncertainty that at least might see his involvement in a mediated settlement and possibly his own return to Savoy. Scaglia was astute enough to realise that the duchess would not simply turn to France for military assistance and thus offer the two princes an excuse to return to Savoy as legitimate defenders of their home state from foreign intervention.[65] But equally, if she could persuade the princes not to dispute the regency by returning then there would be no compelling reason to request immediate French aid. Despite her Bourbon ties, as the mother of the infant duke she had, after all, a powerful personal stake in the future integrity of the Savoyard duchy independent of overly strong French influence. The papal nuncio in Turin to be sure went so far as to report Marie Christine's suspicions of Richelieu's ambitions in Savoy (probably affected by his hostility to her favoured confessor, Monod), claiming that the cardinal wished to take control of the duchy and adding that 'Cardinal Richelieu is a great enemy of this House.'[66]

As Alessandro Scaglia predicted, Marie Christine soon sent envoys to Cardinal Maurizio in Rome and to Prince Tommaso Francesco in her efforts to seek a peaceful solution to the dynastic crisis, and equally to divide the two brothers. Baron Pesieu, the representative sent by Marie Christine to Brussels, arrived in the Spanish Netherlands in November 1637 with letters for Tommaso Francesco and the abate. The dowager duchess also knew that Richelieu would have been suspicious of

---

[64] Claretta, *Storia della reggenza*, I, pp. 211–13, 239–40; Quazza, *Tommaso*, pp. 186–7. While in Brussels, Tesauro stayed with Scaglia. This contact is frustratingly under documented; it is certainly possible that one of the reasons for their contact was that Tesauro shared Scaglia's literary and cultural interests.

[65] AGR SEG 598, ff. 233–6, Scaglia to Olivares, 30 October 1638; 599, f. 1, Scaglia to Philip IV, 18 January 1638; ASV SS Savoia, 59, ff. 345–6, S. Severina to Barberini, 31 October 1637.

[66] ASV SS Savoia, 59, f. 395, S. Severina to Barberini, 4 March 1638; Capriata, *Wars of Italy*, pp. 636–7. The fear that Richelieu had territorial ambitions in Savoy was repeated on several occasions. For example, ASV SS Savoia, 59, ff. 345–6, S. Severina to Barberini, 31 October 1637; f. 358, S. Severina to Barberini, 7 December 1637; f. 380, S. Severina to Barberini, 12 January 1638. According to Tesauro, Marie Christine's suspicion of Richelieu was compounded by the cardinal's hostility towards Pietro Monod, the dowager duchess's confessor. Tesauro, *Origine delle guerre*, p. 49.

any contact with them, because of the possible implication of a separate dynastic arrangement that excluded France, and to deflect criticism Pesieu travelled first to Paris to report to Louis XIII and the cardinal-minister. Once in Brussels the duchess' agent informed Tommaso Francesco that his sequestered appanages in Savoy were to be handed over to his officers and the arrears paid on them, in return for which he was to demonstrate his loyalty to the new duke Francesco Giacinto under her tutelage. Both he and Cardinal Maurizio were furthermore advised to avoid presenting the French with a pretext to take direct control of Savoy. Marie Christine intended quite obviously to persuade Tommaso Francesco to stay away from north Italy.[67]

The duchess also used Pesieu's mission to warm her relations with Alessandro Scaglia, marking his overt integration back into the realm of Savoyard court politics after three years of working informally with her brothers-in-law, Tommaso Francesco and Maurizio. Pesieu was instructed to express Marie Christine's condolences on the death of Verrua, whom she claimed she had prized as a faithful adviser, and her hope that Scaglia would be equally valuable to her, hinting of a possible return to official favour. This was repeated in her own letter to the abate, and to emphasise the integrity of her sentiments the duchess wrote in her own hand, a telling political gesture.[68] Her objective once again was clear enough. While no doubt she valued the services of the Scaglia di Verrua as a powerful and experienced court clan in Savoy, and may well have felt the loss of the count of Verrua as an experienced and loyal military commander, the abate, in the Spanish Netherlands, was known to have a large amount of credit with Prince Tommaso Francesco and the Spanish regime. He was therefore the best person to contact as part of the diplomatic process of preventing the return of the prince to the duchy.

Alessandro Scaglia responded in kind to the dowager duchess. In his correspondence with her, copies of which he also sent to Madrid to avoid any suspicion, the abate was carefully polite and even complimentary, styling Marie Christine as 'your royal highness'. Although Scaglia said little of her generosity to his family he did write, with a calculated show of modesty, that he expected no solid rewards from her since her generous words and affection were reward enough for one who was ever faithful. He also affirmed his unceasing loyalty to the new duke of Savoy, Francesco Giacinto, whom he similarly described as 'the royal duke my lord'. As with Marie Christine's letter, Scaglia's reply was calculated to

---

[67] Quazza, *Tommaso*, pp. 184, 189–96; AST LMF m. 37, fasc. 4, pp. 41–2, instructions to Pesieu, October 1637; Capriata, *Wars of Italy*, p. 631.

[68] AST LMF m. 37, fasc. 4, pp. 76–7, copy of instructions to Pesieu, 28 November 1637; p. 76, copy of Marie Christine to Scaglia, 27 November 1637.

transmit easily understood messages. The Savoyard duke, aged only five, was of course too young to appreciate the gesture, but it was not immediately meant for him. Styling Francesco Giacinto with a royal title was recognition of the House of Savoy's earnest desire to reassert its claim to the kingdom of Cyprus, something that was automatically expected of subjects of the duke and duchess of Savoy after the declaration of the *trattamento reale* of 1632.[69] Alessandro Scaglia's very deliberate epistolary language informed Marie Christine about his relationship with the sovereign prince of what by inference was still his home state at a time when potentially he had a role in settling the disputed regency even from the vantage point of exile in the Spanish Netherlands. If he had not recognised the royal claim then it would have represented a serious slight to the ruling House of Savoy. The abate was waiting to see if some kind of political settlement could be obtained, very possibly with his participation. Early in 1638 Fulvio Pergamo was sent by Tommaso Francesco to seek Scaglia's advice, who by this time had moved from Brussels to semi-retirement in Antwerp. The abate advised Prince Tommaso Francesco that Marie Christine would turn to the French regime if she were antagonised, and he furthermore suggested that the prince should delay his return, complying with her request.[70] Tommaso Francesco retreated into caution, postponing his return home so that he could seek more definite information about what he might expect from his brother and Savoy.

That is not to say that the political crisis was resolved – 'sixteen extremely turbulent months' was how Emanuele Tesauro described the period between Vittorio Amedeo I's death and the spring of 1639 in his account of the origins of the Savoyard civil war.[71] In the early months of 1638 Savoy entered a period of cold war within an atmosphere of suspicion, secret negotiations, and considerable posturing between the three corners of the duchess and the two princes. The tense situation was not helped by the lack of a clear-cut settlement to the regency question or a binding declaration by either the duchess or the princes, or by the fact that in the Spanish Netherlands Tommaso Francesco was bombarded by differing advice from a range of self-interested clients.[72] As an experienced

---

[69] AST LP 'S' m. 48, Scaglia to Marie Christine, 17 and 20 December 1637. It should be noted that since Marie Christine was also a legitimate member of the French royal house she was of royal status, while recognition of the Savoyard royal title was a much more powerful gesture. On Savoy's royal claims see also ASV SS Savoia, 57, f. 1, Gallo to Barberini, 1 January 1633, where Vittorio Amedeo I was reported to have added 'the covered crown', to his arms; f. 31, Gallo to Barberini, early 1633.

[70] AGR SEG 599, ff. 1–v, Scaglia to Philip IV, 18 January 1638.

[71] Tesauro, *Origine delle guerre*, p. 3.

[72] As the Cardinal-Infante noted: 'the prince is an excellent person, however he has many bad advisors who give him twenty different opinions'. ACM, the Cardinal-Infante

political figure Scaglia was repeatedly approached by the prince for advice.[73] But while the abate counselled caution, Emanuele Tesauro was back in Brussels from Italy attempting to persuade Tommaso Francesco to return to Savoy and leave the service of Spain. Tesauro, bluntly described by the Cardinal-Infante as an 'enemy of the House of Austria', maintained that while serving in the Spanish Netherlands Tommaso Francesco had not enjoyed the authority due to him, that Pierre Roose, the president of the council of state in the Spanish Netherlands, was working against him, and that the Spanish regime was not paying him his financial subsidy on time. More seriously, he suggested that France and Spain actually wished to divide Savoie and Piemonte, with Savoie going to France and Piemonte to Spain. Quite possibly this was a resonant fear in the minds of some Savoyards since, given its geo-strategic position across the Alps, the duchy of Savoy could function as a buffer between France and Spanish-controlled Milan.[74] Tesauro's assertion was nevertheless unfounded and in all probability unrealistic. Quite apart from the fact that France and Spain were at war and unlikely to co-operate over a division of the Savoyard state, early seventeenth-century sovereigns generally did not seize other territories without recourse to some kind of legal, dynastic or moral reason, as the Gonzaga succession dispute had only recently demonstrated. That did not, however, settle the matter. The Spanish regime felt that his sensational claim was serious enough to advise the Cardinal-Infante to ask Piochet and Scaglia, himself unmoved by Tesauro, to persuade Tommaso Francesco otherwise.[75]

In October 1638, almost a year to the day after the death of Vittorio Amedeo I, the political crisis in Savoy deepened still further when the unfortunate Duke Francesco Giacinto died, aged only six. Once again Marie Christine sent envoys to her brothers-in-law, Tommaso Francesco and Maurizio, to avoid a civil war and again she contacted Alessandro Scaglia, describing herself emotively as 'the most afflicted princess on earth this day'.[76] The dowager duchess reaffirmed her affection to his

to Olivares, 26 January 1639. I am grateful to John Elliott for showing me this correspondence.

[73] AGR SEG 599, f. 8, Scaglia to Philip IV, 8 March 1638; f. 16, Scaglia to Olivares, 3 May 1638; ACM, the Cardinal-Infante to Olivares, 6 April 1638.

[74] In 1634, Testi suspected that French control of the fortress of Pinerolo was part of a wider policy of territorially incorporating into France the entire duchy of Savoy up to the fortress. Testi, *Lettere*, II, p. 100.

[75] AGS Est. K1418, 159, the Cardinal-Infante to Philip IV, 22 November 1638; 163, consulta of council of state, 18 December 1638; 164, Olivares to Philip IV, 26 December 1638.

[76] AST LMF m. 37, fasc. 4, p. 531, Marie Christine to Scaglia, October 1638. On the death of Francesco Giacinto, an anonymous *avviso* from Milan touchingly reported

House, sentiments, she added, that were demonstrated by her generous treatment of Carlo Vittorio Scaglia (the new count of Verrua) in the face of opposition from other noble clans at the court. No names were mentioned but those opponents might well have included the long-standing rivals of the Scaglia di Verrua, the S. Martino d'Agliè, the family who perhaps enjoyed her highest favour at court. To underscore her point, Pesieu was instructed to inform the abate that she had granted a pension of 600 écus to Maurizio Scaglia, who had spent three years in the Army of Flanders fighting in active duty against France but who had returned to north Italy – in fact in May 1637, while he was still in the Low Countries and serving in the Army of Flanders, it seems that he had been appointed as a colonel in an infantry regiment serving to protect Marie Christine's regime.[77] Her appeals to Alessandro Scaglia's family loyalties formed one half of her strategy for avoiding a contested regency as she went on to express her dislike of Spain's military presence in north Italy. Again, the message would in all probability have been clear to the abate. The duchess' expressed warmth to the Scaglia di Verrua carried the implication that the abate might return to favour with a suitable show of loyalty to the regency regime. At the same time she suggested that if there were to be a peaceful settlement to Savoy's dynastic crisis then the princes should not provoke a civil war that would by extension involve France and Spain. The duchess was banking on Scaglia's political credit and his capacity to operate as an informal mediator with Tommaso Francesco.[78]

Whether Alessandro Scaglia was influenced by Marie Christine's heavy hints or not, he still maintained that Tommaso Francesco should avoid contesting the regency. Pesieu, the Savoyard envoy sent once again by the duchess to her brother-in-law, acknowledged that Scaglia had attempted to dissuade him from returning to north Italy.[79] The Spanish too believed that Tommaso Francesco should consider delaying a return, even though the prince obtained a licence from Madrid to travel to the Italian peninsula. True enough Tommaso Francesco's practical value to them in the Spanish Netherlands was open to doubt. Any promise that he had initially brought of generating opposition to Cardinal Richelieu through his marriage had failed to produce anything of substance, just

that the infant duke Carlo Emanuele II, 'although aged only four said laughing that, I am now the duke, and her highness [Marie Christine] remembering the death of her other son and her other tragedies, replied with tears in her eyes that he was the duke.' ASV Avvisi, 87, f. 111, 27 October 1638.

[77] AST Sezione Riunite PCF 1637, f. 19, 6 May 1637.
[78] AST LMF m. 37, fasc. 4, p. 332, Marie Christine to Scaglia, 30 May 1638; p. 337, copy of Marie Christine to Scaglia, June 1638; Claretta, *Reggenza*, I, p. 344.
[79] AST LMF m. 37, fasc. 2, 5, Pesieu to Marie Christine, 21 January 1639.

as the French exiles around Marie de' Medici and Gaston d'Orléans had ultimately proved worthless. The Cardinal-Infante for one expressed his disappointment over the failure of anything to come from his French contacts.[80] But even if Tommaso Francesco was in practice of less value than he initially appeared, the Spanish were still concerned that his sudden departure from the Low Countries might endanger their military position there. Carignano was after all in the middle of a relatively successful campaign with the Army of Flanders, and the Spanish moreover feared that he would be totally lost to them if he were to return to north Italy, implying that they believed he might settle unilaterally with Marie Christine back in Savoy.[81]

The impulsion to return to north Italy was nevertheless too great for Tommaso Francesco. While the regency directing Francesco Giacinto under Marie Christine's guidance was barely acceptable to the two princes, her control of the regency on behalf of the frail Carlo Emanuele when she had no other male children was intolerable. On 17 March 1639 Tommaso Francesco and his elder brother, Cardinal Maurizio, who also returned to Savoy from Rome, entered an alliance with the Spanish to eject the French from Piemonte and take control of the regency. For her part, Marie Christine, who still wished to remain independent from overly strong dependence on Richelieu, had already been forced to renew the treaty of Rivoli in 1638, that bound Savoy to a military alliance with France, taking 'poison for medicine', as Capriata put it.[82] The Savoyard state was thrown into civil war. The princes, with Spanish military aid and backed by considerable popular support in Savoy, quickly gained control of significant areas of the region. Maurizio occupied the county of Nice and parts of Piemonte, as far as Chieri to the south of Turin, while Tommaso Francesco took control of Asti, Trino, Ivrea, Biella and Aosta, to the north and east of the capital city. By late July 1639 Turin itself was under siege by the prince of Carignano at the head of 8,000 infantry and 2,500 cavalry, forcing Marie Christine to retreat first to the citadel, and then from the city to her brother Louis XIII in Grenoble. In the meantime Leganés, governor of Milan, began a siege of the fortress of Casale in Monferrato, still occupied by French troops since the war for Mantua

---

[80] The connections between Tommaso Francesco and Soissons can be pursued in Patrucco, 'Intorno alle relazioni'; Quazza, *Tommaso*, pp. 125–63. Scaglia followed the course of the negotiations in 1636, which he discussed in his correspondence with Madrid. AGR SEG 599, *passim*.

[81] ACM, the Cardinal-Infante to Olivares, 21 February 1636; Lonchay and Cuvelier (eds.), *Correspondance*, III, p. 295; Brulez (ed.), *Correspondance*, p. 349.

[82] Capriata, *Wars of Italy*, p. 638; Dumont (ed.), *Corps universel diplomatique*, VI, part I, pp. 162–3.

and Monferrato. When that fortress was eventually relieved by the count of Harcourt, the French commander began his own siege of Turin. After a five-month operation between May and September 1640, the Turinese capital was once again in the hands of Marie Christine, and she returned to the seat of her court in November. The Spanish were by this point suffering again from the inescapable problem of logistical overstretch; the nightmare of the unconquerable Casale had returned, the Dutch campaign was faltering, while more seriously the monarchy was facing revolts in Portugal and Catalonia. As winter drew in and Spain's military power waned, the princes agreed in December 1640 to a three-month temporary cease-fire.[83]

Although Tommaso Francesco had wanted Scaglia to return with him to Savoy, the abate cautiously remained in the Spanish Netherlands. But while Alessandro increasingly distanced himself from the worsening situation in his home state, the death of Augusto Manfredo Scaglia and the crisis in the duchy prompted the two nephews who had been with him to return to north Italy. Maurizio Scaglia had returned to Savoy from the Spanish Netherlands sometime in 1638, and it seems that he resumed formal service to Marie Christine.[84] In June 1636 the other nephew, Abate Filiberto Scaglia, had left Brussels for England and Spain, and in February 1638 he landed in the port of Genoa. Shortly after arriving he wrote to Olivares that he wished to remain in the service of Madrid, and in his letter he explained that he had been in contact with his elder brother, adding that it was clear that the duchess of Savoy wanted to avoid a civil war that would draw in the French.[85] Not everyone was convinced that Filiberto Scaglia could still be trusted; in the previous year Antonio Costa, an adviser to Tommaso Francesco, had written to Madrid claiming that Filiberto had secretly been in touch with Marie Christine. When Filiberto arrived back in Italy the accusation was repeated, whether out of jealousy of a potential political rival or out of genuine concern, by the Savoyard secretary of state, Giovanni Tommaso Pasero, and Cardinal Maurizio's treasurer, Masserati, both leading *principisti*, as supporters of the Savoyard princes were styled. Even Alessandro Scaglia expressed concern following the break of contact with his favoured nephew. When the elder abate heard from friends in Madrid, rather than his nephew, that

---

[83] *Ibid.*, VI, part I, pp. 195–6.
[84] AST Sezione Riunite PCF 1637, f. 19, 6 May 1637.
[85] AGS Est. 3347, f. 116, Filiberto Scaglia to Olivares, 26 February 1638. The most detailed treatment of the civil war can be found in Claretta, *Reggenza*, I. See also Augusto Bazzoni, *La reggenza di Maria Christina, duchessa di Savoia* (Turin, 1865); Quazza, 'Guerra civile'.

Filiberto had returned to the Italian peninsula, Alessandro Scaglia could not understand what he was doing.[86]

It is impossible to know with precision Filiberto's intentions, and there were certainly some grounds for suspecting his complete honesty. There was at least one occasion after his departure from Brussels in 1636 when he had been in contact with the regime in Turin, if only, it seems, to explain that he was continuing a detour from the Spanish Netherlands to the Iberian peninsula.[87] Yet Abate Filiberto's journey to and from the Spanish Netherlands had also generated suspicion in Paris. The dowager duchess moreover stated that Filiberto could not return to the court in Turin because of the ill-feeling generated by his stay in Brussels, suggesting that Abate Scaglia's exile remained a politically contentious issue at the court of Savoy. She added that Filiberto was still planning to visit Rome, as if his visit to the Spanish Netherlands had meant nothing, and that he had stopped in Genoa simply to organise some financial matters with his elder brother, Carlo Vittorio Scaglia.[88]

During the civil war the three brothers appear to have been divided in their loyalties out of genuine affiliation to the competing regents and, it seems, out of political calculation. Carlo Vittorio Scaglia, the new count of Verrua after 1637, and his youngest brother Maurizio fought for Marie Christine. Verrua was one of the leading commanders of the duchess' troops and he was seriously wounded at the siege of Turin, defending the ducal capital against the Spanish-backed princes, though an anonymous *avviso* from Rome also recorded that he miraculously survived. Maurizio, himself in command of a regiment, was also involved in direct action against the Spanish in whose army he had fought in the Low Countries and was killed in 1640 fighting with the French to recapture Turin from Tommaso Francesco.[89] In contrast, the middle brother, Abate Filiberto, supported the Spanish-backed princes. The options taken by two of the brothers were set out in an important paper that recorded members of the competing factions in the Savoyard state.

[86] AGS Est. K1418, 86, memorial of President Costa, 1637; 3349, f. 71, Leganés to Olivares, 27 November 1638; AGR SEG 598, f. 10, Scaglia to Olivares, 8 March 1638. On Pasero's Spanish sympathies see Ginate González, *Conde de la Roca*, pp. 181–2.

[87] AST LP 'S' m. 48, Filiberto Scaglia to 'the royal highness', 1636.

[88] AST LMF m. 37, fasc. 4, p. 463, Marie Christine to S. Maurizio, 5 September 1638.

[89] ASV Avvisi, 87, f. 421, 29 June 1639; Claretta, *Storia della reggenza*, I, pp. 403, 413, 426; Manno, *Patriziato Subalpino*, XXIV, p. 247. In one of the last explicit references to his family, the abate expressed his sense of loss to Olivares on the death of Maurizio Scaglia at the siege of Turin. AGR SEG 599, f. 108v, Scaglia to Olivares, 24 September 1640. Following the capture of Turin by the Spanish-backed princes, Marie Christine fled in the company of her lady-in-waiting Francesca d'Hermance, the countess of Verrua. Claretta, *Storia della reggenza*, I, p. 499

The anonymous document analysed the political preferences of leading court and political figures, including three of the illegitimate sons of Duke Carlo Emanuele I, describing those preferences with some subtlety. The count of Verrua was both 'obedient to Madama [Marie Christine]' and 'of the French faction', although he was defined as being 'opposed to the D'Agliè', reflecting the fact that powerful family rivalries at the Turinese court could cut across other political affinities. The count was significantly not described as 'opposed to the princes', Prince Tommaso Francesco and Cardinal Maurizio – he was not categorised as being hostile to the legitimate male members of the House of Savoy, adding a further layer of complexity to his position. The 'abate di Verrua' referred to Abate Filiberto, the name regularly used to denote him, and in clear contrast to his brother he was described as 'disgusted with Madama' and 'of the Spanish faction' as well as an overt supporter of the princes and actively opposed to the D'Agliè, and, revealing the political affinities of the document's anonymous author, a 'true Piedmontese'.[90]

It is difficult to accept that Filiberto was covertly working for the duchess, given such open support for the princes. But once again it is more plausible that he and his brothers had at the same time agreed on some private family strategy as a response to the civil war, just as they seem to have done after 1634. The outcome of civil war in Savoy, which was eventually settled in Marie Christine's favour in 1642, was far from certain. The course of the war went in favour of the Spanish-backed princes, at least until Tommaso Francesco lost control of Turin in November 1640, and it was only when the revolts in Catalonia and Portugal significantly weakened Spain that the extent of aid from Madrid to the princes' war effort began to diminish.[91] If the Scaglia di Verrua had offered total support to Marie Christine they might have suffered badly as a court clan in the event either of her defeat or of a political settlement that favoured the princes. This might indeed explain the reluctance in 1639 of both Carlo Vittorio Scaglia and Maurizio Scaglia to accept the pensions offered as a reward for their services by Louis XIII and Richelieu.[92] If such a strategy had indeed existed then it was ultimately

---

[90] AGS Est. 3349, f. 71, Leganés to Olivares, 27 November 1638; Bodleian Library, Clarendon State Papers 5, ff. 15–v, anonymous description of the factions of Savoy. By internal dating the document was drawn up between 1639 and late 1640.

[91] The cease-fire broke down after its expiry in March 1641, though it marked the point at which the French-backed Marie Christine gained the upper hand as Spanish aid to the princes floundered. Biraghi and Pollone, *Chrestienne di Francia*, p. 114. On the eventual settlement of the war, and Maurizio's subsequent marital arrangement, see Dumont (ed.), *Corps universel diplomatique*, VI part I, pp. 253–60.

[92] Claretta, *Storia della reggenza*, I, pp. 532–3; AGR SEG 599, f. 68, Scaglia to Philip IV, 3 December 1639. Scaglia added in this letter that the refusal by his two nephews to

successful. Following the conclusion of the war and the integration of Tommaso Francesco and Cardinal Maurizio into the regency regime, the Scaglia di Verrua, united again, resumed service to the House of Savoy. At Duke Carlo Emanuele II's first public act on reaching his majority on 21 August 1648, Carlo Vittorio Scaglia was promoted to the *Annunziata* shortly before his appointment as general of the ducal cavalry, the last promotion from the Scaglia di Verrua to the sovereign order until the eighteenth century.[93] Filiberto Scaglia was himself well treated after the civil war, despite supporting the Spanish-backed princes against Duchess Marie Christine. He soon resumed diplomatic service on behalf of the Turinese court, and his first significant diplomatic mission was ironically to the French court, a position that of course fitted into the francophile pattern of interest established by other members of the Scaglia di Verrua during the seventeenth century.[94] For her part, the dowager duchess no doubt wanted to re-establish a basis of support in Savoy, or perhaps more correctly within the political elite that embraced the Scaglia di Verrua, just as Emanuele Filiberto had attempted after his restoration in 1559. Since at least part of the Scaglia di Verrua had remained overtly loyal to her there were few reasons to destroy Filiberto's career, or to punish the family as a whole.

From the comfort of his home in Antwerp Alessandro Scaglia had reacted favourably to the actions of the princes in the initial stages of the conflict in Savoy. Despite the fact that his home state had fallen into civil war, something he had seemingly wished to avoid, he presented it to his Spanish correspondents, Philip IV and Olivares, as a justifiable action, basing his evidence at least in part on France's military failures. God had given his judgement – 'Divine Providence', Scaglia wrote, had clearly set itself against French aggression in the Italian peninsula.[95] As for his nephews, two fighting for the duchess and one siding with the princes, the abate remained almost silent. By late 1640, just as the war in Savoy had been suspended, he had almost withdrawn from the public world and had retired to the convent of the Franciscan Recollects in Antwerp.

---

accept the pensions would no doubt be interpreted (by his enemies) as a sign of his malign influence over them.

[93] Manno, *Patriziato Subalpino*, XXIV, p. 247; Gallina, 'Vicende di un grande favorite', 22 (1920), 115.

[94] Although his mission did not pass without problem. Cardinal Mazarin repeatedly accused Filiberto of being sympathetic to the interests of Spain, not least because he employed Juan Antonio Canapero, the Spanish secretary used by his uncle Alessandro during his exile in the Spanish Netherlands. Claretta, *Storia della reggenza*, II, pp. 47–8, 167–8.

[95] For example AGR SEG 599, ff. 44–v, Scaglia to Philip IV, 23 June 1639; ff. 48v–9, Scaglia to Olivares, 21 July 1639; ff. 60–1, Scaglia to Olivares, 19 October 1639.

Yet despite his refusal to return to Savoy and his steadfast opposition to the French, blood affinities still remained strong, and he did not express hostility towards his nephews for supporting Marie Christine as the civil war ultimately ended effectively in her favour. In his will, drawn up eleven days before his death, he gave a number of presents, mostly financial gifts and paintings, to personal friends in the Spanish Netherlands, but he made his two surviving nephews, Carlo Vittorio (the new count of Verrua after 1637) and Filiberto, the main beneficiaries. In death his sense of loyalty towards his family assumed priority beyond the wide political differences that seemed to have separated the exiled abate from his elder nephews.[96]

What remains striking about Abate Scaglia's decision to enter self-imposed exile in the Spanish Netherlands in 1632 was that it never signified retirement from Savoyard court politics for an individual who had a demonstrable political agenda, and who moreover was provided with chances to pursue it. The abate remained hopeful throughout the 1630s that Duke Vittorio Amedeo I, and even his Bourbon consort, would redefine their relationship with the major powers of France and Spain to establish stability (as he understood it) in Savoy, and allow him also to regain some kind of public position for himself. The arrival in Brussels of Prince Tommaso Francesco and the uncertain fortunes of Savoy within north Italy after the outbreak of war between France and Spain in 1635 fuelled the hope that Vittorio Amedeo I would reconsider his alliance with France, and the abate sought to use his role as an informal agent of Spain to cultivate the right circumstances to bring about his own political aspirations.

Alessandro Scaglia was of clear importance to other political figures – he had too much experience and potential value to remain totally or permanently excluded from the political plans of Turin, Brussels, Madrid and, by extension, Paris. The disintegration of the sovereign House and duchy of Savoy into dynastic and political crisis during the course of the 1630s ensured that the abate's role as a mediator in both the internal and international problems of his home state remained active, just as the Savoyard state remained a live issue in north Italy and Europe. For different members of the House of Savoy – Prince Tommaso Francesco and Cardinal Maurizio, Marie Christine, and perhaps even Duke Vittorio Amedeo I – Scaglia represented a channel for negotiating beyond the arena of official diplomacy, though the continuing suspicions of the French regime always made direct contact delicate to say the least. Correspondingly, while the exile could prove embarrassing and

---

[96] ASB Archivio Scaglia di Verrua, Testamenti XCVI, 2537, will of Alessandro Scaglia, 10 May 1641.

dangerous for the Scaglia di Verrua clan within the context of the court in Turin, it also created certain political opportunities, as the ambiguity of Scaglia's public status in the Spanish Netherlands could be exploited to help safeguard the interests of his family during times of internal crisis within Savoy. The Scaglia di Verrua seem to have operated strategies, whether or not they were pre-planned, for dealing with crisis both before and after the deaths of Vittorio Amedeo I and the count of Verrua. At certain points during the 1630s Abate Scaglia formed an important element in their plans. Although the war for the succession of Mantua and Monferrato had significantly changed balances in the relationships between Savoy, France and Spain, the dispute had by no means neutralised north Italy as a contentious international problem, not least because the dynastic crisis within the sovereign House gave the impression that the duchy might again switch alignment away from France to either neutrality or Spain. Alessandro Scaglia's exile brought to the fore the kinds of wider issues faced by Savoy during the Thirty Years' War as both a regional power in north Italy and a power that had constant contact with the leading powers. And like political exile more generally, his sojourn in the Spanish Netherlands must be set in context: it was not so much the decline of a diplomatic career to the point of retirement and death in Antwerp but rather the continuation of that career by other means.

CONCLUSION

The conclusion of the Savoyard civil war in 1642 marked the end of an exceptionally difficult period for the Scaglia di Verrua as a court clan, as it did for the Sabaudian dynasty as the ruling House. The two senior members of the Scaglia di Verrua, Augusto Manfredo, count of Verrua, and his younger brother, Abate Alessandro, had both died within a short period of one another (one in 1637 and the other in 1641), while Maurizio Scaglia, the second of Verrua's three sons, had been killed fighting the Spanish in the war. The quick resumption of state service by members of the clan after 1642 indicated the continuing intimacy between the aristocratic and ruling families, not least as Marie Christine attempted to bind the elites to her 'restored' regency regime, just as Emanuele Filiberto had done after his restoration in 1559. But it was arguably not until the end of the seventeenth century that the Scaglia di Verrua again enjoyed prominence at the very pinnacle of Savoyard society when a later count of Verrua, Augusto Manfredo, married Giovanna Battista, daughter of the duke of Luynes, one of the members of the high French nobility. As countess of Verrua she infamously became Duke Vittorio Amedeo II's mistress, and through their relationship bore two illegitimate children. The son was established as the marquis of Susa, following his legitimisation in 1701, while the daughter, *Madama Vittoria*, notoriously married the prince of Carignano – himself a member of the ruling Savoyard dynasty – after eloping to Paris. A fitting climax, perhaps, to a century of service to the sovereign House.

Drawing wide-ranging conclusions about state history from the fortunes of the Scaglia di Verrua might seem misguided. After all, not every court clan was comparable in the extent of their success and power, and not every family had such a close relationship with the ducal family. Having said that, it seems instantly clear that a narrow approach to so-called 'state formation', stressing the paramount importance of high politics formulated by invisible ministers with little or no personality, would be

273

unsatisfactory for understanding early modern Savoyard foreign policy. Nor, indeed, would the particular historiographical traditions that have often shaped studies of the duchy seem adequate for interpreting the subtly interwoven patterns of court politics during the sixteenth and seventeenth centuries. Even if the Scaglia di Verrua were exceptionally successful compared with most of their immediate rivals at the Turinese court, their case study alone reinforces the view that the political history of the Savoyard composite state was closely related to the histories of its elite social groups and political clans. 'Dynasty and diplomacy' for early modern Savoy encompassed more than the ruling House alone.

The social, cultural and political history of the Scaglia di Verrua indeed tells a similar tale to that of the House of Savoy – the fortunes of the two family clans were inseparable, from the restoration of the ducal regime after the peace of Câteau–Cambrésis in 1559 until the end of the civil war in 1642. The family's emergence as a leading court clan had reflected the growing importance of the new capital city of Turin and the principality of Piemonte within the wider composite Savoyard state in the second half of the sixteenth century and the early seventeenth century, where Piedmontese elites who committed themselves to the Savoyard dynasty had come to dominate their rivals from Savoie. From the later sixteenth century the Scaglia di Verrua had recognised the fundamental importance of their association with the sovereign dynasty as a rich source of power and patronage. That relationship was in turn reciprocated by the House of Savoy as it correspondingly drew on the resources and expertise of family members, especially through diplomatic service. The family's social, political and cultural success during the first decades of the 1600s, with the significant expansion of its horizons into the realms of international court culture, had much to do with Carlo Emanuele I's long ducal reign from 1580 until 1630. The duke had conferred enormous favour on Count Filiberto Gherardo as a reliable courtier and minister, and this favour had carried through to his two sons. Augusto Manfredo and Alessandro successfully maintained the family's close connection with the sovereign dynasty through service in a series of overseas missions and court offices, while expanding the influence of the ducal regime through their own international contacts and client networks. The Scaglia di Verrua had moreover benefited from the *relative* consistency of Carlo Emanuele I's foreign policy during the early seventeenth century, with his aspiration of expanding towards the east and south into Monferrato and the Spanish-protected Lombardy. This consistency had given members of the Scaglia di Verrua a guide by which to direct their own interests, and it quickly established the family's francophile credentials both at the Savoyard court and in Paris, not least through repeated missions to the Bourbon court.

What unsettled the Scaglia di Verrua as a court clan were the shifts in policies that marked the twilight years of Carlo Emanuele I's reign as he fought for the dynastic claim to Monferrato – pursued, it should be said, in part because of Alessandro Scaglia's own diplomatic strategies that sought to play France and Spain off against one another through their wars with England – followed by the profound uncertainties of the 1630s. These were indeed problems that openly divided the Scaglia di Verrua and the sovereign House alike, as the duchy and its political clans and factions descended into civil war after the twin deaths of Augusto Manfredo Scaglia and Duke Vittorio Amedeo I.

If the Scaglia di Verrua's family history was woven into that of early modern Savoyard history, then the career of their most famous member, Abate Alessandro Cesare, was bound into these themes even more tightly. It had been as a result of the favour enjoyed by Filiberto Gherardo Scaglia that the abate had gained his ecclesiastical positions at a young age and, very probably, his first diplomatic posting, to the papal court. But while his early career had been shaped very much by his father's close relationship with Carlo Emanuele I, the abate's individual qualities soon established their own pattern of service at the papal court and later in Paris. His role as a patron and broker, operating on behalf of members of the Savoyard House, Carlo Emanuele I and Cardinal Maurizio most importantly, merged an expertise in the high arts with power politics and reinforced Turin's cultural campaigns to underline its identity as a leading Italian, and European, court. That relationship between patronage and power was also borne out in the abate's own commissions. The abiding image of Alessandro Scaglia has been as the patron of Van Dyck, whose importance to the abate may well have been accentuated by the artist's close association with members of the Stuart court and the Savoyard ruling House. But Scaglia's association with other artists like Peter Paul Rubens (even though there were no commissions), Jacob Jordaens, Daniel Seghers and Frans Snyders, and writers such as Alessandro Tassoni and Fulvio Testi, were no less significant, and enabled the abate to self-fashion a distinctive identity. Through direct contact with artists and writers and through his identification as a patron of these prized craftsmen (Van Dyck most strikingly), Scaglia placed himself in a system of court culture and politics that crossed not only international boundaries but, in the case of the Caroline court, the boundary of confessions. The abate could participate in a cultural language that, within a fairly small world of like-minded courtiers – typically from dynastically related courts – strengthened his own political standing. Friendships, both personal and political (if they can at all be separated as formal categories), were crucial to Alessandro Scaglia's identity and the key to his successful emergence as a diplomat of international standing during the 1620s and to his career even during the years of exile.

It might however be tempting to return to the comments of less well-inclined historians who have been critical of the abate and, by extension, of the duchy of Savoy as a European power during the Thirty Years' War. 'Like master like servant' – was Abraham de Wicquefort fair to characterise the abate's career, like the reign of the ostensibly unpredictable Carlo Emanuele I, as one of cunning opportunism, if not of measured political wisdom? Or was Roy Schreiber correct to suggest that Scaglia and indeed Savoy were punching above their weights in the arena of power politics dominated by big hitters like France and Spain? After all, if Scaglia's diplomatic influence depended more on 'friendships' than 'material' force afforded by troops and Savoy's geographical position, then *a priori* that influence seems weak and precarious. The fragility of Anglo-Savoyard relations after the death of Buckingham indeed implies that political friendships, and perhaps even the dynastic affinities between London and Turin, only had power so long as there were more concrete reasons to co-operate. But Schreiber in particular makes a significant historiographical assumption about the marginal importance of second-rank states in early modern Europe and about how they related to more significant powers. Neither France nor Spain, easily identifiable as leading powers, believed the duchy to have been unimportant. To a considerable degree this was because Savoy was a sizeable regional power in north Italy, capable in the 1620s of raising over 20,000 troops and in possession of valuable Alpine passes.

The cultivation of Savoy also reflected the long-standing rivalries for territory and prestige between the Valois and Bourbons on the one hand, and the Habsburgs on the other, in north Italy. The ruling dynasties of Spain and France repeatedly married into the Sabaudian dynasty and went to great lengths to curry the favour of members of the ruling House, and indeed of leading families like the Scaglia di Verrua. In part this was because of their earnest desire to work in coalition with other Catholic powers to legitimise their own power politics to potentially critical domestic and international audiences. Yet there was also the implicit recognition of the fact that Savoy was not a passive power or a punch-bag for France and Spain. Dynasticism had its own energy. Indeed the same marriage alliances between Savoy and the leading powers that France and Spain hoped might win Savoy's loyalty furthered the Sabaudian dynasty's considerable efforts to acquire royal status, typically in heated opposition to rival powers in north Italy. Added to this, the ruling House of Savoy had too many outstanding dynastic claims, whatever the likelihood that these claims would actually be satisfied, for it to sit back from regional

and European power politics, or to be disregarded by the leading powers, fearful as they were of losing influence in north Italy. Heads of the
Savoyard House had a responsibility to acquire territories to which their
dynasty had legitimate claims, a fact that imbued their foreign policies
with a particular vitality.

But this in turn begs another question that perhaps too often has been
left unanswered in accounts of international relations. How should success
and failure be measured in the diplomacy of this period? One obvious,
and quite understandable, yardstick would be by its measurable outcomes,
what treaties were signed and what materially was achieved. By these
terms, Savoy's fortunes during the early seventeenth century were mixed.
True, the duchy made some territorial gains in Monferrato after the
conclusion of the 1628-32 war, and had obtained financial compensation
for the claim to Zuccarello, but on the other side of the equation the
dynasty's royal claim was not recognised and from 1630 French troops
remained in the fortress of Pinerolo. Such a conclusion might, however,
misrepresent the dynamics of dynasticism, by viewing family interests
through a relatively small frame of diplomatic time encompassed by the
Thirty Years' War. Certain Sabaudian claims had been active for generations; while sovereigns like Carlo Emanuele I and Vittorio Amedeo
I may well have seen themselves as duty-bound to realise at least some
dynastic aspirations during their reigns, they may also have felt responsible for maintaining those aspirations for their successors. After all, while
Savoyard royal status, so vigorously pursued by the two dukes, was not immediately achieved in the seventeenth century, it was eventually obtained
in the early eighteenth century by Vittorio Amedeo II.

It also seems at first glance that Scaglia's ambassadorial success was not
great. As a Savoyard diplomat he achieved exceptional prominence across
Europe during the 1620s. and he was involved in the fomal settlement
of the Anglo-Spanish war, as the wording of the treaty of Madrid had
recorded. But, arguably, his most significant political achievement came
not in service to Savoy but as an exile, when in 1633 he broke the
aristocratic fronde in the Spanish Netherlands. Yet measuring his success
by the immediate outcomes of his initiatives alone itself offers only a
partial understanding of the character of diplomacy in the age of the
Thirty Years' War and, again, does little to contextualise the roles played
by states like Savoy. Abate Scaglia himself did not operate according to
easily discernible goals at all times. After the treaty of Monzón the abate
adopted a position of diplomatic equivocation, while following the war
for Mantua and Monferrato and the treaties of Regensburg and Cherasco
he believed that a reputable peace could only be obtained for Savoy
by the application of armed force. This reflected the significant shift of

opinion that had taken place in these central years, as the abate moved from promoting the anti-Spanish 'common cause' and 'Italian liberty' to a position defined against France, or at least Richelieu. Throughout the period he applied a brand of political pragmatism informed by his own sets of political assumptions and a conception of what he thought were Savoy's best strategic interests. Indeed, during the 1620s in particular, he seems to have been less concerned with obtaining definite political objectives than with temporising to see what circumstances might offer, a flexible approach to diplomacy that mirrored the variety of his prince's dynastic claims.

If generalisations can be made, diplomacy, as ever, was as much about the dead-end negotiations, deliberate smokescreens and unfulfilled pipe-dreams of the competing powers and players, as about negotiations they undertook and treaties they concluded. Diplomacy was also far more than 'state' politics alone, even though typically it was considered to be a fundamental expression of legitimate sovereignty. Abate Alessandro Scaglia, strikingly recorded for posterity in the Van Dyck portraits, stands as a political and cultural emblem of his paradoxical and multi-layered age. Dynasty and diplomacy for Scaglia and Savoy constituted a complex interplay between the sovereign family and elite subjects, a synthesis of political pragmatism and moralised aspirations, of tangible and intangible influence, and of state power and personal creativity.

APPENDIX: CODES AND CIPHERS

The growth in diplomatic traffic from the fifteenth century and the gradual creation of permanent embassies in different sovereign courts generated problems about the transmission of diplomatic information – how could an ambassador operating in the field send any sensitive documents without a hostile person reading them before their arrival in the home state? While it was probably impossible to guarantee total security, to reduce the risks to correspondence diplomats and their regimes increasingly employed various espionage strategies, the most common of which was to encode written documents. This development in the character of international relations was reflected in the fact that regimes began to make use of secretaries who were specialists in the encryption and decoding of documents. The papal court had a secretary of ciphers as early as the fifteenth century, while a comparable office was created in Spain during the reign of Philip II.[1] As a further reflection of these changes, the leading writers on diplomatic practice in the early seventeenth century also referred to the use of ciphers in a context of whether a Catholic diplomat could justifiably use deception while representing his sovereign prince. Hiding information was comparable to dissimulation, a moderated form of deceit that was not only necessary but indeed positively beneficial in political practice, given the wider moral uncertainty that pervaded the fallen world.

Abate Scaglia, in common with other diplomatic representatives in early modern Europe, employed ciphers in his correspondence. While the practice of some regimes, notably the Spanish and papal governments, was to use general ciphers which were common to all their diplomats and which were changed periodically, Scaglia had his own codes which he used with particular correspondents. He used one, for instance, in corresponding with his secretary, Pietro Barozzio, while he used another with Olivares during the 1630s, no doubt so that he could operate as the count-duke's special confidant in the Spanish Netherlands during the abate's exile there. The examples of his ciphers that survive are all complex ciphers, as they were termed in the seventeenth century. Rather than simply substituting single symbols (typically numbers) for corresponding letters with a

---

[1] Mattingly, *Renaissance Diplomacy*, pp. 235–9; Devos, *Les chiffres de Phillipe II*.

total of around twenty-four symbols – the letter 'u' and 'v' were interchange-able, while 'x' was not employed – complex ciphers used multiple symbols for letters in addition to symbols for common combinations of two or three let-ters and also for entire words. This meant that the total number of symbols in a cipher could run into the hundreds, obviously increasing its effectiveness as a cover, though seventeenth-century treatises on codewriting and breaking pointed out that these too could be broken and accordingly included sections of the frequencies not only of individual letters but also of combinations of letters in the three major diplomatic languages of French, Spanish and Italian to aid codebreakers.[2]

One example of Scaglia's cipher is given below to give a clearer idea as to how complex codes worked, and the key is as complete as possible from the surviving documentary evidence. Fortunately, the deciphers were made by secretaries at the time, who wrote the translation above the original encoded letters, though I have used these keys on previously undeciphered correspondence (presumably duplicates of letters where the other copy had been deciphered but had not survived).

CIPHER

Scaglia used this code in the late 1620s, particularly during the war for Mantua and Monferrato. While there are clear gaps in the key below, it can be presumed that there was a fuller numerical sequence that covered not only the individual letters, but also the combinations of letters and complete words.

a = 30, 32, 96	b = 33
c = 36, 37, 38	d = 39
e = 43, 44	f = 47
g = 50	h = 51
i = 54, 55, 56, 57	l = 58, 59
m = 60	n = 63
o = 61, 66, 67, 68	p = 69, 70
r = 75, 76, 77	s = 78, 80
t = 81, 83	u = 84, 85, 86

The following number has a '^' above it

11 = gli

[2] For two examples of seventeenth-century treatises on deciphering see Antonio Cospi, *L'interpretazione delle cifre* (Florence, 1639); J. P. Devos and H. Seligman (eds.), *L'art du deschiffrer: traité de dechiffrement du XVIIe siècle de la Secrétairerie d'Etat et de guerse espagnole* (Louvain, 1967). See also the comments in Charles H. Carter, *The Western European Powers, 1500–1700* (London, 1971), chapter 6.

All the following numbers have a '+' above them

01 = ve	02 = vi	03 = vo	04 = za	07 = mente
08 = chi	09 = in	10 = à	11 = ad	12 = al
14 = alli	15 = alla	17 = dell'	18 = dal	19 = del
21 = della	22 = et	23 = é	24 = ha	25 = ho
26 = fatto	27 = sono	28 = stato	29 = non	40 = per
41 = perche	42 = che	43 = con	44 = col	46 = quale
48 = qual	49 = li	50 = il	51 = esse	53 = sempre
54 = detto	56 = quando	57 = di	58 = la	59 = le
65 = da	66 = de	68 = do	69 = du	70 = ma
71 = me	72 = mi	73 = mo	74 = nu	76 = ne
77 = ni	78 = no	81 = qui	82 = que	84 = ra
85 = re	86 = ri	87 = ro	89 = sa	90 = se
91 = si	92 = so	93 = su	94 = ta	95 = te
96 = ti	97 = to	98 = tu	99 = va	

All the following numbers have a '−' above them

11 = Italia	15 = Piemonte	16 = Savoia	30 = Monferrato
32 = Nevers	34 = Casale	35 = Genova	36 = Genovesi
37 = Milano	39 = Venetia	40 = Venetiani	42 = Imperatore
50 = Danimarca	57 = Holandesi	60 = Fiandra	64 = Spínola
76 = Francia	77 = Francesi	78 = Re	81 = Monsieur
82 = Richelieu	98 = Spagna	100 = Spagna	102 = Olivares
104 = Inghilterra	117 = Ambasciatore	118 = Lettere	125 = V. A.
131 = Io	132 = Negotio	134 = Trattato	143 = Roan
150 = Pace	152 = Guerra	153 = Dissegno	156 = Olandia
158 = Aprile	159 = Maggio	181 = Re	182 = Duca
186 = Conte	198 = Armata	206 = Corona	207 = Clausel
209 = Coriero	210 = Ciampagna	214 = Essendo	217 = Gonzalo
223 = Ungheria	225 = Inimico	230 = Milano	241 = Re
243 = Signore	246 = Troppe		

Thus, the first line of the letter AST LMS m. 21, 215, Scaglia to Carlo Emanuele I, 22 June 1629, in code starts:

```
   +       +    + +  __  +        + +  _ +     + +    + +       +     + _
   43 68 38 91 67 76 57 209 42 70 30 78 89 09 60 01 77 84 82 80 89 40 58 96 02 30 57 76
```

The decipher is:

Con occasione di corriero che passa in fiandra verrà questa per la via di francia

BIBLIOGRAPHY

I MANUSCRIPT SOURCES

Archives Générales du Royaulme, Brussels

Sécrétairerie d'Etat et de Guerre, 196, 197, 212, 213, 214, 221, 222, 402/2,
    596, 597, 598, 599, 600

Archives du Ministère des Affaires Etrangères, Paris

Correspondance Politique
  Angleterre, 42
  Espagne, 15, 16
  Pays-Bas Espagnols, 7
  Sardaigne, 7, 8, 18, 20, 21, 22, 24, 25

Archivio Segreto, The Vatican

Armarium, XLV
Avvisi, 8, 9, 80, 87
Segretario di Stato
  Fiandra, 19, 21, 22
  Francia, 52, 65, 68, 71, 73, 74A
  Savoia, 44, 46, 47, 55, 59, 60

Archivio di Stato, Biella

Archivio Scaglia di Verrua
  Testamenti, XCVI

Archivio di Stato, Bologna

Archivio Malvezzi-Lupari, 369

Archivio di Stato, Turin

Cerimoniale
  Roma, 1
Lettere Forestieri
  Inghilterra, 48
Lettere Ministri
  Francia, 18, 19, 23–8, 30, 31, 33, 37
  Inghilterra, 4, 5
  Milano, 17, 18
  Roma, 21, 26, 28–31, 33
  Spagna, 19–24
  Venezia, 6
Lettere particolari 'S', 48
Lettere principi diversi, 15, 46, 51
Lettere principi, duchi e sovrani, 33, 46, 48
Materie ecclesiastiche
  Abbazia di S. Giusto di Susa, 10
  categoria 28, nomina del Cardinale
Negoziazioni colla Francia, 8
Negoziazioni coll'Inghilterra, 1, 3

Archivio di Stato, Turin: Sezione Riunite

Articoli, 219
Insinuazione di Torino, 1627: book 3, 10; 1629: book 12; 1630: book 1; 1634: book 1; 1636: book 6
Patenti Controllo Finanze, 1561, 1608–10, 1614–15, 1618–19, 1627, 1632–3

Archivo de la Casa Miraflores, Madrid

Correspondence between the Cardinal-Infante and Olivares.

Archivo General, Simancas

Sección de Estado y Guerra, 2041, 2042, 2047, 2051, 2153, 2240, 2517, 2519, 2520, 2574, 3336, 3347, 3349, 3437, 3444, 3445, 3646, 3647, K1415, K1418, K1424, K1433, K1434, K1437, K1457, K1665, K1480, K1481

Biblioteca Apostolica, The Vatican

Barberni Latini, 5883

Biblioteca Reale, Turin

Archivio Scarampi, 3755

Bibliothèque Nationale, Paris

Nouvelles Acquisitions Français, 3109

British Library, London

Additional Manuscripts, 34,311, 36,778
Egerton Manuscripts, 1820, 2597

Bodleian Library, Oxford

Clarendon State Papers, 6, vol. 15.

Public Record Office, London

State Papers
  Flanders (77), 19, 22, 23, 24, 25, 28, 31
  France (78), 80, 81, 82, 86
  Savoy (92), 11, 12, 13, 14, 15, 16, 18, 19
  Spain (94), 34 35, 36, 37
  United Provinces (84) 134

Staatsarchief, Antwerp

Notarissien Rousseau, 1641

II PRINTED PRIMARY SOURCES

Aldea Vaquero, Quintín (ed.). *España y Europa en el siglo XVII. Correspondencia de Saavedra Fajardo: 1631–1633*, 2 vols. (Madrid, 1986).
Algay de Martignac, Etienne. *Mémoires du duc d'Orléans* (Paris, 1756).
Assarino, Luca. *Delle guerre e successi d'Italia* (Turin, 1665).
Baudi di Vesme, Alessandro. 'La regia pinacoteca di Torino', *Le Gallerie Nazionale Italiane*, III (Rome, 1897), 3–68.
Berado, Antonio. 'Difesa del Marchese di Caluso Governatore di Vercelli per la dedizione di questa Città nel 1617 scritta da esso stesso ed esposta al Duca Carlo Emanuele I', *Archivio Storico Italiano*, XIII (Florence, 1847), 519–28, and the 'Relazione dell'assedio della Città di Vercelli fatto nell'anno 1617 dell'esercito di Spagna', *ibid.*, 453–519.
Botero, Giovanni. *Della ragion di stato*, ed. Luigi Firpo (Turin, 1947).
Bragaccio, Gasparo. *L'Ambasciatore in sei libri* (Padua, 1627).
Brulez, Wilfred (ed.). *Correspondance de Richard-Pauli Stravius, 1634–42* (Brussels and Rome, 1955).
Calendar of State Papers, Domestic.

Calendar of State Papers, Venetian.

Capriata, Pietro Giovanni. *The History of the Wars of Italy from the Year MDCXIII to MDCLIV in XVIII Books, Rend'red into English by Henry, Earl of Monmouth* (London, 1663).

Cigna-Santi, Vittorio Amedeo. *Serie cronologica de' cavalieri dell'ordine supremo di Savoia detti prima del collare indi della Santissima Nunziata* (Turin, 1786).

Cospi, Antonio. *La interpretazione delle cifre* (Florence, 1639).

Couvreur, Walter. 'Daniël Seghers' Inventaris van door hem geschilderde bloem-stukken', *Gentse Bijdragen tot de Kunstgeschiedenis en de Oudheidkunde*, 20 (1967), 87–158.

Davies, Randall. 'An inventory of the duke of Buckingham's pictures, etc., at York House in 1635', *The Burlington Magazine*, 10 (1906), 376–82.

de Bassompierre, François. *Mémoires*, 2 vols. (Cologne, 1665).

de Bourdeille, Claude. *Mémoires de monsieur de Montresor* (Leiden, 1665).

de Callières, François. *The Art of Diplomacy*, ed. H. M. A. Keens-Soper and Karl W. Schweizer (Leicester, 1983).

de Rohan, Henri. *Mémoires du Duc de Rohan sur les choses qui se sont passées en France depuis la mort de Henri le Grand jusqu'à la Paix faite avec les Réformés* (Amsterdam, 1646).

de Wicquefort, Abraham. *L'ambassadeur et ses fonctions*, 2 vols. (The Hague, 1681).

Declaration de la Reyne Mere du Roy tres-Chrestien contenant les raisons de sa sortie des pays-bas (London, 1638).

della Chiesa, Francesco Agostino. *Catalogo di tutti li scrittori Piemontesi et altri dei stati dell'altezza sereniss. di Savoia* (Turin, 1614).

   S.R.E. cardinalium, archiespiscoporum, episcoporum, et abbatum Pedemontanae regionis chronologica historia (Turin, 1645).

Devos, J. P. and H. Seligman (eds.). *L'art de deschiffrer: traité de dechiffrement du XVIIe siècle de la Secrétairerie d'Etat et de guerre espagnole* (Louvain, 1967).

Dumont, Jean (ed.). *Corps universel diplomatique du droit des gens, contenant un receuil des traitez d'alliance, de paix, etc. faits en Europe depuis le régne de Charlemagne jusques à présent*, 8 vols. (Amsterdam, 1726–31).

Elliott, J. H. and José F. de la Peña (eds.). *Memoriales y cartas del Conde Duque de Olivares*, 2 vols. (Madrid, 1978–80).

Fairfax, Brian. *A Catalogue of the Curious Collection of Pictures of George Villiers, Duke of Buckingham* (London, 1758).

Ferrero, Ermano (ed.). *Lettres de Henriette Marie de France, Reine d'Angleterre, à sa sœur Christine, Duchesse de Savoie* (Turin, 1881).

Finet, John. *Finetti Philoxenis* (London, 1656).

Guichenon, Samuel. *Histoire généalogique de la Royale Maison de Savoie*, 2 vols. (Lyons, 1660).

Giuglaris, P. Luigi. *Funerale fatto nel duomo di Torino alla gloriosa memoria dell'invittissimo, e potentissimo prencipe Vittorio Amadeo Duca di Savoia Prencipe di Piemonte Rè di Cipri, & c.* (Turin, 1638).

Historical Manuscripts Commission, Eleventh Report, appendix, part I (Salvetti correspondence) (London, 1887).

Lonchay, H. and J. Cuvelier (eds.). *Correspondance de la cour d'Espagne sur les affaires des Pays-Bas au XVIIe siècle*, 6 vols. (Brussels, 1923–37).

Loomie, Albert J. (ed.). *Ceremonies of Charles I: the Notebooks of John Finet Master of Ceremonies, 1628–1641* (Fordham, 1987).

Magurn, Ruth Saunders (ed.). *The Letters of Peter-Paul Rubens* (Cambridge, Mass., 1955).

Monod, Pietro. *Trattato del titolo regio dovuto alla serenissima Casa di Savoia. Insieme con un ristretto delle rivolutioni del Reame di Cipri appartenente alla corona dell'Altezza Reale di Vittorio Amedeo, Duca di Savoia* (Turin, 1633).

Orbanni, J. A. F. *Documenti sul barocco in Roma* (Rome, 1920).

Passamonti, Eugenio. 'Le "instruttioni" di Carlo Emanuele I agli inviati sabaudi in Roma con lettere e brevi al duca dei pontefeci suoi contemporani', *Bollettino Storico-Bibliografico Subalpino*, 32 (1930), 167–430.

Puget de la Serre, Jean. *L'entrée de la Reyne Mere du Roy Tres-Chrestien dans les villes des Pays-Bas* (Antwerp, 1632).

Histoire de l'entree de la reine Mere dans la Grande Bretagne (London, 1639).

Richelieu, Jean Armand du Plessis, duc de. *Mémoires du Cardinal Richelieu*, 10 vols. (Paris, 1907–31).

Rooses, Max and C. Ruelens (eds.). *Correspondance de Rubens et documents épistolaires concernant sa vie et ses œuvres*, 6 vols. (Antwerp, 1887–1909).

Sainsbury, William Noel. *Original Unpublished Papers Illustrative of the Life of Sir Peter Paul Rubens, as an Artist and a Diplomat* (London, 1859).

Saint-Germain, Abbé de (ed.). *Diverses Pièces faictes pour la défense de la Royne Mère et de Monseigneur, Frère unique du Roy tres-chrestien Louys XIII., contre les violences et calomnies du Cardinal Richelieu* (Antwerp, 1632 and 1644 edns).

Scaglia, Filiberto Gherardo. 'Avvertimenti politici per quelli che vogliono entrare nel corte', *Miscellanea di Storia d'Italia* (1889), 333–52.

Scamozzi, Vicenzo. *L'idea dell'architettura universale* (Venice, 1615).

Siri, Vittorio. *Memorie recondite dall'anno 1601 sino al 1640*, 8 vols. (Lyons, 1677–9).

Tassoni, Alessandro. *Lettere (a cura di Pietro Pulliati)*, 2 vols. (Rome, 1978).

Prose politiche e morali, 2 vols. (Rome and Bari, 1978).

Tesauro, Emanuele. *Inscriptiones, quotquot reperiri potuerunt* (Brandenburg, 1671).

Origine delle guerre civili del Piemonte, in seguimento de'Campeggiamenti del principe Tomaso di Savoia (Cologne, 1673).

Historia dell'Augusta Città di Torino, 2 vols. (Turin, 1679–1712).

Testi, Fulvio. *L'Italia all'invittissimo e gloriosissimo prencipe Carlo Emanuel Duca di Savoia* (Rome, 1617).

Lettere (a cura di Maria Luigi-Doria), 3 vols. (Bari, 1967).

van Dyck, Anthony. *Icones principium virorum doctorum, pictorum, chalcographorum, statuariorum nec non amatorum pictoriae artis numero centum* (Antwerp, 1646).

van Meerbeck, Lucienne (ed.). *Correspondance du nonce Fabio de Lagonissa, archevêque de Sonza, 1627–1634* (Brussels and Rome, 1966).

Vera y Figueroa, Juan Antonio de, count of La Roca, *El enbaxador* (Seville, 1620).

III SECONDARY SOURCES

Adair, E. R. *The Extraterritoriality of Ambassadors in the Sixteenth and Seventeenth Centuries* (London, 1929).

Adams, S. L. 'The Protestant cause: religious alliance with the West European Calvinist communities as a political issue in England, 1585–1630' (DPhil thesis, University of Oxford, 1973).

Adamson, John (ed.). *The Princely Courts of Europe, 1500–1750* (London, 1999).

Adriani, G. B. *Memorie della vita e dei tempi di Monsignor Gio. Secondo Ferrero-Ponziglione Referendario Apostolico, primo Consigliere e Auditore Generale del Principe Cardinale Maurizio di Savoia* (Turin, 1856).

Albion, G. *Charles I and the Court of Rome* (London, 1935).

Alcalá-Zamora y Queipo de Llano, José. *España, Flandes y el mar del norte, 1618–1639* (Barcelona, 1975).

Aldea Vaquero, Quintín. 'La neutralidad de Urbano VIII durante los años decisivos de la guerra de los treinta años', *Hispania Sacra*, 139 (1968), 155–78.

Alexander, M. C. *Charles I's Lord Treasurer: Sir Richard Weston, Earl of Portland (1577–1635)* (London, 1975).

Amoretti, G. *Il ducato di Savoia dal 1559 al 1713*, 2 vols. (Turin, 1985).

Anderson, Jaynie. 'National museums, the art market and Old Master paintings', *Wolfenbütteler Forschungen, Kunst und Kunsttheorie 1400–1900*, 48 (1991), 375–404.

Ansaldi, V. 'Giovanni Botero coi principi sabaudi in ispagna (da lettere inedite)', *Bollettino Storico-Bibliografico Subalpino*, 35 (1933), 321–40.

Ashton, Robert. *The Crown and the Money Market, 1603–1640* (Oxford, 1960).

Babel, Rainer (ed.). *Frankreich im europäischen Staatensystem der frühen Neuzeit* (Sigmaringen, 1995).

Barberis, Walter. *Le armi del principe: la tradizione militare sabauda* (Turin, 1988).

Barbero, Alessandro, 'Savoiardi e Piemontesi nel ducato sabaudo all'inizio del Cinquecento: un problema storiografico risolto?', *Bollettino Storico-Bibliografico Subalpino*, 87 (1989), 591–637.

Barnes, Susan J., Piero Boccardo, Clario di Fabio and Laura Tagliaferro (eds.). *Van Dyck: grande pittura e collezionismo a Genova* (Milan, 1997).

Batiffol, Louis. *La duchesse de Chevreuse: une vie d'aventures et d'intrigues sous Louis XIII* (Paris, 1913).

Baudi di Vesme, Alessandro. *L'arte negli stati sabaudi*, Atti della Società Piemontese di Archeologia e Belli Arti, 14 (1932).

Schede Vesme: l'arte in Piemonte dal XVI al XVIII secolo, 3 vols. (Turin, 1963–8).

Bazzoni, Augusto. *La reggenza di Maria Cristina, duchessa di Savoia* (Turin, 1865).

Beladiez, Emilio. *España y el sacro imperio romano germaníco: Wallenstein, 1583–1634* (Madrid, 1967).

Beldon Scott, John. 'Seeing the Shroud: Guarini's Reliquary Chapel in Turin and the ostentation of a dynastic relic', *The Art Bulletin*, 77 (1995), 609–37.

Bell, Gary. *A Handlist of British Diplomatic Representatives, 1509–1688* (London, 1990).

Bély, Lucien. *Espions et ambassadeurs au temps de Louis XIV* (Paris, 1990).

Bergadani, Roberto. 'Rivalità tra stato e chiesa per intrighi politici alla corte di Vittorio Amedeo I di Savoia', *Bollettino Storico-Bibliografico Subalpino*, 24 (1922), 251–70.

Bergin, Joseph. *Cardinal Richelieu: Power and the Pursuit of Wealth* (New Haven and London, 1985).

 The Rise of Richelieu (New Haven and London, 1991).

Bergin, Joseph and L. Brockliss (eds.). *Richelieu and His Age* (Oxford, 1992).

Biraghi, Giuliana Brugnelli and Maria Bianca Denoyé Pollone. *Chrestienne di Francia: duchessa di Savoia, prima Madama Reale* (Turin, 1991).

Bireley, Robert. *Religion and Politics in the Age of the Counterreformation: Emperor Ferdinand II, William Lamormaini, S.J., and the Formation of Imperial Policy* (Chapel Hill and London, 1981).

 The Counter-Reformation Prince: Anti-Machiavellianism or Catholic Statecraft in Early Modern Europe (Chapel Hill and London, 1990).

Bourgeon, Jean-Louis. *Les Colbert avant Colbert: destin d'une famille marchande* (Paris, 1973).

Bozza, Tommaso. *Scrittori politici italiani dal 1550 al 1650: saggio di bibliografia* (Rome, 1949).

Brants, Victor. *La Belgique au XVII siècle. Albert et Isabelle: études d'histoire politique et sociale* (Louvain, 1910).

Braudel, Fernand. *The Mediterranean and the Mediterranean World in the Age of Philip II*, 2 vols. (London, 1986–7).

Brayda di Soleto, P. 'Il titolo di Eminenza ai Cardinali ed i Duchi di Savoia (tre documenti inediti del 1630)', *Bollettino Storico-Bibliografico Subalpino*, 24 (1922), 230–50.

Brown, Christopher. *Virgin and Child by Anthony van Dyck* (London, 1971).

Brown, Christopher and Hans Vlieghe (eds.). *Van Dyck, 1599–1641* (London, 1999).

Brown, Jonathan. *Kings and Connoisseurs: Collecting Art in Seventeenth-Century Europe* (New Haven and London, 1995).

Bussmann, Klaus and Heinz Schilling (eds.), *1648: War and Peace in Europe*, 3 vols. (Munich, 1998).

Carmona, Michel. *Marie de Médicis* (Paris, 1981).

Carter, Charles Howard. 'Belgian "autonomy" under the archdukes, 1598–1621', *Journal of Modern History*, 36 (1964), 245–59.

 The Secret Diplomacy of the Habsburgs, 1585–1625 (New York and London, 1964).

 The Western European Powers, 1500–1700 (London, 1971).

Carutti, Domenico. *Storia della diplomazia della corte di Savoia (dal 1494 al 1773)*, 4 vols. (Rome, 1875–80).

Cassetti, Maurizio. 'L'Archivio S. Martino-Scaglia', *Studi Piemontesi*, 10 (1981), 198–202.

Chatellier, Louis. *The Europe of the Devout: The Catholic Reformation and Formation of a New Society* (Cambridge, 1989).

Church, William F. *Richelieu and Reason of State* (Princeton, 1972).

Cibrario, Luigi. *Origini e progresso delle istituzioni della monarchia di Savoia sino alla costitutionze del regno d'Italia* (second edition, Florence, 1869).

Cifani, A. and F. Monetti. 'New light on the Abbé Scaglia and Van Dyck', *The Burlington Magazine*, 134 (August, 1992), 506–14.

I piaceri e le grazie: collezionismo, pittura di genere e di paesaggio fra Sei e Settecento in Piemonte (Turin, 1993).

Claretta, G. *Storia della reggenza di Cristina di Francia, duchessa di Savoia*, 3 vols. (Turin, 1868–9).

La successione di Emanuele Filiberto al trono sabaudo e la prima ristorazione della casa di Savoia (Turin, 1884).

Dell'Ordine Mauriziano nel primo secolo della sua ricostruzione e del suo grand'ammiraglio Andrea Provana di Leynì (Florence, 1890).

Clarke, J. A. *Huguenot Warrior: The Life and Times of Henri de Rohan, 1579–1638* (The Hague, 1966).

Cogswell, Thomas. *The Blessed Revolution: English Politics and the Coming of War, 1621–24* (Cambridge, 1989).

Constant, Jean-Marie. *Les conjurateurs: le premier libéralisme politique sous Richelieu* (Paris, 1987).

Continsio, Chiara and Cesare Mozzarelli (eds.). *Repubblica e virtù: pensiero politico e Monarchia Cattolica fra XVI e XVII secolo* (Rome, 1995).

Croce, Benadetto. *La storia dell'età barocca in Italia* (Milan, 1993).

Cruickshanks, Eveline and Edward Corp (eds.). *The Stuart Court in Exile and the Jacobites* (London, 1995).

Cruzada Villaamil, G. *Rubens, diplomático español: sus viajes a España y noticia de sus cuadros, segun los inventarios de las casas reales de Austria y de Borbón* (Madrid, 1874).

Curti, Giovanni. *Carlo Emanuele I secondo i più recenti studi* (third edition, Milan, 1897).

Cust, L. *Anthony van Dyck: An Historical Study of his Life and Works* (London, 1900).

Cuvelier, J. 'Les préliminaires du traité de Londres (29 août 1604)', *Revue Belge de Philologie et d'Histoire*, 2 (1923), 279–304, 485–508.

de Besancenet, Alfred. 'Henriette de Vaudémont, princesse de Phalsbourg', *Revue de l'Est (l'Austrasie)*, 3rd series, 25 (Nov.–Dec., 1866), 267–86.

de Castro, Giovanni. *Il conte Fulvio Testi e le corte Italiane nella prima metà del Seicento* (Milan, 1875).

de Léris, G. *La comtesse de Verrue et la cour de Victoire Amadée II de Savoie* (Paris, 1881).

Dessert, Daniel. *Fouquet* (Paris, 1987).

Dethan, Georges. *Gaston d'Orléans: conspirateur et prince charmant* (Paris, 1959).

Mazarin et ses amis (Paris, 1968).

Mazarin: un homme de paix à l'âge baroque (Paris, 1981).

La vie de Gaston d'Orléans (Paris, 1992).

Devos, Jérôme P. *Les chiffres de Philippe II, 1555–1598, et du despacho universal durant le XVIIe siècle* (Brussels, 1950).

di Macco, Michela and Giovanni Romano (eds.). *Diana Trionfatrice: arte di corte nel Piemonte del Seicento* (Turin, 1989).

di Tocco, Vittorio. *Ideali d'indipendenza in Italia durante la preponderenza spagnuola* (Messina, 1926).

di Vigliani, F. 'Gli Scaglia e Giovanni Battista Luynes VI Contessa di Verrua', *Rivista Biellese*, 4–5 (1954).

Duerloo, Luc and Werner Thomas (eds.). *Albert et Isabelle, 1598–1621* (Brussels, 1998).

Echevarría Bacigalupe, Miguel Angel. *La diplomacia secreta en Flandes, 1598–1643* (Leoia, 1984).

Elliott, J. H. 'A question of reputation? Spanish foreign policy in the seventeenth century', *Journal of Modern History*, 55 (1983), 475–83.

    The Count-Duke Olivares: The Statesman in an Age of Decline (New Haven and London, 1988).

    Richelieu and Olivares (Cambridge, 1989).

Elliott, J. H. and L. W. B. Brockliss (eds.). *The World of the Favourite* (New Haven and London, 1999).

Erba, Achille. *La Chiesa sabauda tra Cinque e Seicento: ortodossia tridentina, gallicanesimo savoiardo e assolutismo ducale (1580–1630)* (Rome, 1979).

Ernst, Hildegard. 'Geheimschriften im diplomatischen Briefwechsel zwischen Wien, Madrid und Brüssel 1635–1642', *Mitteilungen des Österreichischen Staatsarchivs*, 42 (1992), 102–27.

Externbrink, Sven. 'Richelieu und italien Studien zur französischen Politik in Norditalien 1624/31–1642' (MA thesis, University of Marburg, 1993).

Fell, H. Granville. 'Some topics of the moment', *The Connoisseur*, 101 (February 1938).

Fernández Alvarez, Manuel. *Don Gonzalo Fernández de Córdoba y la guerra de sucesión de Mantova y del Monferrato, 1627–1629* (Madrid, 1955).

Fernández-Santamaría, J. A. *Reason of State and Statecraft in Spanish Political Thought, 1595–1640* (Lanham, 1983).

Fichtner, P. S. *Protestantism and Primogeniture in Early Modern Germany* (New Haven and London, 1989).

Foa, Salvatore. 'Il trattato di Rivoli', *Bollettino Storico-Bibliografico Subalpino*, 28 (1926), 133–94.

    Vittorio Amedeo I, 1587–1637 (Turin, 1930).

Fraga Irabarne, M. *Don Diego de Saavedra y Fajardo y la diplomacia de su época* (Madrid, 1955).

Frigo, Daniela. *Principe, ambasciatori e 'jus gentium': l'amministrazione della politica estera nel Piemonte del Settecento* (Rome, 1991).

Frigo, Daniela (ed.). *Politics and Diplomacy in Early Modern Italy: The Structure of Diplomatic Practice, 1450–1800* (Cambridge, 2000).

Gachard, L. P. *Histoire politique et diplomatique de Pierre-Paul Rubens* (Brussels, 1877).

Gallina, C. 'Le vicende di un grande favorito (Filippo S. Martino d'Agliè)', *Bollettino Storico-Bibliografico Subalpino*, 21 (1919), 185–213, 292–305; 22 (1920), 63–157.

Gardiner, S. R. *History of England from the Accession of James I to the Outbreak of the Civil War, 1603–42*, 10 vols. (London, 1883–4).

Genet-Rouffiac, Nathalie. 'Jacobites in Paris and Saint-Germain-en-Laye', in Eveline Cruikshanks and Edward Corp (eds.), *The Stuart Court in Exile and the Jacobites* (London, 1995).

Ginate González, Ventura. *El conde de la Roca, 1583–1658: un diplomatico estremeño en Italia* (Madrid, undated).

Gossart, Ernest. *L'auberge des princes en exil: anecdotes de la cour de Bruxelles aux XVIIe siècle* (Brussels, 1905).

Greengrass, Mark (ed.). *Conquest and Coalescence: The Shaping of the State in Early Modern Europe* (London, 1991).

Hanlon, Gregory. *The Twilight of a Military Tradition: Italian Arisotocrats and European Conflicts, 1560–1800* (Basingstoke and London, 1998).
  Early Modern Italy, 1550–1800 (Basingstoke and London, 2000).

Hanotaux, Gabriel and Duc de la Force. *Histoire du Cardinal Richelieu*, 6 vols. (Paris, 1893–1947).

Haskell, P. 'Sir Francis Windebank and the personal rule of Charles I', (PhD thesis, University of Southampton, 1975).

Havran, Martin J. *Caroline Courtier: The Life of Lord Cottington* (London, 1973).

Henrard, P. *Marie de Médicis dans les Pays-Bas, 1631–1638* (Antwerp, 1876).

Hibbard, Caroline. *Charles I and the Popish Plot* (Chapel Hill, 1983).

Humbert, Jacques. *Une grande entreprise oubliée: les Français en Savoie sous Louis XIII* (Paris, 1960).

Huxley, Gervas. *Endymion Porter: The Life of a Courtier, 1587–1649* (London, 1959).

Inglis-Jones, J. J. 'The Grand Condé: power politics in France, Spain and the Spanish Netherlands, 1652–9' (DPhil thesis, University of Oxford, 1994).

Inscriptions funéraires et monumentales de la province d'Anvers, vol. 6 (Antwerp, 1871).

Israel, Jonathan I. *The Dutch Republic and the Hispanic World, 1601–1661* (Oxford, 1989).

Janssens, Paul and Luc Duerloo. *Armorial de la Noblesse Belge de XVme siècle au XXe siècle*, 4 vols. (Brussels, 1992).

Johnson, James Turner. *Ideology, Reason and the Limitation of War: Religious and Secular Concepts, 1200–1740* (Princeton and London, 1975).

Jouanna, Arlette. *Le devoir de révolte: la noblesse française et la gestation de l'état moderne, 1559–1661* (Paris, 1989).

Jover Zamora, José María. *1635: Historia de una polémica y semblanza de una generación* (Madrid, 1959).

Kagan, Richard L. and Geoffrey Parker (eds.). *Spain, Europe and the Atlantic World: Essays in Honour of John H. Elliott* (Cambridge, 1995).

Kettering, Sharon. 'Friendship and clientage in early modern France', *French History*, 6 (1992), 139–58.

Kleinman, R. 'Charles Emmanuel I and the Bohemian election of 1619', *European Studies Review*, 5 (1975), 3–29.

Koenigsberger, H. G. *Politicians and Virtuosi: Essays in Early Modern History* (London, 1986).

La Rocca, Luigi. 'L'aspirazione del duca Carlo Emanuele I al titolo di re di Piemonte', *Archivio Storico Italiano*, series 5, 46 (1910), 375–92.

Lechat, Robert. *Les réfugiés anglais dans les Pays-Bas espagnols durant le règne d'Elisabeth, 1558–1603* (Louvain, 1914).

Lefèvre, Joseph. 'Les ambassadeurs d'Espagne à Bruxelles sous le règne de l'archiduc Albert (1598–1621)', *Revue Belge de Philologie et d'Histoire*, 2 (1923), 61–80.

  La Secrétarerie D'Etat et de Guerre sous le régime Espagnol (1594–1711) (Brussels, 1934).

Leman, Auguste. *Urbain VIII et la rivalité de la France et de la maison d'Autriche de 1631 à 1635* (Lille, 1920).

Levy Peck, Linda. *Court Patronage and Corruption in Early Stuart England* (Boston and London, 1990).

Levy Peck, Linda (ed.). *The Mental World of the Jacobean Court* (Cambridge and New York, 1991).

Litta, Pompeo. *Celebri famiglie Italiane*, 11 vols. (Milan and Turin, 1819–99).

Lockyer, Roger. *Buckingham: The Life and Political Career of George Villiers, First Duke of Buckingham, 1592–1628* (London, 1981).

Loomie, Albert. *The Spanish Elizabethans: The English Exiles at the Court of Philip II* (Fordham, 1963).

  'The *Conducteur des Ambassadeurs* of seventeenth century France and Spain', *Revue Belge de Philologie et d'Histoire*, 43 (1975), 333–56.

  'The Spanish faction at the court of Charles I, 1630–38', *Bulletin of the Institute of Historical Research*, 59 (1986), 37–49.

Lublinskaya, A. D. *French Absolutism: The Crucial Phase, 1620–1629* (Cambridge, 1968).

Lusso, M. 'Filiberto Gherardo Scaglia, conte di Verrua, 1561/2–1619' (tesi di laurea, University of Turin, 1957–8; in the Biblioteca Provincia, Turin).

Lutz, George. *Kardinal Giovanni Francesco Guido di Bagno: Politik und Religion im zeitalter Richelieus und Urbans VIII* (Tübingen, 1971).

Malvezzi, A. 'Papa Urbano VIII e la questione della Valtellina', *Archivio Storico Lombardo*, 7 (1957), 5–113.

Manno, Antonio. *Il Patriziato Subalpino*, 32 vols. (manuscript copies in the Archivio di Stato and Biblioteca Reale, Turin).

Marini, Lino. *Savoiardi e Piemontesi nello stato sabaudo, 1418–1601* (Rome, 1962).

  Libertà e tramonti di libertà nello stato sabaudo del Cinquecento (Bologna, 1968).

  Libertà e privilegio dalla Savoia al Monferrato da Amedeo VIII a Carlo Emanuele I (Bologna, 1972).

Mattingly, Garrett. *Renaissance Diplomacy* (London, 1955).

Mauquoy-Hendrickx, Marie. *L'iconographie d'Antoine van Dyck*, 2 vols. (second edition, Brussels, 1991).

Merlin, Pierpaolo. *Tra guerre e tornei: la corte sabauda nell'età di Carlo Emanuele I* (Turin, 1991).

Merlin, Pierpaolo, Claudio Rosso, Geoffrey Symcox and Giuseppe Ricuperati (eds.). *Il Piemonte sabaudo: stato e territori in età moderna* (Turin, 1994).

Merolla, Riccardo. 'L'Accademia dei Desiosi', *Roma Moderna e Contemporanea*, 3 (1995), 121–55.

Millar, Oliver. *Van Dyck in England* (London, 1982).

Moir, Alfred, Francise de Nave and Carl Depauw (eds.). *Antoon van Dyck & Antwerpen* (Antwerp, 1991).

Monballieu, A. 'Cesare Alesandro Scaglia en de "Bewening van Christus" door A. van Dijk', *Jaarboek van het Koninklijk Museum voor Schone Kunsten* (1973), 247–68.

Montañez, Maria. *El correo en la España de los Austrias* (Barcelona, 1972).

Morford, Mark. *Stoics and Neostoics: Rubens and the Circle of Lipsius* (Princeton and Oxford, 1991).

Mozzarelli, Cesare (ed.). *'Familia' del principe e famiglia aristocratica*, 2 vols. (Rome, 1988).

Mozzarelli, Cesare and Giuseppe Olmi (eds.). *La corte nella cultura e nella storiografia: immagini tra Otto e Novecento* (Rome, 1983).

Noailles, Viscount de. *Le Cardinal de la Valette, général des armées du roi, 1635 à 1639* (Paris, 1906).

Oberli, Matthias. *Magnificentia Principis: Das Mäzenatentum des Prinzen und Kardinals: Maurizio von Savoyen (1593–1657)* (Weimar, 1999).

O'Connell, D. P. 'A cause célèbre in the history of treaty making. The case of the treaty of Regensburg, 1630', *British Yearbook in International Law*, 42 (1967), 71–90.

Oresko, Robert. 'The question of the sovereignty of Geneva after the Treaty of Câteau-Cambresis', in Helmut G. Koenigsberger (ed.), *Republiken und Republikenismus im Europa der Frühen Neuzeit*. Schriften der Historischen Kollegs Kolloquien 2 (1988).

'Bastards as clients: the House of Savoy and its illegitimate children', in Charles Giry-Deloison and Roger Mettam (eds.), *Patronages et clientélismes 1550–1750 (France, Angleterre, Espagne, Italie)* (London, 1995).

Oresko, Robert, G. C. Gibbs and H. M. Scott (eds.). *Royal and Republican Sovereignty in Early Modern Europe: Essays in Memory of Ragnhild Hatton* (Cambridge, 1997).

Osborne, Toby. 'The diplomatic career of Abbot Scaglia during the Thirty Years' War' (DPhil thesis, University of Oxford, 1996).

'Abbot Scaglia, the Duke of Buckingham and Anglo-Savoyard relations during the 1620s', *European History Quarterly*, 30 (2000), 5–32.

'"Chimères, monopoles and stratagèmes": French exiles in the Spanish Netherlands during the Thirty Years' War', *The Seventeenth Century*, 15 (2000), 149–74.

Ossola, Carlo, Claude Raffestein and Mario Ricciardi (eds.). *La frontiera da stato a nazione: il caso Piemonte* (Rome, 1987).

Parker, Geoffrey. *The Army of Flanders and the Spanish Road, 1567–1659* (Cambridge, 1972).

Spain and the Netherlands, 1559–1659 (London, 1979).

Parker, Geoffrey *et al. The Thirty Years' War* (London, 1984).

Parrott, D. A. 'The administration of the French army during the ministry of Cardinal Richelieu' (DPhil thesis, University of Oxford, 1983).

'The Mantuan Succession, 1627–31: a sovereignty dispute in early modern Europe', *English Historical Review*, 112 (1997), 20–65.

Parrott, D. A. and Robert Oresko. 'The sovereignty of Monferrato and the citadel of Casale as European problems in the early modern period', in D. Ferari and A. Quondam (eds.), *Stefano Guazzo e Casale tra Cinque e Seicento* (Mantua, 1997).

Passamonti, E. 'Relazioni Anglo-Sabaude dal 1603 al 1625', *Bollettino Storico-Bibliografico Subalpino*, 36 (1934), 264–317, 488–543; 37 (1935), 94–124.

Patrucco, C. E. 'Intorno alle relazioni del conte di Soissons col principe di Carignano (1636–1641)', *Bollettino Storico-Bibliografico Subalpino*, 1 (1896), 309–24.

'L'antifrancesismo in Piemonte sotto il regno di Vittorio Amedeo 1', *Bollettino Storico-Bibliografico Subalpino*, 1 (1896), 158–73.

'Sulle relazioni della Casa di Savoia colla Republica di Venezia durante la reggenza di Maria Cristina', *Bollettino Storico-Bibliografico Subalpino*, 1 (1896), 209–12.

Perrero, Domenico. *Il conte Fulvio Testi alla corte di Torino negli anni 1628 e 1635* (Milan, 1862).

Pithon, Rémy. 'Les débuts difficiles du ministère de Richelieu et la crise de Valteline, 1621–1627', *Revue d'Histoire Diplomatique*, 74 (1960), 289–322.

Pollak, Martha D. *Turin 1564–1680: Urban Design, Military Culture, and the Creation of the Absolutist Capital* (Chicago and London, 1991).

Prawdin, Michael. *Marie de Rohan, Duchesse de Chevreuse* (London, 1971).

Pulliati, Pietro. *Bibliografia di Alessandro Tassoni*, 2 vols. (Florence, 1969–70).

Quazza, Guido. 'Giulio Mazzarini mediatore fra Vittorio Amedeo I e il Richelieu, 1635–1636', *Bollettino Storico-Bibliografico Subalpino*, 48 (1950), 53–84.

'Guerra civile in Piemonte, 1637–1642 (nuove ricerche)', *Bollettino Storico-Bibliografico Subalpino*, 57 (1959), 281–321; 58 (1960), 5–63.

La decadenza italiana nella storia europea: saggi sul Sei-Settecento (Turin, 1971).

Quazza, Romolo. 'Nevers contra Nemours nel 1624', *Atti e Memorie dell'Accademia Virgiliana*, 30 (1920).

'La politica Europea nella questione Valtellinica (la lega Franco-Veneto-Savoiarda e la pace di Monçon), *Nuovo Archivio Veneto*, 42 (1921), 50–151.

Mantova e Monferrato nella politica europea alla vigilia della guerra per la successione, 1624–1627 (Mantua, 1922).

La guerra per la successione di Mantova e del Monferrato, 1628–1631, 2 vols. (Mantua, 1926).

La politica di Carlo Emanuele I durante la guerra dei trent'anni, Carlo Emanuele I Miscellanea 1 (1930).

Margherita di Savoia, Duchessa di Mantova e Vice-Regina del Portogallo (Turin, 1930).

Tommaso di Savoia-Carignano nelle campagne di Fiandra e di Francia, 1635–1638 (Turin, 1941).

Storia politica d'Italia: preponderanza spagnuola, 1559–1700 (Milan, 1950).

Randi, Luigi. *Il Principe Cardinale Maurizio di Savoia* (Florence, 1901).

Ranum, Orest. 'Richelieu and the great nobility: some aspects of early modern political motives', *French Historical Studies*, 3 (1963), 184–204.

The Fronde: A French Revolution, 1648–1652 (New York and London, 1993).

Reade, H. G. R. *Sidelights on the Thirty Years' War*, 3 vols. (London, 1924).

Reeve, L. J. *Charles I and the Road to Personal Rule* (Cambridge, 1989).

Rivoire, Pietro. 'Un diplomatico Piemontese del secolo XVII', *Bollettino Storico-Bibliografico Subalpino*, 2 (1897), 317–70.

Ródenas Vilar, Rafael. *La política europea de España durante la Guerra de Treinta Años, 1624–1630* (Madrid, 1967).

Rodriguez-Salgado, M. J. *The Changing Face of Empire: Charles V, Philip II and Habsburg Authority, 1551–1559* (Cambridge, 1988).

Rodríguez Villa, Antonio. *Ambrosio Spínola, primer marqués de los Balbases* (Madrid, 1904).

Romano, G. (ed.), *Le collezioni di Carlo Emanuele I di Savoia* (Turin, 1995).

Rosso, Claudio. *Una burocrazia di Antico Regime: i segretari di stato dei duchi di Savoia, I (1559–1637)* (Turin, 1992).

Russell, Jocelyne G. *Peacemaking in the Renaissance* (London, 1986).

Sahlins, Peter. *Boundaries: The Making of France and Spain in the Pyrenees* (Berkeley, Los Angeles and Oxford, 1989).

Schlugleit, L. 'L'abbé de Scaglia, Jordaens et "l'Histoire de Pysche" de Greenwich-House (1639–1642)', *Revue Belge d'Archéologie et d'Histoire de l'Art*, 7 (1937), 139–65.

Schreiber, Roy. 'James Hay. The First Earl of Carlisle', *Transactions of the American Philosophical Society*, 74 (1984).

Sella, Domenico. *Seventeenth Century Italy* (London, 1997).

Sharpe, Kevin. *The Personal Rule of Charles I* (New Haven and London, 1992).

Shaw, Christine. *The Politics of Exile in Renaissance Italy* (Cambridge, 2000).

Skinner, Quentin. *The Foundations of Modern Political Thought*, 2 vols. (Cambridge, 1993–4).

Smuts, R. Malcolm. 'The Puritan followers of Henrietta Maria during the 1630s', *English Historical Review*, 93 (1983), 26–45.

Smuts, R. Malcolm (ed.). *The Stuart Court and Europe: Essays in Politics and Political Culture* (Cambridge, 1996).

Stango, Cristina. 'La corte di Emanuele Filiberto: organizzazione e gruppi sociali', *Bollettino Storico-Bibliografico Subalpino*, 85 (1987), 445–502.

Storrs, Christopher. *War, Diplomacy and the Rise of Savoy, 1690–1720* (Cambridge, 2000).

Strachan, Michael. *Sir Thomas Roe, 1581–1644: A Life* (Salisbury, 1989).

Stradling, R. A. *Philip IV and the Government of Spain, 1621–1665* (Cambridge, 1988).

Spain's Struggle for Europe, 1598–1668 (London and Rio Grande, 1994).

Straub, Eberhard. *Pax et Imperium: Spaniens Kampf um seine Friedensordnung in Europa zwischen 1617 und 1635* (Paderborn, 1980).

Stumpo, Enrico. *Finanza e stato moderno nel Piemonte del Seicento* (Rome, 1979).

'Finanze e ragion di stato nella prima età moderna. Due modelli diversi: Piemonte e Toscana, Savoia e Medici', in *Finanze e ragion di stato in Italia e in Germania nella prima Età moderna*, Annali dell'Istituto Storico Italo-Germanico (Bologna, 1984).

Sutherland, N. M. 'The Thirty Years War and the structure of European politics', *English Historical Review*, 107 (1992), 587–625.

Symcox, Geoffrey. *Victor Amadeus II: Absolutism in the Savoyard State 1675–1730* (London, 1983).

Tabacco, Giovanni. *Lo stato sabaudo nel sacro romano impero* (Turin, 1939).

Thomas, Werner and Bart de Groof (eds.). *Rebelíon y resistencia en el mundo Hispánico del siglo XVII* (Louvain, 1992).

Thomas, Werner and Luc Duerloo (eds.). *Albert and Isabella: Essays* (Brussels, 1998).

Thuau, Étienne. *Raison d'état et pensée politique a l'époque de Richelieu* (Paris, 1966).

Thys, Augustin. *Historique des rues et places publiques de la ville d'Anvers* (Antwerp, 1873).

Tomlinson, H. (ed.). *Before the English Civil War: Essays on Early Stuart Politics and Government* (London, 1983).

Trevor-Roper, Hugh. *Princes and Artists: Patronage and Ideology at Four Habsburg Courts, 1517–1633* (London, 1991).

Tuck, Richard. *Philosophy and Government 1572–1651* (Cambridge, 1993).

Vaes, M. 'Il soggiorno di Antonio Van Dyck alla Corte di Torino: 4 Dicembre 1622–Febbraio 1623', *Bollettino Storico-Bibliografico Subalpino*, 43 (1942), 227–39.

Valle, Domenico. 'Il Padre Pietro Monod della Compagnia di Gesù, consigliere di stato e istoriografo della Casa di Savoia, e le sue relazioni col Cardinale Richelieu', *Miscellanea di Storia Italiana*, 14 (1910), 269–366.

van der Essen, A. *Le Cardinal-Infant et la politique européenne de l'Espagne, 1609–41* (Brussels, 1944).

Vester, Mathew. 'The Piedmontese restitution: Franco-Savoyard diplomacy from 1515 to 1572' (MA thesis, University of Virginia, 1992).

'Territorial politics in the Savoyard domains, 1536–1580', (PhD thesis, UCLA, 1997).

Vita, G. 'Carlo Emanuele I e la questione del marchesato di Saluzzo (1598–1601)', *Bollettino Storico-Bibliografico Subalpino*, 24 (1922), 22–84; 25 (1923), 71–143.

Waddington, A. *La République des Provinces-Unies, la France et les Pays-Bas Espagnols de 1630 à 1650*, 2 vols. (Paris, 1895–7).

Walker, Joseph Cooper. *Memoirs of Alessandro Tassoni* (London, 1815).

Walsh, T. J. *The Irish Continental College Movement: The Colleges at Bordeaux, Lille and Toulouse* (Dublin and Cork, 1973).

Waquet, Jean-Claude. *Corruption: Ethics and Power in Florence, 1600–1770* (Worcester, PA, 1991).

Wheelock, Arthur *et al. Van Dyck Paintings* (London, 1991).

Williamson, Hugh Ross. *Four Stuart Portraits* (London, 1949).

Woolf, Stuart. 'Sviluppo economico e struttura sociale in Piemonte da Emanuele Filiberto a Carlo Emanuele III', *Nuova Rivista Storica*, 46 (1962), 1–57.

  Studi sulla nobiltà Piedmontese nell'epoca dell'assolutismo (Turin, 1963).

Yates, Frances. *Astraea: The Imperial Theme in Sixteenth Century Europe* (London, 1975).

Zanelli, A. 'Le relazioni fra il Ducato Sabaudo e la Santa Sede dal 1631 al 1637 nel carteggio della Nunziatura Pontifica', *Bollettino Storico-Bibliografico Subalpino*, 41 (1939), 133–212; 42 (1940), 1–59.

Zemon Davies, Natalie. *The Gift in Sixteenth-Century France* (Oxford, 2000).

INDEX

Aerschot, Phillipe Charles d'Arenberg, duke of, 210, 219, 220
Aimone, count of Savoy, 29, 145
Albert, archduke of Austria, 35–6, 127, 196–8, 200
Aldobrandini, Pietro, cardinal, 68
Alessandria, siege of, 64
Alessandro Cesare Scaglia
  abbeys, 66–7, 180, 189, 202, 211, 254
  and Anglo-French relations, 95–7, 98–9, 102, 105–13, 115–22, 132–3, 135–40, 151, 152–4, 157–60, 182–3
  and Anglo-Spanish relations, 106–7, 120–1, 122–33, 138–40, 151, 152–7, 159, 160–2, 164, 179–81, 191, 199, 205–6, 232–4
  aspirations for a cardinal's hat, 67–9
  and Buckingham's death, 153–60
  and Cardinal Maurizio, 66, 79–80, 184–6, 188, 191, 192, 242–4
  Catholic piety, 221–6
  childhood and education, 69–70
  and the civil war in Savoy, 269
  cultural patronage and brokering for Savoy, 76–82
  exile and his family, 246–57, 266–7, 270–1
  family role and responsibility, 66–7
  friendship with Alessandro Tassoni, 79–81, 209
  friendship with Balthasar Gerbier, 124–5, 127, 129, 154, 197, 210, 227, 232–4
  friendship with the duke of Buckingham, 84–6, 97–100, 112–13, 132, 134, 153–4, 160
  friendship with the earl of Carlisle, 92–3, 97–8, 100, 133, 134, 155, 157, 197, 232
  friendship with the earl of Holland, 155–6, 232
  friendship with Endymion Porter, 154, 197, 227, 232, 233
  friendship with Peter Paul Rubens, 124–6, 127, 129, 234
  and the functions of exile, 196–202, 205, 208, 235, 241, 245–6, 270–1
  and the Huguenots, 95–7
  and Olivares, 189, 190, 204, 208–9, 241
  as a patron and collector of art, 78, 212–13
  patronage of Van Dyck, 213–21, 227–32, 239
  political patronage and brokering, 74–5, 117
  and the Queen's House, Greenwich, 234
  reputation, 64–6
  and Richelieu, 65, 69, 99, 103–7, 109–12, 117–18, 119–21, 122–3, 135, 136–8, 140, 151, 154, 178, 183–5, 186–90, 191, 195, 204, 205–6, 241, 244, 245, 247
  rivalry with Pietro Monod, 185
  service to Savoy, 70–1, 73, 175, 179–80, 190, 191, 195
  and Tommaso Francesco, 239–42, 261–3, 264, 266
Alfonso III, duke of Modena, 44, 60
Almerigi, Bernardino, 74
Altemps, villa, 79
Alva, Antonio Alvarez de Toledo, duke of, 190
Amedeo VIII, duke of Savoy, 36–7
Angoulême, Charles de Valois, duke of, 82, 117
Anne of Austria, consort of Louis XIII of France, 54, 118, 183
Anne of Denmark, consort of James I of England, 234
Annunziata, order of, 61
  exclusion of ducal bastards, 44–5
Anthony of Padua, St, 222
Antonio, illegitimate son of Carlo Emanuele I, 46
Antwerp, 198, 221–2, 213–14
  and Jacob Jordaens, 234
  Scaglia's retirement there, 210, 212, 262, 269

298

Family power and public life in Brescia, 1580–1650
The foundation of power in the Venetian state
JOANNE M. FERRARO

Church and politics in Renaissance Italy
The life and career of Cardinal Francesco Soderini, 1453–1525
K. J. P. LOWE

Crime, disorder, and the Risorgimento
The politics of policing in Bologna
STEVEN C. HUGHES

Liturgy, sanctity and history in Tridentine Italy
Pietro Maria Campi and the preservation of the particular
SIMON DITCHFIELD

Lay confraternities and civic religion in Renaissance Bologna
NICHOLAS TERPSTRA

Society and the professions in Italy, 1860–1914
Edited by MARIA MALATESTA

Herculean Ferrara
Ercole d'Este (1471–1505) and the invention of a ducal capital
THOMAS TUOHY

Numbers and nationhood
Writing statistics in nineteenth-century Italy
SILVANA PATRIARCA

The Italian garden
Art, design and culture
Edited by JOHN DIXON HUNT

Reviving the Renaissance
The use and abuse of the past in nineteenth-century Italian art and decoration
Edited by ROSANNA PAVONI

Railways and the formation of the Italian state in the nineteenth century
ALBERT SCHRAM

English merchants in seventeenth-century Italy
GIGLIOLA PAGANO DE DIVITIIS

Aristocrats in bourgeois Italy
The Piedmontese nobility, 1861–1930
ANTHONY L. CARDOZA

Italian culture in northern Europe in the eighteenth century
Edited by SHEARER WEST

The politics of ritual kinship
Confraternities and the social order in early modern Italy
Edited by NICHOLAS TERPSTRA

War, diplomacy and the rise of Savoy, 1690–1720
CHRISTOPHER STORRS

Politics and diplomacy in early modern Italy
The structure of diplomatic practice, 1450–1800
Edited by DANIELA FRIGO

The politics of exile in Renaissance Italy
CHRISTINE SHAW

Florentine Tuscany
Structures and practices of power
Edited by WILLIAM J. CONNELL and ANDREA ZORZI

Naples in the eighteenth century
The birth and death of a nation state
Edited by GIROLAMO IMBRUGLIA

Church, censorship and culture in early modern Italy
Edited by GIGLIOLA FRAGNITO

Convent theatre in early modern Italy
Spiritual fun and learning for women
ELISSA B. WEAVER

Court and politics in papal Rome, 1492–1700
Edited by GIANVITTORIO SIGNOROTTO
and MARIA ANTONIETTA VISCEGLIA

Dynasty and diplomacy in the court of Savoy
Political culture and the Thirty Years' War
TOBY OSBORNE